The
Foursome

The
Foursome

John D. Spooner

HOUGHTON MIFFLIN COMPANY

BOSTON/NEW YORK

1993

For information about permission to reproduce selections from
this book, write to Permissions, Houghton Mifflin Company,
215 Park Avenue South, New York, N.Y. 10003.

Library of Congress Cataloging-in-Publication Data

Spooner, John D.
The foursome / John D. Spooner.
p.   cm.
ISBN 0-395-41952-2
1. Businessmen — Fiction. 2. Golf stories. I. Title.
PS3569.P6F68   1993   92-42798
813'.54 — dc20   CIP

Printed in the United States of America

Book design by Robert Overholtzer

MP 10 9 8 7 6 5 4 3 2 1

For SUSAN
still the beautiful muse,
and for LARRY ANSIN
who plays life
to scratch

My gratitude for the many people
who moved the process along.

THE PEOPLE WHO PROVIDED
THE TOUCHES:

Robert Scott	*Harry Gittes*
Dale Jelley	*Fritz Hobbs*
Roger Feingold	*John MacAuliffe*
David Barrett	*Mark Cohen*
Ed Linde	*Howard Fine*
Don Chiafaro	*Bobby Gorin*
Ted Berenson	*Robert Sprung*
Rupert Hitzig	*E. J. Hyson*
Richard Greene	*Luise Erdmann*
Joseph Saliba	*Godfrey Wood*
Robert Banker	*Tony Medaglia*

THE PEOPLE WHO PROVIDED
THE MECHANICS:

Yvonne Russell
Dianne Tassinary

THE PEOPLE WHO FED ME:

Vinicio Paoli and
John Hauck at
Ristorante Toscano

MY EDITORS:

Mike Janeway
Dick Todd

AND MY MENTORS:

Austin Olney and
Llewellyn Howland III

"Golf is the only thing you'll ever do in life where you get what you deserve . . ."
— *Old golf expression*

"Great sex is almost as good as bad golf."
— *Attributed to Sigmund Freud*

"Money Honey"
— *Rock 'n' roll song, 1953, sung by Clyde McPhatter and the Drifters*

PART I

The Front Nine

○

Spring 1950

They were four wise guys. Even though they were twelve years old. When it came to being wise, you either had it or you didn't. They carried other people's golf clubs to make money, satisfy their parents and build character. Their parents told them that the last reason was the most important one. So they were caddies, after school and on weekends, and they hated Hartigan the caddie master. He was the man who gave the caddies their assignments, and he was a bully. But that was okay with Stanley Singer, who loved a challenge and several times let the air out of the caddie master's tires. Dickie Rosenberg kept lookout when Stanley did it, not wanting to help, afraid of Hartigan, but more afraid of the jibes of Stanley Singer.

The caddie master smoked cigars. He wore a white T-shirt and a Red Sox cap. He rolled up the sleeves of the T-shirt. "He rolls up the sleeves, he can get a good red," said Stanley Singer, the wise guy.

" 'A good red'?" said Francis "Little Duke" Hennessey, not understanding.

"You schmuck," said Singer. "The Irish don't get a tan. They burn red: red blotchy arms, white hairless chests."

"You've got red blotchy arms, you asshole, and red hair," said Hennessey.

"That's great," said Rosenberg. "You can grow up to be a caddie master. Red Singer, the Jewish caddie master, who broke his mother's heart."

"You're too young to break *anyone's* heart," said Freddie Temple.

"You're too young to break anything except your pecker pulling on it." Temple said "pecker" like an English gentleman, not like the other boys, who made it sound like "peckah."

"If I didn't know you better," said Little Duke Hennessey,."I'd think you were saying not nice things about the Irish. If you weren't my friend I would be forced to beat the shit out of you, just on general principles."

"Hey," said Red Singer, "we all God's chillun."

They laughed sitting side by side on a bench in the caddie shack. They flipped cards into Freddie Temple's baseball hat for pennies as they waited to be called by the caddie master.

"Hennessey and Rosenberg," Hartigan yelled, and the two boys snapped to the first tee.

"You two carry doubles. Eighteen holes. Watch the balls and the bullshit. You're out there to *work*, not to flap your gobs."

"I can't carry eighteen," Dickie Rosenberg said. "I've got to be home by six."

" 'I've got to be home by six,' " mimicked the caddie master. "This is a municipal golf course, not a country club. You want to work or you want to hang out down the circle? 'I've got to be home by six,' " he mocked again. "Temple," Hartigan called, and the tall blond boy ran up to the tee. "Take Dr. Foster's and Dr. Swett's bags. If I get a single who has to be home by six, Rosenberg, I'll keep you in mind."

Dickie Rosenberg preferred flipping cards into a hat. He sat back down on the bench next to Stanley Singer.

"You having them to the bar mitzvah?" Singer asked.

"They're my friends, aren't they?" Dickie said. "You can't leave 'em out."

"I had to put the Hebe up," Hartigan said to Temple. "He was the next in line."

"Don't call him 'Hebe,' Mr. Hartigan," Temple said. "He's my friend."

"He's my friend, too, Mr. Hartigan," Francis Hennessey said, lifting two golf bags, one onto each shoulder.

"Well, pardon me," Hartigan said. "I didn't realize that the fucking United Nations was coming to Brookwood, Massachusetts."

The boys moved off down the hill toward the first green, a par three, 180 yards away. Hartigan turned to one of the doctors who was teeing up his ball at the white markers. "I don't know what's happening to kids today, doctor," he said. "Nobody wants to work. I don't know what's going to happen to golf."

Dickie Rosenberg and Stan Singer were on the putting green when their friends finished the eighteen-hole loop. "We each did a nine with women," Dickie said. "I got a buck tip, and she told me I must have nice parents."

"Rosenberg kisses ass through life," Singer said. "In school, on the golf course. He kept telling that lady what a natural she was, what a great follow-through . . . what a suck-up."

"But I got the buck," Dickie reminded him.

The four boys putted for dimes. Freddie Temple had a putter. So did Rosenberg. They carried them to the golf course, held them while they waited their turn to caddie, then put them into the bags they carried, fingering the leather handles while they waited to watch the shots of the golfers who hired them. Temple called his putter "Calamity Jane," the name Bobby Jones called *his* famous putter. Dickie Rosenberg called his putter "Excalibur." Francis Hennessey always borrowed Excalibur. Red Singer borrowed Calamity Jane, and they usually putted the pants off the owners. The boys played the putting green long after the doctors' foursomes had faded, long after the sporty women had gone home to prepare for the maids' night out.

The boys putted the practice green from the first hole until the ninth: Winner takes dimes from the losers. "We should double up for the ties, double up and carry over till the next hole," said Hennessey.

"Sure, double up, Little Duke," said Freddie Temple. "Why don't I just pay you double before we start? You win every time we play."

"What do you give a shit, Freddie? You got the money, I got the skill."

"How can anyone so big and fat be so good at sports?"

Hennessey only looked fat to a newcomer. He was solid, an immovable object even at twelve and fast to anger.

The boys putted until it was dark and the only thing they could be sure of was that the golf balls were white. They quit and got Cokes from the pro-shop machine and sat in a pine grove looking out over the eighteenth fairway.

"I found a frenchy in the parking lot last night," said Red Singer.

"People get *laid* in that parking lot. *I'm* going to get laid in that parking lot."

Dickie Rosenberg had heard the word "fuck" barely three years before for the first time. He was ten when someone told him a joke about "Johnny Fucker-Faster," with the punchline: "Can I put my car in your garage?" Dickie was going to be bar mitzvahed in two weeks. He felt totally unprepared for the ceremony, and the only thing he could truly comprehend about the process was the phrase, repeated to him over and over by friends of his parents, "Today you are a pen and pencil set." This, and the advice not to be surprised when people shook his hand and left money in his palm.

"Someday I'm going to have a front lawn just like the eighteenth fairway," said Stanley Singer. "And I'm gonna hire Hartigan to clip every blade of grass with a scissors."

"There are three things in life that are really important," Little Duke said, chewing on a long blade of grass and lying on his back staring at the sky.

"A new joke," Dickie said. "Here it comes."

"Look up there," Duke said, pointing now with the blade of grass. "That's going to be my house when I grow up. King of the Mountain. Remember when we played that game in the winter? Three of us trying to throw the guy on top off the snowbank? So that we could be King? That white house is number one. Number two is having a three handicap."

"What about a scratch handicap?" asked Freddie Temple. "Scratch is the best, you're a pro if you play to scratch."

"If I play to scratch, I *am* a pro," said Duke, disgusted. "You think I want to end up like Hartigan, or Jimmy O'Neil, the pro here? A couple of rummies. Dumb shits. All they can do is hit a golf ball. If I'm a three handicap I can play with anyone in the world and probably whip their ass, too."

"The King of the Mountain," Dickie Rosenberg said. "You've got it all figured out."

"I know what the third most important thing is," said Red Singer, joining in.

"Get your mind out of the gutter," Freddie said.

"Yeah," Red said, "and come down in the sewer with me." They all laughed, knowing what Red's choice would be. "The third most important thing in life is getting into Judy Hirshberg's pants."

"How about getting her to say hello to us first," Duke suggested.

"That's you, Duke," Dickie said. "Practical."

"I never liked fairy tales," Duke answered.

"That's cause you are one," Red yelled and jumped on top of Duke, trying to pin his arms.

"Takes one to know one," Duke responded, throwing the red-head over onto Temple. Then they all jumped on Duke, yelling "King of the Mountain, King of the Mountain."

When they unpiled, Hennessey added, "I'm going to have a putting green on my front lawn. Just a putting green. Everything else will be hardtop painted to look like grass so it takes no maintenance. Or I'll invent something to do all the work."

"I'm going to live in the city," said Freddie Temple. "Never worry about lawns."

"You don't worry about lawns anyway. I seen all the Ginzos at your house," said Duke. "They come in the truck; they do all the shit work. You and Rosenberg get everybody else to do your shit work."

"Temple and Rosie can't help it if they're born rich," said Red Singer. "But I'll tell you, when I have to unload my old man's sample bags because he can't lift them one more time, I swear to God I'll never do that when I grow up; I'll never be poor."

"Dreams of glory," said Dickie Rosenberg. "That's what my father says to me when I tell him how my life will be different from his. Dreams of glory." Rosenberg was the student, the boy philosopher. He often used big words when they were unnecessary. But they learned to stay close to him; he always had money for movies, for ice-cream sodas, for comic books. And he took them along for the ride. The boys finished their Cokes.

"What does he say when you don't get home by six?" asked Hennessey. "That was a crock, wasn't it?"

"You can't get in trouble two weeks before your bar mitzvah." Rosenberg smiled. "It's part of the Jewish religion."

"You're full of it, Dickie," said Singer.

"Well, I'm going home to test it," Dickie said. "Think I can have my putter back?" he added to Little Duke.

"I won it on the putting green," said Hennessey, putting the club behind his back. It was a usual routine for the friends. Dickie jumped on Hennessey, and they wrestled for the putter until Singer and Freddie Temple pulled them apart. They left the golf course on the late May afternoon. Hennessey and Red Singer threw the Coke bottles against big rocks in the woods next to the parking lot. "Jesus, don't do that," said Fred Temple. "You don't want to mess up the woods."

"You don't walk barefoot in the woods," Red Singer said, "you don't have any problems."

Hennessey hitchhiked home. Temple loped back across the fairways to climb a wire fence separating Brookwood Municipal from his property, which adjoined the course. It sometimes embarrassed him that he was richer than the others. But most of the time he took it for granted.

"You really having them to the bar mitzvah?" Red again asked Dickie Rosenberg.

Rosenberg nodded. "You're nothing without friends. That's what my father says."

"Expressions, always expressions. My old man, too," Red said.

They walked up the hill opposite the golf course. Dickie's street. Rosenberg whacked stones with his putter, as if he were hitting baseballs out of his hand.

"You watching Milton Berle?" Singer asked at the foot of Rosenberg's driveway.

"I've got the Hebrew lesson and two chapters of *Silas Marner*."

"Can't you get the Classic comic?"

"They don't make Classic comics of boring books, Red."

"I wouldn't know, brain. We're not up to that in English yet."

"When you get through Huey, Dewey and Louie, let me know," Dickie said. Red Singer gave his friend the finger and walked on to his own house, a half mile away, in back of the traffic circle with the drugstore, Chinese restaurant and bakery.

"You're late, Francis," Mary Hennessey said to her son.

"Let him up, Mary," her husband said. "You're never late if you bring in money or an idea." Francis "Big Duke" Hennessey worked for Boston Edison, "The Edison" they called it. Big Duke had been a quick amateur boxer, with fast hands, undefeated in the Pacific navy during World War II at 165 pounds. When he came out in 1946 with a wife and three children at home and The Edison paying

$100 a week as a meter reader, there was no contest about what he had to do. Big Duke couldn't afford to get his brains scrambled in a quest for glory. Now he punched a light bag in his cellar and watched Gillette's "Friday Night Fights" on television. He could still punish the light bag.

"There's no excuse. You can make it home by family dinner, Francis," his mother told Little Duke. "I can warm it up till the cows come home; it doesn't taste like it does fresh from the oven."

"Ma, it doesn't matter. I told you a million times. If the players are slow I can't get home till late. You can't tell 'em, walk faster, don't lose any balls, too many practice swings. I work for *them*, Ma, not the other way around." She slid a plate full of chopped meat, mashed potatoes and lima beans in front of him. Francis O'Connell Hennessey, Jr., wolfed them down. A serious eater, Francis, at thirteen, was already five feet ten inches and 170 pounds. He had the hair of the black Irish, straight and thick, and the ability to see the absurd. He got low C's in school when he couldn't stand the teachers. But he always got A's in math. Math was a shrug for Francis Hennessey; math rolled off his back.

His father was a big man for his time, called "Duke" when he fought because of *his* straight, slicked-back hair and the way he affected secondhand double-breasted suits that fit him like The Boston Strong Boy, a perfect 44 regular. He called his oldest son "Little Duke," hoping for perfection in his firstborn, wanting his child to be what he saw as the best of himself. Francis "Little Duke" Hennessey, the math brain, and hopefully good with his fists.

The floodlights on the garage lit the area. "Gimme a big target, a *bigger* target, Little Duke," his father commanded. Francis squatted in the backyard after dinner, holding up a man-size catcher's mitt with a sponge inside the big pocket for protection. The mitt was Big Duke's old one. "You're gonna be a catcher, Little Duke. The catcher runs the ball club; he's the holler guy." Francis caught his father, who could burn it in. The son snapped throws back to the pitcher from the crouched position, whap, whap. He could make the throw to second, hard and low, even in the seventh grade.

"You're a good player, Little Duke," his father would encourage him. "But better, you're a *smart* player. You got the *head*."

Mary Hennessey arranged her son's schoolbooks on the kitchen table and waited for the "whap, whap" to stop and her lessons to begin.

Freddie always looked like a dream come true. Frederick M. F. Temple. Frederick Myles Fahnstock Temple. He lived in an English Tudor brick home with slate roof and leaded glass windows, a cook named Jenny and two dogs, one large and one small. His house bordered The Golf Club. That was the name of it, *The* Golf Club, where his parents were members and where members' children were not allowed to caddie.

"You will caddie at the municipal course, and you will go to public schools until you leave the eighth grade," his father told him long before Freddie knew the difference between public and private school. "Building character was how my father raised me, and building character is how you will be raised," his father went on. "You will know history. You will know all the enemies so that you will understand how to react to them." George Fahnstock Temple III, or Georgie Three Sticks, as his friends called him, was a Boston banker who served on many boards of directors. He invariably voted "No" on every point raised at board meetings so that ever afterward he could say, "I told you so." Once a friend of Georgie Three Sticks told him that the best day of his life had been when his son was born. "Nonsense," said Georgie. "The best day of a man's life is when he shoots his first grouse." Freddie was the youngest of three children. His brother, George IV, was in the foreign service in Chile. His sister, Phoebe, was at Smith in medieval studies. When they were home they either ignored him or made passes at teasing him in unoriginal ways. Freddie was determined, when he became older, to go by them like a shot. The Temples dined at eight each evening. Freddie sat with them. His mother, Elizabeth, called Lizzie, had been a Myles from Salem. She was athletic and perpetually tan. "How much did you bring home today?" his father asked him, chewing on a lamb chop he held in both hands.

"I made seven dollars and fifty cents." Freddie did not tell George Temple III that he had lost $2.20 to Little Duke Hennessey on the putting green.

"I expect you will be thinking about how to invest that money," his father said. Freddie began to pick up his own lamb chop and gnaw on it.

"Down on your plate with that," Lizzie Temple said. "When you run your own household you can pick up a chop. Until then you cut it with a proper knife and fork."

"But you can't get all the meat cutting it off."

"So be it," said his mother.

He listened to them talking about friends, social events, the lack of style of President Truman and their own game of bridge, which they played every Thursday evening *après* dinner at The Golf Club. After dessert (rice pudding) and coffee, George Temple and his wife rose. "Frederick," he said, "we move to the North Shore the day you get out of school. You intend to caddie each weekend until then." It was a statement, not a question.

"Everything but two weeks from Saturday," the boy said. "I'm going to a confirmation."

"People don't get confirmed on Saturday," Lizzie said.

"It's Dickie Rosenberg. He's Jewish," Freddie answered.

"Well, for God's sake, George," his wife said.

"It's fine," he said. "It's part of understanding history. You have to know everyone's habits in order to deal with them, in order to master them. The smartest English commanders learned Indian, Pushtu, tribal Afghanistan dialects, Hindu. You must go and learn, Fred."

After dinner, Freddie read a bit of *Silas Marner,* a lot of Goren's book *The Elements of Bridge,* checked the closing New York Stock Exchange prices in the evening edition of the Boston *Traveler.* Freddie Temple was going to be tall. He was already five-eleven and skinny, with straight blond hair that no one else in the seventh grade, boy or girl, possessed in such fineness or color. He putted on the living-room Orientals, thirty feet into a crystal water glass. After a half hour, he thought that he would never be as good a putter as Red Singer or Little Duke Hennessey, and, on impulse, he smashed the glass with his putter, Calamity Jane. "You don't walk barefoot in the woods, you don't have any problems," he remembered Red Singer saying that afternoon.

Stanley Singer constantly fought with his parents. Everybody fought constantly in the Singer house, but perhaps that was caused by an abundance of love. Stanley had two older sisters, who, seemingly by some miracle, were the best-looking girls in their respective school classes. The girls, Florence (Flossie) and Loretta (Lorrie), were dark, big-eyed, big-bosomed and long of leg. They were both at Brookwood High School, and the boys flocked around the Singer household like kids around ice-cream trucks in August.

Harry Singer was broken down at forty-eight. He was a salesman, and he sold anything that anyone would hire him to sell. From age fifteen he had been selling: newspapers, laundry supplies, pharmaceuticals, sporting goods, used cars. Now he was representing a line of women's sportswear, traveling upstate New York and all over New England four days a week, home on Thursday evenings. Wherever he went he gave Tootsie Rolls to the receptionists or the secretaries. Some called him Harry the Tootsie. Some called him "Toots." Harry had been a redhead, just like his son. But the hair had disappeared even before the color faded, and now only a few puffs of white curled around his ears and settled at the bottom of his head at the collar. Harry's wife, Millie, a tall, austere woman, worried constantly about her children and had been nicknamed years ago by wise-guy boyfriends of Flossie, "Oy vey" Singer, after her constantly used phrase.

"Every night we wait for *you*," Flossie Singer said to her brother. "We're starved; we've got homework; it cuts into our phone time."

"I *work*, okay?" said Stanley. "I bring home *money*. You two do nothing. You know about one subject: hair. Let's see either of you lift a golf bag, lift a *finger*, do *anything*."

"Stop," yelled their mother. "Stop hucking each other. Your father comes home any minute. I won't have the craziness." Every time Millie Singer turned her back to bring forth seconds of meat rolled in cabbage, thirds of potato pancakes, the children itched each other: about pimples, grades, friends, rights to the bathroom, the car, the telephone, the television, the radio. "Is this what I get in America?" their mother pleaded. "One large oy vey?"

The Singers had moved to South Brookwood in 1948, two years previous. They moved from Dorchester, a neighborhood of Jewish families, mostly immigrants from the ghettos of Eastern Europe. Harry Singer had really been moving the goods for the sportswear company. He had two hot years back to back and in 1948 made $26,000. He bought the three-bedroom brick Colonial built on spec, near the temple at South Brookwood Circle, for a shade less than he had made that year. Millie missed the neighborhood, the friends in Dorchester. But it was worth it to look at her brick house. When no one was home she would go into the driveway and touch the rows of brick around the garage door. "Rich," she would say to herself. "Safe."

Harry Singer dragged his weary tail into his brick house at quarter till nine. He sat at the kitchen table and poured himself three fingers of Canadian Club, a habit he acquired over the years selling in upstate New York. "Business stinks," he said to his wife. "Fall is shaping up a disaster. I am a weary Tootsie Roll pedlar." He brightened when he saw the meat rolled in cabbage and his redheaded son. "You are one wise guy, Stan the Man," he said. "You know I named you for Stan 'The Man' Musial, don't you, sonny?"

"Yes, Daddy," Stanley said as his father hugged him and rumpled his son's hair, red as lox.

Stanley Singer didn't give a damn about homework; he only went through the motions. He cared about sports and girls in that order, and he had a brashness that teachers found intimidating. He wasted the evening listening to his sisters' phone conversations, sneaking peeks at the television, itching his mother to make cheesecake. "Stanley has to go to bed; it's ten-thirty," his sisters clamoured finally, and he was dispatched to his small bedroom, its walls covered with pictures from *Sport* magazine: John Lujack, Joe Louis, Ted Williams, Roy Conacher in a Chicago Blackhawk shirt. All the sports in color portraits the way he saw himself: the Red Flash from South Brookwood, Massachusetts. His father came in and shut off the radio, just at the end of an episode of "The Great Gildersleeve." "What kind of a hit today, Stan the Man?" his father asked, sitting on the end of his son's bed.

"Twelve and change caddying, three and change putting."

His father sighed. "Can you lend me ten until tomorrow night? I couldn't cash a check on the road. Just till tomorrow night."

His son jumped up to his bureau.

"I hate to do it, Stanley."

"Hey, Daddy, what's a son for?"

His father loved him for what he thought he remembered about himself. "For a wise-guy boychick, you got a heart, Stan the Man."

Stanley Singer lay awake, worrying about his father. Usually he would make the effort to spy on his sisters through a hole he had drilled in the back of his closet. Tonight they were safe. He forced himself to think about baseball. He recited the Red Sox lineup to himself until he fell asleep.

When Dickie Rosenberg walked late into his dining room, his parents were sitting silently with Mr. Grossman, the Hebrew teacher.

"You're out of luck," his father said. "Mr. Grossman ate your dinner."

"That's okay, Richard," the Hebrew teacher said. "There's plenty left."

"There's *nothing* left for irresponsibility," Dickie's father said. "There is no excuse, and I've heard plenty of his over the years. There are *no* excuses, no dinner and you can go into the study with Mr. Grossman and go over your haphtarah until it's perfect."

Dickie said nothing.

"What did you say?" his father demanded.

"Yes, *sir*," Dickie said. His little sister, Judy, drank water to stifle her laughter. She loved it when Dickie caught hell.

Dickie and Mr. Grossman studied the passages from the Torah the boy would recite at his bar mitzvah. Dickie did not actually read the Hebrew. Mr. Grossman had provided a phonetic translation written out with the Hebrew letters above the English pronunciation below.

"I realize, Rueven," Mr. Grossman said, using the Yiddish for "Richard," which he thought was affectionate, "that your father has very strong ideas about a variety of subjects. This speech he has written, however, goes farther than sermons at bar mitzvahs usually go."

The Rosenbergs were Reform Jews. They had followed the preachings of Rabbi Joshua Loth Leibman at Temple Israel in Boston and believed that modern Judaism should be (in David Rosenberg's term) "more American." David Rosenberg had written Dickie's sermon, welcoming the guests and stressing community involvement and service embracing all peoples and urging Jews to avoid what David referred to as the "ghetto mentality." David Rosenberg had gone to the Wharton School and took over his father's business when he came out of the Army Signal Corps after World War II. He manufactured maternity sportswear, voted for

Dewey over Truman, read *U.S. News & World Report* and despised the International Ladies Garment Workers Union. His wife, Sylvia, had gone to Pembroke College in Providence, was a flapper in the 1920s and had been a Baer (her maiden name), one of the ten leading German-Jewish families in Boston. The Baers were not pleased with her marriage to David Rosenberg. They considered the immigrants from Poland and Russia to be "peasants" and themselves to be Jewish aristocracy. Sylvia, in her flapper days, extended her liberation to writing poetry, smoking Murads and dating peasants, like David Rosenberg, whom she thought were racy.

"If you could have some influence, Richard," Mr. Grossman was saying, "upon your father to make your sermon a trifle more traditional. For instance, you don't play with Gentile boys . . ."

Dickie laughed and thought of his best friends. "I think we'll do it the way my father wants," he said. The Hebrew teacher looked at the young man. Dickie Rosenberg had curly thick black hair like a Mediterranean street urchin. In the summers he turned so dark that his mother sent up doctors' notes to his summer camp to allow him to drink special vanilla milkshakes that supposedly would counteract the blackening process of his skin. Grossman stared at Dickie a moment longer and sighed. "Back to the haphtarah," he said. "We have to be perfect."

When he was leaving, as was usual, Mr. Grossman had to be assisted in backing down the driveway. He hit the usual trees and bushes and eventually got the gray Plymouth down the sloping drive into the street. David Rosenberg and Dickie had directed him during this operation.

"Taking me home for $29.95," said the father.

"What do you mean by that?" asked Dickie.

"It's the ghetto mentality," said his father. "The off-price boys. They smell of overcooked vegetables and families living in two-room apartments with coal stored in the one bathtub. You finish your homework?" David Rosenberg now thought himself a perfect German Jew.

"Dad, I just finished my Hebrew lesson."

"Well, what's keeping you from real homework?"

Dickie shook his head. His father took him by the shoulders and jerked him around. Pointing to their house, he said, "This is what the struggle is all about. The house, the grounds. If I seem harsh to you, it's for a purpose. It's how you come back from the kicks in the tail that are the measure of the man."

Dickie tried to concentrate on what his father was saying, but all he could think about was going to school, to the golf course, to Hebrew lessons. "I haven't had dinner, Dad," he finally said. Unlike Freddie Temple, Dickie didn't accept his father's lessons. He listened, but he didn't want to walk in his shoes.

His father clenched. "He's always clenched," Dickie thought.

"I told you it builds character," his father stated.

Later in the evening, Dickie's mother brought a tray to his room: roast-beef sandwich with the crusts cut off the bread, sweet gherkins, milk and Nabisco vanilla wafers.

"I'm starved," he said.

"Don't complain," Sylvia Rosenberg said. "Your father has had to struggle, and he wants you to know how it feels to struggle also." She smoothed her boy's curly dark hair. "You're a beautiful, sensitive boy," she said. "And I always want you to remember that you're a *Baer*."

His mother smoothed his hair for a while longer, then kissed him good night. She loved his dark skin, even though it was not the skin of *her* people.

Dickie finished his milk and sandwich, ignored the gherkins, ate one cookie and sailed another across his room. He repeated several phrases from his haphtarah portion. Then he said to himself, "I'm a Baer . . . I'm a bear. I'm a *bull*." Dickie Rosenberg laughed, and he knew he was building character. Then he went after the second cookie. Dickie Rosenberg never wanted to waste an opportunity, even if it dealt with dessert.

CHAPTER TWO

O

When Dickie Rosenberg was young, he really thought that anyone who wasn't Jewish was poor. Only Freddie Temple didn't seem to fit into that slot. Temple was a Martian, as far as Dickie was concerned, and sometimes he called him just that, "The Martian." Everyone had nicknames growing up in the suburbs; kids had nicknames everywhere. When life got serious, when you got older, nicknames disappeared or you ordered them to disappear. But the early nicknames were usually right on the money.

The only people in Brookwood, Massachusetts, in 1950 who didn't take bar mitzvahs for granted were the grandparents, who, in most cases, paid for them in full, or partly paid for them. Mothers thought of them as excuses for new clothes. The clothes could point out to friends and relatives that the friends could eat their hearts out (if the mothers had money) or that they could sacrifice for their children (if they *didn't* have it). For the fathers it was a business opportunity ("I'm glad you came to our celebration, Max, because I've been meaning to call you about the new man who's going to be covering the south for us"). For the bar mitzvah boys it was something to be endured, to get through. It was a rite of passage with presents at the other end of that passage. No one ever thought that when the ceremony was over they would be men. There was only one act that could make them men, and they were all dreamers about that. The boys would say they were being bar mitzvahed for their parents, for their grandparents. It was difficult to get the religious significance when they memorized their Torah portion phonetically and when Saturday School (Sunday School) meant an enforced dress code and spitballs and tricks with yo-yos in the corridors of the temple's classrooms. Many of the bar mitzvah boys in Brookwood in the 1950s ended their involvement with temples after the ceremonies. Many of them didn't really feel Jewish until many years later, when parents died, when friends developed cancer, when children married Gentiles, when the old neighborhoods were gone. The concept of *bas* mitzvahs, bar mitzvahs for girls, was unheard of in the 1950s. An adult friend of Dickie's years later claimed that the bas mitzvah was an invention of the liberals, particularly the affluent suburban liberals of the 1960s and '70s. He was a mean-spirited man who claimed, "*Bas* mitzvahs, what a crock. They're not even in the Bible. They're a creation of the pinko Commie fags in Cambridge. Along with strep, no one ever used to even *hear* of strep and labels for everything. What a crock of an excuse. No one can even have a plain old *dumb* kid anymore."

Temple Shalom Aleichem didn't look as if God belonged there in 1950. It was the first contemporary-design temple in the Boston area. At least it reminded no one of a church. It wasn't grand, with buttresses or domes reaching up to a Jewish heaven. It was long and low with sharp angles and stained-glass windows that seemed more comic book than holy. It was a Reform temple: women and men sat together in the congregation. The services were mainly in English. Attendance was obligatory only on the high holy days, Yom Kippur and Rosh Hashanah. The board was dominated by lawyers and doctors who had been educated at Ivy League schools and who dealt everyday with Gentiles. David Rosenberg was on the board. He wore tab-collar shirts and challis ties and thought often about running for selectman in Brookwood. There was much controversy about the new temple's design, but David Rosenberg cinched its completion by saying in a board meeting, "Do we know who we are? If we're secure enough in our own lives to say, 'Damn the torpedoes,' then who in the community is to say to us nay? Arguably, we are the community." Even the lawyers who dealt daily with Gentiles could not disagree.

Dickie Rosenberg's bar mitzvah day was warm and sunny, the kind of spring morning in May that Boston rarely sees anymore. In the middle of a walk outside the temple with his father before the ceremony, Dickie felt like being sick. "I hate this," he told his father. "I feel like going from both ends. And I don't remember *anything*." His father put his arm around Dickie's shoulders, which made the boy uncomfortable aside from feeling sick. But it would not do to have David Rosenberg annoyed on bar mitzvah day, even though Dickie had a feeling that once you were a man you shouldn't accept open affection from another man, especially if he were your father. It should be a time to stand alone.

"Obviously," David Rosenberg was saying, "you're not exactly a *man* today, which means you're not *responsible* for anything. But this *sick* feeling is important for you to remember, probably more than anything that happens today because today will be a blur, the way your wedding day will be a blur. How you come through the times you feel like throwing up is what makes you a man. Now let's turn around, go into the pulpit and, by God, let them hear you in the last row."

"Dad's right about a blur," thought Dickie, looking out on the crowded temple from his seat onstage, a stage he had been on many times in years past, starring in Sunday School productions, satires on the Bible and on Jewish life with such titles as *Pincus Pinocchio* and *Zaydie Knows Best*. Across the stage sat the other bar mitzvah boy, "Fat Louie" Gordon, a prig if there ever was one, with the self-satisfied little smirk on his face that seemed to be the hallmark of really smart little boys who were fat. Dickie had no choice about who shared his pulpit. He only hoped he would be first and could get it over with. He saw his parents and his sister, Judy, in the front row. His grandparents sat alongside them, his father's parents and his mother's mother, whom everyone called "The Countess," sitting tall and fingering her pearls as if they were a rosary or worry beads. But the only thing The Countess worried about was that the wrong people would come in contact with her family. She always sat in front rows so that she would not have to acknowledge the presence of others. She wished that her grandson had straighter hair.

Dickie picked his friends out of the crowd, but he tried hard not to focus on them. Red Singer was trying to catch his eye, giving Dickie the finger from behind his prayer book. Singer was in a row of ten or twelve boys, all dressed uncomfortably in jackets and ties. They all looked as if they had been wrestled into their clothing by a strict warden as a punishment for being boys. Freddie Temple was the exception. He was not wearing stripes on stripes, or rayon tie with Abbott and Costello checked jacket. He wore gray flannel slacks with a navy blazer that had sterling-silver buttons. His regimental striped tie had come from J. Press in Cambridge, and he was the only boy in that row in the synagogue who was not wearing white athletic socks. Temple was also the only boy not whispering and giggling and making farting noises with his lips. He was not even passing notes to the row of twelve- and thirteen-year-old girls who sat in front of them. The girls were their classmates at the Hathaway School in Brookwood, invited to Dickie's bar mitzvah against Dickie's better judgment. "No girls," he had pleaded.

"You may have ten boys and ten little girls," his mother had said. "We want to see *all* your friends at the party. The relatives want to see little people dancing and having fun. If you only have boys, their behavior will be, well, the girls will keep them calmed down." Mothers knew best about boys coming of age.

Freddie Temple took it all in like a witness to a hanging: the smell of prayer books and the perfume of the guests, the smell of old people, of Eastern Europe, the look of antique jewelry and new money, the sense that here was an inside joke and that he, of all the guests, was very much alone. His armpits were damp, and he wished he were anywhere but where he was. He kept glancing down at Duke Hennessey, trying to get a reaction. But Hennessey was taking it seriously, was not getting sucked into Red Singer's antics. Hennessey didn't want to take any chances that a Jewish God would report back to Jesus that he was fucking around in a place where religion went on. He didn't even want to confess that he had gone to the goddamn thing. It was something you had to do for friends, like helping them in a fight, even if you didn't want to do it. No one was happy giving up a Saturday to a bar mitzvah.

Dickie Rosenberg took it all in, but was able to suspend belief in where he was. He spilled through the ceremony by rote, trying to hit the back rows with his voice, which cracked badly only twice, and he concentrated on the clock underneath the far balcony, the clock with Roman numerals, which he always thought was so ironic because of the years that the Romans persecuted the Jews. He finished his sermon in English, the speech that his father had insisted on writing.

His haphtarah was from Ezekiel, Chapters 15 through 31, and it accorded God's ordinances for the priests of the Holy Temple. David Rosenberg liked the part that translated: "They shall have linen breeches upon their loins; they shall not gird themselves with anything that causes sweat." David loved that. He knew that God truly loved those in the garment business. He worked his son's speech from the next part: "And they shall teach my people the difference between the holy and profane, and cause them to discern between the unclean and the clean."

Dickie Rosenberg talked in English of the differences between right and wrong and the necessity of an upright moral life according to Jewish law: "If we as a people have survived for thousands of years by our wits and our willingness to work hard, who am I to go against history? I shall make my mark and strive to know between right and wrong. I shall also do my best fighting perspiration."

He had played errorless ball, through his haphtarah, through his sermon, and his father had even given Dickie a small pat on his behind as he left the stage after finishing his Torah portion.

"Follow *this* act, Fat Louie Gordon," Dickie thought, sitting down and allowing himself the luxury of looking at his parents, who were looking around, taking nods of approval from their guests, and at his friends, who were still sticking out their tongues and sticking up their fingers at him. Only his grandmother, The Countess, was staring straight at him, smiling. She gave him, very gracefully, the V for Victory sign that she had learned during the war from newsreels of Winston Churchill. Churchill wasn't a German Jew, but she felt that, in this case, she could make some concessions to her very high standards.

Fat Louie Gordon was predictably boring. All of the Gordon guests were on the left side of the synagogue. His family was busy all morning during Dickie's portion, checking the numbers of people on the Rosenberg side as well as their clothing and jewelry. Fat Louie's father was a dentist, no match for a manufacturing family like the Rosenbergs. Most of the Gordon guests were patients who never liked visiting Dr. Gordon in his office let alone watching his kid on a Saturday morning in May, which included (in most cases) a present that cost anywhere from $10 to $30. This was the acceptable range for bar mitzvah presents in 1950, except for family, whose gifts had no limitations on cost and would be monitored closely.

After the Kaddish, the prayer for the dead, the rabbi blessed the congregation and the people filed into the aisles. The Gordon guests smiled at the Rosenberg guests as they pushed together toward the exits. "He was very good," they said to each other. "He was very nice," they said, "Good Yontef," they said, which meant "Happy

Sabbath." Red Singer ran amuck in any crowd, even when he was standing still. He pinched bottoms and smiled away innocently; he grabbed at crotches and appeared indifferent. "Good Yontef," Red said to everyone while he did this. "Good Yontef."

There was a tent set up on the Rosenbergs' lawn, blue and white stripes in the sunshine, the grass mowed that morning. A trio of musicians were seated in one corner playing Broadway show tunes on bass, saxophone and drums. Three waitresses in white uniforms, hired by the caterer, passed platters of cold shrimp, sweet and sour meatballs and hot knishes.

A bar mitzvah is never the bar mitzvah boy's show. It is the parents' show. The boy can never believe it is happening to him. The parents know it isn't happening to *him*. It is happening to *them*. Is the music right? Are the napkins in the right colors with the name spelled properly? Are the matchbooks done correctly? (Blue and white with "Richard B. Rosenberg" done in block letters with the date.)

Dickie wandered through the tent feeling like Huck Finn at his own funeral.

"You were great, Rosie," Duke Hennessey told him. "What the fuck did you say?"

"Come on, Duke," said Dickie nervously. "No swearing. And do me a favor, *please* tell Singer not to smoke."

"I didn't bring you a present," Temple said. "But I'm going to give you a book."

"You don't have to do anything," Dickie responded.

"You were terrific, Dickie," said Enid Goldman, one of the famous Goldman twins who had tits, and big ones, before anyone else in her class. "Red is drinking liquor," she added.

One of the big prayers of youth is "Please don't let my friends disgrace themselves in front of my parents." Dickie allowed himself to be turned around by a cousin of his father's, who stuffed an envelope into the inside pocket of his suit coat. "Don't be a nud-nick," he said, wagging his finger under Dickie's nose. "When you grow up and take over the business, listen to advice from other people. And remember that blood is thicker than water." It was a day for people to give advice. Presents gave all the bar mitzvah guests the right to philosophize, to give Dickie a send-off into the adult world with the benefits of their experience. Dickie got a lot of

advice, almost all of it from men. The women told him how much
he looked like a Rosenberg or how much he looked like a Baer, and
they all told him how handsome he looked and he smiled at everyone and thanked them very much. His mother's brothers, his un-
cles, were the only people who treated him like a man. His Uncle
Irving from California gave him a watch and told him, "Sooner or
later you've got to satisfy yourself, not everyone else. Everyone who
talks to you today has failed in some way and doesn't want you to
make the same mistakes. Don't act because you think you're going
to please everyone; you end up pleasing no one. You think California is heaven? I stand in line at restaurants and I know nobody else;
I just stare straight ahead. I know *everyone* at your bar mitzvah
from years ago and I don't know anyone where I live." He added,
"Don't mix fruit juices with your whiskey." Uncle Howard lived in
Boston and was a doctor with a specialty in gastroenterology.
"Learn the sciences and math," he told Dickie. "Don't tell me that
you're lousy in math. No one is lousy at anything if you have
discipline. The mind can focus enough to learn any subject. I'm not
saying be a doctor. There's nothing wrong with the rag business.
I'm just saying that if you don't know sciences and math you basically know nothing." A woman friend passed by. "How's the back
of your belly?" Uncle Howard asked her. He and his wife, Aunt
Marsha, gave Dickie a clock radio. None of his friends had a clock
radio that you could set to shut off automatically, turn on automatically.

Grandparents made the most fuss over Dickie because they cared
the most about form and ritual. For them, the bar mitzvah was
proof that the blood flowed on and the Jews would endure for at
least another generation before sloppiness and the world's bad habits set in to make the Jews like the goyim. They saw the celebration
as proof that *they* existed, that *they* had raised a family in the
proper way, that *their* lives had meaning because the traditions
were observed. His Grampa and Nana Rosenberg were both immigrants, his grandmother from Russia, his grandfather from either
Poland or Russia, depending on the interpretation of generals on
opposite sides. His grampa used rough language sprinkled with
Yiddish expressions and smoked cigars; his nana worried constantly about everything and had a maid from Galway who would
brush her long gray hair one hundred and fifty times a day while

she sat on a stool in the middle of her kitchen listing out loud her family worries: "My husband is fooling with that stitcher; my daughter never learned to cook; my son is killing himself at an early age; my grandchildren never wear hats when they go out." Then the maid from Galway would pin up Nana's hair in a coif that Nana thought made her look rich and important and Nana would go off shopping for slips and corsets and dresses that she knew the stitchers at her husband's factory could never afford.

No one was good enough for Dickie's maternal grandmother Baer, The Countess. If she didn't have a penny, still no one would have been good enough for her except Dickie's grandfather, Jacob "Jack" Baer, the furrier who died when Dickie was a baby. If Jack Baer wasn't a Prussian, he certainly acted like one, inspecting the fingernails of his employees each morning and the nails of his family each evening when he got home. "Scrubbed and shining," he would repeat constantly, wishing everyone and everything around him to be in those conditions. Children were put somewhere else when Jack Baer was around because he "needed order in which to think." After he died of an abdominal aneurysm, his widow carried his principles around like the living flame, her back stiff, her manner austere, admitting no weakness, no sorrow, no loneliness, although she was stricken with all of these. But when Jack was alive, he was the man with whom she never made love without afterward feeling sick and abandoned. It was her lot.

Dickie was terrified of her critique of his performance. "If you're not going to be a tall man, Richard," she began, "at least always stand straight. You must give the illusion of height." The Countess strung out her words for effect so that "illusion" sounded like "illooosion." "If you stand straight and pick your words carefully, people will always listen to you. I think you have great potential to make your grandmother proud. Pray that I live to see that day."

"You know, Dickie," his mother told him. "It would be polite for you to ask your little girlfriends to dance. *And* your sister and your grandmothers, even if they say no. My mother will say no anyway, but your nana will want to do something if it's nice and slow. Your mother also," she said. "I won't embarrass you for long." She hugged him and gave him a little push in the direction of his classmates, who all stood around the edge of the area where people danced. Nancy Constantine and Enid Goldman were doing the jitterbug together, Enid conscious that she had the best bosoms in the Hathaway School and did not hint of pimples.

"I've got to dance with the girls," Dickie told Duke Hennessey.

"Jesus, Dick, I thought this was in your *honor*."

"I can see dancing with your mother or your sister," said Freddie Temple, "but with *them?*" He indicated the jitterbugging young-sters. Freddie Temple was an instinctive lover, even at twelve years old. He often said things that he thought you wanted to hear, then did the exact opposite. He had the moves designed to please his elders and, in years to come, his superiors at work, his bosses. He danced with Dickie's mother before the bar mitzvah boy did. They moved to "The Anniversary Song" from *The Jolson Story* until Mr. Rosenberg cut in on them. Dickie swallowed and danced with his sister while the photographer popped away between grabs at the passing trays of hors d'oeuvres.

"Does it take a *sheygets* to teach our son manners?" said David Rosenberg.

"He's a lovely boy and I think a good influence," Dickie's mother said. "Do you remember we saw *The Jolson Story* four times?"

"I think the caterer did a superb job. And how many people do you know who would ever do this reception in a tent? These new Jews coming from Manhattan and hitting their T's when they talk, a disgrace."

Friends and relatives filled the dancing space now, people with names you seldom hear anymore: Milton, Sylvia, Ira, Edith, Mar-ion, Sy, Esther, Harold. They were common names in the twenties and the thirties, old-sounding names then for young people who were handsome and pretty and successful and who saw *The Jolson Story* four times the way kids in the 1970s would travel thousands of miles to see concerts by the Grateful Dead, grandsons and grand-daughters of the Miltons and the Sylvias, who would all shake their heads and wonder at the foolishness of the next generation who would never work as hard as they did.

In the happiness of the dance, with these guests in their early and midforties beginning to feel prosperous, the musicians suddenly broke into the hora, the Jewish dance of joy and harvest, "Hava Nagela." It was Red Singer who did it. Red Singer, as drunk as any father of the bride, had grabbed Dickie's Aunt Marsha by the hand and yelled at the bandleader, "Hava Nagela." Aunt Marsha grabbed Freddie Temple, who had been surreptitiously throwing back gin and orange juice, a habit his parents had always thought cute. Freddie also began yelling, "Hava Nagela," having no idea what it meant. But since he felt as if he were in a foreign country anyway, he was throwing caution to the winds. The circle of hand holders, happy kickers and drunken chorus didn't figure on both David Rosenberg and his mother-in-law, The Countess, forming one of their few alliances, a shocked alliance, and descending together on the trio. "Stop," yelled Rosenberg. "Enough," commanded The Countess.

No one who was there ever forgot Dickie's bar mitzvah because when the music stopped in midbeat, Red Singer threw up, not a small reaction, but an all-timer, a heart-stopper of a vomit. Duke Hennessey saw it and immediately left the party, running away from Dickie's driveway as if he had just stolen a jackknife from the hardware store and was terrified at being caught.

"Peasant music produces peasant reactions," said The Countess later.

The party didn't stop after Red Singer's attempts to make the Rosenbergs more ethnic than they wished to be. But it was over for Red. Uncle Howard and Aunt Marsha said they would drive him home, and they did, wrapped in one of Mr. Rosenberg's old raincoats, Red's clothing piled in a pillowcase that the Rosenbergs used in their maid's room and that he kept in a smelly bundle on his lap. Freddie Temple kept him company, laughing hysterically whenever he dared look at Singer, then quickly shifting his gaze out the window to control his glee. "What am I going to tell my folks?" Red whispered to Freddie.

"I'd rather tell 'em I pissed my pants from the comedian they had at the party than tell them I got drunk and blew my cookies."

"They're gonna know there wasn't any comedian at a goddamn bar mitzvah."

"Then you tell 'em food poisoning."

They pulled up opposite Red's house. "Thanks, Freddie. That's a perfect idea. You know, I did eat about twenty knishes. Maybe it was food poisoning. Thanks a lot, Aunt Marsha," he said much louder. "I'm sorry for the disgrace." Red jumped out and slammed the door. He ran up his walk in the oversized raincoat, looking like a redheaded refugee from Halloween. He stopped and looked back at the car. "But it was worth it to dance with Aunt Marsha," he yelled and ran toward the safety of his front door.

"Isn't he adorable?" said Aunt Marsha.

"He stinks," said Uncle Howard. "Nobody loves a wise guy. Who does he think he is, drinking liquor at twelve years old?"

Freddie Temple sat in the backseat, burping silently to himself, drunk as a skunk.

"You live around here, sonny?" Uncle Howard asked him. "It's been a long day."

"About two miles from here, sir," Freddie said, enunciating each word carefully because he knew he was slurring. "I'll be happy to get off and walk."

"No, no," said Uncle Howard, "just point me in the right direction." He glanced in the rearview mirror. "What does your father do?" While he asked the question he was poking his wife on the thigh with his right hand; pay attention the gesture said.

"He works in a bank," Freddie said. "It's your next left and the fourth driveway on your right."

The homes in Freddie's neighborhood were called "mansions" by everyone in the seventh grade. Even by Uncle Howard. "That your house?" he said. "You live in a mansion."

Freddie felt guilty about his house. Even Dickie lived in a house seemingly half the size of *his*. All he could think of to say was "It's not my fault." He thanked them for the ride and ran straight for his house, wanting to shower off the smell of Red Singer's pukey clothes, wanting to wash off the entire day when he should have been out in the sunshine playing ball instead of celebrating with strangers something that for Freddie was incomprehensible. His parents would *never* understand it, and he wondered, while he rubbed himself down in the shower with Lifebuoy soap, if *he* would ever understand it either. He thanked God that he never would have a bar mitzvah.

Little Duke Hennessey played sports every day of the week, and he never got winded. But when he got to the bottom of Dickie's street he felt as if his heart and lungs were going to explode. He stopped for a moment to calm down, then stripped off his tie and unbuttoned his shirt collar. Then he began running again, slower now, pacing himself, and he ran all the way home.

"Are you okay, Francis?" his mother asked him. "You're soaked. Dear God, what have you been doing?"

"I ran home from the Rosenbergs. Are you going to confession this afternoon?"

"No, I'm not going to confession. Are you sick? You're burning up."

"If I wanted to go to confession today, could I?"

"Go talk to your father," she said. "*Dear God.*" Little Duke went upstairs instead and came down in dungarees and a sweatshirt. He went outside with a red rubber ball and played baseball against the stairs with himself, fielding smoothly and without error.

Big Duke Hennessey came into the kitchen. He had been listening to the Red Sox playing the Cleveland Indians. "Lou Boudreau has more brains in his little finger than all the Red Sox put together."

"Did you see your son? He's hysterical about something."

Big Duke started to laugh. "It's his day with the sheenies. Enough to upset anyone."

"It's not funny, Frank. And I wish you wouldn't use that word. Francis said he wanted to go to confession."

Little Duke's father laughed again and grabbed an apple from the icebox. "He's having trouble with the money is all. He's seen the devil today, he thinks, and he's starting to grow up. That's always a dangerous day."

Dickie Rosenberg learned on his bar mitzvah day about paying dues, that nothing ever turned out the way you anticipated. So little in life was actually *his*. He realized that the best thing about his coming of age really *was* the presents. He shut the door to his room and lined the gifts up on the floor, on his desk and on his bed. There were lots of reference books: *Reader's Encyclopedia,* Oxford dictionaries, *Roget's Thesaurus, The Columbia Encyclopedia.* His grandparents gave him the *Encyclopædia Britannica.* He looked up synonyms for penis and vagina in his thesaurus, but they were not included. There was not one present he didn't like; he appreciated them all, from leather stud box to photo albums to the gold watch from his parents that was inscribed on the back: "A man. May 17 1950." The measure of a man was his possessions, Dickie thought and counted his presents again. He also counted the money he had collected from various relatives and friends of the family. It was almost $1,400. At the time, Dickie's allowance was fifty cents a week, which he supplemented by caddying. Almost $1,400. He could buy fourteen thousand comic books. Then he could trade them, the biggest dealer in school. His father interrupted his thoughts without knocking.

"First thing Monday morning," he said. "Bang. In the bank. Better let me have all that cash." He noticed his son hesitating. "What's the matter, you don't trust your father?" He laughed. "I know. You were just getting used to it. You know, today marks understanding more than anything else. You're expected to understand things now. I can tell you that whenever you get used to something, it either changes or it disappears."

"Do you think I did a good job today?"

"I told you I thought you were fine. We were all very proud, Dick, the first of life's hurdles."

"I was thinking about what to do with some of the money."

"You're going to *invest* it. You're going to think about what companies interest you, and you're going to tell me what stocks to buy. The only way you learn about money is to be emotionally involved with it. Reading about money teaches nothing; moving it around teaches everything."

His father gave him an awkward hug. Dickie thought that his father smelled of heavy beard and hair tonic and rough woollen.

"How much money did you get?" Red Singer asked him later, on the phone.

"It doesn't matter," Dickie said. "I've got to invest it in the stock market."

"Shit, Rosie," Red said. "I know a guy can buy a car for you, hold it in a garage till you're sixteen. My old man doesn't give a shit what I do with the dough I make as long as I kick some into the family."

"How's your stomach?"

"I suppose I'm banned from your house forever now," Red said.

"Only until you die."

"Is that what your father said?"

"Of course not."

"I bet he did. Poor Rosenberg."

"Now wait a minute, Singer. What if I threw up at *your* bar mitzvah?"

"We'd take you to the fuckin' hospital because I'd know it wasn't from booze."

"Thanks for the handkerchiefs, Red."

"Is that what I gave you? Ma does that. I didn't have any idea. Go beat off into one."

Dickie looked up a few more words in his thesaurus before he turned off his light, happy at least that tomorrow was Sunday and he could sleep late. He could hang onto the $1,400 for at least another day. Maybe he'd buy a few shares of General Motors. If they were good for America maybe they'd be good for him.

CHAPTER THREE

O

There are various methods to measure the passage of time. There is the calendar year. Most people in business measure time by quarters ("We were off two percent for the last quarter") and speak seriously of their fiscal year ("Our fiscal year ends May thirty-first"). But most people secretly measure their lives by the school year, time that begins in September and ends in June, with July and August eternally vacation, regardless of how many hours put in on the job. School was out in Brookwood the last week in June, and the four friends met the next morning on the tennis courts in back of the Hathaway School, their grammar school, to play some basketball. There was a net erected on top of a steel pole with a steel backboard where half-court games could be played. No one could use that particular tennis court if basketball was in progress, but that was never a problem because only fairies played tennis in 1950. That's what the foursome thought, anyway. People who played tennis were no good at real sports like football, hockey, basketball and baseball, sports for *men*, not fairies. Not homos. Not freaks. That's what the foursome thought, anyway.

The boys wore dungarees in the sunshine. They wouldn't have been caught dead wearing shorts, even though it was humid and almost seventy-five degrees at ten-thirty in the morning.

They had drifted down to the tennis courts from the playground above them beside the sprawling red-brick school. They had been looking to play baseball. But only a handful of other kids were around, not even enough to pick up sides. Marty Shea was there hitting fungoes to a couple of sixth-graders. Marty Shea was in high school, but he always hung around younger kids, getting them to shag flies for him, to pitch batting practice to him. Shea would hit for hours, and his fungoes were things of beauty—long, high flies that looked as if they would never come down. He could hit out of his hand like Ted Williams, but he couldn't hit a pitch. Marty Shea was a weird guy, and his contemporaries got tired of his fungoes. Little kids thought it an honor to chase his balls to the steel wire fence bordering the field, to the stone water fountain, a thrill to camp under one of his sky balls and watch it plummet with a "smack" into a glove.

Duke Hennessey was usually prepared for all eventualities in sport. He carried his catcher's mitt, a bat, a baseball and a basketball in case they were forced to shift games. "So we'll take off our shirts and play 21 or Horse," he said. He never would play baseball with his shirt off. He didn't think it was proper uniform. And Duke, more than the others, understood the etiquette of sport.

Twelve-year-old bodies didn't yet have any muscle definition. They were groping for everything at twelve. The only thing that gave the boys any solace was playing sports and the knowledge that they were all in the same boat. "You're the skinniest fuck-face I've ever seen," said Hennessey to Singer. "But *you've* got tits," Little Duke said to Rosenberg, who was embarrassed about his body and reluctant to shed his shirt. So they played 21 and Horse, which was a game where one player took a shot of his choice and, if it went in, the next player had to duplicate that shot. If he missed, he became an "H." Then the next player initiated a new shot until the cycle spun out, the player with the fewest letters of Horse becoming the winner. Freddie Temple, being the tallest, could hit hook shots all day, a shot Dickie Rosenberg found impossible to duplicate. He sat down first, followed by Temple, who could never sink the underhand lay-ups perfected by Singer, who eventually won with a half-court two-handed set shot that "swished" and that Hennessey followed with a board-rattler nowhere near the net. Then they played two-on-two, Singer and Temple against Hennessey and Rosenberg, moving the ball in, going up for shots and rebounds, pushing and shoving under the backboard, bear cubs in a sunshine that shone all the brighter now that school was over. They never really noticed the strangers until one of them grabbed a loose ball and held it behind his back.

"A little shirts and skins, Jewboy?" a new boy said. There were six of them, tough Irish kids from across the tennis courts, which was the border separating Brookwood from West Roxbury. They were all of high school age, kids who had paper routes and worked jobs after school when they weren't playing hooky. They went to parochial high schools and lived in two- or three-family homes, wooden frame triple-deckers full of children and blue-collar fathers with one white shirt apiece for church. Periodically these teenagers raided across the border into Brookwood, busting a few heads, breaking windows in the synagogue, stealing some bats and gloves, grabbing a few wallets that invariably would contain no more than several dollars, school pictures and some hot-lunch coupons.

"Let's have the ball, Reilly," said Little Duke Hennessey, who called everyone from West Roxbury "Reilly." The strangers all looked fifteen or sixteen years old. They dribbled and ran and passed away from the four friends, toward the basket at the other end of the courts. Two kids playing tennis gathered up their racquets and balls and headed quickly up toward the Hathaway School. Hennessey headed after his basketball, followed by Temple and Singer. Rosenberg brought up the rear. He hated it when the Reillys came over the border. He had been caught alone several years before and been held by two boys while another lit matches and stuck them in his shoes, a hotfoot. Dickie's heart was thumping then, thumping now. The older boys played keep-away. Every time the one with the ball was approached, he would pass to another of his friends. The leader of the Reillys had a wiffle haircut for the summer and a face as full of pimples as a dermatologist's illustrated textbook. "C'mon, you rich sheeny assholes; you want a game, we'll play for the ball, give you a sportin' chance. This is a free playground; you can't monopolize the courts." One of them pinched Rosenberg's left nipple and laughed. "This black one needs a bra."

"One more time, Reilly," said Hennessey. "Let's have the ball back."

The leader moved toward Duke, who stood his ground. He towered over Hennessey. The leader had muscles — the sleeves of his white T-shirt were rolled up. He bounced the ball off Hennessey's head and caught it on the rebound. "My name's not Reilly, fartface."

Red Singer always had more emotion than brains. He suddenly took a flying start and leaped onto the back of the leader, then tried to rip the nose off the field of pimples to which it was attached. The leader fell to the concrete surface of the court from the surprise attack and Hennessey grabbed the basketball. He whipped it to Temple and then also jumped onto the fallen leader, whacking him in the face and throat with his fists. Then they were all in it, whether they liked it or not. There was a time you had to fight on the playground, and there was no way around it for the heroes or for the cowards. When you are raised in a sensitive way, you are going to get destroyed in a fight. You have no idea that someone would dare kick you or gouge your eyes or bite. Dickie Rosenberg was kicked in the shins and smashed in the eye before he believed it was real. It was a great lesson for him in later life; there are people out there who feel no compunction about kneeing you in the balls before you have shaken their hand and long before the bell has rung. Temple took the worst beating. Two of the Reillys held him down, and a third had a few seconds free to pound his mouth, making him spit up a tooth, before Hennessey ran to grab his Louisville Slugger and teed off on the bigger boy's shoulder. Duke screamed and swung the bat from side to side, "Clear out, you cocksuckers. Clear out or I'll kill you." Singer was sobbing and punching, the smallest of all and, with Hennessey, the most frenzied. A teacher from the Hathaway School, staying on for administrative duties after the school year ended, appeared on the stairs leading to the tennis courts. She had gray hair pulled back in a bun and wore sensible shoes. She taught music. There was a pitchpipe attached to a silver chain hanging between her breasts. She blew it and then yelled, "I've called the police, you boys. They're on their way. You boys stop." She blew the pitchpipe again, a shrill sound like police whistles in Germany. The Reillys backed off, cursing the younger boys. "My nose never bleeds," the leader yelled, blood running down his face. "We'll come back and tear you apart."

"The only thing you could tear apart," Singer called at them, "is your sister's legs." The leader strained to come back, but his friends prevented him. A police car pulled up above them, and the Reillys ran, out of the tennis courts, back across the border into West Roxbury, where they knew they had priests and nuns and justice on *their* side. "I don't think those guys were Jews," one of them said, puffing as they ran.

"Bullshit," said the leader. "That's what's over there, Jews. Except maybe the guy with the bat and that crazy fucking redhead. What the Christ was he? I'm gonna kill that little prick if I see him again. We cruise in Jackie's car next time. And we bring our own bats. Those cops comin'?"

"Brookwood cops don't come over here. Boston cops never would pick us up. They're all our cousins. They don't like the Jews any better'n we do."

"I don't know," one of the Reillys said. "I still think they weren't Jews. Pretty good moxie for little kids."

"Maybe they was visiting. On a field trip to Jewtown." They picked up the pace, running deep into St. Joseph's parish across the VFW Parkway, safe among the triple-deckers and the big bellies that hung out down the corner opposite the Tam O'Shanter Grille and Brian Kelly's father's package store, where anyone short of ten-year-olds could buy Dawson's beer without an ID, safe near the pool hall and the cemetery, where they played Buck-buck up against the big tree near the Curley Mausoleum.

Later that night, Red Singer's father insisted they drive around West Roxbury looking for the boys who had attacked them. The Brookwood police had taken their reports, although the foursome were reluctant to talk. "Forget 'em," Hennessey warned the others. "Those guys will think twice before coming back, and the cops will never do anything. They're all the Reillys' cousins." Duke knew when to cut losses; it was Red who always pushed things over the line.

But Harry Singer insisted they go prowling. "No one's going to bully my kid," he said, "and not be punished." Mrs. Singer dragged at one of her husband's arms, and her daughters dragged on the other one. "No, Daddy," they pleaded.

"No, Harry," said Millie Singer. "They'll kill you. What can you do against the young Irish? They'll *kill* you. Call the police, girls," she sobbed to her daughters. Millie thought that any enterprise you took up with the goyim somehow marked you for death. The Jewish tradesmen, butchers and tailors could cheat you, but the goyim had the ability to put you in your grave.

"This is America, Millie," Harry Singer said to her. "We'll be all right. Go into the den. Watch television, Kate Smith is good. If you have to do anything, make brownies, make tollhouse, make something *sweet*."

They picked up Dickie Rosenberg because Mr. Singer insisted they needed him to help with the identification. Red made him go, but Dickie told his parents he was being taken out for ice cream by the Singers.

For Hennessey, talking with the police was an end to the matter. It had happened, they fought, it was over. The best athletes never brooded about the last pitch or a missed shot. They went on to what was next, the past a blank.

Freddie Temple had lost a tooth in the fight and told his parents he had caught a baseball in the mouth. "How could you miss a throw right at you?" was what his father wanted to know. His mother said she'd try to get him to a dentist when they moved to the North Shore for the summer and in the meanwhile wrap some ice in a towel, hold it on the damaged spot to stop the swelling and boys will be boys.

Parents who were strangers never called each other in the early 1950s. Residents of Brookwood mixed no more with people outside their ethnic backgrounds than did immigrants to New York or the West End of Boston in the early 1900s. In Brookwood the Hennesseys would never have communicated with the Singers or the Rosenbergs. They were dimly aware that people like the Temples existed. Even the Singers and the Rosenbergs belonged to different temples. Their forebears came from different villages, took different routes to America. They would walk around each other like animals sniffing intruders in a cave. Their boys might grow up to be different, but the parents never strayed from their kind. When you strayed from your kind you got burned.

Dickie knew that if he told his parents they would call Town Hall, demand some action, call the Anti Defamation League and try to get the incident in the local papers. It was enough that he would never forget it, but he was determined to identify no one, even if they did see the teenagers hanging out on a West Roxbury corner. Physical confrontation made Dickie feel sick to his stomach. He didn't think himself a coward. It was surprises he didn't like. If only he had known that the Reillys were going to interrupt their game, there were *fifty* things he could have thought of doing.

Harry Singer really had no idea where he was going. But he had a tire iron on the floor of the backseat just in case. He drove around aimlessly in the foreign country that was West Roxbury, just next door from his safe haven, the neighborhood where he lived and where he knew the druggist, the women in the bakery, the cleaner who also sold rayon neckties for twenty-five cents. Red and Dickie sat in the backseat nudging each other whenever they came to a corner where youngsters stood in groups. Dickie tried to scroonch down in his seat; Red pressed his face right to the glass, squinting at every face, hoping to see the bullies. After forty minutes they came up empty. "I didn't realize this was such a big place," said Harry Singer. "These people have got no money, boys. You have to understand, they want to hit out at people who have things."

"We're not really rich, Dad," said Red.

"We're richer than the thick Micks," said his father. "No one's going to push my family around without them knowing who they're dealing with."

Red was proud of his father and proud that he was as feisty as his old man. Red picked up the tire iron and whacked it against a free palm. "You'd have used this, Dad? What would you have told the cops?"

His father pulled over to the side of the road and idled the car. "I'd have said, 'Justifiable homicide,' " said Harry Singer. "How about Howard Johnson's for some ice cream?"

Dickie was sitting tall in the backseat now. He went after the Reillys and he survived and he didn't lie to his parents. He *was* going out for ice cream.

○

CHAPTER FOUR

Summer 1950

If you were a male child of Big Duke Hennessey in the summertime, there were two things you did, no choices. You worked and you played ball. There was no Little League in Brookwood in 1950, no parents jockeying for position and living out fantasies through their children. Parenting was done at home, period. Outside the home children were on their own, but they knew what was expected of them. There was an American Legion baseball team in Brookwood, VFW Post No. 142, but it was strictly for high school boys. Little Duke had a cousin who played third base for the Legion team and got Duke the batboy job. Duke also got to catch batting practice and, because of it, got voted a Legion jacket by the team, blue with the American Legion emblem over the left breast in yellow. There was no finer piece of clothing in all Brookwood for a thirteen-year-old. Francis Hennessey, Jr., used it as a blanket over his sheets, even in the hottest July nights. All the guys on the team went to Brookwood High or to St. Joseph's. "You're gonna be the varsity catcher someday," the older guys would tell him. These were the greatest words Francis Hennessey could ever hear. Going into the eighth grade he could already throw as hard as George Sabatini, the Legion's regular catcher, who could fart the first few bars of Vaughn Monroe's hit, "Ballerina." Francis would keep his mouth shut and keep the bats in order, put out the bases, lug the equipment bags and listen to the players talk about sex — and baseball. Francis never thought anyone in high school could lie about anything, so he believed the tales of french rubs and hand jobs, blow jobs in the Veterans of Foreign Wars parking lot from Elsie Paige, who would take on everyone as long as they were polite and didn't use bad language. Francis listened to their stories and memorized their songs: "Don't know why, there's no meat behind my fly, sloppy rabbi," without knowing what they meant, only knowing that the tune was "Stormy Weather."

"You get a boner yet, kid?" Sabatini would ask him, and the other team members would whack Sabatini in the arm and tell him not to be an asshole and leave Hennessey alone. "But does he get *boners?*" Sabatini would yell. "He can't be a catcher unless he's got the biggest hard-ons on the team." Duke's cousin John Mahoney would drop him off after the games. Little Duke was the last stop for Mahoney, who was too skinny to play football but could hit singles all day and night. Mahoney got to use the family Plymouth, which had seven St. Christopher medals stuck above the rearview mirror. "What's a french rub, Jack?" Little Duke asked his cousin. Silence. Finally, Jack said, "Some kind of massage."

"Come on, Jack. I'm not a kid, for Christ's sake. I can throw as hard as Sabatini. What's a french rub?"

"I don't know what a fucking french rub is, okay?"

"Come on, Jack, I'll retape the grips on your Bob Elliott bat."

"Okay, for Christ's sake," Mahoney said. "It's when she puts your pecker between her tits and rubs 'em back and forth till you come." Mahoney had never described it to anyone before. It was dark when he was dropping his cousin off. Darkness was a late surprise in Massachusetts summers. You could get seven innings finished before it was impossible to see the pitches. Mahoney could never have told his cousin what he told him unless it were totally black. He blushed anyway, knowing that he would never have a french rub as long as he lived, even though he could hit singles forever, even in the ninth-inning darkness on Massachusetts summer nights.

"Sabatini and those guys really have that happen to 'em?" Hennessey asked.

"You know those guys are full of shit, Francis. They just play ball and talk, you know? And that's what you should do. Just play ball and don't get your balls all in an uproar."

But Francis Hennessey's balls *were* in an uproar when he got home and got into his bedroom. For the first time in his life he didn't want to listen to the radio with his father and he didn't want Fig Newtons with milk. "What's the matter?" his father asked him, coming into Little Duke's room without knocking. There was no privacy in this Catholic home, no secrets that your parents didn't have a right to share, no sins that shouldn't be the possession of all. "The team lose?"

"We won six to four, not as close as it sounds."

"You wanted to play; you hate watching."

"There's nothing wrong, Dad. I'm tired. I carried doubles at the golf course this morning. Guys had every club in the book, and they only used drivers, a couple of irons and the putter."

His father put his hand on Francis's brow. "Feels hot. You sure you're okay?"

His son assured him that he was fine, and his father left the bedroom. Little Duke's legs hurt with the aches his mother told him were "growing pains." He thought about baseball and heroics in games he had watched, heroics in games he had played. He fought to erase images of what older boys talked of when they weren't talking of the Red Sox and the Braves and the importance of keeping up the chatter in the infield.

"It's summertime fever," Francis Hennessey, Sr., said to his wife, Mary, who was sitting on the porch swing listening to distant cars on the parkway and the nearby swishing of leaves on the elm trees lining their street.

"You mean he's working himself too hard," she said.

"There's no such thing as a young man working himself too hard," Hennessey said. "What I mean is the older boys are filling him with stories of girls."

"You don't think, Frank . . ." she said.

"God, no," her husband laughed. "You remember what I used to say about all those boys hanging around your porch . . . all that meat and no potatoes."

"Oh, Frank." She blushed, making motions to quiet his irreverence and at the same time making room next to her on the swing. It would creak with his bulk when he sat, and it made her think of the creaks and squeaks of everything he sat on or lay upon with his great strengths, and she was happy that they had a son.

The youngest boys in camp were singing in the mess hall. "Ai-yi-yi-yike us, nobody likes us, we are the boys of the freshman group. Always a winning, always a grinning, always a singing ai-yi-yi." As soon as they quieted down, dessert was served by the waiters:

chocolate cake, for which all the campers had been told to "save their forks" from the macaroni and cheese. Why wash two forks for the same meal? Dickie Rosenberg liked the milk *really* cold with his chocolate cake.

On rainy days, the boys at Dickie's camp, Wah Hoo Wah, sat in the mess hall after lunch and sang songs. The boys sang the college fight songs: "Hail to the Victors Valiant; With Crimson in Triumph Flashing; On, Brave Old Army Team, on to the fray; Bulldog, Bulldog, Bow Wow Wow, Eli — Yale." At thirteen years old, Dickie Rosenberg saw himself lugging a football for any of these schools, twitching his skinny hips, his soft breasts hardened into the pecs of an all-American. The opponents he didn't run around he would jump over or fake out or just smash into and leave them grabbing for a jersey or a leg or a cleat that was suddenly no longer there. When the afternoon was beginning to play out, when the boys had sung their guts out on "The Outlaws, Frank and Jesse James" and "In the moonlight, Rahdy Doo Dah, in the moonlight, Rahdy Doo Hah, you can hear those banjos strummin', Rahdy Doo Dah," then the boys' hands on the tables began to pound. The sound built until every table in the mess hall jumped from the pounding of boys' hands on the edges of those tables, the tables themselves moving on the linoleum floor scrubbed each day with wax and green Pine-Sol from the State of Maine that made everything smell as if there weren't a germ in the world. Uncle Henry, the owner of the camp, had been a baseball star at Dartmouth and never forgot it. The camp colors were green and white. The camp itself, Wah Hoo Wah, was named after a Dartmouth cheer. During color war, the last two weeks of the season, the entire camp was split into teams, green and white, and the boys would go at each other, hated enemies, as if it were the Rose Bowl. "Life is like color war," Uncle Henry said, and he meant it. Uncle Henry was hairy; almost every part of him was covered with black hair. It sprouted everywhere as if he were a fairway on a not very manicured golf course. This would have been fine with Henry, as golf courses were green, and it would have made him into an even better son of Dartmouth, The Big Green. In the mess hall, on rainy days when the songs and cheers went on into the afternoon, Uncle Henry did a fair imitation of a hairy Mussolini. He pounded on the table himself, jumped out of his seat and threw his arms into the air. The boys went wild cheering him, and the counselors egged him on, smiling to each other as if to say, "Let's humor the old fart. Look where Mussolini wound up."

"You boys-a good boys," Uncle Henry would say. "Let'sa all go backa to the bunks and pray fora sunashine." It was a butchered Italian accent, and it worked with the campers. It even worked with Aunt Sandy, Henry's wife, who would often say to her husband when they were in their bed made in Camp Wah Hoo Wah's own Arts and Crafts cabin and the air smelled of pine boughs, "Talk Italian to me, Henry. Make me think you're Mussolini." Uncle Henry always did his best, a quality he knew he had learned at Dartmouth.

Dickie Rosenberg loved camp. He had started when he was nine and cried himself to sleep for the first week without letting anyone else know about it. When he discovered that most of the other boys were homesick also, and that several of his bunkmates still wet their beds, and that one would take blankets to the latrine and sleep on the floor because he needed the light, he discovered a great truth of life: there were always people worse off than you, no matter how miserable you were. Dickie became a leader at camp because he subtly lobbied for it: president of the freshman group, a serviceable shortstop, a fine backstroker, winner each summer in color-war quiz night and at the extemporaneous speaking contest: "How would you manage the Red Sox?" He idolized older boys who were the best athletes and the counselors with the sweatshirts that said "Property of HAA" (Harvard Athletic Association). He longed for the day when he could be captain of one of the color-war teams and bury the hatchet into one of the ten-foot totem poles that stood outside Uncle Henry's cabin. After each day's color-war competition, the entire camp assembled there before dinner. The scores were announced, and the captain of the leading team got to smack a hatchet higher than the hatchet of the other team stuck into one side of the pole. Atop this ceremonial totem was the carved figure of an Indian. The wooden Indian wore a painted green sweater with a big "D" emblazoned on it. Dickie thought these two team captains were young Jewish gods. If the green side were on top, the entire team would march into the mess hall chanting, "Green team will shine tonight, green team will shine. Green team will shine tonight, all down the line. When the sun goes down and the moon comes out, green team will shine." Then the white team would march in, building its chant to drown out the greens: "Boola, boola, boola, boola, that's the war cry of the white team. We will drown them, we will crown them, till they holler, *Boola Boo*." Louder and louder until the cold cuts and punch were served and the little warriors left off cheering to eat. Uncle Henry and all the boys loved punch night. Punch, Uncle Henry was delighted to tell Aunt Sandy, was a lot cheaper than milk.

Rainy days at camp were like rainy days for the operators of ski resorts: they ruined business, they made people uncomfortable. They made children long for home. After a lengthy song fest in the mess hall and a long rest hour in the bunks where letters written home were mandatory, the entire camp reported to the Rec Hall for indoor games. The rain turned the lower campus into a sponge and the wind whipped it off the lake so that it seemed the world would be wet and gray forever. Through the storm you could see patches of yellow light moving up and down and converging upon the big wooden ark of a rec hall. A hundred boys in yellow slickers and yellow rain hats were escorted by their counselors to this huge building with a stage and bleachers and a gym floor where every evening activity took place, from talent night to quiz night to movies to Friday night services ("Thank you for the blessing of field and lake, court and riflery range, that we are so happily privileged to enjoy here . . .").

On one of these rainy days, somewhere between Simon Says, Red Light and a game like Limbo in reverse, where a broomstick is held higher and higher and one had to jump to reach it, Dickie Rosenberg felt that he was going to be sick to his stomach. He was prone to anxiety and to stomach problems.

"Use the bathroom in back of the Rec Hall stage," said Steve Goldberg, one of his counselors, from Haverhill, Massachusetts, who could hit jump shots all day from practically midcourt and walked with a rolling slouch like a high school hotshot. "I feel sick *now*," said Dickie, "and there are four kids waiting in line."

"Okay," said the jump shooter. "Get back to the bunk. But either lie down and cover yourself with your extra blanket afterwards, or come back here for Attack-ball. We need you for Attack-ball, Dick. We want everybody building their bodies."

Dickie didn't feel so sick when he was reminded that he should build his body, and he leaped in his yellow slicker and rain hat all the way back to his bunk. If he built his body he would lose those tits.

There is something scary about an empty building in a storm. The shutters were down on Dickie's cabin against the rain blowing in. Wet bathing suits, attached to a clothesline, swung from their pinned crotches like little nylon flags. Dickie came into Bunk 11, his home for the summer, and it was a dank household with beds messy from rest hour: comic books, nose clips, camp sweaters and dust bunnies all over the floor along with the equipment of the summer: tennis racquets in presses, rubber balls, Ping-Pong paddles, sneakers, bats and baseball gloves. Seldom, if ever, was the bunk empty. Dickie was tempted to check everyone's cubbyhole for special comics he loved: *Blackhawk, Tales from the Crypt,* Classics Illustrated. The bliss of being alone to rifle through everyone's things was overcome by again feeling sick to his stomach, and he headed for the latrine at the back of the cabin. He pushed through the swinging door with some urgency and saw something he would never forget as long as he lived: his bunkmate, little Barry Goldstein, was pulling the pecker of one of their counselors, Aaron Brodie, a consensus all-East guard from Penn State, as fast as one could ever pull a pecker without tearing it from its roots. Little Barry, crooked grin with a hint of premature mustache and very red lips, was an odd presence at camp: not an athlete, not a brain, he was the kind of kid who would be silently unhappy at Wah Hoo Wah for a couple of years and then move on to work at some suburban Howard Johnson's or in his father's business, where he would hang around an office or deliver a few packages or seal a few cases until it was time to go home. Barry Goldstein stopped immediately and turned to Dickie with his little sly smile intact. Brodie, the counselor, saw his job, his career and his life fly out the shuttered windows. All he could think of to say was "Dickie, I had a problem."

"It's okay," Dickie said. Brodie was big and acted stupid, but he was not a mean counselor. Dickie wouldn't dream of telling Uncle Henry. He used the other latrine in the bunk, sick to his stomach, very nervous that someone would come in on him. He put on his yellow slicker and headed back to the Rec Hall. Aaron Brodie, in shorts and a T-shirt, ran after him. "Dickie," he said, trying to put an arm around him, "there's a reason for everything." Dickie shrugged off the arm and kept walking. He could hear a song from the Rec Hall, a song that usually signaled the end of games:

"Friends, friends, friends, we will always be . . . whether in fine or in dark stormy weather, Camp Wah Hoo Wah, will keep us together . . ."

He was aware of Brodie babbling at him, telling him he could have fifty-yard-line seats for every Penn State home game next year. The rain was slanting down now, soaking Brodie to the skin. Dickie was walking faster. "I don't give a shit about Penn State, Aaron," Dickie said, and began to run.

Freddie Temple never caddied in the summertime. Even his father's quest for the perfect son let up in the summers to the extent that Freddie was free to run with his friends, to play golf and tennis at the Club, to throw footballs on the beach and wish like mad that he were older. He felt gawky and out of control.

But life was less of a question mark for Freddie than for any of his friends in Brookwood. Freddie and his summer contemporaries on the North Shore of Boston had no doubts at all about where their lives were going. The boys were going away to boarding school, then to Harvard or Yale if they were reasonably presentable, Williams or Amherst if they were dumb but good at obscure sports like soccer or squash, Dartmouth or Penn if they were only dumb and a place had to be available for four years to hide them until the service. Princeton was a *Southern* college, Cornell was somewhere on the frontier, Columbia was for radicals, and Brown was not only beneath contempt, it was in Providence, Rhode Island. That was college for men in 1950, as far as Freddie Temple's parents and friends were concerned. Female children of the North Shore were also slated for boarding school or for day schools like Winsor or Beaver or Brimmer & May in Chestnut Hill. They were slated for the Seven Sisters at one level or acceptable junior colleges at the next but with one goal in mind: get an education, but get married. Read philosophy or history; study biology or physics; learn typing, shorthand, sing in the chorus or dance around the maypole in a sheet. But get married. That was it. And the blond beauties on the North Shore of Boston in 1950 wouldn't have had it any other way. There was an order to one's life. That was the way things were. Not that they wouldn't have their rebels, their Harry Crosbys, their writers and artists and actresses. But these creative people were often thought fools, people to be slightly pitied, tolerated, gossiped about. One's bank would send them trust checks. For the social population of Boston's North Shore, life was too wonderful. They were in charge, and you would have to be an idiot to rock the boat. Here was Freddie Temple's typical summer's day: up at eight for blueberry muffins, off to the Yacht Club for sailing drills in a 210, hotdogs and Cokes at the Beach Club for lunch, followed by tennis on grass courts or hitting drivers on the practice tee or putting in bare feet for lime rickeys at the bar until his mother finished her golf round and was ready to take him home.

Lizzie Myles Temple didn't know *anyone* she or her husband hadn't grown up with. She never considered that there was a life away from her world. She could not describe the man who filled her prescriptions at the drugstore, or the man who took her grocery-order delivery at S. S. Pierce, or the teachers who taught her children. They were there to serve, and their bills were paid reasonably on time. There was no need to encourage *anyone*. Just be decent and slightly chilly. Lizzie had golf balls to hit and cards to deal and dance cards to fill.

"You're crewing in the regatta Saturday, darling," she said to Freddie. A statement, not a question. Lizzie was filling in the blanks on the ride home, making conversation. Her baby boy was beautiful, but his life was his own and she had many more problems than he, thank you very much, and she couldn't hit a short iron to the greens to save herself and what really mattered in relation to *that*?

"We drew the boats today, Mummy," Freddie said. "I'm crewing for John Damon."

"Your father loves children's silver trophies in the house, remember that."

"The skipper gets the silver, Mummy," Freddie said.

"Yes," said Lizzie Temple, thinking that perhaps her grip was the problem. Too much right hand on the short irons.

Freddie and a number of children from their club were being driven that evening to a dance at Prime, the junior yacht club associated with the American Yacht Club in Marblehead. Several chauffeurs were available for this job, along with Mr. Gallo, who did the lawn and the gardens for the Temples in the summer. Mr.

Gallo did all kinds of jobs for the Temples, and his children wore the cast-off clothes from Freddie and his older brother and sister.

Freddie sat up front in the old prewar Buick his family kept for use at the summer house.

Five kids were stuffed into the backseat: the Shaw twins, Eric and Ian, who really didn't like anyone but themselves; Albie Crook, who was usually looking for a fight and talked only of playing football someday for Harvard; and two best girlfriends, Vickie Styles, on the heavy side but the best sailor of the lot, and "Thin Min" Bridges, taller than all the boys her age but also funnier and much admired for her spunk. Freddie kneeled on the passenger seat, facing backward so he could jabber with the others on the way to the dance. He was wearing the uniform of the summer, white duck pants with a blue blazer, blue oxford button-down shirt and a striped tie of his brother's stained with years of boarding school and college dining hall meals. On the ride they talked only of sports, mostly sailing but also of their instructors that summer. They all took lessons at various clubs, in various activities that they would pursue all of their lives.

The dance at the Yacht Club was a record hop.

One of the older kids, a college sophomore, played 78 records on the Club's victrola. All over America at this age, boys stood in one corner, girls stood in another, and that evening at the Prime Yacht Club was no exception. As the evening progressed, the lights were dimmed, several girls danced with each other, several of the smaller, more adventuresome boys took a spin on dares with several girls and the lover of the group (there is always one) held a girl close, danced slow, upper bodies pressed together (a scandal at thirteen), hips separated by the width of another person. Freddie stayed in the corner with the Shaw twins, shifting his weight, drinking Cokes and wishing he could press his upper body against any girl, but particularly Allison Bennett, who had dimples and short blond hair that Freddie felt deserved to be nuzzling his cheek. But Freddie didn't dance. He watched the dancers, and he went onto the porch, where the boys were sneaking drinks of rum mixed with Coke and puffing on cigarettes cupped in their palms against the breeze. Billy Coleman was the disc jockey and also the commodore of the junior sailing program. Coleman was popular and a champion sailor in his family's 210 named *Havana-Banana* with painted cigar and banana on either side of the hull. Coleman was a leader, but he was also a practical joker. He adored teasing the younger kids. Coleman was responsible for making rum available from a bottle he brought to the dance and kept in his blue ditty bag. His girlfriend wandered in and out during the evening, beaming at the younger kids, helping to choose the records. Her name was Julie Hall, and she lived across the street from the Yacht Club in her grandparents' house that they shared with three generations of Halls. Every time she left the room where the dance was being held, she took the ditty bag with her. Periodically, Coleman and Julie Hall would take to the floor to show their younger charges how it was done when you were in college, full of experience and technique. To the crooning of Nat "King" Cole, they swirled and dipped low and showed the kids their future. Julie pushed Freddie Temple to dance with Allison Bennett. Everybody at a certain age wants to be a parent, even if it is only to push somebody around.

Freddie did his best on the dance floor, a fox trot with heavy emphasis on what his dancing classes stressed: the box step. Allison Bennett made the same effort. They both wanted it; they both hated the awkwardness of adolescence. But the "it" they wanted was to be *smooth*.

"You had to go to those dancing classes at home?" Allison asked.

"Every fourth Friday night," Freddie said. "When am I ever in my life going to waltz?"

"I know," she said. "It's so . . . old."

They bumped another couple and awkwardly danced on.

"I'm going to ask Coleman to play a Spike Jones record," Freddie teased.

"Don't you dare. It's about time you and your friends grew up. Are you coming to the clambake Sunday night?"

"What do you care if my friends and I act like children?"

"Just asking. I don't care how you act."

They were cut in on by Julie Hall, who made everyone in the room laugh by pulling Freddie in close to her and swirling him around in exaggerated turns. He had never danced so well, and his blushes meant nothing against his tan. His mother often smelled from a smell that sickened him when she kissed him good night. It was a smell that was heavy and dark, a sweaty smell that was not female, not male, just unpleasant. The smell was rum. Julie Hall smelled almost the same. But it was mixed with the mystery smells of a twenty-year-old, and Freddie was thrilled with the combination.

"It won't be long, Freddie," she said. "Take it from an old lady. The girls will be standing in line. Is that what you want?"

Freddie surprised the college girl. "It's *part* of what I want," he said.

Coleman spun Doris Day singing "Sentimental Journey" and came over to them. "No dancing with the same person more than once. You want to take him outside on the porch, take him outside."

Coleman also smelled of rum and after-shave lotion. Alcohol was the magic potion of Boston's North Shore. It was elixir for young and old in the Temples' set and socially; it set the tone for everyone. There were famous drunks and characters on the North Shore the way there were famous business people and philanthropists in other communities. Tommy Allen, Georgie Temple's summer golf partner, was fond of saying, paraphrasing Herman Melville, "A martini was my Yale College and my Harvard." Liquor was a measure of acceptability. How you held it, dealt with it, managed it was often the mark of a life. It was not shocking that introduction to alcohol started early on the North Shore. It was a fact of life and one you should get on with as quickly as possible.

Julie Hall swayed back and forth and mocked her boyfriend. "You want me to take Freddie out on the porch?"

"*Kiss* him," Coleman hissed at her.

She grabbed Freddie by the hand and dragged him out of the Yacht Club onto the porch overlooking Marblehead harbor. Chinese lanterns swung from hooks, the lanterns put there just for the evening, decoration for the youngsters. Julie put her mouth against Freddie's, which was shut as tightly as the vaults of the State Street Bank. She licked her tongue around his lips, quickly, probing for entry, then withdrew. "That's it," she said. "Someday, you'll do a lot better." Julie ran back into the dance, where "Sentimental Journey" was winding down.

Encouraged beyond belief, Freddie asked Allison Bennett out onto the floor. She gave him the first of many hurt responses he would get in his life. "You stick with *older* women, Freddie.

Don't waste your time with *little* girls." And she was gone, leaving him again with the Shaw twins, who were throwing fingers for pennies, "bucking up" to amuse themselves until they were allowed to go home.

On the ride back, Mr. Gallo and the kids sang songs. They sprawled over each other in the backseat of the old Buick singing patriotic numbers because Mr. Gallo had a son with the marines who had just been shipped off to fight in Korea. They sang "Over There," "Comin' in on a Wing and a Prayer," "Johnny Got a Zero" and more choruses of "Over There" because they could thump on the seats and have contests about who could sing the loudest, which Mr. Gallo won because he was drunker than any of them. Thin Min Bridges insisted on "America the Beautiful" as they approached her house, and it came out just fine with Albie Crook and Mr. Gallo singing bass and Vickie Styles, who studied voice, hitting high notes and even the Shaw twins joining in, carried away by the spirit of distant wars.

When all the others had been dropped off, Mr. Gallo and Freddie did not sing. "I pray for my boy every day," Mr. Gallo said. "You have a son someday you know what I mean."

Freddie didn't know what Mr. Gallo meant. All he did know was that he had had one of the great nights of his life, kissed by a college girl and the chill up his spine that he felt singing "Over There." And he hadn't just been *kissed*. Julie Hall had run her tongue over his lips. Freddie was feeling no pain when he slid into the kitchen for milk and brownies that he knew the cook would leave for him in the icebox, the brownies wrapped in wax paper. His parents had given a dinner party, and he could hear someone playing "Sentimental Journey" on the old upright piano in the living room. He went into the kitchen quietly, not wanting to have to go into the living room to make the rounds of his parents' friends. He snapped open the handle of the icebox and jumped back in fright as someone else yelped, "Oh my God," in equal fright. Falling back into the midst of the kitchen, he saw his mother. She had been leaning against the back of the icebox, and her dress was pulled up to her waist. She was with his father's lawyer, Morris Hawkins, whom Freddie had never seen without both a vest and a frown. This time his vest was unbuttoned, as were his trousers, and Freddie knew there was no way to button one's trousers quickly. Morris Hawkins turned away. Lizzie Temple straightened herself immediately and turned to the attack. "What the hell are you doing up, young man?"

"I'm just back from the dance, Mummy."

"Well, for Christ's sake, don't go around in the dark frightening people to death. Get whatever you're getting and go to bed."

Freddie grabbed the dish with the brownies and left the milk alone. He could drink water if it came to that, and he hustled with his late-night treat up the back stairs. His mother remained in the kitchen, as far as he knew. And he didn't want to know. Freddie had his own memories.

Red Singer hung out in front of the drugstore at night with older guys, guys who tolerated a squirt like Red because he would do anything. The girls who walked by the drugstore hated Red because he was that most disgusting of all combinations, young and dirty. "Dirty" was what the girls called anyone foul-mouthed and foul-minded.

"Pant for this one, Singer," commanded Philly Miller, the leader of the gang who hung out at the corner. A teenaged girl walked by, wearing a sweater two sizes too small. Red Singer made loud panting noises like a dog begging for food. He followed the panting with a long howl. The other boys also howled and laughed. The girl stopped and looked at Red. "I'm going to tell your sisters how dirty you are, Stanley," she said, and then smiled at Miller. "Hi, Philly," she said, and walked slowly on. Cool Philly; dirty Red.

This is how it went in the evening at Matonquit Beach, where the Singers spent every July and August. Red's father rented one floor of a white clapboard triple-decker house in the Alphabet Section of Matonquit. Matonquit was a seaside town on Boston's South Shore, a small pinkie of a point sticking out into the Atlantic Ocean next to Quincy, but well above Plymouth and Cape Cod. During the 1920s it was a haven for the Irish who were beginning to accumulate money: the Fitzgeralds, the Kennedys, James M. Curley. It was also the closest beach community to Dorchester, Roxbury and Mattapan, where immigrant Jewish families moved when they left Boston's North and West Ends. As these families began to prosper and move once again, they chose grassy suburbs like Brookwood and Newton, where their children could have yards and houses and where neighbors didn't gossip over clotheslines strung from back porches and the smell of Sabbath cooking didn't permeate an entire street. Many of these people bought summer houses along the beach in Matonquit. The poorer Jews, working still to bust out of Roxbury and Dorchester, scraped up money to rent apartments in the "Alphabet Section," streets lettered A to Z, where they could live as they lived at home: crowded, families in two or three rooms. But with sea breezes and a wonderful white sandy beach with clear, chilly water and nights that gave the illusion of freedom away from different kinds of ghettos, it was a breather in lives full of hard work and sacrifice.

It was also a stretch for Harry Singer to rent the top of a two-family house on Q Street, but it was a stretch he made for his daughters. The rooms cost him more than he made, and August's rent he had to borrow from his brother, which killed him because every nickel he ever borrowed from his brother came with a sermon about "living beyond his means." The house was on the bay side of Matonquit, the wrong side of that spit of land, split by Powhatan Avenue. The right side was the ocean side. But the houses there belonged to the people who owned the businesses, not the people who sold the goods or who needed to give Tootsie Rolls to the secretaries in order to get in to see the boss. Someday he would have a business, Harry knew, and a house on the ocean side. In the meantime, his daughters, Flossie and Lorrie, could get around, be exposed to the right people. You could meet anyone on the beach, and his girls were the most beautiful girls in Matonquit. Everyone said so, and his brother could go fuck himself. He'd pay his brother back in the fall. *One* good month and he was home, he could get a little ahead.

Stanley Singer worked his sisters for all they were worth. He realized early in life what an asset they were to him. Every hero in Brookwood and Matonquit hung around their house, hoping for the secret to the Singer sisters. Millie Singer served more milk and ginger ale and homemade goodies, blueberry pies, apple strudel, chocolate cake, than any mother in Massachusetts. "Does she like me, Mrs. Singer?" they would all ask.

"Of course she likes you," Millie Singer would say to all of them. "Another piece of strudel?"

Stanley took money from his sisters' suitors for giving them information. He basked in their praise. No one could bully him, or lean on him, or rag him for anything. He could call on all the big men in Brookwood High School and even some from Newton High and Boston Latin. Everyone knew Red Singer, the brother of Flossie and Lorrie with the long legs and the magic tits whom no one could touch but everyone dreamed of.

Red had odd jobs in the summer. He had to bring money into the house, about that there was no debate. He took work as a fact of life. He adored his father, and his father instilled in him the need to take care of the women in the family. He worked in Spiegel's fish store that summer, from eight in the morning until two in the afternoon, six days a week. He stocked the shelves, stamped prices on boxes, swept the store and mopped the back room, where the fish was delivered fresh every morning. When he got out of work it was beach time, and he rode his bike fast down Q Street to the dunes, leaving it on the sand and running first into the surf to wipe out the smell and the memory of fish and Old Man Spiegel. ("Yes, Mrs. Hoffman, the pollock is nice. We got some nice sole, too; you want some whitefish, and we moved the jars of herring. *Stanley,* bring some jars herring.") Every time a housewife left the fish store, Spiegel would comment on how cheap they were, how stupid they were, how chintzy were their husbands. Red prepped himself this way for jumping into the social life of the beach. His solitary swim was his rehearsal for outdoing the other kids, for mouthing off, for daring to risk anything. He rode a wave in lying on his belly, riding in all the way to where he scraped himself on small stones and shells at the water's edge. He would do this several times until he was ready. Then he proceeded down the beach, which was three miles long with white sand that at low tide turned gray and hard, perfect for ball games of any kind: stickball, running the bases, boxball, tag football. The crowd of kids hung out at Kendall Street about a mile away from where Red had left his bike. Everyone was a teenager on Kendall Street, and most of the crowd was Jewish and smooth in the best high school sense. They were strutting their stuff, hair slicked back, combs in the elastic waistband of their bathing suits, cigarette packs just beginning to be rolled into the rolled-up sleeves of their T-shirts, biceps flexed. Their parents piled together in the tenements of Roxbury, Dorchester and Mattapan. Their children at their ease on Kendall Street piled together in the sand, their heads lying on neighboring tummies, back to back playing cards, digging holes, building castles, smoking, petting, kissing, wrestling, messing around with summer on their hands. Red Singer walked into the group on *his* hands, balancing easily, cocky grin fixed in place. Philly Miller pushed him over onto the sand. "You smell like pussy, Singer."

"You're sniffing your own fingers, Miller, not me," said Singer, taking his chances with the toughest guy on Kendall Street. The guys from the old country, which these kids called Roxbury and Dorchester, played on the streets at home, and their edges were rough. You were a sissy if your family had moved to Brookwood or Newton; you had lost the edge of the streets. The kids talked about cars and dates and the Red Sox, who were currently six games behind the New York Yankees. They talked about their hair and clothes and who liked them. Flossie and Lorrie took turns combing and braiding each other's hair and pouring lemon juice into their hands and rubbing it into their scalps in the hopes that the juice would act with the sun, streaking their dark hair blond. Their parents didn't want them dating boys from Dorchester now that they had moved up in the world. "Do you have to sit near us, Stanley," Flossie said to her brother. "You'll be sixteen someday. You don't have to be the mascot of our crowd."

The muscle boys took this as a signal to shoo Red away. This led to pushing and arm twisting and Flossie saying to the muscle boys, "Hey, leave my brother alone."

"Yeah, don't hurt him," echoed Lorrie, which made the boys roll their eyes and say, "But we thought . . ."

Red Singer needed to make a splash. He knew that ultimately it was up to him to care for everyone in his family. His father was weighed down with too many bosses, too many sample cases. Getting there he needed people to pay attention to him. When Wolfie, the ice-cream man, rang the bell on his truck, Red jumped to his feet, "I'll treat for everyone, coconut-covereds, chocolate-covereds, sandwiches, Fudgsicles," and he ran across the sand to Beach Avenue, which ran the length of the dunes. Ice-cream trucks cruised the avenue, white refrigerator trucks, with college boys working summer jobs at the wheel and representing the major milk distributors. Wolfie was an independent, a character with thinning black hair and a sarcastic mouth, especially about the young ladies of the beach. "What a lovely pair of . . . eyes you have, darling," Wolfie would say, staring at a teenage chest and handing over a Hoodsie with a picture of ballplayers underneath the ice-cream coating of the inner lid, DiMaggio, Warren Spahn, Musial. His truck was painted white enamel with a big red-lettered sign proclaiming "Wolfie's Frozen Treats" on both sides. He had a bell and a horn that did go "ahhooga," bought from an army surplus store. The kids hated Wolfie, but he worked his route hard. He *did* have the biggest chocolate-covereds on the beach, and he had something no other truck sold . . . sundaes with hot fudge.

"Six sundaes, five chocolate-covereds, five Popsicles, all colors," said Red.

"You're getting to look more like Woody Woodpecker every day," said Wolfie, reaching deep into his freezing compartment for the goodies.

"And you look like just the last two syllables — Pecker."

"What?" said Wolfie, holding back the ice cream until he saw Red's money. Red had no intention of treating anyone. He knew, indeed, that he would be the one who was treated. His sisters would see to that. "Two dollars eighty-five cents," said Wolfie.

Red fumbled two fingers in the small pocket of his bathing suit. "I hope I didn't get those bills wet."

"C'mon," said Wolfie. There was a line of little kids behind Red, clutching their nickels and dimes.

"Wait a second, Wolfie, I got it." Right on cue, Flossie and Lorrie Singer came over the dunes looking exasperated and delicious. "You're not going to pay for anyone's ice cream, Stanley," Flossie said. "You can't throw your money around like some big shot."

Wolfie held out his hand, took $3.00 from Lorrie and made sure he touched her skin while he did it. "Any time you girls want *free* ice cream just say the word. But make sure you leave Junior Birdman at home."

Flossie batted her eyes. "How about tossing in a couple Creamsicles, Wolfman?"

Flossie was a tease, and her brother couldn't stand it. Red thought that everything he got, he got the hard way.

"I'll give you a Creamsicle you'll never forget," Wolfie leered.

"Just give her the goddamn ice cream, you son of a bitch," Red yelled at him. Wolfie made a motion, drawing back his fist at the boy. They were standing in back of the truck with kids spilling out, lined up behind them, on the hot asphalt of the road. Red suddenly ran around the ice-cream truck, hopped in the driver's seat and locked the door. He started the ignition and jammed it into first gear. He popped the clutch, and the truck jumped down the beach road with a wonderful whine and scrape of engine and tires and bellows from the outraged Wolfie.

There wasn't a young man who had reached his thirteenth birthday and hung around the drugstore at night in Matonquit who didn't know how to hot-wire an ignition. This was easy. Red realized that he had been wanting to drive off with Wolfie's truck all summer. "The pig insulted my sister," he thought as he careened down the beach road. In the rearview mirror he saw Wolfie running after him. Wolfie would not stop running until he saw cops, that's what kind of a guy Wolfie was. But after three blocks, all Red could see to his rear was the heat shimmering off the pavement in waves. He stopped the truck when he reached the spot where he parked his bike. "Hero for a day," he thought. "Worth a half-assed beating from Dad." Pleased with what he saw as a no-risk deal, Red left a note for Wolfie stuck beneath a windshield wiper. "WATCH YOUR MOUTH," it said. Red fished in his bathing-suit pocket and found a dime. He put it on Wolfie's driver's seat, got out and took a coconut-covered from the freezer. Putting the wrapper in a trash bin, he hopped on his bike and began to pedal slowly home to face the music. "Wolfie is a prick," he thought, "but he's got the best coconut-covereds."

Red pretended he was riding a horse, knowing he was going to the movies that night with the guys to see Jimmy Stewart in *Winchester '73*. Riding no hands, he sighted along an imaginary rifle and shot old women rocking on their porch chairs. He made the sound of gunfire echoing in canyons. Movies were his favorite things.

Eighth Grade, Autumn 1950

There was one tree on the playground, a tall sugar maple, whose September leaves only hinted at autumn change of life. The boys sat underneath its shade. They had just finished a buck-up game of tackle football, and they were gathering their strength to trudge home. Red Singer had lit a cigarette, and he puffed happily, looking foolish in cast-off football pants with an old torn wool sweater pulled over his prized pair of shoulder pads bought at Sears Roebuck with earnings from the summer.

"You're getting to be a pro at smoking," Duke Hennessey said, "but easier to tackle."

"You're full of shit, Duke," Red said. "I'm the fastest guy in the school, and you know it."

"If you ever want to play in high school, you'll give them up," said Dickie Rosenberg. "You'll lose your wind. Plus you're not the fastest guy in Brookwood. This town is loaded with talent in the other sections. Guys who don't smoke."

"You tell him, you tell him, Rosie, you're the expert," said Hennessey. "Red smokes to be a hot shit when he's really just a cold fart."

"We can tell who became men this summer and who stayed boys," said Freddie Temple, motioning for Red to throw him a cigarette. Freddie snapped it out of the air and lit it with matches he kept in his rolled-up corduroy trousers.

The boys wore patchwork football equipment. They all had shoulder pads and helmets. That was it. None of them had jerseys with numbers; none of them had cleats, merely hightop basketball sneakers. They didn't even wear jocks, only the cotton briefs they all had worn to school. (This was a time when boys played on playgrounds, when they amused themselves, picking up games in each season and practicing for hours, not just showing up for games expecting to be perfect at the first whack. At most levels, nothing was organized. There were no coaches, no equipment that you did not provide for yourselves. There was no Pop Warner football in

1950, in Brookwood no Little League. The parents worked, and the kids played. No fuzzy lines between parent and child in 1950.) The boys talked about the usual subjects: "Does she like me?" "Will Billy Goodman of the Red Sox win the batting title?" "Our homeroom teacher's BO" and always, "Does she like me?"

They were telling each other jokes as the wind blew chilly and the sun began to fade when Bob Newman, principal of the Hathaway School, walked quickly across the field toward them. "The butts," warned Hennessey. Temple and Singer squashed their cigarettes and put them into their pockets. Bob Newman was no fool, a tough, no-nonsense educator who understood that adults always knew better than children. He blasted them.

"You think you're kidding me?" he said. "I'm surprised at you, Temple. The *body* is your temple, you ever hear that phrase? You smoke and that temple is ruined. Nobody, underline *nobody*, smokes in my playground. Singer, I'm not surprised by anything you do. Let me have those cigarettes."

"They're mine. I paid for them," Red said. But he said it feebly.

"I want the cigarettes, and I want the name of the store that sold them to you."

Bob Newman could hurt you a dozen different ways. He could stare down every mother in the Hathaway School district, and Red Singer was never going to be a problem for him.

"I stole them from my mother," Red said. "You're going to have to ask her where she bought them."

"I intend to do that very thing, Singer. Now on your feet, and you're going to run around this playground ten times. You, too, Temple. Every time you puff on a coffin nail I want you to remember Bob Newman and ten laps."

All the boys stood. Duke Hennessey elbowed Dickie in the stomach lightly and jerked his head toward the other two, who had already started jogging away, not questioning their sentence. "Come on, Dickie," Duke said.

"What the hell for? I wasn't smoking."

"You're in the same backfield," he said. "One suffers, we all suffer."

Duke took off behind the other two with a steady, ambling gait that looked easy. Dickie shook his head and double-timed to catch up with his friend. "Stupidity," he muttered to himself, but he ran nevertheless.

Bob Newman headed for his car, knowing that they would do the full ten laps whether or not he stood around to supervise. Hennessey would see to that.

During dinner that evening, Newman's wife told him he seemed preoccupied. "What thinkest thou?" she said in the usual banter that they had adopted years before.

"I was thinking that the eighth grade is the first test of manhood," her husband said. "For these boys it's the top of the heap in grammar school before the lowest of the low at high school next year."

"*Quelle profondeur,*" she said. "You want to tell me the next four tests of manhood?"

She loved games like that, and he was happy to oblige.

CHAPTER FIVE

O

High School, 1951

The quadrangle was where everyone in high school gathered. Everyone except for the "knuck-knuck" division, the youngsters who were taught trades in the manual training building. They hung around on the steps of the building. These were the students who were going on to work or into the military after high school. Segregated and made to feel stupid even if they were not, the knuck-knucks made everyone else pay who dared walk their sidewalk. Duke Hennessey knew many of these tough guys because he had played ball with them in the summers. Duke came to Brookwood High School with a reputation for athletics, and any friend of Hennessey's was okay, not to be ridiculed or challenged from the steps of the manual training building.

"Knockers, knockers," yelled boys from the steps as girl students walked by carrying armloads of books in front of them cradled under their bosoms. "Fairies, fairies," they yelled at boy students lugging green book bags. Duke was immune, walking with Red Singer and Dickie Rosenberg, by the baseball field toward the four-story institutional brick buildings topped by the clock tower with the large block letters inside the casing that read "BHS." "Are you nervous?" Dickie asked.

"What have I got to be nervous about?" said Red Singer. "I got shitty marks at Hathaway. I'll get shitty marks in high school. What difference does it make? This is a bus stop for the redhead on his way to greatness."

"Who are you kidding, Stanley?" said Hennessey. "You're scared shitless. Brookwood High is going to chew you up and spit you out."

They went to separate homerooms and then to separate classes, engulfed by the size of the school: two thousand students who generally assumed they would toe the line, study what was required, go out for school organizations and sports, fall in love and move on to some college or job without much help from parents except financially. The heat on students at Brookwood High was not the heat of academic excellence or the heat of competing for college entrance. The real pressure involved the same two questions from the eighth grade: "Does she like me?" and "Does he like me?" Everything else in high school was secondary to that.

When classes let out, students poured into the quadrangle, the outer courtyard surrounded by the brick class buildings that formed its outline. The groups in the quadrangle congregated by cliques: athletes, cheerleaders, recent arrivals from the Jewish ghettos of Roxbury and Dorchester in sharp clothes with pegged pants and turned-up collars. *The* girls and *the* boys, as they were called, the most popular of school leaders, and their hangers-on were in another corner. Freshmen milled around, uncertain of where they belonged. But they stayed in small groups of friends they had known at one of the seven grammar schools they had attended. It was much too early in the first days of high school to stray from what was familiar.

The kids who had gone to the Hathaway School crowded together trying to look nonchalant. "I'm going to freshman football," Hennessey said. "I don't want to hear any shit about you two not going out for it."

"I may have to get a job after school," Red said. "Depends on my father's new territory."

Hennessey and Rosenberg said nothing. They knew that Red's father struggled and that the family often had to put on the good face.

"My parents won't sign the permission slip," Dickie said.

"So we'll forge it for you. Like you'll sign my report cards," said Red Singer.

"Look. It isn't the Hathaway pickup games. They got kids from all over town playing football. I'm too small, too slow, my best sport's basketball and I want to practice that all fall."

"Chickenshit, right?" said Hennessey.

Suddenly there were whistles in the quadrangle, high-pitched shrills made by fingers in the sides of mouths, sounds learned on playing fields and street corners. Students who had stood in distinct groups now all surged to the middle of their brick-topped space. "It's a shoot-out," Red said.

Two boys stood in the middle of a circle of students, stalking each other, looking for openings. They were tall boys with close-cropped hair, one with pimples on his forehead, the other with a sport shirt and a tie hand-painted with palm trees. "To the death," the boy with the hand-painted necktie yelled, and they circled each other with their green book bags swinging from their hands. "To the death," the crowd began to chant as Pimples crashed his book bag off the chest of his opponent. Painted Necktie countered with a looping smash to the side of Pimple's head. Pimples carried the lighter load of books in his bag and was able to react much faster than the other boy, swinging his book-bag club early and often, connecting with stinging blows that made the crowd think, "An eye, he could knock out an eye."

Painted Necktie had a lumbering load of books in his bag and while the crowd continued to chant "To the death," he muscled his load with a grunt of effort into a swing that sent Pimples sprawling to the ground. "They're certainly doing everything they can to give us an exciting first day," Red said.

"Can you kill somebody with a book bag?" a girl next to them asked.

"Only if you pull the bag over their head and tighten the straps," said Hennessey.

"All right, youngsters," a high-pitched voice rose over the shouting. "Enough brutality." The voice sounded like the scream of the radio-soap-opera grandmother whose audience knows that the jig is up. Pimples was scrambling to his feet, knowing that high school code said that no one could be beaten while he was down. An elderly woman pushed through the crowd. Her sensible blue wool dress was draped over monumental bosoms and flowed down to equally sensible heavy black shoes. The shoes had thick heels that allowed her to stand for long hours teaching Latin to dullards who preferred hanging out in the quadrangle and fighting with book bags. Miss Forbes had been teaching Latin at Brookwood High School for years. She thought in Latin. "Hoodlums," she yelled, and the seas parted. The students backed off. Miss Forbes pulled

Pimples to his feet by his left ear. She reached up to pull Painted Tie by his right ear. "Schola Brookwoodensis non in tres partes divisa est," she exclaimed. "Unius domus membra sumus, quae nullo modo a pueris rusticis rudibusque divelli possunt." Then in English: "Shake hands and be men, not boys." Then again in Latin, "Dispergite profanum vulgus! Turbarum dementiam abicite!" The students, Latin-oriented or not, understood the gist and wandered off again to their own corners of the quadrangle. A boy's voice called out clearly, but with his back turned to Miss Forbes and dozens of kids milling about. She could not tell who yelled, "Is it true you marched with Julius Caesar?"

The boy she held by the right ear snickered. "You think that's funny?" she said. "You both march with me to detention hall. We'll write some Latin on the blackboard."

"But I take Spanish," said Painted Tie. "We were only fooling," said Pimples. "That was part of club initiation. You know, the Sheiks and the Goths clubs? We pledge in the fall."

"I know nothing of clubs, only of education," Miss Forbes said. "Si ego cum Caesare, vos tamen cum Forbes ista iter facitis. If I march with Caesar, *you* march with Miss Forbes." They snickered, but they marched to detention.

"I always wanted to be a Sheik," Rosenberg said. "I used to look up to those guys in camp, the older guys from high school who had warm-up jackets with SAA written on them. Sheiks Athletic Association."

"Yeah, I know what they say. The Sheiks, safest club in Brookwood," said Red. "Typical, you'd go with the rich snobs. I like the Goths, they got the best athletes."

"They use ringers, I heard. They use the goys."

"Oh," Hennessey said. "I can play for them, but I don't get to wear a jacket."

"They're all Jewish clubs, Duke," Rosenberg said. "Like fraternities."

"Well, you guys go beat each other with book bags. I've got a football meeting." Duke walked away, swaying a little from side to side the way he had seen older high school jocks swagger when they walked, rolling shoulder muscles, popping pectorals as if everyone noticed.

"Subtle they call that, subtle, Rosie. He's got eyes," Red said. "He can see. You don't have to hurt his feelings for Christ's sakes. Everyone knows the clubs are all Jewish."

"Do you think we're going to be as friendly with Duke now?"

"You mean because of what you said?"

"No, you jerk, because we're older, because of high school."

"I think a friend is a friend," Red said. "I think you're a real asshole to even say something like that. After all we did together at Hathaway. Makes me wonder about you, Dickie."

"Okay, what about Temple? You think he thinks he's too good for us? He goes away to fairy school."

"You forget so soon we were brothers. It doesn't matter where you go, what you do. You think Duke forgets or Freddie forgets? Blood flows and it hurts. But it's all red. You remember. The fairies at fairy school with Temple didn't caddie together."

"You want to take the bus home or hitch?"

"You change the subject whenever you know you're wrong," Red said.

"Let's take the bus. No one will pick us both up in a car hitching."

"You go," Red said. "I may go to the meeting for the cross-country team."

"You want to run over golf courses in sweatpants?"

"You go home and study. You see those girls? You see those guys standing with them with the letter sweaters? Go stick the pages of the Latin book together beating your meat. We're studying equations in algebra. One letter sweater equals one piece of ass. You think I can't count?"

Dickie walked alone to the corner of Route 9 and knocked on windows of cars stopped for the traffic lights. "You going towards South Brookwood?" he yelled to be heard behind rolled-up windows. Everybody else could play. He would study and keep his eyes open.

There was chapel service every morning at St. Luke's School. Freddie Temple and the other third-formers, the first-year students, had to be there early to plump cushions, line up prayer books, do odd jobs to make sure that cleanliness was next to godliness. A Bach fugue ushered in the students. "This is a jail in a blazer and tie,"

Peter Lorenzo whispered to Freddie as they rubbed with polish the brass plaques screwed into the backs of the wooden pew seats, the plaques that bore the names of wealthy donors to St. Luke's. Lorenzo came from Long Island, where his father did mysterious things that made lots of money, things that Lorenzo could never really describe. Lorenzo was lumpy and not a good athlete, one of the true unforgivable sins at St. Luke's. "You left polish on that brass," boomed a voice down at Lorenzo. It was Dr. Lewis, the rector of the school, a tall patrician from Yale Divinity School who knew that the other unforgivable sin at St. Luke's was to be from a middle-class Italian family on Long Island, no matter how mysterious one's sources of money. There was one God, but some people were more equal than others in His sight, and to be a High Episcopalian surely set you above all others. "One of the reasons to be at St. Luke's," the rector continued, "is to learn that whatever is worth doing is worth doing right."

During the chapel service Freddie felt as he had many times that fall, that the only reason he was at St. Luke's was because his father had gone there. He mouthed the words to the hymn they were singing, "Joyful, Joyful, We Adore Thee." He knew the words because his father would always sing them when he was drunk. He mouthed the words because he thought that singing was for fairies. Duke Hennessey had convinced him of that. All during the rector's announcements Freddie's mind wandered, torn between lack of sleep and the feeling that he wasn't really there, that he had been dropped from the sky into a bad dream. He was away from home, fourteen years old and miserable. The night before, sleeping in his cubicle, surrounded by his closed cotton curtain, the kind that surrounded all the third-formers in his dormitory, he had been awakened with a rush of fear. Where was he? There were whispers around him and laughter suppressed by quick hisses of command. The boy in the next cubicle came from New York City, but his parents were French and spent the greater part of the year everywhere but in New York City. He looked like a child, with a sweet, small-featured face and skin the color of a soft leather wallet made in Florence. When Freddie and the boy met, Freddie asked him if he liked sports. "Oh, yes," the boy said. "I'm a bathing enthusiast." His name was Marcel de Bayle, and when Temple woke up de Bayle was being carried out of the dormitory by at least five boys hooded in pillowcases with holes for their eyes and mouths. There were twelve students to a floor in Temple's dormitory: one enormous room separated into cells by the curtained enclosures. Each boy had a bed, desk, small bookshelf and chair in his area, which was approximately eight feet by eight feet. Privacy was possible by pulling the curtain around on its overhanging rod, much like a shower curtain. Other than the muffled cries of de Bayle and the giggles of the pranksters, the dormitory slept or pretended to sleep, too afraid of retaliation from big boys in pillowcase hoods. De Bayle was carried out of the room, fighting all the way. Temple jumped from his bed and followed them. In the landing outside, there were brass knobs on the wall, covers to old gas lights with ornamental nipples in their midst. The intruders held de Bayle up to the ornament. "Kiss the nipples, de Bayle," they hissed at him. "Kiss the nipples and show you're a man. Make noise and you're dead."

"Come on, Miss de Bayle," they said. "Suck the nipples off your brass dorm mother."

De Bayle was whimpering, terrified. Then he was sucking away on the brass nipple of the fixture.

"Leave him alone," Temple said in as loud a voice as he dared. De Bayle was dropped to the floor.

"Get to bed, Temple," one of them said. "Or you'll get your turn after Miss de Bayle."

Two of them shoved Temple back toward the dormitory entrance. Temple reached out instinctively and grabbed, ripping the hood off one face. Temple knew the face, Louis Clark, a hockey player and a bully. The heroes and the bullies are always known and pointed out early to new boys at every private school. Clark was heavy-set, with dark hair combed back in a pompadour that he would measure with a ruler. He had a perpetual sneer on his face as if to ward off any good feelings for his fellow man.

"Come on, Clark," one of the hooded figures said. Clark stared at Temple as if photographing him for the future. Then they raced down the staircase and off to their rooms, the privilege of the upperclassmen after the cubicles of the third form. "You okay?" Temple asked the crumpled de Bayle, who still sat on the floor.

"They think I'm a girl," he said. "How can you be all right when you're in a boys' school and they think you're a girl?"

"Look," Temple said. "You keep kicking and punching. Bite if you have to, every time they give you a tough time. They don't like anyone who fights back. Sooner or later they get tired of anyone who scraps. You do that, and they won't call you a girl."

"I'm too small for football."

"You have to force yourself, de Bayle, or you'll never be free. Names *are* much worse than sticks and stones."

In the chapel Temple played over the events of the previous night. Then he read the names carved into the granite wall, names of former students who had died in the battles of the two world wars. The rector was dismissing them for morning classes with his usual inspirational message. "These are initiation days at St. Luke's School. The schoolyard is a club, and we all belong sooner or later. As Samuel Johnson said, 'Boswell is a very clubbable man.' You will all be very clubbable men if you play by the rules." The service, which also served as morning assembly and announcement period, closed with a hymn. Then the boys filed out, goosing each other, shoving, babbling, eager to get out of chapel, not eager to get to class.

Freddie Temple had grown almost an inch and a half over the summer. It seemed as if his arms and legs had been stretched by clowns. Several old boys at St. Luke's dubbed him "Plastic Man" during his first week of school. But they had said it admiringly because of his blond good looks and because long arms and legs at St. Luke's meant only one thing: a potential oarsman, a member of the crew. Freddie stepped out into the sunshine of prep school fall in Massachusetts, a different sunshine it seemed than in Brookwood. Everyone wore ties and jackets; some teachers lit pipes walking across the green toward classrooms. It was a world without parents and without girls. Freddie knew that Rosenberg and Hennessey and Singer would hate St. Luke's. Worse, they would laugh at it.

Two older boys came up on either side of Temple, walking swiftly. They boxed him between their bodies and nudged him with their elbows. "Don't screw around with initiations, Temple," one of them said, and Freddie recognized the voice from the night before. It was a friend of Louis Clark's. "We have high hopes for you, Temple," the other boy said. "But there are traditions here, things that have been going on for a hundred years."

"You don't screw around with history, Temple," the other boy said. "You play football; you'll row. When you're an old boy you'll want to initiate the newbs, the new boys, yourself."

"We're on your side, Temple," the other said. "Leave little girls like de Bayle to us. It's for their own good. You'll see that in time." They each gave him whacks with their elbows, but friendly whacks, conspiratorial whacks, and hurried on by.

Freddie walked slowly along granite paving stones toward the old building called Schoolhouse, where classrooms waited. It seemed to him that the pathway was part of the road map of his life, already charted for him, already preordained. He smiled, thinking what Red Singer would do at St. Luke's and what the school would do to Red.

It was Friday night.

Red and Dickie Rosenberg sat erect on dining-room chairs moved into the cellar of Sonny Newman's house and placed in a row. Ten boys sat in the chairs, nervous in the service. A tall young man wearing the red and blue letter sweater of Brookwood High stood in front of them. "You guys are lucky, you know it? You are being pledged by the Sheiks club. How do you get to be so lucky? It's a miracle if you ask me. Sit up straight in those chairs."

Clubs had been big in Brookwood for fifteen years, dominating the social life of the Jewish teenage population. The Sheiks, "the safest club in Brookwood," were the sons of doctors, lawyers and manufacturers. They lived mostly in single-family homes, wore white bucks or saddle shoes and Shetland sweaters and aspired to Ivy League colleges. Several of them had gone to Camp Wah Hoo Wah, where Dickie had idolized them in their jackets that proclaimed them members of the SAA. They had members like Harry Gitman, president of the student council, Bill Hacker, head of the court of justice, Pernicious "Pernie" Cohen, who had moved in from Atlanta and was one of the best tennis players in the state. Big men. Dickie had been selected because of friendships made at camp. Red Singer was there because of his grammar school reputation as a hot ticket and because of the influence of his sisters. The boy speaking to them was the president of the Sheiks, Bobby Starr, who played basketball and was voted Most Personality in the class poll run by the yearbook staff.

At Camp Wah Hoo Wah, Uncle Henry was always looking for the Jewish white hope, a camp athlete who could make it in the high school ranks, then move on to play ball in college. Such an occurrence was rare, other than in track, but the admiration in the Jewish community for an athlete in their midst was extraordinary.

Dickie Rosenberg desperately wanted to be a Jewish white hope athlete, to belong to the Sheiks, to strut with a letter sweater. Red Singer didn't give a damn, and he wanted people to know that he didn't give a damn.

Bobby Starr raised his right hand and a basketball flew at him over the heads of the pledges. They all flinched. Starr slowly dribbled the ball in front of them, talking as he dribbled. He dribbled right hand, left hand, between his legs like Cousy. Then he tossed it quickly at Red Singer. The boys on either side of Red ducked, but Red caught it easily and spun it on the end of an index finger. Then he flipped it back to Starr. Several members applauded and yelled, "Togo, Togo," the name of a current Holy Cross all-American player.

"The point of this exercise," the president went on, "is to demonstrate that the Sheiks have specialties; they're doers — athletes, student government leaders. If you're not eventually going to run the school, you better not even think about wearing the SAA jacket." He glared at the pledges. "Forget that I ever knew any of you before tonight. From now on I'm *Mister* Starr. And all the members are Mister to you. You're on your own to prove you're good enough. Mr. Dorfman, our sergeant at arms, will give you your first assignments."

Punchy Dorfman was crazy. Everyone knew that. No one else would dare lock "Feathers" Hiat, the physics teacher, in the chemistry lab closet. No one else would fart noisily during the pledge of allegiance to the flag and do it on purpose. No one else would go into the girls' locker room after gym class to ask for aspirin.

"What's Mr. Dorfman's specialty?" Red asked.

"My specialty is blackballs," Dorfman said. "Now on your feet." He barked the order. The pledges jumped from their chairs. "Stay absolutely still now," said Dorfman, "no matter what happens. Discipline is one of the symbols of the Sheiks; out of control is for the goyim. Nobody speaks but me. You will be blindfolded and told to perform a task. A slip of paper will be placed in each of your pants pockets. I mean one slip of paper will be placed in one of each of your pockets. I mean look for the fucking piece of paper when you leave here and you're on the sidewalk. That paper will have an assignment written on it which you must complete before the next pledge meeting. This is history talking here, you twerps. I had to do this; Bobby Starr had to do it. Only it was much tougher then. This is a pussy pledge class, I can feel it. Now complete silence between this instant and the time you leave this house. Stare straight ahead, except for you, shit-for-brains Pollack. Pledge Pollack, step forward and remove your pants and your underpants."

Ira Pollack was small, too small to go out for high school sports, but, as his cousin, who happened to be Bobby Starr, the president of the Sheiks, told him, "You got the perfect build and the perfect name for cross-country. All the cross-country guys are small and dopey with dopey names."

"But I'm your cousin," Ira pointed out. "Your mother will kill you if I don't get in the Sheiks."

"Make cross-country, don't whine. Run like a bastard and you'll get what you deserve."

Ira Pollack looked like a small Arab boy, dark skin, curly hair. But his thick glasses removed him from any image of the bazaar, and it appeared as if he were going to cry in front of the pledge class, trying to cover up his nakedness with his hands. "Hands on your hips, shit-for-brains," Dorfman yelled, and as he yelled, blindfolds were placed over the eyes of the nine remaining pledges. "Breathe a word about what happens here," Dorfman added, "and give up forever joining the brotherhood. This is men's business, and men keep their yaps zipped. This ceremony binds us forever because no one violates the code."

Red whispered to Rosenberg, "Have I come this far to have my first piece of ass be Ira Pollack?"

"Silence, Singer."

Little Ira was led to the first pledge in line. Dorfman took the pledge's right hand and moved it until it touched the flesh on Ira's bare bottom. Then Dorfman held the pledge's right index finger. "Bend over and open up those cheeks, Ira," he commanded. The pledge master jammed the unsuspecting pledge's finger into a Dixie Cup full of mayonnaise, careful not to let the digit feel the sides of the container. "Ugghh," came the sound of gagging disgust from the pledge. Dorfman repeated the process all down the line, and all down the line came the sounds of gagging, choking and revulsion, except from Dickie Rosenberg, who did what he had to do without a sound and would have done more if it would get him into the Sheiks.

"What's your assignment say?" asked Dickie when they were out on the street walking quickly away from the meeting.

"I don't give a shit what it says," said Red. "You think I'm ever going back to have those bastards dump all over me?"

"Dump all over *you*. It was all of us."

The nights were getting chilly in Boston. It was the end of September, and the boys hurried along, heading for the Howard Johnson's at Coolidge Circle, the hangout.

"The difference," Red said, "is that I hated it. You'd probably love to put your fingers up somebody's asshole. Maybe even your dick for that matter."

"Some things you do because the reward is worth it. You want to go through high school a lone wolf?"

"I don't want to go through anywhere eating someone else's shit."

"Okay, Red. What's your assignment?"

Singer fished in his pants pocket and pulled out a folded piece of paper. Without unfolding it he rubbed it around on his crotch, along his rear end, crumpled it up and put it down a sewer opening in the street. "The Sheiks can blow up a Sheik and pull it over their heads as far as I'm concerned," he said.

Dickie couldn't think of anything clever to say to his friend. So he unfolded his piece of paper and read aloud. "You are to knit a perfect jockstrap for delivery to the next meeting." Red got hysterical. Then Dickie got hysterical.

"I got better things to do with my life," Red concluded.

"And I do, too," Dickie responded. "The Sheiks are part of the way I'm going to get there. If I got to eat shit for a while, I can pretend it's covered with Marshmallow Fluff."

"Why don't you run for president of the class?" said Red, "and kiss everyone else's ass on the way."

"Why do you have such a hard-on?"

"I hate to see you being such a phony."

"Because I care about different things than you, Red? We're not still in the seventh grade."

"No shit, Dick Tracy," said Singer, and they hurried along in silence, each feeling the strain in their stomachs about silences that stand for bitterness and misunderstanding.

Howard Johnson's at Coolidge Circle was where the boys and girls went to meet each other on weekends. Or rather it was the parking lot of that restaurant, after the boys would be kicked out of Ho-Jo's for loitering or littering or fighting or flirting or for just being noisy and not spending enough money. A hotdog was twenty-five cents, a Coke was a dime. A frappe (an extra-thick milk shake) was thirty cents. No one had much pocket money, and several of the high school kids held part-time jobs. There were guys who set pins at the bowling alley or bagged at Star Market. There were girls who baby-sat. When it was not spring and Singer and his friends didn't caddie, they squeezed the money they had saved. Rosenberg had an allowance of $1.25 a week. Red Singer got a buck. Duke Hennessey got no allowance, but he saved from his summer's employment. Freddie Temple received $10 a month in cash from his mother, who sent it to him at boarding school, faithfully folded in letters written in a perfect hand that told of weather and sister and brother and family dinners and included warnings to stay warm, dry and remember to study.

The girls stood in one group in the parking lot, careful not to lean on automobiles. The boys lounged on the cars, leaning against doors, sitting on other people's fenders, the fancier the better, in the hopes that passers-by might think the cars belonged to them. They found Duke Hennessey sitting on a green Oldsmobile surrounded by teammates from the freshman football team. None of them came from South Brookwood, and conversation stopped when Red and Dickie walked over.

"So?" one of the football players said, as if he owned the parking lot.

"So?" said Red. "So you're a putz, that's what's so." The player didn't waste any time. He went right for Red, who held his ground. Hennessey, moving faster than a big man had the right to do, leaped from the fender where he sat and wedged himself between the two. "These are my boys, Clint. My boys from Hathaway School."

"Nobody calls me 'putz,' " Clint muttered. "I know what that is."

"Yeah," said Duke. "I got news for you. He just did. This is Red Singer and Dickie Rosenberg. They're okay; they're my friends."

"What do they play?" Clint said, backing off, thinking that any friends of Hennessey had to play ball.

"Right now they're playing at being putzes themselves," Hennessey laughed.

"How's it going, Frank?" Rosenberg asked Hennessey, one of the cosmic questions friends ask friends without looking for any answers.

"I suppose you guys went to a pledge meeting. Secret stuff."

"It's a bunch of crap, Duke," said Red.

"What do you think, Dickie, a bunch of crap?"

"I don't have a problem with it. I think it's okay."

"I think Dickie's beginning to like boys," said Red. "They taught him at summer camp, and he likes the taste." Red flicked a punch at Dickie's shoulder, a noogie with the middle knuckle extended. Everybody laughed.

"First *you* couldn't go out for football," said Duke, "now *you* like boys. Look over my shoulder; don't be obvious. See those girls over there, next to the beach wagon, those five or six girls? See the one with the short blond hair and the freckles?"

"I see pimples," said Red.

"Not that one," said Hennessey, grabbing Red, then, whirling around, pointing right at the girl he meant. She was the prettiest in the group, a laughing blonde, a kidder with green eyes and a turned-up nose.

"I can't see any freckles," Red insisted. The girls saw Hennessey pointing. They made jokes and giggled and turned their backs.

"Come on," Duke said. "We'll get a close-up of Rita Cronin, and I'll show you freckles and the first girlfriend any of us has had."

"She's in my human relations class," Dickie said. "I've been thinking of dreaming about her."

"You dream about her, Rosie, I'll hear about it and come after you." Duke led Red and Dickie by the arms over to the group of laughing girls. "Miss Cronin," he said with exaggerated politeness, "you know Stanley Singer and Richard Rosenberg, two famous Jewish homos." The girls broke up. They were all Irish or Italian. Most of them wore little gold or silver crosses on chains around their necks that they wore outside of their sweaters that were all a size too small. Rita's white sweater was a hundred percent wool, but she would never wear angora. Angora was for fast girls, girls with money from South Brookwood who had clothing allowances and were being given listings in the phone book for themselves that said "children's phone."

"What do you think of her, Rosie?" asked Hennessey. "Is this a future head cheerleader or what?"

"Come on, Francis," she said, "I can't even do the flying split yet."

Red rolled his eyes at Rosenberg, and Duke looked at him with the menace that young men have for anyone who is potentially rude to a girlfriend. "I know Dick," Rita said. "He's in human relations. Red Singer everybody's heard about. My girlfriends say that Red Singer's dirty and that we shouldn't be seen with him."

"You got to know him," Duke said. "He's not like that on the inside."

"I don't need to know him," Rita said. "I know you."

Duke turned to his friends. "That excites me more than anything I ever heard. I swear to God."

Duke Hennessey had become a hero during the fall. He was a starting guard on the freshman football team, playing both ways. The varsity coach was predicting that next year Duke would be a varsity starter. Old-timers, retired men who sat in the stands and watched all schoolboy sports, compared Duke to the grand linemen of their memories and predicted greatness. In his first game, Duke's reputation spread throughout the school. They were playing Waltham, a tough town loaded with three-family houses and working-class people. Brookwood's team was known in the Boston papers as "the affluent towners," which tended to inflame members of opposing teams. Losing fourteen to nothing at the half, Brookwood's players seemed intimidated by the mouthing-off at the line of scrimmage by their opponents. "We'll stuff your balls in your mouths, you pansy fucks," they would say. "You shit your pants during the game, wait till you see what we'll do to you afterwards," they called. The kickoff for the second half came to a running back nicknamed Mike the Bike for his speed. As the Waltham defenders poured down the field toward him, Mike the Bike panicked. Afraid of being killed, he handed the ball to Hennessey, who was preparing to block for him. "Trick play, Duke," Mike muttered and actually ran backward, away from the wild Waltham kids, away from the totally surprised Hennessey. Mike's cowardice elevated Hennessey to legend. He was, in his words, "so pissed off at the Bike for being chicken, I straight-armed one kid in the jaw, ran over two more, got a couple of great blocks and carried one little sucker twelve yards with someone else dragging on my leg." Duke scored the only touchdown of his life on sheer tenacity and the adrenaline pumping from anger at his own teammate. His act so energized the team that they pushed Waltham all over the field for two quarters and won twenty to fourteen. It was only a freshman football game, but the story spread through Brookwood High the next day, both Duke's triumph and the coach's words after the game. The speech became a subsequent motto for Brookwood coaches down through the years. The freshman coach never used profanity. He taught English when he wasn't coaching. But in the postgame meeting he was so excited that he jumped on a rubbing table and yelled at them: "Boys. You conquered chickenshit." This phrase was written on chalkboards after every Brookwood win and has lived much longer there than "Kilroy was here," "Off the pigs" or even "Paul loves Molly 4 ever," spray-painted on bridge crossings. Mike the Bike lost his wonderful nickname and through his life thereafter was known as "Trick Play" Mike, something he never got over trying to rationalize. The varsity coach called Duke into his office to congratulate him the next week. "Looking forward to you playing for me next year, Hennessey," he said.

"Coach," Duke said. "Johnny Turco from Holy Cross scored seventeen touchdowns in nineteen fifty. I scored one lousy touchdown."

"Hennessey, Lincoln only freed the slaves once," the coach said.

Duke laughed forever at that line. But he never forgot the purity of his act or how it was perceived. He also never forgot that most memorable moments in people's lives have been provoked by accident.

Rita Cronin and Hennessey tossed a tennis ball back and forth to each other in Howard Johnson's parking lot. Duke always carried a ball with him; he always had to be tossing or catching. Mating dances.

"The boys should come first," Red said to Dickie. "This has been some shitty evening that probably only fried clams can cure. Loan me a buck?"

"I got enough for one order," Dickie said. "Oh, Christ, it's my father." David Rosenberg was working his way through the maze of cars and high school kids looking like a conscientious objector dropped in the midst of a platoon of marines. "Rosie," Red said. "I hate to say it, but sometimes it seems as if your parents are trying to fuck up everything for you."

The lights were going out in Howard Johnson's. "It's eleven-fifteen, Richard," Mr. Rosenberg said. "You were due in the house at ten-thirty." He was oblivious to anyone else around them except his son.

Dickie's defense was wan, but he tried it anyway. "Dad," he said, "I'm in high school now."

"The poorest excuse in history," said his father. "Get in the car."

All Dickie could hope for was that his father would walk by himself and not totally drive him into the dust. No such luck. They marched together, Dickie with his eyes on the hubcaps of cars, his father still oblivious. Red Singer shook his head and let them go without comment. To get the taste of the evening out of his mouth he had to act. So he was already stooping down to let air out of unsuspecting tires. Hennessey was in another land, in the company of girls. Pinned down in the gray Oldsmobile with hydromatic drive, Dickie listened to the listing of his punishments:

"No music, no movies on Saturday afternoons. There will be

raking of leaves, bed by ten o'clock, no radio in bed, reading of the *New York Times* on Sunday, including doing the answers to ten crossword puzzle words, and some understanding of companions in life, some sense of who your people are and who they should not be."

Dickie had heard it all before. His only thoughts were about getting a Sheiks jacket and if by any chance his mother would help him knit a goddamn jockstrap.

Spring 1952

The boys stood on the elevated tee looking at the long fairway of Brookwood Municipal's eighteenth hole. It was a Saturday in June, just after school had let out, just before summer camps and jobs began. The boys had caddied earlier and snuck back onto the course late in the day to illegally play the last three holes.

When you're young you're hitting out. Slow backswings are for old men. Only Dickie Rosenberg, dark and brooding, tried to control the ball somewhat, tried to steer his drive into the fairway. He had taken instruction from counselors at camp, extra instruction paid for by his father, who told him he should learn carryover sports, tennis and golf. The others watched golfers and instructed themselves, adjusting their swings by trial and error. Dickie sliced to the right, into heavy rough bordering woods full of fir trees. "Virgin," cried Hennessey and Red Singer. "Virgin" was the word of the moment. Singer said it was what he would call them all until it were no longer true.

Freddie Temple had been home from school for almost a month, caddying every day to pick up extra money and because his father expected him to be active until the family moved to the North Shore for the summer. After hanging around for two days, he called Dickie. "It seems strange," he admitted. "So much has happened this year." Freddie had rowed in a four-man shell with a coxswain, a sport completely unknown to his old classmates from Brookwood. Dickie had not made the freshman baseball team, the first spring in his life he did not play the sport. Duke Hennessey was both the captain and catcher on the freshman squad. Red Singer trained in a half-assed manner for spring track, gearing up for the mile, but at the same time he was up to almost half a pack of

Camels a day. Red took a mighty swing at his ball and drilled it way left, out-of-bounds. His second drive, a provisional, split the fairway and, with a slight draw, ended up in A-plus position almost two hundred yards out. "Same man," said Rosenberg, aping what everybody always said after a successful second chance. "Too bad he's lying three," said Hennessey. Duke took an unorthodox whack at his tee shot, swinging like a clean-up batter with too much stomach, too many beers the night before the game. He topped the ball, barely hitting it at all, and it still bounded straight down the fairway about a hundred and fifty yards. "You are a fucking gorilla," said Red.

Freddie Temple, taller now by an inch than he was in the fall, sliced his shot a mile to the right. "Jesus, Freddie," said Red, who was his partner playing for twenty-five cents a hole, "you couldn't make double bogey with a cannon from there."

"I got a good partner, Red," he said. "I don't need a cannon."

"I'm lying three, you schmuck," said Red. "You're so fucking polite. Get worked up, Temple. This is money we're talking about."

They sliced and mishit and joked their way up the fairway as the sun went down and then got chased off the green before they finished by the manager of the clubhouse, who was old-fashioned and believed that people who played the course should pay for the privilege. "One contest," said Red, "then let's go over to Chink's Garden for egg rolls."

"One contest," agreed Hennessey. "Then I'm going to Rita's."

"You got a date every goddamn weekend, Duke," said Red.

"It's not a date. I'm just going over her house."

"Her parents at home?" asked Temple.

"Her parents are always home," Duke said. "We go for walks, sit on the steps."

No one asked the question that was in all their minds. Getting anything? You never expected that question if you liked someone. You never asked that question of friends.

"It's too dark for the contest," Dickie said.

"Chicken," Duke answered. "We'll all hit at the same time."

They dropped four golf balls onto the grass at the side of the clubhouse. The idea of the contest was to chip a ball, with a wedge or a nine iron, over the main road going by the course. The road was a major thoroughfare, heavily traveled by fast-moving traffic.

The target, across the road on the grassy median strip, was a sign that warned of an approaching traffic circle, a green and white metal sign put in place by Brookwood's Department of Public Works. The shot closest to the sign won a quarter from everyone else. Automobiles raced along the road over which they would hit.

They dropped their balls. "Okay," Duke said. "A couple practice swings, and we hit together when I say." And the four boys swung their nine irons or their wedges.

John Paul Sullivan had the world by the balls. He was driving a new Cadillac Coupe de Ville. He was virtually unopposed in his run for Congress. His father's money from theater chains, bowling alleys, pancake restaurants and his political influence ensured that John Paul could outspend any other Democrat or Republican for that matter. He had a beautiful wife who had graduated from Juilliard and could play everything from a Beethoven sonata to Gershwin. He had two adorable little kids. So why was he fucking around on Saturday night when he could be eating a lobster in Kenny's on Cohasset Harbor with his wife and the group who would be his brain trust and bankrollers in Congress and eventually in the governor's seat or the Senate and God knows what next. John Paul Sullivan had been a football player at Boston College, been with the First Marine Division in Korea. That was enough for Massachusetts and he knew he had the world by the balls, but it didn't matter a bit that the young woman kneeling on the front seat next to him and fishing with her hand in his fly was not his wife. He was on his way to give a brief speech, a fund-raiser in front of a group of Jewish businessmen at Temple Mesada in South Brookwood. Sullivan was late and guided on the occasion by one of his aides, Belinda Gold, who had majored in government at Sarah Lawrence and longed to work in Washington. They had been lovers for six months. Belinda knew she was good for J. P. Sullivan, and she had no intention of disturbing his marriage. That would have fouled up the election and forced her to look for another job. And even if J.P. asked her, she would never consider marrying a Catholic. He pulled her head down onto his lap as they raced along the road, the streetlights just starting to blink on. Belinda took him in her mouth, wondering if she could finish him off before they got to the temple. If she did she would have to be neat; wouldn't do for the next congressman to appear with pecker tracks on his trousers. She could feel him caressing her hair with one hand as her head bounced with greater speed. She never heard the crack on the front windshield as the golf ball hit, but she felt J.P. jump in her mouth and the car lunge as if he had spun the wheel with great force. Her mouth was still full of him as she heard him scream and then a crash as she was thrown underneath the steering wheel, which had broken. Its column tore into John Paul Sullivan's chest, killing him almost immediately.

Instantly the boys heard the squeal of brakes, the crash, the blowing of horns, other cars screeching to stops. They took off in the opposite direction, running, running, their hearts on fire, around the clubhouse, to the safety of the woods bordering the eighteenth hole. "Jesus. Jesus Christ," they cried to themselves.

An hour later, Rosenberg and Singer sat in a booth of the China Garden eating egg rolls and drinking tea.

"I swear I didn't do it," Dickie said. "I hit a great shot."

"Well, I always hit it straight," Red answered. "It was probably Temple."

"He's changed," Dickie said. "He's got nothing to say."

"You think he likes other boys? That's what happens they say when your parents send you away to school. Only kids who can't make it have to go to private school, you know."

"What's the matter with you, Red? Temple was a star. He didn't have to go to private school."

"I heard my father say all my life to my sisters, no one is too good for you. You're as good as anyone. Then my mother says to the girls, you're much too good for that boy or this bum or something like that."

"You think Freddie thinks that?"

"I think he's going to feel bad he's not at the high school."

They sipped their tea with lots of sugar and ate their egg rolls. Dickie didn't take off his Sheiks jacket, even though it was warm in the restaurant. "I hate being a freshman," Dickie said finally. Red looked at him, pouring more tea. "No shit, Dick Tracy." Red said that to everyone when he was feeling superior. He knew he didn't shank the shot. They were silent for a while.

"I'm scared we killed someone," Dickie said.

"Shit. Everyone's okay. Insurance will pay for the car. It was an accident. Everyone's okay."

Freddie Temple kept running through the woods after they drilled the automobile. The last thing he needed was trouble from his father when he had to live with his parents all summer. He ran across fairways and greens and climbed the tall wire fence separating the Brookwood Municipal golf course from the private links of The Golf Club, where his parents were at a dance. "My old friends think I'm a jerk," he thought to himself. "And I think *they're* jerks." As he ran, his balls bounced around inside of his boxer shorts. "They're probably still wearing Jockey briefs," he thought. He had no intention of hitching back to the Chinese restaurant. And he knew he didn't kill anyone because he always was good with the wedge. He had trouble with his woods but never his irons. He knew also that he never should've called the others, not after going away to St. Luke's.

They met the next day at the tennis courts in back of the Hathaway School. Duke had to call Freddie three times to make sure he got the message. "Meet us," Duke said. "I don't give a shit what you say. If I have to, I'll come over there and drag you by the hair."

They sat on the grassy bank overlooking the courts. "Remember the time," Red said, "when we beat the shit out of those guys from West Roxbury?" They laughed and then fell into an embarrassed silence.

"What were you going to do, Temple, tell your father?" Red said.

"I went to church today," Duke said. "I thought everyone in the place was looking at me. But I know I hit the ball straight."

"It was dark, Duke," Dickie said. "How the hell do you know if you hit it straight?"

"It was probably you, Rosie. You're the only one hits shanks all the time. You and Freddie. What happened to you, Temple?"

"I didn't want to see any of you ever again," he said. They were quiet. "The guy died. He was running for senator."

"Congress," said Duke.

"What's the fucking difference?" Red said. "He's dead. And we did it."

"We didn't do it," Dickie insisted. "Maybe he had a heart attack or something. A million things could have happened. And I didn't shank my shot. I felt it go straight. I would have won the contest."

"You want to tell us you *won* the contest, you asshole," said Duke. "You'll probably put us all in jail."

"Wait a minute," Red said. "Let's just hold your water. The point is, what do we do now?"

"We should go to our parents and tell them," said Freddie. "Just make a clean breast. This is going to get worse. That Sullivan was rich. My father had some business with his father, and he says that they are rich and tough. Someone's going to find out."

"What's to find out?" Red asked, talking very fast. "Who said it was us? It was dark. How do we even know?"

Dickie was thoughtful. "What if we say we saw it happen but say nothing about hitting the shots? The car smashed up. No one knows about the golf ball except us. It was an accident."

"But he died, Rosenberg," Temple said. "One of us killed him."

"Look," said Duke, who sat on the grassy hill and threw small stones in the direction of the tennis courts. "One of us shat the bed and if he knows he ain't telling. What's the biggest thing we can swear on?"

"My Jewish word of honor," said Red.

"You know how stupid you are, Red?" said Duke.

"What's wrong with that? It's sacred."

"We can't swear on that," Freddie said.

"Yeah," Red said. "I guess."

"If we go in now," Duke reasoned, "and tell our folks or tell the cops, we're dead. It was a stupid accident. Maybe we didn't even cause it. Maybe only God knows. If we're not going to mention it, we have to swear a pact on our mothers." He took a needle stuck into a piece of beeswax from his pocket.

"Wait a minute," Red said, giving Duke a book of matches. Solemnly, Duke sterilized the needle and pricked the ball of his thumb, squeezing out drops of blood. "Each of you do it," he said, handing the needle to Rosenberg. "And say like I'm saying. 'I swear on my mother's life that I'll never say anything about the contest to anyone, so help me God.' " They all did it. They all said it. And they all pressed their thumbs together, mixing the blood, making them feel that they would be struck down if they broke the vow.

Dickie wondered if it would be he or his mother who would feel the wrath if he told. It took a lot for him to stick the needle in himself. But he had to do it. They suspected him, he knew, of hitting the shanked shot, but he knew he had hit the ball true, whatever they thought.

"The guy would have made a shitty congressman, my father says," Red said.

Duke stuck a finger in his face. "You don't talk about the dead that way."

Temple said nothing. They held handkerchiefs hard against their thumbs and walked together, away from the tennis courts.

CHAPTER SIX

O

Senior Year, Fall 1954

Red Singer's cellar was a good place for a party. It was a finished cellar, called a playroom by the Singers, with a linoleum floor, pine-paneled walls, a bar with cardboard coasters stamped with names of foreign beers from Italy, France and Mexico on it. No German beer coasters would ever be in the Singer playroom. There was a pool table, with eight cues and a lot of little pieces of chalk for the cues. Window seats, several couches and two easy chairs completed the furnishings. Everything was covered in heavy-duty red corduroy fabric. It was a place built for children to entertain friends, a place to brag about to neighbors who didn't have finished playrooms.

It was Christmastime, but the Singers' playroom never looked any different regardless of season. Red's sisters had insisted on the renovation. They used it during high school for boy/girl parties with a record player standing on a card table, equipped to play 78s and 45s. They used it as a place to make out with dates since everyone knew that the Singer girls would not go parking. Their mother, Oy Vey Singer, didn't care what the girls did in their own house, as long as the boys they dated came from approved (wealthy) Jewish families and had prospects for going into a family business.

All young people are transformed by senior year in high school, one of the few twelve-month periods in one's life where he can feel both immortal and certainly smarter than any adult whoever came down the pike. Red Singer was no exception to this rule. He had, by senior year at Brookwood High, developed being a wise guy into fine art. His hair was Rubens red and often combed into a modified DA, duck's ass cut, arranged to give a rouge ripple down the middle of the back of his head. His black chinos were pegged, narrow at the ankles and flaring out toward the middle. He wore a black Garrison belt, thick leather with a brass buckle whose edge he had sharpened with a file. The belt was worn pulled around so the buckle was over his right hip, the approved mode. Cool. Like everyone's role model that year, Marlon Brando in *The Wild One*. "Want to drag for beers?" was the question of the season, even for the good little boys and girls of the Boston suburbs. "You look like a greaseball from Dorchester," Rosenberg had told him. "Every mother in Brookwood says a prayer when she sees you coming."

"Hey," Red would say, "tough is tough."

Dickie Rosenberg was president of the student council, swam the hundred and the free-style relay on the swimming team and was usually seen in button-down shirts, Shetland sweaters, chinos and severely scuffed white bucks. He had run for everything and volunteered for everything. When he lost an election for class secretary or for homeroom chairman, he ran again the next season for class vice president and hall monitor. He joined the student forum, which invited speakers on current events like Senator Leverett Saltonstall or the head of the Brookwood School Committee, speakers to make the youngsters better-informed citizens. It would also look good on college applications. Something else happened to Dickie Rosenberg that made popularity in high school inevitable: he became good-looking. Every girl in high school, from the first day of classes, knew who the best-looking boys were. His complexion had darkened as his features had become harder over the last four years. His hair was black, and grammar school braces had been removed to reveal white, even teeth. He kept his hair longer than his classmates, even during swimming season when everyone else adopted whiffles. He kept two combs with him at all times, one in his back pants pocket, another in a plastic book cover that protected his U.S. history text. Anyone who looked dark all year was a lover, and the Brookwood girls would all vote for lovers.

Red's finished cellar became, with winter and spring track, the focus of his senior year. *If* he could bring girls to the cellar, *if* his father was on the road selling, *if* he could help keep his mother from bringing down Cokes and brownies, it could be like having his own apartment. He never figured that it would be ballroom dancing in gym class that would trigger his dream.

Several times a year the physical education department at Brookwood decreed that it would be good for the mental and physical health of all high school children to learn the social graces. Brookwood provided sessions in both ballroom and square dancing. The girls loved it; the boys hated it. But twice a week for forty-five minutes, from Columbus Day until Christmas, gym classes became co-ed. Mrs. Parker, the girls' gym teacher, who looked exactly like Cyrano de Bergerac, lined up the students in their street clothing and stocking feet (so they could not scuff up the gym floor) and paired off the boys and girls. "Give yourself room," she commanded. "One needs room to dance." She pirouetted in her gym suit, blue bloomers over black woollen tights, to a small record player and put on an RCA red label edition of Strauss waltzes. "One, two, three, one, two, three," she commanded herself and waltzed alone around the paired-off couples who stood, mostly silent and miserable, waiting for her to stop. Red was partnered with someone he didn't know, a new student, almost as tall as he, dressed in a long plaid skirt with a big safety pin on the side, white sleeveless turtleneck jersey and the standard white athletic socks, rolled down twice at the top. "I'm Loretta Mirsky," she said. "My blond hair is all natural, and I just moved here a month ago from Cleveland, Ohio." Red had a feeling that all Midwesterners were amazingly polite. "I'm Red Singer," he said. "I been here all my life."

Mrs. Parker danced herself over to the record player and took off the Strauss. "I wanted you to just get a hint of the great Empire period of the waltz: costumes, gowns of velvet and silk, officers in full dress in Vienna, tortes and vats of whipped cream. I want you to know that dancing is glamorous, has history and is wonderful fun. Now you see. Boys, grasp your partners firmly around the waist, holding your fingers also firmly for guidance, at the lower back. You, come over here." She indicated Barton Gold, a klutz if there ever was one, who got pubic hair at eleven and used to hide in the locker room in his own locker so the other boys wouldn't see what he had. "Me?" Barton Gold said, blushing as if he were being asked to display his childhood pubic hair.

"Yes, you," Mrs. Parker responded, putting Patti Page's "Tennessee Waltz" onto the turntable. "You're plenty old enough to be a gentleman. All gentlemen must know how to waltz."

"Waltz me around again, Willy," Red Singer called out from his position at the rear of the young couples.

"That's a dirty song," Loretta Mirsky said to him, with a face as serious as Patti Page's must have been when she recorded "Tennessee Waltz."

"How do you know that?" Red asked her.

"Because of my brothers," she said, then sang softly to him. "Here comes another verse, it's worse than the first verse, so waltz me around again, Willy."

Red sang, "There once was a man from Calcutta . . ." Loretta Mirsky continued, amazing Red, "who liked to beat off in the gutter. The noonday sun beat down on his gun and turned all his cream to butter."

Mrs. Parker was leading Barton Gold around in large circles, she leading and Barton taking the girl's role in a grotesque waltz. Barton was still a klutz whether he was acting as a boy or a girl. "Follow us, class," Mrs. Parker yelled at them, and the class made a semblance of pushing partners in half walk, half stumble in vague time with Patti Page.

Loretta came closer to Red than any girl had ever come to him in his life. Even in the best of dance-floor embraces at boy/girl parties, the most one could expect was a tight upper body embrace coupled with far separation of anything below the waist. A green book bag could be passed between pelvises without touching any pant or skirt material. This was a teenage rule. Loretta Mirsky put one leg between Red's legs, and Red was wearing tan chinos.

"You feel what I feel?" she said.

When Red got angry or blushed, everyone called him Rudolph. He was now so flushed his face could be a car flare in the breakdown lane. "You busy Friday night?" was about all he could blurt out before he had the presence of mind to say, "Turn around, stand in front of me. Don't move," when the waltz was ended.

After class, Red was standing near the water fountain in the gym with half a dozen guys, bubbling to them about his unbelievable good luck. Mr. Remis, the aged gym instructor, sarcastic and hating his work, walked by with his high bouncing walk. If he liked anyone, he liked them for their ability to do one thing: climb ropes. Anyone who could clamber up the thick gym ropes like a monkey could win a friend in Mr. Remis. Red Singer was a great rope climber because he was all legs, the key to that exercise. Arms were really useless in climbing ropes. "Looks like you pissed your pants, Singer. You shake it a few more times, tends to prevent that. Or wear darker pants."

"He likes you," said Dickie Rosenberg.

"Go down to the training room, Red," said Hennessey. "Put the heat lamp on it."

Mrs. Parker walked by them with her clipboard. "You boys will always thank me. Once you learn the waltz you know it forever. Like riding a bicycle."

Red looked down at his chinos after she passed by. "Is this love?" he asked his friends. Two guys held his arms then, and Hennessey splashed water from the fountain onto the front of his pants.

Freddie Temple drove his parents' blue V-8 De Soto Firedome to pick up Rosenberg. Dickie had called him early into Christmas vacation, hoping they could get together.

"We're going skiing, Dick. Whole family to Wildcat. Then I've got a few parties in New York."

"I got the picture," said Dickie. "I thought we'd talk about college; you could see the guys."

"At St. Luke's they tell you to apply to one college unless they can actually see daylight between your ears."

"I'm applying to six schools."

Freddie felt daylight between himself and his old friends from grammar school. He wanted to kiss them good-bye, yet he didn't, he couldn't. Freddie had a heart that his parents, so austere, hadn't hardened completely to his public school past. The boys at St. Luke's shut out worlds that were not Park Avenue, Hobe Sound, skiing in Vermont, ranching in Wyoming, worlds of their grandparents' and parents' making. The only boys at St. Luke's who had not grown up identically were foreign students, sons of exiled Spanish royalty, sons of Greek shippers, Japanese merchants, Latin American dictators. These boys were bullied if they were shy or threw themselves into studies. They were idolized if they gambled and tossed around money and talked of fast red cars and faster dark women. As far as Freddie could tell, there were two Jewish boys in the entire school, both sons of New York investment bankers, both brilliant in their studies and entirely miserable at St. Luke's.

"As soon as we're back from skiing," Freddie said to Rosenberg, "I'll call you. I'd like to see the guys, see what's happening."

"I'm applying to Harvard," Dickie said. "I didn't think I would."

Freddie drove to pick up his friend wearing a tie and jacket. After his third-form year he didn't find it a pain to dress up. Now he looked down on youngsters he saw in his hometown who didn't wear a coat and tie. And they felt the same about anyone who *did*. He waited in the street below the Rosenbergs' house. "Don't drive up the driveway," Dickie had told him. "My father gets too pissed if anyone touches a branch on one of his trees with a car." Fred couldn't help it. He heard Dickie pronounce it "cah," and he himself knew how far away he had gone from the playgrounds of the Hathaway School in South Brookwood. "What do you say, Blondie?" Dickie asked as he slid into the front passenger seat of the De Soto.

"I say *this*," Freddie said, reaching under the seat and handing Dickie a flask full of screwdrivers. Dickie never drank liquor. He associated it too much with Red Singer throwing up at his bar mitzvah, with Red throwing up in the back of trolley cars late at night coming back from Boston. And he hated the taste of beer. Dickie sipped from the flask. It was no time to get the disapproval of his fancy friend from childhood. It tasted like the orange juice his mother used to lace with cod-liver oil when he was a kid.

It is possible for any of us to be seduced out of anything. All that is needed is the right timing. Dickie would be goddamned if Freddie Temple would think him anything but cool. He took three long swallows from the flask after his first tentative taste. "Hey," said Temple. "Leave a little." He grabbed it back and swigged, his eyes leaving the road for an instant. The car veered toward a light pole, then righted as Temple took control and laughed when Dickie jammed his foot against the floorboards. "That brake doesn't work," he said. Dickie took the flask back and drank deeply.

"These are the biggest guys in the school. What are we supposed to do?" asked Nancy Stout, who couldn't wait to finish her cigarette so she could start another. She was driving her father's Dodge. "Whatever you feel like," said Loretta Mirsky. "It's no big deal.

Just watch me. And we can talk about it during the night. See how things go."

"Have you been all the way?" Nancy asked.

"That's for me to know and for you to find out."

"I don't care if you did move here from Cleveland. Kids out there don't do it any more than kids here. It's a lot of crap."

"Yeah." These last two comments were from the backseat. Two girls recruited by Nancy Stout for the party, girls known as fast, girls whispered about in the quadrangle. They were Claudine Forrest, whose father was a hairdresser, and Diane Dust, who, when she smiled, showed one tooth missing, a back molar. They all wore slacks except for Loretta Mirsky, who was looking her best, tight tweed skirt and loafers with the inevitable white socks. Her sweater was black lamb's wool pulled tight across her chest, as if she had purposely washed it in hot water to make it shrink.

"You can think what you want," Loretta said. "But the girls in Cleveland, what they know makes this town look like Mother Goose." She turned around and stared at the two girls in back. Her lipstick was as bright and fresh as Easter Sunday. "You can watch if you don't believe me. I don't care."

"Hi, Dickie," Loretta said later to Rosenberg. They had all gotten out of their cars, parked opposite Red's house. "Who's your friend?" she asked. The other girls giggled. "He going to a dance, all dressed up?"

"He always looks this way," Dickie said. "This is Fred Temple. Private school, can you tell?"

"Funny, he doesn't look Jewish," Loretta said.

"Temple isn't a Jewish name," Dickie said. "It's a Jewish place."

"I don't get it," said Diane Dust.

"You'll get it," smirked Loretta, and, taking Dickie's arm, she pulled him toward the house.

Duke Hennessey was shooting pool in the basement room next to where Red was choosing records for the evening. "All slow stuff," he called to Duke. "We don't give them a chance to be anything but close." He had pulled out Billy Eckstine, Nat "King" Cole, Sinatra. Songs his sisters had collected. They were the songs he remembered listening to in cellar parties around Brookwood when he used to stand with the boys cracking jokes, conscious of the girls but true to the code of drinking the sodas, eating the sandwiches, never dancing, thinking Johnnie Ray was sappy. "This time," Red thought, "it'll be different." His parents were at the movies; his sisters were in college. And God had moved Loretta Mirsky from Shaker Heights, near Cleveland, to Boston.

It had taken Red a long time to convince Hennessey to come to the party. He felt he had to offer him something to renew their old friendship. Duke was considered one of the best athletes in the history of Brookwood High, still a math brain, still going with Rita Cronin, who was finally a drum majorette and could really do a split way down low so her legs were actually parallel with the ground. "Watch her pick up the grapefruit," wise guys would say at pep rallies. "Watch it disappear." But they wouldn't dare say this in front of Duke.

"Come to my house, Duke," Red had pleaded. "Look, love is one thing. I know you're going with Rita. At the very least Friday night you'll get a hand job. I guarantee it."

"Are you saying Rita and I don't do anything?" Duke had said. "Or are you saying that we do and I need variety? Either way I'm probably going to punch you out. Why did I even come over here?"

"Because you're a horny bastard," Red said. "And you're sick of me yelling virgin at you since you've been seven years old."

"You didn't know the word till you were thirteen," Duke said. "I just came to watch you make fools of yourselves. I wouldn't take a hand job on a silver platter." He broke a rack of balls with a crash. Two balls jumped off the table onto the floor. "I think I'll leave now and go over to Rita's. Or go home is better." But that's when Dickie, Freddie and the girls walked into the playroom and Red dropped the needle onto Billy Eckstine singing, "If I Told a Lie." Red immediately grabbed Loretta Mirsky and spun her around, holding her close. He dipped her low to the ground, low, low. They both fell to the floor, he unable to pull off the dip, she unable to keep her balance. Red nibbled her neck, little nibbles meant to be funny. The other three girls huddled together as close as they could get without touching. Freddie reached his flask toward them. "Screwdrivers," he said.

"You got beers or anything?" asked Diane Dust, trying not to open her mouth wide enough to reveal the missing tooth.

Red jumped up and ran behind the bar. He lifted up a plastic baby's bassinet filled with ice cubes and cans of Budweiser. "I got beer," he announced. "I got pretzels," he said, throwing packages onto the bar top. "I got potato chips" — pronouncing it paddada chips — "I got nine church keys," he said triumphantly, lining up beer can openers. "And I got a pack of cards." Billy Eckstine crooned on and everyone got their own church key.

Loretta Mirsky was thrilled to be hostess. Only four months living in Brookwood and she was out with the biggest guys in the class. She introduced her girlfriends, whether they were known before or not. It was the polite thing to do. Freddie Temple was the only guy she didn't know by reputation, but he looked better than any reputation he could have had. "I'll give him to Nancy because it's her car," she thought. "Claudine should have Dickie Rosenberg because I know she's got a crush on him, and I'm amazed Duke Hennessey's here since he goes with Rita Cronin so I know they either broke up or he's jealous and whatever the reason he'll never go near Diane so he probably deserves me, but then again he doesn't dress anywhere near good enough for me." Everyone drank beer except Dickie, who was feeling like king of the world on half a flask of screwdrivers. Everyone danced except Hennessey, who was feeling both superior and faithful to Rita Cronin. "Would you like to dance?" Diane Dust asked him.

"I don't dance," he said. "I play ball." He had downed three beers, more than he ever had in his life.

"I don't care if you don't do it well," she said. "I can do the lindy. I can do anything and teach you. Even the cha-cha. Dancing with somebody ain't going behind anybody's back if that's what you're nervous about."

"The last time I was nervous," Duke said, "was when Father Joseph up to St. Anne's gave us the sermon about the flesh."

"I don't go to St. Anne's."

Duke laughed. "What a dipshit," he thought. "I got to get out of here." But he stayed and opened another beer.

It was almost completely dark in the playroom. Two dim lamps were lit on tables at either end of the couch. Red had put on a Jackie Gleason album, *Songs for Lovers Only,* and he was swaying with Loretta in the middle of the floor. Both of his hands were underneath her sweater, rubbing her back. They were kissing, tentatively at first and then full-bore, tongues, chewing bottom lips, top lips, licking each other's mouths. "I'm a natural at this," Red thought. "I knew it. I'm a natural."

"It's okay," Loretta Mirsky whispered, allowing Red to steer her to the couch, allowing him to unhook her bra, allowing him to move his hands to her breasts. "Soft," Red said as if they were a tremendous surprise. "So soft." Loretta moved so that she was lying down on the couch. She pulled Red next to her, grabbing his pants legs and tugging him closer.

Everyone else was pretending to be occupied with what they were doing. But no matter what they were doing they were all really watching Red and Loretta. Claudine was trying to maneuver Dickie into the next room. "It's rude to stare at people making out," she said, eager to watch but wanting Dickie to herself. Claudine was tall and one of the few girls in high school who enjoyed accentuating her height. She piled her dirty blond hair on top of her head, and she wore medium heels because her mother wouldn't allow her to wear anything higher. Claudine wanted to be in the Ice Capades. She danced and she skated to exercise her legs. She was a loner who didn't have a pack of girlfriends, but she was smart enough to know that Loretta Mirsky could open up her life to boys if she paid attention. Nancy Stout was inclined to *be* stout, but she made up for it in the high school hierarchy by having her own car, which was usually full of freeloaders, and by having high, rounded large bosoms that boys would reroute their paths to classes to see in the corridors of the school. None of this mattered to Freddie Temple. She was there; he would give it a whirl. They danced, and his hands were everywhere. Halfway through the song "Two Purple Shadows," an oldie they all remembered, he had Nancy's melons out of her bra and was actively massaging them while she puffed away like a sprinter. Freddie eased her over to the other couch in the dark, the lamps having been killed earlier by Red.

"What are you getting?" Red yelled out through the quiet and the sounds of "Two Purple Shadows." "Sing out, Freddie," he called. "Sing out, Rosenberg."

"Second base inside the shirt," Freddie yelled back. "Shhh," Nancy Stout giggled, clamping a hand over his mouth. "All the way," Dickie called.

"Nothing at all," Claudine rebutted. "Bare knuckle," she added, then made it okay by fiercely kissing Rosenberg and allowing his hands to roam freely outside her clothing.

While the reports came back from the darkened basement, Red had two of his fingers inside Loretta Mirsky's crotch and she was rolling her hips around so enthusiastically Red thought she'd throw them both off the couch.

Duke Hennessey was frozen at the switch, wanting to leave, wanting to stay, affected by the beer, by the songs, by the darkness. He could hear the whispers of Red and Loretta from the couch. He could hear their panting, the noise of fabric, of zippers, of shoes hitting the linoleum floor, shoes kicked off in haste, flipped across the room. "You want to go somewhere else?" Diane Dust said softly. "We can go in the back of Nancy's car. You want to make out?"

Duke said nothing. He stood against the wall under the framed French prints of dogs playing cards, dogs playing croquet, dogs peeing against a fence. Cute prints that Red's father knew would finish off the playroom perfectly. He stood and listened and strained to watch, unable to move, thinking: "I'm the catcher. I call the pitches; I control the game; I'm on top of everything and I can't walk out of here."

"I can do things for you," Diane Dust said, frightened by his silence, knowing that she had to be doing something because the other girls were doing something and she wanted to come to the next party. She reached over and touched the front of Duke's pants. Duke reacted instantly, pushing his lower body toward her hand as if it held the secret. With that encouragement from Brookwood's baseball captain, Diane Dust unzipped Duke's pants and put her hand inside, rubbing him outside of his Jockey briefs, wanting a light on so she could see, wanting more than that for Duke to touch her, to kiss her, to acknowledge that she was there, other than by thrusting his body toward her hand. "Kiss me," she said. But Duke kept his code, a code ruled by thinking of both Rita Cronin and his parish priest. "No kissing, no touching," he whispered. "I don't touch you or kiss you. Just do it," he urged. "Use both hands." So he stood against the wall of the playroom, nothing as simple as baseball or football, and allowed himself to be masturbated while he stared through the darkness at the shapes on the couch, shapes allowed to kiss and touch, shapes without a code.

"No, Dickie," Claudine said, stopping his hands from straying inside of her sweater. "I don't do that stuff."

"Come on," he said. "You got desires; you got feelings. Why are we in Red's cellar, to shoot pool?" He didn't stop trying to touch her.

"I came to get to know you," she said, pushing him away. "This isn't even a date. You never even bought me fried clams, never even took me to a movie."

"This is better than a first date," Dickie insisted. "It's in a house, no parents at home. You show me that you're really interested and they'll be plenty of movies, dozens of fried clams. All you can eat."

"I have to see what Loretta is doing. I don't do more than Loretta."

At the moment, Loretta Mirsky was trying to roll a Trojan over the erect penis of Red Singer. "It's gonna be me," he kept thinking. "It's gonna be me. The first."

That's when he came, not able to resist, his dick with a mind of its own. "Jesus H. Christ," he yelled out loud, pulling off the safe and trying to force himself into Loretta, who was having none of it. "Are you crazy?" she said. "I thought you knew what you were doing."

"I did know what I was doing," Red insisted. "It was you who didn't know. This was supposed to be fucking, not a Goodyear commercial." Laughs came from all over the playroom. Except from Duke Hennessey, who hissed in a strained voice that was magnified as if coming from a bullhorn out of the blackness: "Don't stop."

Diane Dust felt humiliated, but she kept pulling on Duke's penis, pulling and stroking. The act for her was a disembodied ritual, a blind routine that she could not define, one that had no meaning. Hennessey shot his wad in spurts that seemed to him to have been saved up for seventeen years, falling upon the carefully laid linoleum squares of the Singer playroom floor. Duke could now be disgusted in the dark. He didn't want to see Diane Dust; he didn't want to see his old friends; he didn't care to see his spilled seed on the linoleum. "Don't touch me," he told Diane. Then he zipped up his fly and left the playroom without saying another word, only thinking to himself, "Unworthy of Rita Cronin, unworthy of God; unworthy of the varsity baseball team." He began to run, as he always did when he was either escaping from something or thinking through a problem. Duke was lucky. He understood at an early age that it was through physical effort that he could renew himself, purge himself of sin, original and unoriginal. "Hut one, hut two, hut three," he chanted to himself, recalling the quarterback's cadence, losing himself in the rhythm of forgetting.

Dickie pulled Claudine back into the room with the pool table. "Now you know what Loretta was doing," he said. "How about it?"

"Hey, look," she said. "I never been all the way, so you can forget about that. She's from Cleveland. You can be good-looking and a big shot. I think you're a snob, and you're getting nothing from me until you take me out. Until we go to a movie or to Joey and Margie's Deli after a movie and you introduce me to some of your BMOC's." Sensing she might have slammed the social door too heavily, Claudine came close and snuggled against Dickie. "But we can make out tonight," she said. "And you can have second base."

Freddie Temple was in uncharted waters. He had never been this far before with a girl. He had Nancy Stout's blouse completely off and her bra tossed somewhere onto the floor. She had stopped him whenever he tried to undo the button on the back of her slacks, and they were so tight it was impossible to slide them down without her help. He was lying on top of Nancy, nuzzling her breasts, rubbing his lower body into hers, hoping she would give in but fearing at the same time that he would not have a clue what to do if she let him. As he kissed her, he thought of the old joke that he understood now for the first time. "Hear about the camel who ran out of water?"

"No."

"He had to dry-hump across the desert." Freddie was humping away and Nancy was humping away, but that's when Red Singer turned on the lights. He was dressed in a plaid Viyella shirt, a birthday present, and Jockey briefs. He shuffled a deck of cards with a fancy riffle, a routine his father had taught him. "Strip poker, anyone?" he asked, a wicked grin on his face.

The eternal motto for orgies has been "Come not." It was Red's party. He was satisfied. He could take his ball and go home. Nancy Stout immediately covered herself and, with Diane Dust, they ran for the lavatory, locking themselves in. Claudine shrugged. The lights were on; she flipped through the 45s looking for something she liked and smoked a cigarette. She figured time was on her side. If Dickie liked her, terrific. He'd take her out. If not, she had had a night with some hot shits and she could go back to planning for the Ice Capades.

Loretta Mirsky knew that she was made in Brookwood. She found out the hot-ticket boys in town were all inexperienced; they were children. With her loss of virginity to a Shaker Heights smoothy in Cleveland the year before she moved to the East, she knew she had a lot of lead time before anyone in Brookwood could catch her. She was smart not to wear slacks. All she had to do was smooth down her skirt and she was decent. Her underpants she had stuffed into one of her loafers. Smart. Thinking ahead.

Nancy and Diane emerged from the lavatory. Diane had been crying. Nancy was indignant with the boys. "Duke is a shit," she said. "Where was he raised, who taught him manners? I got a curfew with the car."

Claudine had put on Frank Sinatra's *Songs for Swingin' Lovers* album. "Don't start playing songs," Nancy said. "I got a curfew with the car."

"Well, I don't have a curfew," said Loretta Mirsky. "How about it, Claudine? The night is young."

"The night is young and you're so glamorous," sang Dickie Rosenberg, gone on the screwdrivers and the beer.

"I'm going with the girls," Claudine said, very cool. "Dickie knows where to find me if he wants me."

Loretta Mirsky stayed. She sat demurely on the couch and smiled at the three boys, knowing that she was at least a hundred years older than they.

"You see what you missed going to fairy school?" Red said to Temple. "Lights out at ten, candles out at eleven? That's the story, right?"

Temple laughed. "That's girls' boarding school, Singer."

"You can call me Red," he answered. "It's okay. What is this, only use last names since you've been away?"

"It's the way it happens there," Freddie said. "Everybody uses last names. It doesn't mean anything derogatory; it's the custom."

"Do girls really do that with candles?" Loretta asked. "I'm glad I go to high school. Going away must set you back for years."

Dickie slumped on the couch opposite Loretta. He was combing his hair. The act soothed him. Touching his hair was a comfort to Dickie. "I can't believe I struck out with Claudine," he said. "I got less than any of you guys, even Duke, who's probably in confession now, for Christ's sake."

"You only look like a lover, Rosie," said Red. "That's your problem. The girls don't think you're sincere." He sat next to Loretta and fondled her breasts on top of her sweater. She didn't stop him. "Now *I'm* sincere. You know that, don't you?"

"You better be." She smiled.

"I'm so sincere," Red said, "that I've got an honest proposition for you. You let me get inside your pants, right?"

"You don't have to be so crude, Mr. Singer," Loretta said. "Whatever I did, I did because I like you."

"I respect that," Red said. "And I respect you, you believe that?" He was thinking that his dad would really love to hear this, that his dad would take him on the road to sell if he knew what kind of chatter his kid could deliver.

"You want us to go, Singer?" Temple asked. "This makes us kind of redundant, *n'est-ce pas?*"

"Back when we fought the guys from West Roxbury," Red said, "you would have called anyone who talked like you a schmuck."

"Now I wouldn't call anybody a schmuck," Freddie said.

"Sure," Red countered. "Now you'd call them a '*n'est-ce pas.*' Do you realize I'm working on the ultimate sacrifice, you asshole?"

"What's the ultimate sacrifice?"

"I'm trying to get you laid with my girlfriend."

"You want to suck around Temple, Red?" said Dickie Rosenberg. "I can call you by your last name till the cows come home if that's what it takes."

"I want to get you laid, too," said Red. "What is friendship all about?"

"Do you believe in friendship?" Red asked Loretta.

"I believe in friendship," she said. "It's gang bangs I have a problem with."

They all laughed hysterically, the kind of laughter that happens once in a while, when you can't control it. Like in classrooms, or in Sunday school when you are supposed to be serious. Freddie opened four beers and handed them around. He and Dickie sat on the floor in front of the couch with Loretta and Red crowded next to each other. "Let me tell you something," Red said to Loretta. On the record player one of Red's parents' old 78s had dropped, a hit song by Vaughn Monroe, "Ballerina," 1947. "Anything you do with me, it's the same as doing it with my best friends. Anything you do with me, it's exactly the same as doing it with them." Everyone was very quiet except for Vaughn Monroe, who was singing, "A thousand people here, have come to see the show, as round and round you go, so ballerina dance." The song came to an end, and the needle went click, click, click, click, whirrr, as the record player needed help and no one dared move to help it.

"What the fuck," said Loretta. And the boys drew in very close, surrounding Loretta, the transplant from Cleveland.

Senior Year, Spring 1955

It was traditional, after the senior prom, to have parties at the beach. Not just any beach but Matonquit, where many of the seniors had the most history. The boys had borrowed parents' cars, with strict requirements as to filling of gas tanks, being careful and getting home at a certain hour. The girls had cheap overnight bags shaped like hatboxes, which they kept in their dates' car trunks. Four or five or six girls would sleep over at one girl's house. The strictest parent could not control his child if she were sleeping over. The strictest parent could not control the child who was hostess for the sleep-over. No one could discipline a daughter who had friends for the night. Too many odds against.

The prom was for playing dress-up. Everyone knew there was

something wrong with anyone at Brookwood High who wore a tie. And only at holiday concerts did any girl who pretended to know anything wear stockings and heels. But proms were different. The theme of this senior prom was Under the Sea. "We need a theme," Dickie said as a member of the prom committee, "because life needs a theme and the gym needs to play dress-up probably more than we do."

"First we lower the ceiling with nets," said Elly Markum, the class secretary who got A's in art. "Then we fill the nets with seashells and balloons."

"You either need a mighty fine net," Dickie said, "or the biggest shells in the world to fit in it."

"Papier-mâché shells," Elly said with disdain. "You ever hear of creating fantasy? You ever read fairy tales when you were a kid?"

"That's your department," he said. "I just want to make sure the class makes money on the dance."

"What difference does it make?" she asked. "We're graduating in a week."

"It's what we leave behind," Dickie insisted. "The legacy. You want to leave a deficit?"

"You can worry about breaking even at Harvard next year," she said. "Our legacy will be the papier-mâché shells. That'll be what the kids will remember."

The prom was responsibility: boys stiff in rented tuxedos and tight cummerbunds, girls stiff in low-cut gowns with enough crinolines underneath to ensure that any dancing would be proper, perhaps cheek to cheek but everything else separated by inches of space, layers of clothing, lacquered hair on the girls, Wildroot creme oil laced into the hair of the long-haired boys, whiffle sticks applied to those with crew cuts. Teachers and the parents of class officers chaperoned and were appropriately formal with each other. Parents and teachers respected one another. They chitchatted, drank punch and were entirely ill at ease and dishonest for the long evening, ever sneaking constant peeks for the faces of their own boys and girls: oh, to actually *see* them dance.

The after-parties were freedom: off with the rented formal wear, out of the gowns, save forever the corsages, and everything crushed into suitcases or thrown into the trunk of Daddy's car, motors revved up and rubber left on roads on the procession to Matonquit Beach.

The racier boys packed William Penn whiskey in pints along with Giant Imperial Quarts of Narragansett beer, which they wrapped in blankets. Dickie had petitioned for his father's car six months before the prom, long before he had a date. For Dickie, getting the family car was based on his performance at school: his grades. At home it was his chores: shoveling the driveway, taking out the barrels on trash day, mowing the lawn in the spring, raking in the fall. It was not just a measure of the quality of his work, it was also the measure of the enthusiasm he put into it. "Wheels are freedom, Dad," Dickie had said.

"You think I don't know that?" his father replied. "But freedom without responsibility is a lie, a joke. Alexander Hamilton, Richard. Emulate Alexander Hamilton. 'Your people is a great beast,' Hamilton said. Don't follow the crowd. You want a car, go to work and save the money to buy one." His father still resisted as Dickie was dressing for the prom while his mother escalated her pleas on Dickie's behalf into a battle. "Ruin him more," he heard his father yell.

"He got into Harvard," his mother rebutted.

"Do you get rewarded for doing what you're supposed to do?" his father yelled in return.

His father relented when Dickie came into their bedroom in his tuxedo. "John Gilbert, Junior," he exclaimed, almost all of his comparisons relating to the 1920s. Then Dickie received the rules that, if he obeyed them to the letter, would result in his driving down the driveway and then back up, depositing the keys on the hook in the downstairs coat closet. Dickie was taking a first date to the prom, a gutsy move for so important a night. But his date was Betty Ann Robinson, the Jewish cheerleader, an event in herself. Betty Ann was only the sixth Jewish cheerleader in Brookwood High's history, and her parents couldn't figure out why she would even be interested. "This is not a thing for a nice girl to be doing," they pointed out. "Showing your legs so far, exposing your private parts."

"Mom, for God's sake, I show more in a bathing suit. Cheerleading is the biggest thing in the school — the best girls."

"Fine, Betty Ann. Make a display." So she did. She could do the deepest split, the tightest flip, she could jump the highest and give the loudest yell. "Beat 'em, bust 'em, that's our custom, go, Hennessey, go."

She and Rita Cronin became best friends, and Duke had urged the fix-up date for months.

"He's too conceited," Betty Ann had said about Dickie.

"Not when you get to know him," urged Duke. They doubledated for the prom, and they drove to Matonquit together for the after-parties, down the June roads that were not crowded, a night soft as 100 percent cotton. The two girlfriends sang on the way down, anything that occurred to them but heavy on numbers like "Night and Day," "The Nearness of You" and the duet "You're Just in Love," sung originally by Russell Nype and Ethel Merman in *Call Me Madam*. And they talked. The girls giggled and gossiped with other girls, there was no room for boyfriends; it was that kind of a ride to the beach. Betty Ann Robinson turned around, knees against the back of the passenger seat, and talked to Rita Cronin. Dickie whipped the car to the side of the road and screeched to a stop, grabbing his date to keep her from banging against the dashboard. "Out," Dickie said. "You think I bought an orchid and rented a tux to have you five miles away from me in the car? I waited four years for this night."

The two girls knew how to treat dates who were out of line. "Beat 'em, bust 'em, that's our custom, go, Dickie, go," they yelled, ridiculing the boys. Rita and Duke got into an argument, and they drove the rest of the way with the boys in front, girls in back, mirroring the way Dickie's parents often went out for the evening with friends. It was something Dickie swore would never happen to him when he got married.

"You want to forget about being pissed at girls," Duke said. "Talk about sports. Think about sports."

"Do you believe Hogan got beaten in the Open?" Dickie said.

"By Jack Fleck," said Duke. "How could an unknown beat Hogan in a play-off?"

"You're right. I feel better already."

There were almost a hundred kids at the beach, many of the boys still in tuxedos with the pants legs rolled up, wanting to get the most for their rental money.

It was Red Singer's beach. He had orchestrated the parking on the dunes and had gotten permission from the police for a small, controlled bonfire. It helped that one of the two town lieutenants had dated his sister Flossie and still had a sneaker for her. "You get more mileage out of your sisters than a fucking Studebaker," Duke had told him. Red took this as a compliment.

"Don't be a schmeazuck, Francis," Red said to him, being one of the few people outside of teachers and priests who called Duke by his given name. Red was talking in a language he considered swift, putting "eaz" in the middle of off-color words so that frig became "freazig" and fart "feazart." One day in English class when called upon to read, Red said, "The evil men do lives after them. The geazood is oft interred with their beazones." It was worth it to be sent to the headmaster's office for "insubordination." The headmaster said, "It's not too late to throw you out on your ear, Singer. I see you're going to Tufts. It's not too late for me to write them a letter."

"I don't know what came over me, sir," Red said. "It's the euphoria of graduation."

"Why haven't you ever applied yourself, Singer?" he said. "Anyone who can use 'euphoria' in everyday speech deserves better than seeing me for disciplinary action." He thumbed through a folder: Red's records. "A C-plus average and deportment problems all four years. You finished second in the state meet, the three hundred."

"A bad start, sir. I can really run like a bastard."

"It doesn't even matter what I say, does it, Singer?"

"School and me are marking time," Red said.

"Are you going to end up in jail, Singer? A con man?"

"I hope not, sir."

The headmaster waved him out. "Euphoria," he repeated out loud as Red walked away from the office.

Pausing by the secretary's desk, Red said, "Feazuck yeazou."

"Pardon me?" the secretary said.

"I just got the Latin prize."

"Congratulations." She beamed. He knew that no matter what he did, Tufts would never renege on its acceptance or its scholarship. Because he really could run like a bastard.

The weather was with everyone; the moon was with everyone, half a sliver but enough that they noticed it. Every song they could think of sounded right, even if it was in their minds and not on the portable radio stuck in the sand on "easy listening." It became a night when steadies drifted off away from the fire and first dates sang, did cartwheels, told jokes and maneuvered to make an impression that would also allow them eventually to drift away from the fire.

Betty Ann Robinson had challenged Dickie to a race on the sand. "You want to make up?" she said. "If you beat me at fifty yards, no handicap, I sit in the front seat on the way home."

Dickie did not want games on the night of his senior prom.

"Why do you think I asked you out?"

"Because you've heard about my great personality?"

"Because I've been watching you in the quadrangle and in the halls all year. And I've been curious about what you're really like."

She laughed. "What I'm really like? That's a line I read somewhere. Old as the hills. You heard I was a make-out artist."

"I swear to God I never heard that. Why are you so defensive?"

"You're the smart guy. You're going to Harvard. You tell me." She was five-foot-four and scrubbed like a Camay soap ad, sandy blond hair cut close to her head and a small straight nose that looked as if it deserved to be sucked by a connoisseur of noses.

"I'll tell you," said Dickie. "You've got a crush on me, and you're leaning over backwards not to let it show."

"Yeah," she shot back. "I used to be conceited, but now I'm a great kid." She back-pedaled away from the circle of kids. "Who wants to race down the beach?" she yelled. "Losers in the water." She had a dozen takers who lined up on the line she drew with her toe on the black hard sand of low tide. Duke Hennessey and Rita Cronin, Red Singer and Dickie joined a group of others, some dressed in tuxedo pants, girls with blue jeans under their party dresses, one boy in his Jockey briefs who was feeling no pain. "Ready," Betty Ann said. "On your marks. Go." They took off down the beach and raced beyond the fifty yards with Red way in the lead, followed by Duke, who could travel for all his bulk. Then Betty Ann Robinson. Dickie finished next to last and watched while everyone else threw the boy in Jockey shorts into the ocean.

"Why did you run in the race if you hated the idea?" said Betty Ann.

"I wanted to show my date that I was a sport," Dickie said.

She looked seriously at him for the first time that night. "So you're really human," she said, "not just a greaseball God looking for a mirror to check out his hair." She reached for his hand and gave a quick kiss to his cheek. "Are you human enough to go for a walk with a Jewish cheerleader?"

"I'll never see you next year," Rita Cronin said to Duke. They sat at the bottom of a sand dune, far from the campfire, where they could hear sounds of the Brookwood fight song being sung. Rita was going to Newton College of the Sacred Heart in the fall. It was in the town next to Brookwood.

"For Christ's sake, Reet. I'll be ten minutes away."

"I've done some checking. MIT kids are in a lab for four years. Then they spend the rest of their lives in another lab. I'll never see you play football again or cheer you on the sidelines."

"MIT doesn't have cheerleaders. You can still watch me play baseball."

"It isn't the same. I love you, Francis."

"Like" was a word Duke had used hundreds of times. "I really like you. I like you better than anybody. You know how much I like you." Saying "love" for Duke was like saying "Mary, mother of God" or "Blessed is the fruit of thy womb, Jesus." You never uttered those words without feeling that they were illuminated by the light that was filtered through stained glass. "Can't you say anything else?" Rita asked.

Duke threw small stones at the distant water. "I was raised to work hard and take certain things seriously," he said. "If I call you my friend, you're my friend, you're my friend for life. If I say love it's got to be the same thing."

She started to get up. "Wait a minute," he said, pulling her back down. Her back nestled into the sand, and he pinned her shoulders and whispered into her ear, "I love you." Then he kissed her hard before the words blew away and before he'd have to say them again out loud.

"Why should I be honest with you?" asked Dickie. "It's a first date. Honesty with people is something you earn over a period of time."

"That's not true," Betty Ann Robinson said. "Honest is something you are or you aren't all the time."

"If you're so smart how come you're not going to Harvard?"

"See," she said. "Sarcastic, defensive. When I apply to college next fall, I want to go to Smith. It sounds good; it's got one syllable, easy to remember."

"Would you go out with me again if I struggled to be honest?"

"And if you don't sneak peeks in mirrors?" She softened and rubbed her thumb along the back of his hand as they walked. He wanted the preliminaries over. He hated the rituals of dating and the standard requirements of high school. He was itching for what was next, always for what was next. Rosenberg was feeling that no matter what he was part of, no matter what he belonged to, he was on the outside looking in.

On the race home to return his father's car, everyone snuggled. It looked as if there were two people in the Dodge, not four, and Dickie felt as if he had truly been to a prom the way he had always envisioned it: a girl nestled close to him so that everyone could see that they liked each other, that she liked *him*. He worked the clutch. She shifted the gears. Duke and Rita Cronin kissed and wrestled and rustled in the backseat. Duke knew that because the word "love" passed between them he was now entitled to new territory. But he was a thinking athlete, a heady ballplayer. He knew about cause and effect and had often heard his father, Big Duke, tell him, "Never think with your pecker." He had turned down scholarships to Holy Cross and Michigan State, where he would have played football. Seventeen schools had recruited him for sports, but his father had also told him, "Ivy League or Tech. If MIT will take you, that's where you're going. Then you'll be able to take your life and run with it. You don't end up like your old man, up the Edison for forty years with a beaten-in nose and two bent ears." The baseball coach at MIT made up Duke's mind. "You can play ball here, son, for four years, if you have the time. Think of it. You will never be the smartest kid who ever came here, but you could be the best baseball player in the history of Massachusetts Institute of Technology. That label will open doors for you all over the world." When he accepted MIT, Duke stood six-foot-one and was a sneaky-fast 205 pounds. For years he had never worn his hair in anything but a crew cut.

They dropped off the girls first, Betty Ann, then Rita. Duke and Rita took so long at the door that Dickie leaned on the horn in the dead-quiet neighborhood. Duke came rushing into the car. "You fucking idiot," he said. "We were just saying good night. You wake her folks, my ass is grass and they're a lawnmower."

"I got to get the car home. I'm an hour late. I won't get a sniff of it all summer if my father's awake."

"More important," Duke said, "how did you do? She could have been driving in your pants she was so close."

Dickie passed the speed limit on the way to Duke's house, screeching to a stop down the road so that Duke's folks wouldn't hear a door slam. "You know, I think a lot about that night with Loretta Mirsky in Red's cellar," said Dickie. "You just raced out of that place."

"Well, I think about it, too," Duke said, easing open the passenger door. "I felt so goddamned guilty. Jesus. Diane Dust, for Christ's sake, that pig touched me, and I wanted her to. I couldn't stick around to have what you guys had. But I'm kind of glad, you know?"

"I got news for you, Duke," Dickie said. "I couldn't fuck her. I never told anyone before."

Duke laughed his heady athlete's appreciation for life. "Now you won't burn in hell," he paused. "Freddie Temple was an asshole for going off to private school. You know?" He shut the door carefully so as to wake no parents on the quiet June night.

The party had left Red alone on the beach. His date had responded to his repeated attempts to undo her bra and force his hands between her legs by going home with other friends. "I'm not Loretta Mirsky," she had said, the final blow. "Why didn't you take her?" Red wished that he had, but Loretta had become famous in Brookwood since the winter and was untouchable in public. No one could admit to asking the infamous Loretta out on an actual date, but boys called her house at all hours looking for her and telling her parents in anonymous croaks, "Your daughter screws; your daughter gives blow jobs." Red was angry at his friends, angry at his date. "Everyone should know," he thought, "that if you accept a date to a prom you have to make out." He lay on his back and looked up at the sliver of moon. "That son of a bitch, Rosenberg," he thought, "planning everything, scheming, the politician.

I'm honest, and I get shit on for it." Feeling sorry for himself, he loosened the belt on his jeans and unzipped his fly.

"This is no time to be pulling your pud," said a voice. "It's time to put the fire out and go home." It was one of the cops from whom they had gotten beach-party permission. Red jumped up, embarrassed. "I was just going to go swimming," he said. "Although," he admitted, "it might have been a good idea to be pulling my pud. Sometimes I think I've been doing it for seventeen years."

The cop laughed. "All the guys feel that way," he agreed.

"How do I know I'll like the guy, Temple?" Timmy Buck challenged Freddie. "For Christ's sake, you've got us rooming with a Hebe townie. You can't vote for Franklin Roosevelt anymore, you know." They were on the practice tee at The Golf Club, hitting shots, feeling wise. Freddie was wearing faded khaki Bermuda shorts and a St. Luke's School rowing shirt. He had grown to almost six-foot-three and kept his blond hair long except around the ears. Freddie was gorgeous without thinking about it, without doing anything to help it along.

"You get to know Rosenberg," Freddie said, pausing from hitting long two irons, erratic but far off the tee. "He's smart. He can help us through courses. He knows girls all over the place. You just don't know any Jews, Buck. You're a goddamn bigot."

Buck switched to a nine iron and hit a succession of high, arcing, perfect shots, each landing within several feet of the other. "I know Lester Bloom, that shit who was in the fifth form always talking about his old man's money. How many do I need to know? What do we need it for? We don't have to study at Harvard. You walk in, take some guts, spend all your time in a club, then go to graduate school and get serious. Harvard's a breeze."

"Well, I went to kindergarten with Rosenberg, and you're going to learn to like him. Besides, I really couldn't say no when he asked me."

"I get to suffer because you're a bleeding heart, Temple?" Two young men walked toward them carrying golf bags. "Let's go if we're going to get in eighteen before dark," one of them called.

"That Montgomery," Buck said. "Going to Penn in the fall. He must really be a dumb shit not to get into Harvard from Groton. Even your friend Rosenberg got into Harvard."

"You want to piss me off, Buck," said Temple, "keep it up."

"I want you emotional," Buck said. "People who are emotional can never hit a golf ball straight. Bring your money, Blondie." The four boys headed for the first tee, Buck trying to goose Montgomery with his nine iron.

○

CHAPTER SEVEN

College, Freshman Year, 1955

"**Y**ou're a bunch of overprivileged assholes," Al Capp, the creator of Li'l Abner, screamed at the Harvard freshman class of 1959.

"*You're* an asshole, Al," screamed back hundreds of voices, longing for an outlet, a scapegoat for the pressure of wondering if they could ever make it at Harvard. The collective administrative wisdom of the college in the 1950s thought that two messages were important. The first was fear. Seat the freshman class in an auditorium and say, "Look to your right, look to your left; when you graduate, one of you won't be there." The other message was "Relax, mix it up. This is not a frightening place. But to truly realize this, it would be best learned if you were drunk for the first time in your lives. We'll guarantee this happens in a controlled atmosphere." This atmosphere was provided by the freshman smoker, held each year in the autumn at Memorial Hall, a monstrous Victorian pile used mainly for taking exams, as incongruous a building in its setting as Jockey shorts would be on Douglas Fairbanks, Jr., or Fred Astaire. Al Capp was hired by Harvard for $200 to provide stand-up comedy of the sort that should appeal to young men who would have voted for Walt Kelly's Pogo if they were old enough to vote in the presidential election of 1952. After ten minutes of topical remarks, politically oriented, Al Capp got the impression that he was being treated like a servant. The first paper plane was thrown from the balcony, followed by a squadron from all over the hall. Capp, in sudden retreat, threw several curses and middle fingers to the freshmen and stumbled off the stage on his wooden leg. The crowd, whipped into a frenzy of good feeling, knew that Al Capp could not have gotten into Harvard. But they suddenly appreciated that *they* did and that they were bonding for the first time as a class. So, prodded by faculty and advisers, the class of 1959 went downstairs to get skunked together, the ultimate for eighteen- and nineteen-year-olds. Dickie Rosenberg was sucking up the night as if it were from the nozzle of a keg. Beer was poured into the freshmen. Also onto the floor, all over their clothes, heads and bodies, like the locker-room scenes of a World Series winner. After two hours no one was too intimidated or fearful to talk to anyone else. But Fred Temple only talked to his roommates and to old friends who had gone to St. Luke's. They wore jackets and ties while most of the other freshmen wore sweaters or frayed shirts, over soft khakis, chino pants. Dickie kept his eyes and ears open, the opportunist. He wore a tie and gray tweed jacket. He was on the outside of Freddie's circle, and he pushed a little to break in, knowing first off that his accent was wrong, that he needed to start pronouncing his r's, not say, "Paak my caah in Haavaad yaad." The dead giveaway of the townie, public school boy. So he drank beer after beer and worked on his r's.

"Who are you trying to shit, Rosie?" The voice was that of Roger Wolfe, a classmate from Brookwood, one of the seven from his high school admitted to Harvard with Dickie.

"What are you talking about, Wolfe?" Dickie said, consciously falling into the prep school habit of calling people by their last name.

"You always accused me of answering a question by asking a question," Wolfe said. "I mean the jacket and tie when I'm about to get sick all over my worst sweatshirt." Wolfe was grinning like a fool, slurring his words.

"The answer, Wolfe, is that I have no intention of getting sick all over my tie. Maybe I've learned how to hold it."

Wolfe grinned some more, the grin of honesty. "Tell me, Mr. Fancy Rosenberg," he said, "do you think Judaism is a race or a religion?" Roger Wolfe had graduated number three in Brookwood's graduating class and was going to be premed.

It seemed to Dickie that Fred Temple floated above the crowd, not a hair out of place, not a lapel askew, his tie firmly knotted tightly against his collar. Freddie tasted his beer as if it were champagne. Dickie watched him, surrounded by several of his St. Luke's friends, oblivious to anyone else, indeed, disdainful of everyone, lost in their world, yet standing in three inches of suds and slop on the floor of Memorial Hall. Dickie grabbed two glasses of beer, threw one down quickly and elbowed his way close to Fred Temple's circle. Freddie motioned him in and put an arm around his shoulders. "You all know Rosie," he said, and the way he said it, you *had* to know Rosie. Freshman noise floated upward in the great hall along with smells of sweat, stale brew, cigarettes and, if you could smell it, an easing of tensions built up for two weeks in a strange, intimidating place among strangers. Several football players, breaking training, began diving into the suds, sloshing around the floor as if they were on a beach at very low tide. Timmy Buck was drinking out of a flask, the only freshman who seemed to need more than hops. He offered it to Rosenberg, who shook his head. "No need to ruin the finest," Dickie said, sweeping his arms at the crowd. "This history may be askew, but one fact is very clear, that if you want a better brew, ask for Gansett ale and beer," he chanted, the old ad that used to play on Red Sox games.

"You're a hot shit, Rosie," Buck said and slapped him on the back. Buck roomed with Dickie and Freddie Temple in Grays Hall, a small dormitory originally built in 1863 on the south end of Harvard Yard. Their suite had two bedrooms, a bathroom, a living room with nonworking fireplace, three bureaus, three desks with Harvard captain's chairs. Daily maid service provided by the school had been discontinued a year earlier. The disappearance of servants from Harvard, the "biddies," as they were known, was one of the three topics most discussed in the first week of school by Timmy Buck. The other two were the number of people out for crew and the distressing ugliness of the Radcliffe girls. Fred Temple seemed oblivious to Buck's snobbery. It amused him; he now ignored it. Freddie tolerated Buck's boorishness and Dickie's lack of sophistication with equal unconcern. Temple felt he was the ideal to which they both must aspire. He had become untouchable because he looked so good and made looking good look easy. "I've had about enough of my classmates," Buck said. "Let's head for the Cliffe." "You interested in pig sticking?" he asked Rosenberg. Buck was horrified to be rooming with a Jewish public school boy, no matter how presentable or smart he might be. But with Temple's vote of confidence, Rosenberg became a curiosity to Buck, a collectable, an approved item that perhaps might be useful, like a better corkscrew. After a week, Buck was afraid he might be missing something, and, consequently, Dickie became wonderful for him. Dickie, on the other hand, worshipped what Freddie had become and hated Buck. He didn't actually hate him, he feared that he would walk in on a conversation where Buck would be condemning, patronizing, ridiculing or misunderstanding Jews. Then Dickie would have to take a stand and take a chance on making an enemy. Dickie wanted to seduce at Harvard, not be forced into confrontation.

"I'm sticking around for a while," Dickie said. "I like to see kids from Kansas City blow lunch."

"You're a hot shit, Rosie," Buck said.

Dickie would never admit that he had to work on a paper on Copernicus for nat sci 3. His roommates seemed totally unconcerned about courses or classes. Dickie was convinced he would flunk out at Thanksgiving. What he considered worse was that he thought himself incapable of completing a sentence with a Radcliffe girl, even if she were the ugliest freshman in America. So his roommates left and Dickie took another beer to the side of the room and watched his future. After ten minutes he felt totally out of place, the way he so often did in high school. At Brookwood, Dickie was running in place, ready to head for the horizon, out of the clutches of his family. At Harvard he felt the big swallow, the truth suddenly. "I'm out of it." He walked through the crowd of his classmates, feeling his ears ringing and his stomach slightly distended from the beer. Snatches of passing conversation were absorbed:

"We used to go to Evelyn Waugh's house on New Year's Eve. For the punch."

"You want to go to law school? Have you ever read the Holmes-Laski letters?"

"Who gives a shit about free will versus determinism?"

"I have no classes before ten, nothing on Saturdays and nothing above the first floor."

"In my West Texas home, we'd get twenty-five thousand people to a high school football game under the lights on a Friday night. I'm the first person in my hometown to ever go to Harvard. They all know I'm coming back a full-fledged Communist."

"The smartest guys in the school all went to Bronx High School of Science."

Feeling like the dumbest guy in the school, Dickie left Memorial Hall by himself, nobody in a Sheiks jacket to join him, no one from

Camp Wah Hoo Wah, no one from Brookwood whom he cared to be with. "Liquor is a depressant" was one of the last things his father warned him about when he left for college.

"Don't become like the goys" is what his mother said.

"How do you mean, Mom?" Dickie answered sarcastically. "Rich and handsome?"

"Stupid" was all his mother would say, disapproving one final time of his rooming with Freddie Temple.

Dickie walked through Harvard Yard on his way to Grays Hall. It was the end of Indian summer and windows were open all through the Yard to the warmth. Classical music, none of which Dickie recognized, played from rooms where freshmen studied, the serious ones who either didn't go to the smoker or left early, nervous about falling behind in their work. Dickie counted things on his fingers, checking off the good and the bad. "I don't know classical music; I'm lousy at languages; I'm not good enough to play a college sport; sciences are a mystery." Close to his dorm he heard someone singing along with Sammy Davis, Jr., "That Old Black Magic," at the top of his lungs. Dickie smiled and counted on his other hand. "One. You're good-looking. You're not afraid to push yourself. If they called you an opportunist in high school, be an opportunist. Run for something. That's an area no one seems to care about here. Go for the soft spots." The Sammy Davis imitator had trouble with the high notes. "He's worried and insecure just like me," Dickie determined. "Do I have to take a backseat to classical? They don't know rock and roll. That's my edge."

With his roommates gone to Radcliffe, Dickie went across the hall hearing hoots of laughter from his neighbors' room. Four boys from various public high schools lived next door, brilliant boys, Dickie thought, from Watsonville, California, Pittsburgh, Morristown, New Jersey, and Little Rock, Arkansas. They all wanted to be novelists. As Dickie watched, they drew cards to determine who would get the first novel title they all wanted. "You know the sign in the Harvard Square subway kiosk," the boy from Little Rock said. "The sign says, 'Twelve minutes to Park Street.' That's the title we all want for our novel. So we're drawing cards, Richard." Southerners used formal address, never nicknames, until they knew you well. There was an intimacy to their banter, a secret shared. They all hungered for the same thing, making Harvard a little piece of home. They finally rejected the card drawing and agreed that the first among them to publish anything would own the right to use the title. "What about you, Richard?" he was asked. "What do you want to be when you grow up?" He blurted out the first thing that came to mind. He had no idea. "I want to be the richest man in America." They hooted at him, but they knew they'd meet strange people if they came to Harvard College.

Dickie drifted back to his room and tried to read *Oedipus at Colonus* for his general education course. He read the same speech half a dozen times and gave it up.

"Are you awake, Rosie?" The voice pulled Dickie out of the sour sleep of the beer drinker. Dickie had the upper bunk of a double-decker. Fred Temple slept in the lower. Timmy Buck had a single bedroom, a solution worked out by Fred for many good and noble reasons.

"How was Radcliffe?" Dickie mumbled.

"You got to get up for the ball games, Dick," Freddie said. "The guys who count socially don't go back to the room to study. They go on the prowl. I want them to understand and like you the way I do. Next time we go hunting and I ask you, come along, okay?" Freddie swung into bed in his boxer shorts. Dickie wore cotton summer pajamas from Best and Company. His mother bought him three pair for college. "Well," he thought, "Buck won't see me in my pj's tomorrow morning. He'll never get up for class." He could hear the clickety-clack of a typewriter, the sound coming from the room across the hall, one of the four getting a jump on the rights to *Twelve Minutes to Park Street*. How the hell could he ever make it at Harvard, he thought, when there were guys who worked all night. Temple called them "wonks."

It didn't take long for most of the students at Tufts who didn't live in the laboratories to know about Red Singer. During his first week of orientation he went out for freshman football and found himself totally ignored. The coaches noted him as having no high school reputation, being too small, probably too slow and too weak, someone who would stay out for three days on some dare and then quit. Red didn't quit. He worked in the hot September days harder than anyone. He knocked himself out on a tackling dummy; he launched himself at opponents who outweighed him by fifty pounds in blocking drills; he did extra laps around the field after practice. At the end of the first week, the varsity coach gave the boys a pep talk. "This is a hard sport, not for the weak in spirit. And you boys are at Tufts College. Not for the weak in the head either. Know *why* you're out for Tufts football; know why you want to work this hard." Then he asked if there were any questions. The candidates sat outside next to the practice field, their helmets between their legs. Red jumped to his feet. "I'm not gonna be lost in the shuffle, Coach," he announced. "I may be smaller and weaker than most of these guys. But I'm probably smarter than anyone on this field, and I've got the most spirit. I'm fast as a bastard, and you can't cut me. Besides, I know my reason for playing football at Tufts. I'm playing football to get girls." Red sat down. Then everyone out for freshman football applauded, including the assistant coaches. Red was right. They didn't cut him. But they did keep him on the bench, the last guy on the squad. His comments made the Tufts student paper.

It was a great time to have red hair. Everyone pointed him out.

Red went to his first college mixer that week and added to his reputation for being outrageous. A varsity player told him that "Jackson girls are the ugliest girls in America. But you cut your tusks on them, and you don't need a car."

Tufts was, and is, a fine 4,000-student university with a good reputation, located in Medford, Massachusetts, a working-class neighbor of Boston noted for its manufacturing businesses, mostly in custom furniture. Its mascot was and is the pachyderm, its teams nicknamed the "Jumbos" after the stuffed elephant that stands in Tufts' Barnum Hall. Red delivered sandwiches, snacks, milk and soft drinks at night to the dormitories to help with his college costs. It was another way to establish himself as a campus personality. No one he sold to forgot the redheaded purveyor of ham and cheese and Drake chocolate cakes. Red would sing a song at the top of his voice in the dormitory entrances, a parody of Tom Lehrer's satirical "The Old Dope Peddler." "It's the old sandwich vendor," he sang, "spreading joy wherever he goes."

That fall, Red lived in a rooming house on Powder House Boulevard, right near the main campus. There was not enough dormitory space to accommodate all of the incoming freshmen. Certain local students were assigned to the pleasant wooden dwelling with the smiling Irish grandmother, Mrs. Mulcahey, in charge of keeping order, making tea and cookies and dispensing occasional aspirin and iodine and Band-Aids. Eight students lived in the upstairs bedrooms, sharing two baths and endlessly hoping to befuddle Mrs. Mulcahey enough to sneak girls and beer into their suites. Red's roommate came from a small town in western Massachusetts. He spent his time agonizing over the reading assignments and picking his feet. "Jesus H. Christ," Red would say to him. "If you pick those goddamned feet in front of everyone, what the hell do you do when no one's around?" The roommate would be gone by mid-years, too miserable to study, too lonely for the hills of western Massachusetts to make new friends in the big city of Medford.

Red joined a fraternity in those early weeks of fall, pushed by a football teammate from Haverhill, Massachusetts, a hulking tackle named Ginsburg whose older brother had been a member of Phi Epsilon Pi or Phi Ep as it was known. Phi Ep was a primarily Jewish fraternity, a fast house whose members had cars or access to them, played a lot of cards, had spending money and admitted several black athletes so they could feel even better about themselves. Red spent his mornings sleeping, his afternoons at the Tufts oval for football practice. His nights, when he wasn't selling goodies in the dorms, were spent cruising the junior colleges of Boston, looking for available girls who were not too smart. Red didn't pay much attention to studies, and the only guilt he felt was for the limited tuition his father paid. He rationalized the worst: "I pay Dad back no matter what happens, I sell sandwiches; I get a partial track scholarship; Dad knows I'll do what I have to do." And he loved his father. What he hated was his father's life on the road serving dozens of masters, getting up for the selling game in blizzards, in spring mud season, in fall northeasters, his dad struggling to move the goods and trying to make his salesman's draw. Red had no idea about *Death of a Salesman,* but when he eventually saw the play, it became his single favorite work of art.

What he did care about was making life a game, and his game was getting attention. He hated being alone; he needed a crowd. Even in the library, packed for the first exams of the fall, Red would manage a glorious lengthy fart in the midst of the silence and was glad to accept both the blame and, truly, what he thought was the credit.

No one used the term "entrepreneur" in those days. People who noticed Red called him a "shaper," someone who shows off, someone who practices quick draws or card tricks or flexes his muscles, all in private, rehearsing for the crowd.

Several older men often hung around Tufts oval, watching football practice, shooting the breeze, marking time. One of them, a nondescript in his fifties, always sat apart from the others. He wore a ragged tweed topcoat and a battered felt snap-brim hat that looked as if it had been expensive fifteen years earlier. He would come late to practice, watch until dark, then hang around the gate where the players exited after showers. The Tufts football team dubbed him "Flash." They all suspected he was naked under his topcoat and debated among themselves as to who was the object of his affection. "Who do you love, Flash?" they would call to him as they headed toward Professors' Row, where the fraternities stood. "Tackles have the biggest cocks," guys would yell. But Flash kept silent, watching the boys pass by, pulling down the brim of his hat and smoking cigarette after cigarette. Red twisted an ankle when he got into the freshman game with Trinity and stayed late with the trainer on the following Monday. It was dark as he left the oval, leaves blowing down in the beginning of fall's good-bye. When Red heard a voice say, "You look like the kind of young man who would like to make money," he jumped back against the stadium gate, his heart thump-a-thump. Red's response to everything, from the time he was a little boy, was the wisecrack. It gave him time to think, to regroup and test the opponent.

"I don't suck pricks, Flash," Red said. "I'm even embarrassed to play with myself." Then he half walked, half ran in the direction of his rooming house.

"I'm not like that," the man called.

"That's what they all say," said Red, moving out smartly.

"I mean it," Flash said. "No fooling around. This is money."

Flash went wrong years ago, and what was left was the tweed coat, felt hat with the snap-brim and dozens of 35 millimeter pornographic movies, some, it was rumored, starring Yma Sumac, the Peruvian singer who had a four-octave range. Weeks later, in the sunshine of early November, Red made a deal with Flash for the films, a deal that did not involve cock-sucking on anybody's part.

"Duke," Red said to Hennessey on the phone, "I don't care how many guys you bring. Five bucks a head. You get Mickey Mouse films and all the beer you can drink."

"I want beer, I can get dimeys at Cronin's any time I want," said Duke. "Much as I miss your company, if I want cartoons I can go to the Laffmovie on Washington Street."

"These are dirty movies, Duke. You've never seen anything like these." Sudden silence on the other end of the phone.

"How many guys did you say I could bring?"

Duke didn't know whether MIT was good for him or whether he truly hated it more than he had hated anything in his life. Even though he was only ten miles from Brookwood, MIT was light-years from anything he had known. It was the first fall since he was a baby that he was not playing football. "No one here knows what football is," he thought during an orientation that, for Duke, might have taken place on the moon. The transition from loosey-goosey Brookwood High to the intensity of the Institute shocked Duke Hennessey, and he spent most of that fall worrying, depressed, studying up to six hours a night and doing more praying than he had done in years. "I've been here a month," he told his father on the phone, "and I haven't met one kid here who believes in God."

"You sound like you're about to roll over," Big Duke said. "Hennesseys don't roll over. They may knock us out of the ring, but they ain't going to do it because we were dogging it." Duke knew what his father expected, and he knew what he expected of himself. There were five required courses freshman year at MIT: math, physics, chemistry, humanities and an elective, which in Duke's case was a survey course in government. The size of the classes was not intimidating, lectures to a hundred and fifty students. Smaller sections that explained course work in detail were limited to thirty people, about the size of Duke's classes at Brookwood. Cushioning the shock of the workload freshman year was the rush from the fraternities, then the true nurturing system at MIT. They were also important to the school, which, like Tufts, lacked adequate housing for all of the students enrolled. Duke went with Alpha Pi, a simple decision made immediately after he asked a pledge master at one of the fraternities, "Who has the most athletes?" But it was not a comfortable time. There were signs posted on bulletin boards all over campus, hand-lettered, or written on blackboards or scrawled on the backs of laboratory doors in the library. "Tech is hell," the signs said. And for Duke, it was. He thanked God that MIT didn't have a football team because he never would have had the time to play.

Rush week at the fraternities was all seduction. The brothers had researched the incoming freshmen that summer and knew who were the prizes. They were buddy-buddy during rush week, offering help with courses, taking the most courted out to dinner or to girls' schools on cruises. The competition was intense. Each fraternity sought to entice ten to fourteen bodies into each pledge class, which would then move en masse into the fraternity house to begin almost a semester of hazing. Fraternity Row was along Beacon Street in Boston's Back Bay, bow-front brick houses in which lived the forty or fifty brothers who made MIT bearable for themselves and, through their pranks, occasionally unbearable for others. Duke considered all his assignments during this pledge period to be chickenshit. He had spent his life up to that fall on what he considered to be man's life, playing ball, working hard, studying, true to Rita Cronin. His fellow freshmen at the Institute he took, in the main, to be immature jerks, "babies" he called them. His classmates seemed never to have played a sport, never to have had a date or a fight. The kids he and his friends grew up calling "brains" were all lumped together with Duke on the banks of the Charles River, several miles downstream from Harvard. He felt sorry for himself until he met James Michael Faherty, all two hundred eighty pounds of him, an ex-high school guard like himself who did binomial equations in his head and could rip phone books with his hands. James Michael Faherty came from New Haven, a tough schoolboy town, and escaped Yale only because he and all his high school classmates hated the local college boys on sight. They were taught early that the Yalies were their enemies, and many weekend nights after football season were spent looking for trouble along the campus streets lined with the Gothic buildings of Old Eli. Jamie Faherty was a natural. He had the innate ability to assemble numbers and concepts of numbers in his head. The math and science department of Hillhouse High petitioned his parents in favor of MIT for their big boy, who everyone at Hillhouse called "Beast."

"What the fuck are *you* doing here?" said an incredulous Duke when they first met during rush week. For two minutes after that meeting, they pounded each other's shoulders, the football warm-up exercise usually done with pads on. They were as happy to find each other as long-separated twins, and from that moment they were like giant bookends for hundreds of flabby-limbed, muscular-brained young innocents with big plans. They both pledged Alpha Pi, lived in the same room and shared the chores of the regular pledge class: waking up members at prescribed hours, doing errands, going for Chinese food at midnight or doughnuts from Kenmore Square at dawn, polishing bathroom floors with toothbrushes, shining shoes. If they didn't perform according to the rigid standards of the brothers, they would have to steal panties from the room of a Wellesley College house mother or paint red the balls of George Washington's horse on the statue that stands in the Boston Public Garden across from the Ritz. And always they had to "assume the position," grabbing their ankles with their hands, and be paddled with canoe paddles by the brothers from Alpha Pi, some of whom loved the paddling better than any other part of school.

Duke had never lived anywhere in his life other than in his parents' house. The fraternity brothers took over the parenting role, governing themselves, doling out chores. Tuesday evenings there were coaching sessions at the house in calculus, chemistry and physics. Monday nights, Mr. Sal, the barber, came over to administer haircuts. Mr. Sal worked days in a Copley Square hotel and had moonlighted for years along MIT's Fraternity Row, choosing that school for the simple reason that he liked to build complex model boats, clipper ships, Spanish galleons. Sal could always get assistance from the budding engineers if he didn't take too much off the top. Duke and James Michael Faherty studied and lifted weights in their room, took the hazing in stride and worked their tails off until the night of the Charles River whitefish.

All colleges exerted pressure to some degree on their students. But at most institutions of higher learning you could fake it, borrow a paper, write a C− exam, take a gut course, plead illness in the family to deliver an assignment late. Massachusetts Institute of Technology, the "toot" to its survivors, had the motto "I.H.T.F.P.": "Institute Has the Finest Professors." The faculty all patted themselves on the back. But the students knew that the letters stood for "I hate this fucking place." There were no shades of gray. You were right or you were wrong. There was no way to fake. It was numbers, numbers, numbers. If you had the numbers correct, you were okay. Wrong and you flunked. All the fraternities had Bibles in their libraries, essays from the 1930s in humanities. But humanities were considered a joke at the toot. "Humanities," Faherty told Duke, "are bullshit. A waste of my time." Chemistry was also unpopular, considered boring and not anywhere near as important as math and physics. "Why aren't you taking notes?" a professor in chemistry asked a student in his class.

"I don't have to, sir," the student answered. "I have my grandfather's."

When they played, the fraternity boys played hard to escape the grind and the thought of the grind. At an Alpha Pi pledge meeting in late fall one of the brothers said, "What can we do with these dipshits that is truly difficult and also sophomoric?"

"I know," said Bobby Cobb, who had three pair of white bucks and a pipe collection that lined one wall of his room. "We'll get the rhinos" — what they called Hennessey and Faherty — "to set the whitefish collection record." "Charles River whitefish" was the term in the 1950s used to describe the used condoms found floating by the banks of that fetid stream separating Cambridge from Boston. Oarsmen used to pick them up on the ends of their oars. Trophies.

Bobby Cobb was a mean, superior, pipe-smoking son of a bitch who had gone to Exeter and would never let anyone forget it. He had a sadistic streak that really never surfaced until he got into fraternity life and discovered that pledges had to do his bidding. He got into Alpha Pi before anyone really knew him, riding his reputation as a hotshot sailor in prep school. Indeed, Bobby Cobb was the best skipper at MIT, leading the sailing team on the Charles to an undefeated season in 1955. "You rhinos," Bobby Cobb said. "Take a rowboat out on the river and bring back enough whitefish for a school record, which, by the way, was set in nineteen forty-six after everyone came back from the war and went crazy. The record whitefish for a fraternity was a hundred and twenty-seven used and retrieved. Remember, we have ways of testing, and those safes better be used or else you two giant wonks will be back in the dorms pretending you don't give a shit while you're really dying inside. You go back to the dorms you'll think heaven on earth is Burger's Mystery Hour" — Professor Burger's course on crystallography. "In other words, you'll be redundant."

So the rhinos went out to hunt Charles River whitefish.

"This is fucking ridiculous," said James Michael Faherty. "I've never been in a rowboat in my life. I don't trust boats."

"I've been in a boat. A pedal boat at Norumbega Park with Rita," said Hennessey. "Almost tipped it over reaching for her. It's tough to tip those boats. They're like barges. I hate to swim. Everything I ever did on a playing field was smooth. In the water, I panic." At this, Faherty began laughing and rocking the rowboat from side to side.

"Come on, Faherty," Duke said. "You don't like it any better than me. Don't be an asshole."

Faherty kept rocking, knowing he was intimidating Duke. "I said I didn't like boats. I happen to love swimming." But he gradually stopped rocking, having tested Duke and made him flinch. That was enough satisfaction.

"You really are a schmuck," Duke said.

"What's that?"

"If you have to ask," Duke said, "you've got to be a double schmuck. You have any Jewish kids in your high school?"

Faherty smirked, not so dumb. "Some of my best friends . . ."

It was a Saturday afternoon in early November long after Indian summer, with an east wind that made it difficult to feather the rowboat's oars. "You know they're watching us with binoculars," Hennessey said.

"I'll tell you," Faherty responded, "I don't want to live in the dorms with the weenies. I want to stay in the fraternity house. I'd do anything to make a tackle in high school, bite, claw, grab helmet holes. If they want me to fuck a duck to get into Alpha Pi, I'll fuck a duck. Hey, if they're watching us, dip a little with the net, see if you come up with something."

Hennessey made a big show of dragging a large fishnet behind the stern of the boat. He pretended to get excited as if he had caught a whale, struggling with the net and finally dumping its supposed contents into a bucket.

"What are we going to do, Duke?" said Faherty, concentrating on rowing them farther and farther from the Cambridge shore, out toward the middle of the river.

"What we're going to do," said Duke, "is row to the other side, over near Back Bay. Then you're going to give me enough dough to hop out, run to a drugstore, buy a couple dozen safes and some shaving cream. Then, while you row us back to the guys, I'll fill them with Palmolive and make them look used."

"You don't have to get two dozen. I got three in my wallet."

"You're going to be a great success in life, Faherty. Keep rowing."

The man who jumped off the Mass Avenue bridge almost landed in their boat. As it was, Faherty lost one of their oars, which immediately floated away.

"Jesus, Mother of God," said Faherty at the same time Hennessey was rolling over the side into the chilly, filthy water. They were almost under the bridge that connected Boston to Cambridge. The body of the man surfaced ten feet away, and Duke dog-paddled after him. Duke went into the water instinctively the way he would react to an off-tackle slant or a pitch thrown at his head. He never hesitated. He grabbed the man by his hair and began to carefully swim back to the rowboat, kicking like crazy to maintain momentum. Then the man began clawing at Duke's face, scratching, trying to tear, choking water and sputtering like an ex-husband out of control. Duke, now shocked by the chill of the water, felt himself being dragged down by the desperate fight of the man he was trying to rescue. He swallowed water himself, letting go of the hair he had clutched, trying to snatch at anything that didn't punch back. That's when Faherty bounced the remaining oar off the man's head and pulled him by the collar alongside the boat. Duke hung on also, retching over the side. People walking over the Mass Avenue bridge had seen the man climb the guardrail, hesitate for a moment, then jump feetfirst into the water thirty feet below. Dozens watched, rushing to the rail as Duke and Faherty saved a life, wading with the unconscious jumper until a Metropolitan District Police launch picked them up and sped away, towing the rowboat behind the boat with one oar and no Charles River whitefish.

They were heroes at the fraternity and around the town. Their exploits made the front pages of the *Boston Herald* and the

Boston Globe. The *Brookwood Citizen* published Hennessey's high school graduation picture with the caption "Hennessey the Hero . . . Again."

"You screwed up, pledges," Bobby Cobb said to them at the fraternity house. "You chose to ignore your assignment, which did not include collecting some poor miserable bastard out of the drink who wasn't even a fish. You have anything to say, you poor excuse for Alpha Pi aspirants? Jesus, you don't even look like you belong at the Institute. You look like a pair of Boston College bohunks."

Duke was straining very hard to keep his hands off Bobby Cobb's throat. He could feel himself shiver, remembering the water's shock and the silent retching he endured long after the police towed them to safety. The man hadn't wanted to be saved. He was a graduate student at MIT and, it turned out, brooding about the cosmos and his own sexuality. It seemed perfectly normal to him, all of a sudden when out for a walk, to leap from the bridge. While still in shock, in the police boat, he kept repeating over and over, "The line between life and death is very thin." Duke took several deep breaths to calm himself. He shut out Cobb's words. They rolled around him, meaning nothing as he turned away and left the fraternity house. Cobb was yelling after him, "Hero, Hero."

The hero sat on a derelict couch in a dormitory at Tufts. Cigarette smoke hung in the room like an experiment. The dormitory, Fletcher Hall, a nondescript red-brick building typical of those built in the 1950s in New England, stood across the street from Professors' Row. But no professors were admitted to the room the students called "Club 45," where black curtains hung from the windows and empty beer cans were stretched up to the ceiling, row upon row, as both decoration and tribute to the capacity of the residents. Red Singer didn't live there, but he was the host; it was his party. Approximately twenty-five young men were scattered around the common room of 45 Fletcher Hall, a two-bedroom suite with its connected common room, now draped in black. Various scruffy sofas and chairs were scattered about, acquired from thrift shops or inherited from graduating students. Duke had come to Red's party the week after his heroics, bringing Faherty along for support. It was a Wednesday night. They had borrowed a senior's car on the promise that they would gas it up and, the next weekend, wash it. Duke instinctively knew so much, not only about what base to throw to, what defensive signals to call, but about what made people do what they did. He was born with an instinctive ability to cut through the crap. This was overlaying the innocence of a Catholic boy from Brookwood who had never broken training in his life when a sport of his was in season. Red Singer, he reasoned, was the only person who could rid him of the taste of Bobby Cobb, of the taste of MIT. These were the days when you didn't transfer colleges with impunity; you did not take a year off because you were unhappy. You made the best of it. If you flunked out you automatically went in the service because it would "make a man out of you." Red welcomed Duke and Faherty with noogies to their arms. Then he quickly stepped aside to stop three boys before they could step through the doorway. "You guys," he said. "Five bucks apiece. No one gets the time of their lives for less than five bucks." They were freshmen at Tufts in chinos and white bucks, barely shaving, nudging each other nervously and fumbling to produce the five-dollar entrance fee. "What do we get for the fin?" one of them questioned, trying to justify the payment.

"What do you get for the five dollars?" Red beamed, best friend to novices, charming. "You get a whiff of Paradise. You get beautiful women fucking, sucking and carrying on. You get your wildest dreams on a six-foot screen. You get good fellowship and all the Red Cardinal beer you can possibly drink. It sounds so good you better get in there before I raise it to ten bucks. It looks crowded. I don't know if I can really squeeze you guys in. We have fire laws." That did it. The freshmen were straining against their chinos by now and, relieved of their money, they rushed into Club 45, thrilled by the blackout curtains, the smell of sweat and Red Cardinal beer. Red winked at Hennessey and Faherty. "I charge on a sliding scale," he said. "Three bucks for guys I know; five bucks for suckers. Guys I've known since third grade get in free." He nodded at Faherty. "You can slip in your bodyguard for the same freight as you."

"You're a true white man, Red," said Duke. "What's the beer cost you, ten cents a can?"

"That's why you go to MIT. The numbers. Right on the button. You want to move in the door now, you're holding up progress."

There was a line in back of them, going down the stairwell. Red's Club 45 was clearly not operating with the blessings of the Tufts faculty. Inside you could name your poison. Red had cigars, cigarettes, grainy pornographic movies playing on a bed sheet hung against a wall. He had beer but no hard stuff and a continuous poker game going in one of the bedrooms, quarter limit, three bumps, high-low, down-and-dirty college poker. Duke and Faherty dominated the couch with their presence, watched the films and got drunk. Duke had never seen anything like it in his life, and he felt that he had never been so excited, wishing he were watching the films all by himself. But he was far from alone. All around him guys were cheering on the scenes, laughing uproariously, shaking sprays of beer onto the sheet screen. One Tufts student took his pants off and began rubbing his penis against the sheet until pushed away by friends whose view he blocked. Beyond caring, he continued to play with himself. Several fights broke out about nothing, an imagined insult, a close-quarters shove. They were quickly calmed down, too many people in too small a space, the thrill of brief rebellions against authority. Jazz played on a phonograph, Charlie Parker, The Bird. It was a screaming saxophone night. Above it all, Red hovered, making sure peace was preserved, that the projector rolled, that the beer didn't run out, that the card players had sandwiches. All for a price. "You don't seem too social for a sociable guy," he said to Duke. Red leaned over the back of the couch, tapping Duke on the shoulder, making the big guy jump with surprise. On the screen two naked women were taking turns fondling and sucking the seemingly gigantic organ of an ugly fat man. The images were fuzzy. "Is this what the doctor ordered, Francis?" he added.

"You know something, Red," said Duke, unable to turn from the images, "you are an evil fuck." Duke had finished more beers than he had ever had in his life, draining them, crushing the cans in one hand and tossing them at various bodies in the room. No one would mess with a drunk Duke Hennessey.

"I just know what people want, Francis," Red said. "Even you."

Duke spun around, the first time his eyes had left the screen since he had come to the party. "I'll tell you what I want now," he said, and climbed over the back of the couch.

Later, back at the fraternity house, Faherty was whispering urgently to Duke. It was after two-thirty. All the brothers were asleep, it not being exam time, no need for No Doz and all-nighters. "Don't do it," Faherty hissed. "You want to give up everything?" Duke pushed him aside and, taking off his shoes, tiptoed up the stairs to the bedrooms. While Bobby Cobb dreamed of sailboats on the Charles, Duke Hennessey covered every one of Cobb's pipes, from his umber rough-hewn briar to his General MacArthur corncob, with rubbers collected from Red's party guests. Some of the condoms were in less than pristine condition. Duke did his job silently and left a note pinned to the extra blanket on Cobb's bed. "You asked for it," the note said. "The new Institute record for Charles River whitefish. Put that in your pipe and smoke it."

CHAPTER EIGHT

O

Coming-out Party,
Spring Freshman Year, 1956

"I'm sorry, Red. I couldn't get you on the list," Temple said.
"What about Hennessey? You take Micks on fancy lists?"
"He goes to MIT. *It's* acceptable even if *he* isn't."
"If I even had a hint that you weren't kidding," Red answered.
"Tufts isn't Harvard, but it ain't borscht either. Ooomph," he
grunted as he teed off on The Golf Club's seventeenth hole, a par-
four, dogleg-left, tough four-hundred-forty-yarder. "How do you
like them apples?" Red smiled as his drive cut the corner and moved
left, coming to rest on the right side of the fairway almost two
hundred forty yards from the tee.

"How the fuck does such a little guy hit it so far?" asked Hennessey.

"It's timing and rhythm, fat man," Red said, "like everything else
in life."

"Then how come you're flunking out of Tufts if you're so
smart?"

Red waited until Duke hit his drive, through the fairway into the
rough along the right side of the bend. No one ever, no matter how
furious or offended, ever spoke at the top of someone else's backswing. "Who said I'm flunking out?"

"I took Intuition 13 this year," Duke answered. "Plus I knew
you when you were little and cute, before you got ugly. And I'd
know you'd rather go hustle for bucks than study."

"Bullshit, Duke. I got a C-minus average."

"That's just a little better than me," said Temple, who had

crunched his drive, surprising everyone by the fact that it was in the fairway.

"So if I get better marks than you and I'm a much better golfer, how come I don't get on the list?"

"Because life is not fair, Red," said Dickie, whose drive was his usual slice into the rough.

"But we have a plan," said Temple as they moved off the tee down the fairway, carrying their own clubs.

"This is the party of the decade, Red," said Dickie, "and you're going to be allowed to crash."

"You think I'd go anywhere that I wasn't invited?" said Red. His friends laughed at that one, all the way to their shots.

Sarah "Sally" White's family had planned her coming-out party since she was a little girl. Her father, Penrose White, was one of the largest gasoline distributors in New England and one of the area's most serious duck hunters. In retaliation for his many shooting expeditions during the year, his wife, Barbara (Beezee to her friends), promised herself that Sally's debut would be the most extravagant Boston had seen since the days of the 1930s, when people who had it really knew how to spend money.

Sally White was never a beauty, but she was, as all the boys said, "a hot ticket." She was the first of her friends to smoke, the first to sip a rum and tonic, the first to dance barefoot in her crowd, the first to wear a bra and the first to go without one on a date. She had a face like an adorable puppy dog whose breed you couldn't quite identify. Sally White was the only person in Concord, Massachusetts, who had a swimming pool. Oh, maybe half a dozen other families had pools. But Sally was the only person with a pool who counted, meaning someone who didn't own an insurance agency or a Buick dealership or a contracting firm specializing in Quincy quarry granite. Sally and her mother and Sally's three best friends lay on chaise longues, flat out on their backs with cotton batting on their eyelids at noon the day of the coming-out party. The women lay unmoving, greased from guzzle to zatch in baby oil and iodine. The day was an all-timer for late June, unseasonably hot. Hazy sunshine. Sally thought it was all for her and that everyone in America was coming to her party. "Do you think I'm a spoiled bitch, Mummy?" said Sally without moving. "Vicki always calls me a spoiled bitch." Vicki Wilde rolled over onto her stomach. She reached out to undo the top straps of her two-piece suit.

"I wouldn't call you a spoiled bitch," Beezee said. "Just because you're an only child, have four closets to yourself, your own convertible, a maid and a cook doesn't mean you're spoiled. Also thirty-two pair of Bermudas."

"But I don't have boobs like you, Vicki, so money doesn't buy everything," Sally said.

"Take it from experience, girls," said Beezee White, sitting up to take a long sip from a gin and tonic. "Being spoiled is an art. If you're spoiled as a girl, you can have an adult life ruined by marrying someone who makes you do things. What can be more ruinous than that? Don't be jealous of Sally. It's what happens after tonight that counts. Everything up to now is cotton candy."

"Plus I can never have boobs like Vicki's," Sally said. "Right, Mummy?" Sally stood up. "I creak, for Christ's sake," she said, stretching out. "I'm only eighteen and I creak." She flipped off her halter top and pushed her bosoms up with her hands, pushing them at her mother and her friends. Sally had short dark hair that bounced, and she said whatever she felt like saying.

"For God's sake, Sal," her mother announced to her. "Go take a swim." Mrs. White spoke as if she were announcing things through a megaphone. Sally jumped into the pool. Her mother and her friends passed around the baby oil with iodine and made sure they even rubbed it between their toes. "It's going to be a wonderful party," Beezee White announced in her stereophonic voice.

There were dinners all over Concord that night before the party. For all the young people the idea was to pile on enough booze in a controlled atmosphere before really tying it on at the dance. Parents of the youngsters saw no reason to think that any of this was not right and proper. Freddie Temple and his roommates were invited to dinner at the house of Freddie's current girlfriend, Janey Vaughn, who lived in Concord and was Sally's fourth best friend in the world.

Dickie had gotten his first car for his birthday in May. It was a navy blue Oldsmobile convertible, his reward for getting all A's and B's first semester, an agreed-upon condition for the gift. He had finally worn his father down, pleading almost daily for a car from the arrival of his sixteenth birthday. His mother and all of his grandparents got on the bandwagon when college came and, after a banner first-half fiscal year in the maternity sportswear business, David Rosenberg threw in the sponge. "Cars and college don't build character," he muttered. But he knew when he was licked.

For Dickie, coming-out parties were like masquerades, and he was convinced he was the only one who realized it. He was supposed to drive out to Concord with Duke Hennessey, but Duke called at the last minute. "I can't go, Rosie," he said. "I think we can give up the myth of me being independent."

"What are you talking about?"

"Look," Duke said. "You guys take Rita for granted. I take Rita for granted. I do what I want, and she's always waiting. Well, shit. I go with her. And I have to see her tonight since she just got out of finals. Besides I fucking go with her. I should be with her on Saturday night."

"You're only young once, Duke."

"Yeah, and I figure I only need one girl at a time. Why would I want anyone else when I got Rita?"

That's the kind of question no true friend can ever really answer.

Dickie basked in the reflected glow of Freddie Temple, biding his own time. His mother spoke constantly to him about "being corrupted by Harvard, corrupted by the Gentiles." But Dickie saw these Gentiles, the WASPs, as being the green light at the end of his dock. He identified with Gatsby, although he had never read the novel that spring. He didn't really want to be a WASP. But he wanted to be seen with them, to be with them. *Their* parents didn't call them daily with admonitions about every subject under the sun. "Hello, stranger," Dickie's mother would say if he had missed calling her for more than two days in a row.

Dr. and Mrs. Vaughn greeted their guests at the door. They lived in a rambling white comfortable Colonial house with a long driveway near the Concord Green. "Dick Rosenberg," Dr. Vaughn said. "Mmm. Not Ron Rosenberg's son, the cardiologist?"

"He thinks all Jews are doctors," Dickie thought. "We're off to a great start."

"No, sir," Dickie said. "My father's in the clothing business."

"Well, that's nice," Dr. Vaughn said and looked beyond Dickie toward the next group of arriving people. Dickie was about to be twenty. He needed a drink. He had rented a tuxedo even though Freddie Temple had told him, "Buy a dinner jacket. You're going to be on a lot of party lists; you may as well get used to it." Dickie's father wore a tuxedo once a year, on New Year's Eve at their country-club dance. David Rosenberg had owned his tuxedo since the 1930s, when everyone dressed to go out for an evening in Boston.

The Vaughns' house was long on chintz, overstuffed furniture and order. "Rosie," Janey Vaughn greeted him with a smacking kiss on the cheek. She was standing in front of a long trestle table covered with white cloth that served as a bar. Temple stood next to her, in a crowd of friends. "Screwdriver, screwdriver," Rosenberg said to everyone instead of hello. Their other freshman roommate, Timmy Buck, never quite understood Dickie's lingo. But Temple's laughter reassured him that it was clever, so, unwittingly, Buck became Dickie's loudest cheerleader. "Down to basics, Rosie," he whooped and signaled the bartender. "A large screwdriver for my thirsty friend." Dinner was a mixed bag of parents, parents' friends and young people who all seemed to have known each other and each other's relatives from birth. Dickie was the only one there who worried about which fork to use for salad, which words to choose in conversation. But by the end of his freshman year he no longer spoke like a wonk from South Brookwood. And the liquor always helped. Dinner was served buffet style after almost an hour and a half of cocktails, with peanuts and rat cheese on Ritz crackers available to anyone who wanted to cut off a slab from a plate on the dining-room sideboard. The boys and girls sat in the music room, a room full of books, a Baldwin baby grand and several music stands used when the Vaughns would invite neighbors in for trios. There was a pecking order in the room, three or four of Janey's girlfriends who dated prep school boys sat in one corner with their young men from the Middlesex School or Belmont Hill. These girls did their damndest not to sneak glances over at their classmates dating Harvard boys, who all crowded the other side of the room, on the couch, on the floor, around Janey and Freddie Temple. Dickie had had two screwdrivers and his tongue was loose while his eyes stared at a girl across the room, her head tilted back in laughter.

"Who's that?" he asked Janey, whose mouth was stuffed full of her mother's beef bourguignonne.

"Oh," Janey said, spitting little bits of food and laughing about it, "that's Julia Hepburn. She thinks she's French."

"I take French with her," a girl sitting on the floor next to Dickie said, sitting with her mass of debutante white bouffant dress spread around her. "She may think she's French, but she got a C-minus in the course." Dickie was going with no one. But he needed some permanence to cope with the distressing realization that South Brookwood was probably not the center of the universe. Permanence for Dickie was not deciding what was to be his major. Permanence was having a girlfriend. For the rest of dinner, he saw people he knew dropping cigarettes onto Oriental rugs, accidentally spilling plates full of food onto the floor, laughing, drinking. The adults in the next room were doing the same, the men periodically coming into the music room to beam over their daughters and ogle their daughters' friends. If Dickie Rosenberg had an ideal at that time it had to be Julia Hepburn. Julia had long blond hair, a pageboy cut. Her mouth was considered large, full lips and a lot of white, white teeth. She laughed loudly, a bawdy laugh Dickie noticed, and he wanted to be the one to amuse her. She seemed, he thought, to laugh, look over at him, then quickly glance away. She was tall, almost five-foot-eight, with a figure no one could guess at because of the size of the dresses everyone wore. Dickie grabbed a cocktail napkin and a green Concord Country Club pencil sitting on an end table. He scribbled a note on a napkin. "Could you please deliver this to that girl over there?" he asked one of the older women serving the party. Dickie folded the napkin and pulled open a hard roll that had been on his plate. He closed the roll around the note and handed it to the waitress. The woman delivered the roll, and he could see the blond girl looking at him across the room, as the waitress pointed. He saw her asking people for something to write with, and a boy produced a pen. She bent over the napkin, shielding it from the gaze of others. Then she pushed it back into the roll, stretched back her arm and tossed it across the room. Dickie tried to catch it one-handed and dropped it in his plate, a bad beginning, the napkin note in the gravy of the beef stew. Dickie's note said, "If you don't dance the first dance with me I'll swallow this napkin and choke. Signed the Mysterious Stranger." Julia Hepburn's response, in blue ballpoint ink, said, "So choke, not-so-mysterious stranger."

The first song at Sally White's coming-out party was "The Lady Is a Tramp." Dickie and Julia Hepburn whirled around the floor, elbows pumping like mad in the prescribed manner of debutante dances.

Julia was amazed. "You really know how to dance," she said.

"Arthur Murray taught me dancing in a hurry," Dickie crooned.

"You're not serious."

"If she could have seen dancing classes in Red Singer's basement in the seventh grade," Dickie thought. "Twenty little boys and girls on good behavior with a dancing teacher hired by all the parents because it was part of what polite little Americans should learn."

"It's just natural instincts," Dickie said. The dance was held underneath a vast green-and-white-striped tent erected for the evening. Guests entered through the Whites' house, a massive brick Federal that rambled through several wings, guest quarters, servants' quarters, a house full of English antiques, family portraits, hunting prints and one Corot landscape lit by candles for big parties. Penrose White looked like a duke stuffed into his formal vest embroidered with ducks, framed by his black dinner jacket with wide-peak lapels made for him by Huntsman of Savile Row. He greeted, slapped people on backs, kissed and hugged women and girls and took all compliments on his daughter Sally's debut into society with a grace that he thought reflected a heating-oil mogul with an estate in Concord, Massachusetts.

"Young man" is how he greeted all the boys who came through the receiving line. He paid attention to their handshakes, liking the firm dry hands, dismissing the moist weak palms, thinking about proper matches for his feisty daughter. He watched Sally across the room, surrounded by young people making a fuss over her. He could hear her laughter, raucous like his own, an earthy duck hunter's laugh. "Which of these little bastards are going to penetrate Sally?" he felt himself thinking. "Jesus, she would have been a fine boy."

Freddie Temple wasn't thinking about anything in particular. He was knocking back the vodka and tonics, giving a great imitation of his father. His cheeks were starting to perspire, and his blood was up, ready to dance, ready for the coming-out party circuit that would last most of the month of June. Freddie Temple tried not to think about "down the road." Today was plenty for him, and no one in his life had ever made today anything but pleasurable. "You think all you have to do is stand around looking gorgeous?" Sally White said to him. "Real people think gorgeous is probably dumb."

"Freddie isn't dumb," Janey Vaughn said, grabbing Freddie's hand. "He goes to Harvard."

"Jesus Christ, girl," said Sally, grabbing Freddie's other hand and pulling him toward the music. "It's bunny-hop time. The less we talk the better."

"The more we talk, the better," said Dickie to Julia Hepburn. "We can get at the 'essence de' that way."

"The 'essence de'?" Julia repeated, still pumping her elbows as they swirled around the floor. "I like that. I biked around France last summer but nobody ever said 'essence de' to me."

"That's because you never got off your bike and into the cafés," Dickie said. He wanted to make an impact with everything he said. He couldn't take a chance on losing her by saying anything she could think stupid or boring. He would fake it as much as he had to. "Be cool," he told himself. "Be interesting." She allowed herself to relax into his chest, just a hint of her body, and they danced on. Around them the floor was crowded, people jammed against one another, calling to each other over familiar backs in low-cut gowns and dinner jackets, white and black: "Hiya, Bobby. How were exams, Minot? Golf sometime, Sam? Love your hair, Pussy. Isn't it all a gas?" Boys cut in on Dickie, whirling Julia away, and she didn't seek him out over the new shoulders she grasped. The crowd sucked her away, and he joined his friends at the bar on the edge of the dance floor. The band had turned to the jitterbug with the guests in the high mood of eleven o'clock when the early gin and tonics or martinis had been tamped down by wine and beer or Scotch and sodas.

"What do you know about Julia Hepburn?" Dickie asked Temple.

"What can I know about her, she's a teen queen," said Freddie, blowing a perfect smoke ring from his Camel.

"She's beautiful," said Dickie. "And she acts mysterious."

"Die for love," said Temple. "I've known you since the third grade and what you really think is mysterious turns out to be long blond hair." Dickie laughed and asked the bartender for a beer, which was poured for him down the side of a tall glass. "I can't call her Julia, though. How the hell can you call someone in nineteen fifty-six Julia? It's as if she's right out of *Little Women*. She should be Katharine Hepburn, not Julia. I'll call her Kate."

"Jesus, talk about melodrama," said Temple. "This is a coming-out party not a soc rel class."

Sally White danced by them in her usual frenzied style, dancing double quick time to anything that was played, even slow numbers. One boy actually danced with her, but two others clung to her waist, spinning and pumping their elbows up and down. "Are my boobs on straight?" she yelled at Temple and his crowd at the bar. Sally White was adored by everyone, male and female, the young and the old, who secretly loved that Sally gave their lives a goose.

Dickie kept cutting in on Julia Hepburn. He would get two minutes with her and be tapped in turn on his shoulder. "I'm going to call you Kate," he told her, doing one of his brief flings in her arms.

"No, you're not," she said. "That's what my father calls me."

"He must be a really clever guy."

"He's a drunk." Dickie's dream girl answered just as another young man tapped Dickie's shoulder and moved her away almost in the same instant. All during his freshman year at Harvard, Dickie had developed the burning desire not to be a WASP, but to be *one* with them, to share their ease, their assumption that power in the world was theirs by natural order. This meant sharing their women. Their women seemed far better than the cheerleaders at Brookwood High or the cellar girls or the class treasurer or heads of the prom committee with Vassar and Smith on their minds. Julia Hepburn was what he wanted. How could he be so stupid as to call her an obvious nickname and think it could be original. He had another beer and looked for her on the dance floor. Temple told him at one point, "You want to fuck your way into the Social Register, Rosie."

It was almost eleven-thirty, and the band was as frenzied as the dancers. They whipped the guests, and the guests whipped them. Most of the young men had abandoned their dinner jackets as they flounced about, sweating in shirt sleeves and madras cummerbunds.

After a long South American set, ending with a frantic samba, the band, dying for a break, slumped in their seats as the drummer rolled a long drum roll, quieting the crowd. Penrose White, looking as florid as if he had fallen into a vat of port, lurched to the microphone in front of the band. "Coming out," he said into the mike. But because he was unfamiliar with speaking into amplification, the sound boomed out of the speakers as if it were the sound system at a prison riot. "For God's sake, Penrose," Beezee White yelled at him from the edge of the crowd. Everyone laughed.

"This is why I hunt ducks," Penrose White said, more softly. "They don't shoot back. And you can eat them."

"He can't eat his wife?" The stage whisper right in back of Dickie Rosenberg was directed right at him. Dickie spun around and saw Red Singer grinning stupidly, the way people grin who are ossified. Singer was wearing a white dinner jacket with notched lapels that was at least several sizes too small. He wore this over black chino pants with a clip-on waiter's black bow tie and a red elastic cinch belt that belonged to his mother around his waist. The front of his white jacket was filthy. "Jesus, Red," Dickie said. "Where the hell did you come from?"

"You told me to crash the party of the year, so I crashed," he said. "But I had to crawl through the fucking garden. There are cops outside." He was wearing a sombrero.

"You look like you live in a doorway in Scollay Square," Dickie said.

"Oh," Red responded, "big fucking deal. You walk in the door, super-Hebe from Harvard. You tell me come to the great party, it's black tie. A year ago you didn't know a fucking black tie from a hole in the ground."

Meanwhile, Penrose White was warming to his toast. "Coming out is what we want for all of our daughters, a chance for friends to kick up their heels, a chance for new relationships to form. For the old fogies like us and the young bucks and does to gather in celebration of a girl becoming a woman. Sally," Pen went on, emotional now, in his cups, "welcome to the world of an adult. I couldn't love you more if you were a son." He held out his arms for his daughter, and she came flying into them. They both cried in each other's embrace as the band played "Happy Days Are Here Again" and the crowd whistled, stomped and cheered.

"I'm surprised he didn't name her after a duck," Red whispered. "But she's my girl, Rosie. Just you watch. She's mine."

"What are you going to do?" Dickie asked.

"Don't worry," Red said. "I won't queer your act."

"What the hell are you talking about?"

"You know what I'm talking about," Red said quietly. Then he yelled out, "I was at your bar mitzvah, remember?" Dickie blushed and pulled the sombrero over Red's face. He was gone from Brookwood High forever. Convincing Red to crash the party was a huge mistake. "No one here ever heard the words 'bar mitzvah,' you asshole," Dickie whispered. "They'd think it was Arabic or something."

Red pulled back the sombrero and looked at Dickie with true dislike. "*You're* the asshole if you think you're fooling anyone," he said. "What the hell kind of a name do you think Rosenberg is, English royalty?"

"Smarten up, Stanley" was all Dickie could think of to say. He walked away, hoping to distance himself as much from high school as he hoped to distance himself from Red Singer.

Red was the first man in the history of Boston coming-out parties to dance the hora by himself. After the toast of Penrose White, Red, doing a cakewalk that featured kicking his legs in front of himself like a drum major, moved up to the bandleader and said, " 'Hava Nagela.' " Red loved the hora. It was always a chance for him to show off. The bandleader was Jewish, as were many of the society bandleaders of Boston. Most of them worshipped the WASP and tried to give their own children names they had lifted from their patrons. There were sons of Boston bandleaders named Brattle Gold, daughters named Tenley Rosen. The bandleader at Sally White's party, however, worshipped no God but Benny Goodman and secretly despised being a well-paid servant (in his eyes) of the ruling class. Besides, on his breaks he had had several rye and gingers. The band broke into the unmistakable strains of "Hava Nagela," and since no one in the crowd had a clue how to dance to this foreign tune, Red jumped into the breach. Still wearing the sombrero, he dipped and kicked to the music, his face wreathed in what his old friends would call a shit-eating grin. Guests who talked all through their host's speech stopped to watch Red's demonstration and, thinking it was planned, applauded once again when Sally

White joined Red, kicking and dipping, holding hands and going in a circle, while the bandleader grinned his own grin and whipped his boys into a froth worthy of any wedding of Goldbergs and Cohens.

"Wild one," Sally said. "Who invited you?"

"Do you know the Vanderbilts?"

"Did they do push-ups in the garden also?"

Red spun her around. "I'm an old friend of Freddie Temple's," he said.

"That's too bad. I was beginning to be interested."

"What's the matter with Freddie?"

"No one that good-looking can think about anything but what he looks like. When you're ugly, life holds many possibilities because you're forced to push it."

"*Stop*," Red yelled. Then to the bandleader, "Romantic songs." He scaled his sombrero over the heads of the crowd like a Frisbee and pulled Sally White close to him. "Would you have invited me to this party if you had known me before tonight?"

"What's your name?" Sally asked.

"Stan Singer," Red said.

Sally pulled away and looked at him. "Nobody's named that."

"Where I grew up we'd say that's my name, I swear to God."

"May I have the honor, chicken," said Penrose White to his daughter.

"Daddy," she said, "this is Stan Singer."

The heating-oil baron of Concord, Massachusetts, looked quickly up and down Red's borrowed, rumpled formal wear. Barely nodding, as drunk as Red, he muttered, "Cheap entertainment" and waltzed off with his daughter.

Jitterbugs and the dirty boogie followed romantic songs, which were followed by fat Phoebe Ranson, a cousin of Mrs. White's who had studied opera and always insisted on singing two songs from *The Student Prince* wherever she was invited. She was followed by three boys from Harvard's Krokodiloes singing group, who harmonized "Aura Lee," then lurched off to the bar. At quarter to one, no guests had left. Penrose White had scrawled a check to the bandleader to ensure another half hour of music. Several of his friends were upstairs in bedrooms with people other than their mates, while younger guests were tiptoeing in and out of the same bedrooms looking for places to be sick or to lie down. A few young men had discovered Mr. White's wine supply and were passing bottles of Burgundy out of cellar windows, storing them beside the house for the time they would leave the party. They were too drunk to consider it stealing. They went to Harvard or Yale or Dartmouth. They were entitled to the good life, even if it consisted of Penrose White's vintage wines.

"When am I going to see you again?" Dickie asked Julia Hepburn.

"I'm teaching sailing in Maine."

"I'm teaching golf in Maine. At a boys' camp," Dickie said.

"Shall I let you play through?"

"That would imply that I'm ahead of you."

Three belligerent prep school boys who brought Julia to the party surrounded her then, glaring at Dickie. She linked arms with them and started to lead them away.

"Only chronologically ahead of me." She smiled back at him. "Call me if you're clever." The boys' looks intimidated Dickie, but they allowed themselves to be dragged away.

Red Singer teetered in the doorway.

"When you come again," Sally White said, "my father has some hundred-year-old rum in the cellar."

"How about a twenty-year-old girl in the bedroom?" Red said.

"I don't screw," Sally White, the debutante, giggled at him. "People come see me for my personality and for Daddy's hundred-year-old rum."

"There's always a first time."

On the long gravel driveway leading to the Whites' house, Freddie Temple stood tall, kissing his date. Cars drove by them, flicking high beams, blowing horns. Freddie was oblivious; kissing was everything. Dickie and Red walked toward them. "You've become a real Harvard asshole," Red said. "I know what I want all the time. I'm out to get laid, period. You don't have a clue what you want or even who you are."

"Go fuck yourself, Stanley. Your problem is that you're a simple shit."

"Let's match up in ten years," Red said. "I'm going by all you guys like a shot."

"The only shooting you're going to do, Stanley, is in your pants."
They stood around in the driveway watching Freddie, who did not seem to be coming up for air.

Hennessey had pushed, pushed, pushed since he had started dating Rita Cronin, but he never really believed that the first time would be in the backseat of her father's car. They were parked overlooking the Brookwood Reservoir, where they had gone dozens of times in high school to watch the submarine races.

"You wish you were at the party with the guys," she pouted.

"Jesus, Reet," Duke said. "Would I be sitting in the backseat with you on a Saturday night if I didn't want to? I chose to be with you. You're my girl. Where else would I be?"

"You haven't changed in what you think? With all those brilliant people at your school? They have brilliant girls there, right?"

"Right. With humps on their backs and beards."

Rita laughed and relaxed back into Duke's arms, comfortable in the routine they had observed for the last four years, in one car or another. They even parked in the same place, near a lonely stand of trees where most romantic couples feared to stay. Duke Hennessey feared nothing. Rita reached down to unzip Duke's fly as he explored underneath her skirt, excited that spring was here because it was an end to girdles and stockings for at least three months. Rita Cronin was adorable, still had freckles on her nose, loved jokes but took life seriously. She had overcome her guilt for the umpteen hundredth time and was ready for their mutual masturbation, which would finish with Duke ejaculating into a Kleenex she always provided from her purse. But it felt so good that night that she allowed Duke to pull her onto his lap and let him rub his penis around her inner lips until she could almost sense him inside of her. Duke was thinking, "Ten thousand hand jobs is enough rehearsal. I'm a goddamn engineer now. An engineer doesn't need another hand job." And he was saying, "Just a little, just a little, honey. It won't stay in. One more push; it's not really in." Then Rita was helping, and it was there, in, the one feeling even an MIT student cannot quantify. "Geniuses and fucking morons can all tell when they're in," he thought. "Freud put it in and Adolf Hitler and Newton and Copernicus and the president of MIT and what's the big deal that I want to put it into Rita Cronin?" So Duke did, and they were happy afterward, until they both began to worry. Rita snuggled against his big chest, and they told each other how much they were in love. Duke rolled down the windows in the backseat of Rita's father's car so he could clear the steam from their breath on the glass and look at the sky to see if the stars were out on the first night in their lives that they ever got laid. Cars of high school kids raced by in back of them, late-night dragsters, leaving rubber, oblivious to love.

○

College, Senior Year, 1959

"**C**ome in, boys, come in," greeted Harry Singer, slapping Dickie and Duke Hennessey on their shoulders. "Happy New Year." Harry was always selling merchandise on the road, even when he was in his own living room. "What can I get you guys, you're finally legal, right? We got everything, Canadian, Scotch, we got gin."

"Gin and tonic if that's okay, Mr. Singer," Rosenberg said.

"If you have a beer, fine," said Duke. "Otherwise a Coke would be great."

"We got everything," Harry Singer gushed. "Come on. Stan is downstairs in the playroom. Excuse Mrs. Singer. We're going to a friend's house; she's getting dressed." His voice dropped to a whisper. "Stan is a little nervous about the army. He's got a head start on us. Since five o'clock. I wish you boys might say something. Calm him down."

They went to the basement playroom, Harry Singer first, then Duke and Dickie, who were nudging each other, remembering the time they were there with the girls in high school. It seemed to them a million years ago.

Red sat on a bar stool in the playroom, a white metal Civil Defense helmet on his head, left over from World War II when his father wore the helmet patrolling the neighborhood streets during blackouts, air raid drills, doing his bit for his country.

"Every night is New Year's Eve," Red shouted to them. He was drunk as a skunk. "You think I look like Audie Murphy? You think I look like a hero?"

"You look like you'll get a psychiatric discharge," Duke said. Red laughed as if he were out of control and jumped off his stool to greet them, pumping their hands and slapping their backs. "Where's Freddie?" he asked.

"Now calm down, Stan," his father said, looking shriveled, not the old salesman up for everything. He looked old, with more doubts than optimism. Harry Singer was gray, and his only son had been kicked out of college.

"Happy New Year," Freddie Temple said as he came down the stairway wearing black tie. "I dressed up for you, Red. Believe it?"

Red pounded his shoulders, too. "The *sheygets* with the heart of gold," Red shouted. "The most honest of any of us."

Freddie asked for bourbon. Harry Singer, on his hands and knees behind the bar, could find no bourbon. "Who drinks bourbon?" he said to himself, knowing he would locate none. He pulled out dusty bottles of Cherry Heering, rock 'and rye, presents from customers and bosses going back twenty years. "Will you take Scotch?" Harry asked. "Who drinks bourbon but plantation owners?" Freddie drank Scotch. His parents never warned him about mixing different drinks. It never slowed them down, why should it slow their son? When they all had their drinks, Harry Singer proposed a toast. "A new year, boys," he said. "And a toast to friends. They and family are the most important thing in the world. To friends."

"To friends," they all echoed, clinked glasses and drank.

"I'm leaving you boys," Harry Singer said. "Got to get dressed up. Soup and fish. Happy New Year. Give some good advice to Stan the Man, guys, okay?" He playfully punched his son in the arm and retreated up the stairs.

"Okay, you stupid bastard," Duke said. "What happened?"

"I guess I fucked up," Red answered.

"We've heard all sorts of rumors," Dickie said. "You were pimping and taking money from all the fraternities. Deans were involved. We heard you had all the schools in Boston organized."

Red grinned under his Civil Defense helmet. "It was just me. And two douche bags from Chauncy Junior College who were about to take on one entry in one dormitory. Maybe six guys, for Christ's sake. And they wanted to do it for ten bucks apiece. They were drunk. I was drunk. Two guys had already gone when the dorm master came in. For fifteen bucks, my share, I get kicked out of school. Christmas is no excuse either when you're Jewish. So my choice is the marines or the army. No six-month program in the navy. You'd have to go for three years and fuck that, just to be a sailor-boy. I barely went to college for three years."

"My parents would disown me," Dickie said.

"Yeah," Red nodded. "Well, my parents think I was working so hard on jobs that I didn't have enough time for the books. They're pissed at the school."

Duke lifted his beer and toasted again. "Brass balls, Stanley."

Freddie, practical Freddie. "You going back to school after the army?"

"I've got a bad taste about school. They've got a bad taste about me. Who needs it? Did John D. Rockefeller bother with school? Did Henry Ford? I'm not gonna be a doctor or lawyer. Who needs it?"

"Brass balls," Duke repeated.

"Anyway," Red got serious, "I'm not going to see you guys until you're all out of school. I really appreciate your coming over. But it's important that you know how I feel about us." Duke rolled his eyes. "No really." He took off his helmet, and his red hair in the dimly lit playroom made him look like some grown-up, flesh-and-blood Howdy Doody. He held out the helmet to the others. Money sat in its midst, cash in a neat pile. "It's two hundred dollars." Red grinned. "Money earned the hard way if you know what I mean. Now I say that we all need each other, that all our lives we'll remember Brookwood. But more than that: everything we do we'll be measuring Is this better than Hennessey and Rosenberg and Temple? Am I richer, more successful? Is my wife better looking? This is two hundred bucks. I want all of you to match it. Ten years from now we'll play golf and the guy who's most successful in life takes the pot. What's childhood if you can't push your friend's face into the mud in the playground?" Temple had fifty bucks, Hennessey ten and Rosenberg the same. They signed IOU's for the rest, put their signatures on an agreement that Red had written and tossed it all into the helmet. They finished their drinks. There was no fireplace. Red threw his glass against a wall where the concrete was exposed. The others did the same. Then they went upstairs and out into New Year's Eve and Red hit Temple on the back of his neck with a snowball. They all fired snowballs at each other. Duke used his old trick from grammar school, stockpiling his ammunition, then heaving a snowball high into the air and, as his intended victim watched its high arc, whipping two or three in a straight line, hard and fast. They fell for it in grammar school, looked for it on New Year's Eve and avoided Duke's bullets. But they pummeled each other for fifteen minutes or so until Red ripped his shirt and Freddie slipped and fell into a snowbank and they all piled on, rubbing each other's faces in the snow, laughing hysterically, little boys on New Year's Eve. Then they said good-bye to each other. They all had separate parties, different destinations that night, and it had been understood they would just have a drink for old time's sake, for auld lang syne.

Freddie drove his own blue Chevy to a party at The Golf Club, two miles away. He played rock and roll on his radio and pounded the dashboard as he drove the snowy streets. He played the icy patches in the road, having fun, skidding into turns and easing out of them, thinking about his date and little else but fun with automobiles, his life on automatic.

Duke Hennessey drove an old Morris Minor he had bought from a graduating senior in June for $175. Half his fraternity house could fix any automobile ever made, and several brothers helped him put the car in shape to make it limp through life with Duke. It coughed and sputtered in the cold, and he coaxed it on across Brookwood to meet Rita Cronin, their eighth New Year's Eve together. He needed the stability of Rita, his base. He didn't want to have to think about women, love or sex. He wanted those parts of his life to be like a list he had checked off: college, check. Love life, check. Duke had check-listed his way through MIT: required courses, fraternity, sports, locked them in early so he could get on to the future. Duke realized that he had not been given talents to spend his life working for the Edison Company like his old man. He had been given talents to *own* the Edison Company, and he didn't want things like complicated relationships to sidetrack his dreams.

Dickie still had his navy blue Oldsmobile convertible that his father had bought for him after his first semester of A's and B's, a goal his father had claimed he would never reach as long as he "spent all his time fooling around with the Gentiles." He was a mile from his parents' house but in his mind thousands of miles away. He was driving to Concord for an evening with Julia Hepburn, whom he had pursued on and off since he had met her at Sally

White's coming-out party years before. They had flirted, written to each other, seen each other occasionally, always before she flew off to a year abroad or a summer skiing in Chile or acting summer stock in the Berkshires. But there was something there for both of them, and it burst into that something during football season to the disapproval of both their parents. The Jewish boys at Harvard stayed with the Jewish crowd, the ghetto syndrome: Chicago, New York, Boston. They roomed together, dated Jewish Wellesley and Radcliffe girls together and worked to get into medical or law schools. Julia Hepburn would be Dickie's ticket out of Brookwood and the world of his father's maternity garments. He turned his radio to the same station Freddie had dialed, heard the same song, "That Old Black Magic" by Louis Prima and Keely Smith, sang along with it and floored the convertible along a snowy Route 128 toward Concord and the Social Register. Julia called him a nickname he loved, that he wished everyone would call him: "The Rose."

Red remained outside his house, whipping snowballs at trees and an occasional passing car.

"C'mon, Stanley," his father said, coming outside to get his son. "You're too old to be throwing snowballs at cars. You used to get in trouble when you were a kid."

"It's okay, Dad," Red said. "I'm going in the army. They'll give me every chance to grow up." His father hugged him then, pinning his son's arms to his sides with the embrace. "Stan the Man," Harry Singer said. "Be good. Don't fight the world all the time." Red stood back, swaying slightly, trying to focus on the father he loved. "Musial will be *nothing* on me," Red said. "I'm not going to be good, Dad. I'm going to be great. You wait and see." He made one more perfectly packed snowball and whistled it after a Cadillac that slowly drove by, its snow chains rattling when they hit bare pavement.

PART 2

The Back Nine

O

Dickie's Game

By graduation from Harvard he was no longer Dickie Rosenberg. He felt he was Richard, a full-fledged Richard, never a Dick in any way. In his mind he had left the world of the suburban Jewish ghetto and succeeded in the circle of Gentiles who mattered, the circle of the Social Register. He had been elected to a minor final club in college, The Frog, located over a clothing store on Mount Auburn Street. At his initiation, the members forced all of the initiates to drink what they claimed were daiquiris but in reality were two kinds of cheap rum and lemon extract. At this time there were only a handful of Jews in the final clubs at Harvard. It was a foot in the door. Freddie Temple had taken Dickie as far as he could take him. He couldn't get Dickie into his club, which had been the club of Freddie's father and his grandfather. That would have been too much of a battle, and Dickie sensed the lines over which he could not cross and should not push. He wanted to break ground. But he also wanted to win.

Dickie took his parents to lunch at The Frog during commencement week, both of them skeptical in the enemy camp. "At Penn," his father said, "we had Jewish fraternities, we didn't need to mix. The boys from Deke and Saint A's didn't like us any more than we liked them. Times were much more honest before World War Two."

"At Pembroke," his mother said, "there were four Jewish girls in my class, and we were all best friends. Oooh," she suddenly squealed, a funny noise for a woman almost fifty. They were in line for lunch in the club's dining room, a beautiful day in June, the kind Harvard likes to think is called forth for its graduation ceremonies. David and Sylvia Rosenberg were just about to look down their noses at the tuna salad, the plates of cold cuts, the raw carrot sticks arranged around olives and celery, when an elderly man in tweeds and a club tie, a man given to martinis at lunch in June, goosed Mrs. Rosenberg right through her girdle.

"I beg your pardon, sir," said David Rosenberg, indignant but always giving the other guy the benefit of the doubt. They were guests after all, and the pincher was an older man. "Oh, for Christ's sakes, Bud," the pincher said as if nothing unusual had happened, "if you can't grab an attractive bottom in your own club, where can you do it?" He grumbled. "Women have no business here anyway, don't you know? Serves them right."

David Rosenberg stood there, unable to react. Dickie came up carrying Bloody Marys for his parents, his fingers into the drinks. Clubbies stirred their drinks with their fingers; it was the acceptable thing to do. "He pinched your mother," David Rosenberg said. "What are we going to do about it?"

The pincher glared at Dickie. "Tell them," he said. Then, ignoring the Rosenbergs, he moved ahead in line, piling onto his plate tuna salad, Parker House rolls, stuffed eggs, minipats of butter. His utensils stuck out of the handkerchief pocket of his tweed jacket.

"Christ, Dad," Dickie said, "that's just old Monk Murray. He's ossified and harmless."

"Your mother is a lady."

"Sometimes," Dickie said, "you can look like a fool no matter what you do." The strain between them continued through lunch even though club mates wandered over while they ate, plates balanced on their laps in the club's living room. "Hey, Rose," they said and greeted his parents. "Parents of The Rose?" they said. "Good to see you; nice to meet you, sir, Mrs. Rose."

"It's *Rosenberg*," David said to one young man whose long hair fell over his eyes.

"Well, sure," he said, "but your son is 'The Rose,' " as if they'd fully understand.

Later, out in the sunshine, walking to the stadium to watch Harvard play Yale in baseball, Dickie's parents began their serious talk. "If you had gone to the Wharton School," his father said, "this wouldn't be happening."

"What your father means," his mother said, "is that these are not your people."

His father said, "They're going to stab you in the back someday, show you their true faces."

"It'll be a big shock to you, darling. But no shock to us." His mother tried to put her arm through her son's arm. He pulled away.

"Give me a little credit, would you, for knowing what I'm doing. You spend your life with a ghetto mentality: Jewish clubs, Jewish friends, totally Jewish lives. You don't know anything else, and you act as if anyone who isn't exactly like you is the enemy. I can't lead a life like that."

"You'll learn," said his father.

"Dickie," said his mother.

"Please call me Richard," he told his parents as they walked the dirt track leading to the baseball field. The Harvard team was warming up, coaches hitting grounders to the infield and fungoes to the outfield, the pitchers throwing hard: "whap, whap."

Chills didn't linger in the Rosenberg family. His parents had their say; Dickie had his say. They sat in the bleachers side by side and watched baseball, strangers in the sunshine but looking as if they belonged to one another.

David Rosenberg switched strategies. "I need you with me in the business," he said. "It's all laid out for you to build it up and make it grow. Women are going to get pregnant, thank God, and they'll forever wear dresses or slacks. Why should they look sick when they can look chic? You can bring Harvard to the maternity business."

"We've got time to think, Dad. When I get out of the army." A Yale player lined a double over the shortstop's head.

"You can think in the army. Your brain never stops."

Dickie's brain never did stop, which is why he chose to volunteer for CIC, the Counter-Intelligence Corps. He was part of the reserve program, regular basic training followed by four months' schooling in his specialty. That was the end of active duty for reservists. Then they owed the government one night a week and two weeks every summer for five and a half years. This was 1959. There was a draft in effect that would have meant a regular two-year tour of duty in the army. Six months in the reserves was the alternative that Dickie and thousands of young men chose. The Counter-Intelligence Corps was headquartered at Fort Devens, Massachusetts. Which was very near Concord, Massachusetts. Which was where Julia

Hepburn lived, with whom Dickie had become obsessed. He had his car on the base. Classes finished at four, classes in code craft, history of military intelligence, the principles of communism so that all the budding spies could understand the enemy. They studied surveillance techniques and a variety of other lessons from unarmed combat to survival in hostile terrain with only a mess kit, a compass and an entrenching tool (a collapsible shovel). He was, at this time, only truly at war with his parents. In his mother's eyes the dream, when he was a boy, of someday sending him to Harvard, was replaced by her saying, "That's what you get from your *Harvard* friends." Her dream was the Harvard of *her* youth, Jewish fraternities, tea dancing at the Copley, suppers on the Ritz roof, discussions of Justices Brandeis and Felix Frankfurter, boys from Newton and Swampscott, New York City and Chicago. Harvard was a Jewish place for Sylvia Rosenberg, née Baer, a Jewish experience. Dickie had crossed the wrong lines, and she blamed a Harvard she never knew or wanted to know.

All that Dickie knew, or believed, was that he was in the peacetime service, playing out a charade, with his own car and with virtually no responsibilities other than filling that car occasionally with a dollar's worth of regular gas. Dickie was as free as he would ever be in his life. And all he could think about was Julia Hepburn. Dickie would run into her at dances, at parties, after football games or crew races. She would say to him on their occasional dates, "The readiness is all. That's the key to Hamlet and the key to me. Time isn't right for us. I don't even know why we are out together." But she would look straight into his eyes and smile, challenging him. She knew her stuff. The results were always the same. She'd tease and flirt, putting her hands on his arm or shoulder or knee when she was in conversation, then removing his arm when he tried to hug her close or be possessive in any way. They teased each other in conversation, Dickie trying to be as cool as possible, no wrong steps, never forcing it. All through college he wanted her and had finally given up when, on a whim, he wandered into a dance at the Hasty Pudding Club the night before he shipped out for basic training at Fort Dix. Feeling sorry for himself, he drank Budweisers and stood against the wall, waiting for undergraduates, younger friends, to come to him.

"Rose, what are you doing here?" they'd say. All of his close friends and roommates were gone. Temple was in the navy for three years. Others were in different branches of the service, graduate schools, still in Europe or Latin America, hanging out, putting off whatever inevitable was in store. Then he saw her, laughing with her head thrown back, dancing with elbows pumping and legs doing double time. When she twirled by him, she saw him leaning against the wall trying to look suave, drinking his Bud out of the bottle. Dickie couldn't be sure, but he could have sworn that she stuck her tongue out, smiled, then danced away. He drank some more, then followed her, cutting in on "The Lady Is a Tramp."

"Not an editorial comment, I hope," she said, welcoming him into her arms as if it were the most common event in the world, like kissing a cousin on the cheek.

"Are we going to spend our lives on one drink," he asked, "one-dance dates, little meetings with little greetings?"

Julia made Dickie nervous. He had chased her in his mind since he had seen her at Sally White's coming-out party, and he had played the game of let's pretend ever since. He tried to act detached. He built up an image of himself as the amused sophisticate telling her on several of their dates, "I believe you should be invited everywhere, but very seldom go." By the end of his senior year he knew he had blown it. She was at Vassar, he knew, spending time in New York or, worse, in New Haven with Yalies, those threatening blond guys from Fence or Saint A's who had played hockey in prep school and stood up straight. He was afraid of her saying no, of turning him down. Dickie planned against people turning him down.

Facing the army at 7:00 A.M. the next day, he realized, seeing Julia again, that he may have overstepped playing his cool role. So he took the risk of being honest.

"Would it be boring," Dickie said, "to say that I am going in the army in the morning to make the world safe for democracy and that when I come home I want to see you with more frequency than twice a year?"

She stepped back and stared at him, stopping their dance in the middle of the floor. Couples looped around them.

"That's not boring at all," Julia said. She wore her hair longer than she ever had. It was blonder also, streaked with recent summer and lemon juice assiduously rubbed in by girlfriends on nights without dates. "But you graduated, and a lot depends on what you're going to do with your life. In the boring department, that is."

He still had to play the game. "Law school?" he ventured.

"Jesus," she said.

"I suppose no medical school, divinity school or B school would qualify?"

"Life qualifies," she said, sounding like a junior at Vassar but incredibly provocative to Dickie.

"I am actually going to do something no one you know has ever done or will do." Win her, he thought.

"Then we'll date," she said. "I want to see where four years frittering around leads. Write me," she added. "Win me." Someone would forever cut in on Julia at a dance. In social situations she made her point and moved on, as confident in the use of her wit and her ability to keep men off balance as she was in the appeal of her thick, long blond hair.

Dickie wrote love letters from basic training and felt as if he were at the front in World War II, Julia his sweetheart at home, his pinup, his Betty Grable. After his head was shaved at the reception center, after he got his first M1 thumb, after the kick of his weapon gave him a black eye, after Julie London tapes played at breakfast (she had been married to "Dragnet" 's Jack Webb), after he learned that ex-Korean War sergeants were the funniest men in the world, he wrote to Julia Hepburn: Harvard to Vassar letters.

"We marched up to the firing range today," he told her. "In November, the rains and wind in New Jersey go through you like physics and chemistry go through the sad student, a sharp burst you never understand. I'm wearing army-issue undershorts, long johns, fatigues and field pants. If I ever got the runs it would take me twenty-four minutes to pull off all my trousers. I would surrender to the enemy before the first pair were off. It's cold, and Poughkeepsie, New York, seems like the village somewhere in the Himalayas that dreamers called Shangri-la."

Julia Hepburn would write back. "Audie Murphy," she'd say. "(You may be the antithesis of Audie, you may even be the ubiquitous Audie Schwartz and turn the other cheek, which would be a moon)." Julia's letters were loaded with parentheses. Almost everything she thought was an afterthought.

They met in New York on one of his few weekends off from basic training. She had checked into the St. Moritz Hotel on Central Park South and told Dickie by letter that she would wait for him in Rumpelmayer's, the French ice-cream parlor off the lobby of the hotel. He arrived in uniform, head still shaved, small military overnight bag in his hand, no stripes on his sleeve, a recruit, the lowest of the low in a soldier's world. Julia almost didn't recognize him. He seemed a different person, smaller. He put his cap on her head and treated it all like a masquerade. She didn't kiss him hello. It was awkward, love letters over weeks' time prepared her for more mail, not for face-to-face.

"What kind of name is 'Richard' for a soldier?" were the first words she said. "You should have a nickname. I like 'Hero' Rosenberg." Then, prepared, she kissed him, a quickie on the mouth. He came back for more, holding her tightly with his free hand.

"I like 'The Rose' better than 'the hero,' " he said.

" 'The Rose' is a big thing to live up to once you're out of college. Sounds like a legend to me."

"I need a drink," Dickie said.

"After an ice-cream sundae?"

They sparred, tentatively at first. When they wrote letters they wrote to a fantasy, how they wished things would be. In person it was a shock to have to actually say words. Most love letters in truth we really write to ourselves.

They moved to the St. Moritz bar and drank martinis. Julia saw Dickie, or wanted to see him, as her Jewish Harvard intellectual. He was dark, with dark brown eyes, white even teeth and lips that she thought of as Mediterranean. "Thick with promise," as one of her Vassar roommates described them. There were lots of Jewish girls at Vassar. They, too, as at Harvard, roomed, ate, dated in a group and all seemed to have relatives or friends in common, all over America. Marriage was the last thing on Julia's mind. The first thing on her mind, staying in a hotel in New York City, was that she had never been all the way with a man.

After a month of army life, up at five, running through calisthenics, classes after breakfast, marching out, marching back, chow, cleaning the weapons, polishing the boots, writing letters, Dickie had one martini and almost fell asleep at the bar. He had learned to doze with his eyes open in the military. Millions of soldiers had learned the same from the first campaign of cavemen to the present, cavemen listening to their sergeants lecture them about the dangers of tyrannosaurus rex.

"Do I detect you slurring your words, Richard?" Julia asked. "Or am I so stimulating that I'm putting you in the Land of Nod?"

"It must be all the fresh air at the firing range or falling out in formation on the company street at four-thirty A.M. when it's pitch-black and twenty degrees and career sergeants from Foreskin, Texas, are screaming at you and calling you 'Asshole.' I may be the only enlisted man out of Fort Dix this Saturday night having a martini."

Julia softened and put her hand on his thigh. "Maybe this will wake you up," she said. "I decided I am going to hide you in my room tonight." She rubbed her hand over the black stubbly surface of his head. "I love your haircut. That's what decided me. It's so babyish."

"Is it night yet?" Dickie asked.

She ignored that. "We're going to walk along the park and explore the West Side, looking for the cafés where intellectual Jews drink black coffee, play chess, think great thoughts and argue endlessly."

The word "Jews" sounded naked to Dickie. He was uncomfortable with the word on Julia's lips, the word isolated, as if she held it in her mouth and spat it out as distasteful. Saying "Jewish intellectuals" would have sounded all right to him; "intellectual Jews" seemed to point a finger.

"Do you think I'm an intellectual Jew?" Dickie asked.

She thought for a moment. "You know," she said, "I actually think of you as something exotic. Actually wearing a burnoose or something, dark and desert. If you want to know, exciting and foreign. Yeah. But not so intellectual. That's not an insult. You never wear glasses."

"Except to read."

"I've never seen you reading, only in action, conversation." They walked from the St. Moritz through Central Park to the West Side and over to Columbus Avenue, arms around each other. "We haven't seen an intellectual in twenty blocks," Dickie said. "You think it's too cold?" It was deep November, and the wind of early evening blew toward downtown as if heading to the theaters of Broadway.

"They're in cafés arguing," Julia said, "debating the fates of the Rosenbergs and Alger Hiss."

"Sacco and Vanzetti," Dickie said. They went into a neighborhood bar and sat next to each other in a wooden booth eating hamburgers and drinking beer. She looked so beautiful to him. He had thought about it before, but holding Julia's hand and talking about their lives and not being responsible for anything except showing up for bed check Sunday night at Fort Dix, he couldn't help thinking about changing his name, shortening it. Rose instead of Rosenberg. It would make many things simpler, just by making them ambiguous. "Rosenberg the soldier in his uniform on the West Side of New York," Dickie thought. "Just like a movie in the 1940s. John Garfield." He hugged Julia closer to him again. Again she rubbed her hand over his thigh, covered in government-issue woollen.

Later on, Julia rode up on the hotel's elevator alone, carrying Dickie's overnight bag. He followed ten minutes later, confident. As if he knew exactly where he was going. As he was not checked into the hotel, he didn't want any questions. The lights were out in the room when she let him in. Only a crack of illumination came from behind the mostly closed bathroom door. Dickie didn't want her to be naked, but she was. He wanted to undress her slowly. "How efficient," he thought.

"Hurry and get undressed," she said. "I'm sorry there's no view. We look out on an air shaft." He kissed her then, with all the experience he thought he had over her, and wondered how much experience *she* had. What had she done? Then it was all kiss, all touch, tough to loosen the brass buckle on his belt, kick everything into corners of the room, then dive onto the bed, giddy, drunk, complicated but in love with Julia Hepburn, who lay under him making noises while he kissed her toes and kissed her nipples, equal time, then couldn't wait to put his tongue into her, knowing she would taste like a debutante, and he thought he knew what that taste would be, somehow vanilla, sweet like apples or, rather, cider. "If you can't get it in vinegar, get it inside her," he thought, and he fought against thinking of grammar school and golf and his three friends while he moved inside of Julia Hepburn for the first time.

After that weekend they saw each other whenever they could. But it was at Christmas that their relationship thundered because of her vacation from Vassar and his new station after basic training. Every evening after classes at Fort Devens, Dickie was free to leave before chow. He would bomb down Route 2 to Concord in time for his ration of daily punishment: cocktails with Mr. and Mrs. Hepburn. Benjamin Hepburn was a lawyer who specialized in wills, estates and the secrets of the gentry. These secrets he tucked away under an impeccable façade: superior manners and the impression of keen intelligence. He was demanding of family and friends, demanding perfection and performance to which no one could ever quite measure up. Julia's mother listened for his every word, his every opinion and couldn't wait to utter her favorite phrase, "Yes, Benjamin," in answer to all he said. The first night Julia was home from Vassar, Dickie was invited for dinner, dressed in his civvies. Mr. Hepburn didn't ask Dickie what he wanted to drink. He handed him a small tumbler, slightly larger than a shot glass, filled to the top with an icy-clear Gibson, a drier-than-dry martini with two pearl onions sitting on the bottom like animal eyes. Mr. Hepburn sat in an armchair by the fireplace, crossed his legs, shot the cuffs of his white shirt and watched Dickie as if he were a specimen. "Why would you be an enlisted man?" he asked. "You went to Harvard, my daughter tells me." He spoke as if Julia were not in the room.

"There is a two-year commitment if you're an officer," Dickie said. "In peacetime, best to do six months, then the reserves. No use wasting two years when a career is waiting." Mr. Hepburn took little, perfect sips, and his eyes never left Dickie's face. It was as if he were peering into his brain, knowing he would find it wanting. He made Dickie do most of the talking while Julia laughed violently at every description. Mr. Hepburn waited for a lull in the story, took a small sip of gin and asked, "What does your father do, Mr. Rosenberg?"

Dickie would be damned if he didn't stick right up for his family. "He makes maternity clothing. He owns the business," he added, and realized that this was probably hellish information to give to the father of a girl.

"Then I suppose it will be business school, Mr. Rosenberg," Hepburn said, getting up to pour himself another perfect thimbleful of Gibson.

"Probably, sir," Dickie said. "Right after the President makes me head of the Joint Chiefs of Staff." Mrs. Hepburn took in her breath sharply, as if she had just run over a cat. Did she detect sarcasm in a response to her perfect husband? Julia overreacted with laughter. Benjamin Hepburn shook his head, as if he had just confirmed his original opinion of Dickie. No more drinks were offered to him, and the grilling seemed to be at an end. There was a dinner of lamb chops and asparagus with hollandaise during which Julia did much of the talking, mostly of New York and her school and Dickie's academic accomplishments in college. Mrs. Hepburn looked at her husband for approval after each of Julia's remarks. Mr. Hepburn commented almost solely on the cooking, which was done by Margaret, an elderly Irish woman who wore a white uniform and nudged Julia each time she passed her chair as if to say, "You've got a boy, you've got a boy." Later, Dickie and Julia drove to a roadhouse outside Concord. "We're visiting friends in Cambridge," she told her mother.

The roadhouse was a gathering spot for local tradespeople and for Concord gentry who needed late-evening drinks like they needed new tweeds but who compulsively searched for one or two more because their lives and their livers demanded them. But every man at the bar and in the darkened booths turned to watch Julia when she entered. Dickie loved that she looked as if people should know who she was. They ordered stingers, the preferred after-dinner drink for Fred Temple and his set, and a move Dickie had down pat. When they were drunk together, they reminded him of Scott and Zelda Fitzgerald. It was what he wanted them to be: witty, charming, outrageous perhaps, young forever.

"Daddy shouldn't bother you; he's that way with everyone."

"Anyone lived in a pretty how town (with up so floating many bells down)," Dickie chanted, half remembering E. E. Cummings but knowing it would snow Julia.

She looked at him with big blue eyes. "That's why I love you."

It was out of the bag. Neither of them had said the word before to each other. Dickie got up from his side of the booth and slid in next to Julia. He kissed her neck and ran her thick hair through his fingers, blond hair he couldn't believe. "Are you just saying that because I'm going to be head of the Joint Chiefs of Staff?"

"I am saying that because you answer the requirement I have for loving."

"What's that?" he asked.

"You can never be boring."

Through a haze of stingers he held her and knew that he could never be boring as long as he was drunk. They drove back to Julia's house, a large wooden Colonial painted Salem yellow that looked out upon the town green. Julia led him up to her bedroom, silently with their shoes in their hands, hoping they wouldn't wake either her parents in the wing opposite or the ghosts of Emerson and Thoreau. Julia was daring. She acted as if her wing of the house were her own private apartment. She threw her clothes into the air from her bed. Dickie, drunk as he was, put everything of his in a pile where he could grab quickly for them in the dark if he had to. Julia may have wanted the danger of bringing a man to her bed under her father's nose. Dickie wanted no such confrontation. "I know these bastards from Concord," he thought. "They all hunt, and they probably keep loaded shotguns. Who wouldn't acquit a father who shot someone in his daughter's bed?" Nevertheless, with Julia naked and the combination of brandy and crème de menthe urging him on, he made love to the woman he loved and hoped the springs of the antique bed at midnight wouldn't betray him to the owner of the antique house.

For the next few months, Dickie went through the motions at Fort Devens, going to class, taking exams and living for the weekends when Julia would come up from Vassar, go to parties with him in Cambridge, then smuggle him up to her bed, keeping him there until the small hours when he would tiptoe out to his car parked at the town green and drive in the quiet darkness back to base. This routine flourished unchecked until Passover, which concluded with Julia's spring vacation.

"My parents want to take us to the club for dinner," Julia told him, excited about the implications.

"Julia, honey," Dickie said, "I've got two days off for Passover. I have to have dinner with my folks."

"But it's the club."

"It's like Christmas, Jules. I've got to be with my parents."

"I thought you didn't care about any of that stuff. This is important."

"I can't lie to them. But I can meet you afterwards."

"You do what you have to," she said. Chilly.

Passover was painful for Dickie. "Damned if I do and damned if I don't," he thought to himself. "The family pissed at me if I don't show up; Julia annoyed no matter what I do." He was determined to leave his father's house early, as soon after dinner as he could. He fidgeted through the seder service, faked interest in his sister's stories of high school and his father's problems with the business. When he made his good-byes just after nine o'clock, his grandmother, The Countess, took him into the pantry and kissed both his cheeks. He had told everyone he had to make bed check at Fort Devens and felt rushed. Bad enough to lie, he thought. But to lie on Passover. At least it's not Yom Kippur, he rationalized, Day of Atonement.

"Dickie," his grandmother said, "I am not. But your parents are worried about you. It's wonderful to be a soldier and a Rudolph Valentino. But you have to remember your background." He tried to reassure her, but she pinched his cheeks and continued. "You must know," she said, "no matter how fancy you are, or think you are, no one else will ever forget you are Jewish. Rich or poor, beautiful or ugly, the world lumps us all in one boat. Never forget it. You marry a shiksa. Someday she throws it in your face."

His mouth felt sticky from the sweet Passover wine as he raced his car to Concord.

"You missed the sweetbreads, Mr. Rosenberg," Julia's father said to Dickie. They were having brandy in the room Mr. Hepburn referred to as the library. Mr. Hepburn poured tiny amounts of brandy into large snifters, tiny amounts the way he doled out thimble-sized Gibsons. Then he proceeded to drink what seemed to Dickie to be half a dozen of the little beauties. Dickie thought about how the Hepburns must have made love and he smiled. "You like sweetbreads, I conjecture?" Mr. Hepburn added, noting Dickie's satisfied nod.

Dickie had no idea what sweetbreads even were. "A rare treat," he answered. "We had turkey tonight at my house."

Mrs. Hepburn rarely opened a conversation. She must have been consumed with curiosity to dare upstage her husband. "Tell us please what this celebration of yours is all about," she said suddenly, as if mention of turkey on a holiday other than Thanksgiving or Christmas was too much for her. Julia leaned forward in her chair, eager like a prize student to have her favorite professor destroy the audience with fantastic tales of Passover. Dickie told them about Moses and Pharaoh, the parting of the Red Sea, the plagues, including the killing of the firstborn.

"Cecil B. DeMille," Julia's mother exclaimed when Dickie was finished. "I had no idea."

"Nonsense, dear," her husband snorted. "You know your Bible almost as well as I."

"But I didn't know that that was Passover. I suppose it's a wonderful thing to celebrate. But why the turkey?"

Dickie knew he had to have an answer. "The flight from Egypt," he said. And his audience, who God knows knew symbolism, nodded as if it were there all the time.

Dickie won Julia back with his tales of Passover. He was her hero once again, although she later whispered to him as they climbed the stairs to her room in their stocking feet, "Daddy says that if we get married we can never get into the club. But I'll go to your house for Passover. If it's not the same day as Easter."

"That's bullshit," Dickie whispered. "I was in a club at Harvard, fancier than the goddamn golf course out here with stale cheese and Yorkshire pudding."

"Don't get all pus-sy," she warned. "They serve delicious food. Sweetbreads." He didn't ask her what they were, but if her father loved them you could bet they could be eaten in tiny bites. Jesus, she was beautiful, he thought, tiptoeing down her hallway. Debutante skin, he thought, debutante snatch, like a yellow mitten from Lord & Taylor. But it was also the first time, sneaking down the hall, since he had met her at that coming-out party years earlier that he had any doubts about loving her forever. He couldn't help thinking about his grandmother and her telling him that Gentiles could never really understand anything that he knew. Then he was in Julia's bedroom, the room smelling of talcum powder and Bluegrass, her favorite perfume. The curtains were down for added darkness, but Dickie knew there was always a coffee cup full of water on her night table next to the complete works of Emily Dickinson in one leather-bound volume. He knew that because one night he had knocked over the cup with a kick from the position they were in and Julia had later raised hell about water spots on the cover. Dickie wanted to give pleasure in his lovemaking. It was important to him to satisfy. Julia inevitably ended up straddling his thighs, her preference for penetration, and adored his touching her breasts while she rode up and down noisily, lost in their screwing, taking it seriously. Dickie was both frightened and excited by the risk of being in Julia's room. He loved her noisy love. He always had half an ear out for anyone on the stairs, in the hall. He was sure her cries were amplified throughout the old house. That night it just felt too good to take warning and, as Julia was riding to win, place and show, the overhead light snapped on and froze them in that pose. Woody Allen is wrong, Dickie thought when he reflected on the scene years later: you *can* have a bad orgasm. He couldn't stop himself, even though Julia jumped off him, making a sound like a bathroom plunger. Mr. Hepburn stood in the doorway in a green woollen bathrobe and slippers. "I ought to shoot your gonads off," he said slowly in a voice that meant it. Dickie knew he was dead. One way or another he was dead. Julia threw a blanket around her body and positioned herself in front of Dickie, who only had a few stuffed animals to cover his threatened genitals. She said to her father in an equally determined voice, equally cold: "We're in love, Daddy." At Vassar she probably could have gotten away with it. Mr. Hepburn stared only at Dickie, not at his daughter. And he spoke as both judge and executioner: "You're not fit to speak my daughter's name, to talk with her, to look at her across a room. And I'll see to it that you never do again. I'm calling the police." He walked away in his slippers, down the hall, and Dickie frantically began getting dressed, tripping over his boxer shorts, racing into his pants and shirt.

Julia sat on the bed, watching him. "Where do you think you're going?" There wasn't ever a time that Dickie thought of police when he didn't hear the years-ago sounds of glass cracking and the squeal of tires and the smashing of steel. Now as then, all he could summon up was escape.

"My father told me a smart soldier knows when to retreat. And I say never get caught up by a police chief in a town where your enemy lives."

"You're saying Daddy is your enemy?"

"No. My *friends* all want to shoot my balls off and throw me in jail." Dickie finished dressing. Julia made no motion. "Baby," Dickie said. "Your father just caught us in the act. What do you want me to do?"

"I want you to be a man."

"Christ," Dickie nearly shouted. "I'll call you at school." He quickly walked down the hall and raced down the stairs, tapping his pockets to make sure he had his car keys. He quick-stepped to his car. The night was without moon. Only one dim streetlight lit the town green. Suddenly, lights began to go on all over the Hepburn house. The front door burst open behind him, and he heard a blast in the quiet night that sounded like a grenade. Mr. Hepburn stood on the brick doorstep in his green bathrobe and slippers with a shotgun in his hands. "Stand where you are, you Jewish dog," he said. Dickie took his chances with momentum and kept going. That's when Julia raced from the house, buck naked, running in front of her father after Dickie. "Richard," she yelled into the night. "Richard," as Mrs. Hepburn watched from an upstairs window and Mr. Hepburn put his weapon at port arms as if waiting for the next covey of quail. Dickie didn't wait around. He saw Julia running naked in the street behind him and he laid rubber, leaving the Concord green thinking that the only place he would be safe was back in the army. "If we ever got married," he thought, "they'd kill me."

Dickie always assumed that The Countess really cared very little for organized religion. After breaking up with Julia Hepburn, he went to visit the old woman looking for answers about why he sought to distance himself from the family.

"I don't care for your hair cut so short" were the first words she said to him after he kissed her cheek. "The world doesn't take a man seriously if his hair is too short."

"I'm in the army, Grandma. It's a requirement." She ignored this, lecturing him from a straight-backed chair as if she had been holding back all the good advice in the world for just this moment.

"What would you say, Grandma," Dickie asked, "if I married someone who wasn't Jewish?"

She looked right at him, not blinking. "I'd say you were a fool. Look at that album on the coffee table and you see a young girl. Tough for me to believe also. But it is a young Jewish girl, and now it is an elderly Jewish woman. There are things in life that deserve dilution, like bitter medicine. There are things that should not be diluted, like Jewishness. Look at the album." Dickie thumbed through it, not for the first time. As a child he had looked through all of the available family histories, on both sides. Grandma Baer's family all seemed stern, unsmiling, born to work hard, to prosper and punish their children. "Like it or not," she said, "they are all Jewish faces. The same as in your own mother's albums. Let other people stay with people like themselves. You do the same. Sooner or later, if you are married, the entire life experience comes down to 'Who are your people?' Fools ignore this lesson. Most of what Jewish people *ever* say to each other involves the special knowledge they get in Jewish childhood. Do you want your wife to never know what you're talking about?"

Later, Dickie drove around Brookwood, remembering high school, slowing down opposite old friends' houses, opposite his grammar school. He parked next to the temple where he had had his bar mitzvah and tried to remember the words, any word in his haphtarah, or anything from the sermon his father had written. But all he could think of was Red Singer throwing up at the reception under the tent. He managed to mumble, "Here oh Israel, the Lord our God, the Lord is one." But like most prayers learned by rote, it meant nothing. Fred Temple had told him that when he was at St. Luke's School one of his classmates thought the Lord's Prayer said, "Our Father who art in Heaven, *Hallowell* be thy name."

One of his father's best friends was a profane man, a neighbor in Brookwood who had grown up in the shoe business. Abe Fishman kidded David Rosenberg, calling him "Mr. Fancy" for his University of Pennsylvania manners and his Brooks Brothers clothes. But they shared membership in their temple, in their country club and in their love of manufacturing. Abe had no sons and had often teased Dickie while he was growing up about the dowry he would earn if he married any of Abe's three daughters. For a rabbi, Dickie much preferred Abe to any actual clergyman he had ever met, and he sought him out at the one place he could always be found, Jack's Deli in South Brookwood, early in the morning before the shoe factories opened. "Boy-chick," Fishman cried, kissing Dickie on both cheeks. "You had to go to Harvard to finally realize what a good deal are my daughters." Abe held forth at Jack's Deli as if he were Louis B. Mayer, philosophizing, bullying his fellow shoedogs or anyone else who patronized his early-morning club. Abe had thick wavy hair, so white it looked like an ad for Rinso. He had a wicked little grin that told you to look out for practical jokes. "Marry Jane," Abe said. "She's got the biggest chest and the smallest brain. Marry Jane and I start you at the top . . . of the shipping department. Manny," he ordered, "bring the Harvard boy corned beef and eggs; butter the bagel."

"You know I've always preferred to ask you questions rather than my father," Dickie said, eating what he was told to eat, especially since Abe told him that corned beef and eggs would allow him to keep his hair.

"You haven't been around much for advice," Abe said, "in the last few years. Some of us thought maybe, Mr. Big Shot. But I said no, he'll be back. Jack's Deli is a magnet; the community is a magnet."

"That's what I wanted to talk to you about, being Jewish."

"First of all," the shoe man said, "you don't talk about being a Jew. You are, that's it. The world hates you. Has forever hated you, will forever hate you. Think I'm lying? Ask the German fancy Jews who were above it all until Hitler gave them a shower of gas. You think we ridicule each other? We do it to us before the world does it to us. You understand what I'm saying, Harvard boy? Wrap being Jewish around you like a blanket. It'll be the only thing in your life that will truly keep you warm. You are what you are, boychick. I only make shoes. But I'm not a schmuck. You've got to know what's at the middle of your life."

*

Without his friends and roommates from school with whom he could put on motorcycle boots, act Beat Generation, Dickie put on a navy suit with rep tie and went to work for his father in the maternity business, spending two days a week in the New York showroom at 1410 Broadway. Van, their New York salesman, looked as if he was dressed on Jermyn Street in London and groomed at Bergdorf Goodman. Van was a prince of queens on Seventh Avenue, famous for being outrageously homosexual and for selling more maternity clothes than anyone in the history of the trade. "Richard, my boy, you learn the business from the ground up," Van told Dickie.

"I worked summers in the shipping department," he answered.

"You learn about patterns and fabrics?"

Dickie nodded, being the good boy.

"Well," Van said, "I'm sure your father told you that nothing should go out into the trade until the boss looks at it. You know Abe Shrader, the women's wear manufacturer? Of course you do. Quality control is his obsession. He sees and approves every piece, every dress that goes out of his factory. If we sent Abe Shrader to Detroit no car would ever come off the assembly line anything but perfect. Else back it would go." Van would punctuate his lectures with suggestions that were meant to keep Dickie off balance. After teaching the boss's son about the New York department stores that he sold, Van would say, "Is there any chance at all of us getting married? If I were your father's daughter-in-law, or son-in-law as the case may be, he maybe would kick me up to three quarters of a percent of the showroom's volume. Or is virtue its own reward, sweetheart? Don't tell your Dad I said that."

Dickie stayed at the Waldorf when he was in New York because his father had booked there for years and management gave him a rate. Starting in the business at $9,000 a year, Dickie played at being the big man, making more money than most of his friends fresh out of school or the service. In New York he took dates to dinner and the theater and for late drinks, often at the Monkey Bar in the Hotel Elysée, where a piano player sang dirty songs. Or he went to P. J. Clarke's on Third Avenue, where he had first been taken in college by boys from Park Avenue to drink planter's punches and whiskey sours. One early dateless night, Dickie was having drinks and a cheeseburger at Clarke's with a buyer from Saks Fifth Avenue, a married woman more used to the gentility of a French restaurant than the boisterous sports bar but amused and tolerant and a longtime customer of Rosenberg Maternity Fashions. "I come here for the jukebox," Dickie was saying. "They've got the best songs of any box in New York. Good songs make you think romance, make you ultimately think maternity, right?"

"You got two big seasons, Richard," she said. "You don't have to do a year's business in one night."

"Why not? Let me play something for you. *Porgy and Bess*. 'I Loves You, Porgy.' You'll *want* to give me a year's business." As Dickie walked to the Wurlitzer, Gershwin sounds poured out of the instrument.

"I loves you, Porgy," the song came, "don't let him take me. Don't let him handle me with those hot hands." He couldn't believe it. And he couldn't believe the girl leaning with her hands against the warmth of the jukebox, singing along with the lyrics, mimicking the accents of Nina Simone. She had long dark hair, combed to one side and almost covering her right eye the way Veronica Lake used to wear her hair, like an obvious Russian spy or a woman suspected of murdering her husband. Her lips were painted brighter red than most ladies painted their lips, and she wore a tweed suit. Dickie thought that young ladies only wore tweed suits on interviews for graduate school or for teas at Briarcliffe. "Are you wearing that suit for a graduate school interview or tea at Briarcliffe?" Dickie asked. "I was just coming over to play exactly that song."

She looked at him through her hair. "Well, no shit, Dick Tracy," she said with an accent that said boarding school. "I dress this way because this is New York. What's your excuse?"

Dickie laughed. "I don't know any better. How's that?"

"Life is three songs for a quarter," she said. "You obviously don't live here."

"The provinces," Dickie said. "Boston. I'm Richard Rosenberg," he said.

The way he said it she smiled. "And you went to Harvard, I suppose."

He nodded.

"The papers would say that I *attended* Sarah Lawrence. But I've been other places also. If you couldn't play 'Porgy,' " she asked, "what would have been your second choice?"

He scanned the selections: " 'Money Honey.' The Drifters."

"I'm Adrienne Feinberg," she said, shaking her head to one side, her hair moving off her eye. "Isn't it lucky I approve? Come meet my dad."

A big man, big, bald and slightly in his cups, stood watching them at the bar.

"Are you bringing back a live one?" he bellowed at them. "Don't you bring back a stiff."

"This is my father," Adrienne said. "Max Feinberg. Everyone calls him 'Slapsy Maxie' Feinberg, which he takes as a compliment."

Dickie introduced himself to the big man.

"My daughter," he roared so everyone at the bar could hear him.

"Speaks three languages but costs me twenty-five grand a year. It's okay for you, kid, to hear this if you're a live one. Want to go to the Knicks with us tonight? You come to Clarke's you must be going to the Knicks anyways."

"Thanks. I'm having dinner with a friend. A customer."

"A customer," Maxie bellowed. "Bring him along. You an insurance man, live one?"

"Maternity clothes," Dickie whispered.

"Christ on a crutch," Maxie roared like a regular at the bar, which he was. "A cloakie. A son-in-law. Adrie." He hugged his daughter. "You done good."

She hugged her father back. "Boston and Harvard," she whispered into his ear.

Maxie stood up. "C'mon, youngblood," he said to Dickie. "If you can pee a hole in the ice block at Clarke's, you can be a fit son-in-law."

Maxie was hard to resist.

CHAPTER ELEVEN

O

Red's Game

Red was made for the army. He could hustle. He was twenty-one years old when he took the bus from the Boston Army Base to Fort Dix, New Jersey, for basic training. He was five-foot-ten-inches tall, and his hair was only slightly less on fire than when he had been in grammar school. His skin erupted less frequently now, although his eyes and nose still burst into red when he drank or when he got excited. He felt fully confident that he could talk himself out of any problem or into any door that might be closed to others. And if talk didn't get him out of trouble he could still run like a bastard. Red was nervous on the bus when the kids from Boston's Italian North End were mouthing off, tripping people, snapping paper clips from elastic bands. But he purposely sat himself down next to the biggest punk he could find, a hulking dumb kid from Marblehead, Massachusetts, and when the Italians continued to flip the paper clips, Red got up, turned around and shouted at them, "If one of those fucking things hits us we're going to beat the shit out of you." Thinking Red was the giant's buddy, they calmed down, directed fewer missiles and then only to other, quieter sections of the bus.

Basic training was a breeze for Red, his head shaved, with fresh fatigues, rookie trooper that he was. For he never felt himself a rookie, and while the Italian wise guys, heads now shorn, fainted in the shot line when needles went into both arms simultaneously, Red just took it as routine and moved on to teach his barracks lights-out poker. He got others to make his bed, clean his rifle, do his KP and guard duty. He managed this by teaching card tricks that his father, the classic salesman, had taught him. He wanted his clothes to be standing tall. His father had always told him, "Stanley, if you *sell* anything, be spruced up. Look better, look richer than your prospect. Then you've halfway got the sale the minute you walk in the room." So he spit-shined his boots to perfection and had his fatigues tailored to mold his body. His hair color and his loud mouth completed the picture, assuring that every sergeant and noncom would notice him in any crowd. When he lost at poker, inevitably to guys from New York, it drove him crazy. Then he had to wait for payday for the lousy thirty bucks a month, knowing his father couldn't afford to send down anything extra. When he was broke he had to sit around the company day room or the barracks or the beer hall scrounging quarters for 3.2 brews or coins to play the pinball machines. "I'm as broke as the other dumb fucks," Red thought. He had time to think in the army. Every decision was made for him by people higher up the ladder, the chain of command. In basic training Red thought about his future. But the sky opened for him one night before dawn on bivouac exercises in the field. Red lay awake in a two-man pup tent, needing to take a leak more urgently than ever before in his life. At the moment the only exposed part of Red was his nose. He was inside his cocoon of a sleeping bag wearing all of his clothes, including the army fur cap with earflaps pulled down. Red knew it was at least ten below zero outside of his bag. Should he pee in this warmth, in his clothes? Or should he jump out of the tent, freeze his pecker off? While he debated, he focused on his life, trying not to think about having to pee. He could never lie back and be carried along by his looks the way his sisters had prospered. It was not enough to have money, he decided. He had to have recognition as well, he had to be appreciated for his accomplishments, loved rather than feared. He had never been loved except by his parents, only laughed at for his pranks. "I can't be a lawyer or a doctor," he reasoned. "I could never stay long enough in any school." His mind tripped to a movie he had seen the week before, *Some Like It Hot,* with Jack Lemmon and Marilyn Monroe. To keep himself from peeing and from thinking about the alternative, the frigid morning outside his sleeping bag, Red thought about the movie. At the film's end, Jack Lemmon and Tony Curtis, masquerading as women musicians to escape the Chicago mob's revenge, leaped into Joe E. Brown's speedboat. Brown played a rich, old, lecherous playboy, in love with Lemmon whom he truly believed to be a woman. As the boat sped out to

Brown's yacht, Lemmon stripped off his wig, pulled open his dress and announced, "I'm a man." Brown did a mild double take, rolled his eyes adoringly at Lemmon and said in the film's last line, "Well . . . nobody's perfect." Red exploded from his sleeping bag. He felt as if it were twenty below and he would not dream of going outside the tent. Next to him slept Skip Sweeney, his tent mate, a six-foot-six basketball player from the University of Massachusetts who had been on academic probation and decided to enlist. Sweeney snored though Red's acrobatics and, almost completely covered from the cold, never heard, saw or smelled Red's reckless urine pouring all over his sleeping form. Red didn't even realize that he was peeing all over his mate, and if he had known, he wouldn't have cared. It was 3:00 A.M., black freezing night, and all Red could think about other than relief was a time when he would get out of the army. Then he would go where it was rich and warm. He was going to make movies. Nobody's perfect.

This decision about his life's work allowed him to run wild when basic training was over. He was reassigned to the Medical Corps at Fort Sam Houston, San Antonio, Texas. He felt free to run wild because for the first time he realized he would never again go back to school. He was sure that in California no one would ask him where he went to college. With pain behind him, Red threw himself into Texas. From his first day there, he told everyone he was in the movie business, just doing his duty for his country until he could head west where dreams came true, particularly his own.

"Anyone who's full of shit, we keep our eyes on," the sergeant said about him. But this was the Medical Corps, the army in peacetime. No sweat. Fort Sam Houston was a country club of postings in the U.S. military. Red knew that the first thing to do in any strange place was to get connected. He had a fraternity brother, Bruce Stone, from San Antonio, whose father was a liquor distributor in the Southwest. Red called him before he left for Texas and greased the way.

"If you swear to God," Stone said, "to never get near my sister, we'll show you the best time you've ever had." Bruce Stone got him on the coming-out party list in San Antonio, a season that lasted the entire year, celebrating the young womanhood of a dozen Texas daughters of newly rich parents in an endless round of teas, barbecues, luncheons, small dances and formal balls. Stone also got him the use of his family station wagon on weekends and guest cards to half a dozen private clubs in the area, the only spots where hard liquor (supplied by the Stone family) was legally available. Soldiering was easy: classes in the morning on first aid, splinting, bandaging techniques, triage. The lunch lines at the company mess halls were endless. Red and his buddies almost always chose to eat at the bowling alleys on base, which served cheeseburgers, fries, soft drinks. There was a fat, smiling Mexican working the lunch lines every day selling newspapers. He leered and needled the soldiers, sweat marks on his short-sleeve shirt going down to his waist. He hawked his papers, pointing to the headlines featuring San Antonio news, and his cry was the same every day: "Found the body."

"Someday I'll make a movie about that guy," Red would tell his friends. "The fat Mexican, the chow lines, the boredom."

"Who the fuck would want to see a movie about that?" A boy who had gone to Baylor asked.

"You will, cowboy," Red said, "and you'll stand in a line longer than this."

"Shit. Let's go get us a Dr Pepper. Talk about the pool."

The pool was Red's invention. Each weekend that he had leave, starting Saturdays at two o'clock until ten on Sunday night, Red would take as many as twelve soldiers in his borrowed station wagon to the Mexican border town Nuevo Laredo, only a few hours south of Fort Sam Houston. Each of his passengers would pay $10 for gas and the trip. This was the inside price for friends. The real profit came from the lottery, Red's "pussy pool," conducted after company formation on Thursday nights. Tickets for the pool were $2. Anywhere from $250 to $400 would be raised, with little Tony Antonelli, the company mascot from Buffalo, New York, pulling the winning tickets out of the lucky hat, Red's olive drab soft cap. Two winners received a free weekend in Mexico, including whorehouse visits. Since it was his idea, Red pocketed whatever was left over. But he always bought beer or tequila sours at thirty cents a drink for the friends who traveled with him to the Mexican border town. The troopers would sing in the station wagon, bombing down the Texas highway, "Ninety-nine bottles of beer on the wall, ninety-nine bottles of beer" and "Roll me over in the clover, roll me over, lay me down and do it again." In Mexico Red would lead them from souvenir shops ("Bullwhips just like

Lash LaRue's . . . four dollars") to cafés to Boys Town, where over-the-hill whores, fucked out, played out, would perform unnatural acts upon each other and with small animals and inanimate objects like plastic dolls for the American tourists, who would crowd around a bed in one-room shacks to cheer on the pitiful women. Looking back, Red knew that in Brookwood he would always be considered a weisenheimer; he could never shake off the label from high school. He could be entirely selfish in the peacetime army, mindless marching to class, sharing the low humor of fellow recruits, most of whom had attended college and felt far above their surroundings. They were just passing through on their way to more school and careers in the civilian world, away from candy ass and Mickey Mouse. The sergeants all called him "Woody Woodpecker." The whores in Nuevo Laredo all rubbed his nose and his head, his carrot top buzzed down to a nub by GI electric clippers. Red put up with all of it. "You can eat any shit," his father told him, "as long as you've got a plan. The plan keeps you going. But it's like temple on Saturday. You've got to get up for it."

To this point in his life, no female had ever told Red she loved him except his mother. And she told his sisters many more times than she told him. Red had never told anyone that he loved her either; at least he had never meant it. He had said it several times to bribe dates into coming around. He knew he loved his father. But he wanted a girlfriend more than anything.

He had a sense that he was already in the movies. In San Antonio he was in costume; certainly he was playing a part. His Tufts fraternity brother had gotten Red onto the debutante list, and Red had no anxiety about showing up. He had been unwanted in almost every social gathering since he had been a little boy, at least by parents, and he was determined that, unwanted or not, everyone would remember him. "I'd invite you for the weekend, but I'm afraid you might come," a mother of a girl he dated in college once told him. Everyone laughed who heard the story, but Red knew she was telling the truth. His parents airmailed him a secondhand tuxedo almost in his size. The same package contained a salami and Vermont cheddar cheese. He wore the tuxedo to a country-club dance, a club old in the traditions of Texas; everyone knew the names of the last two men to die at the Alamo. Red was fortified with three Pearl brews, made by a local beer manufacturer that endeared itself to the military by giving tours and free samples to the young men of the air force and army, who considered the brewery the premier tourist attraction in town. The band was actually playing "The Yellow Rose of Texas" when Red was stopped at the door and asked his name by the young ladies in party dresses seated at a long, cloth-covered table. "*Captain* Stanley Singer," he said, snapping to attention. "That's actually *Dr.* Stanley Singer, OBGYN. Specialist in delicate ladies' problems."

"The only delicate problem we have, Doctor" — one of the girls smiled sweetly — "is how we're going to dance with all these handsome boys." Red was in his glory. No one knew him, and, because his name was on the approved list, no one would question his stories. In Texas that would be impolite. He wandered through the country club, first to the bar. "How ya doin'. I'm Dr. Singer from Boston. Tequila and tonic is what I prescribe, and it's what I drink because I'm flat out plain in love with San Antonio." Red knew that the secret of successful salesmen was protective coloration; flatter the natives in original ways, love their hometowns. But Red made two mistakes in his launch into San Antonio society. He assumed that he'd never see any of these people again. And he fell in love. He saw a girl in a ball gown with brown bouncy hair and a nose so small he felt like biting it off, a nose like a white Hershey's Kiss. He didn't ask anyone who she was. He went right over to where she stood, talking with friends, and asked, "Would you consider dancing with a doctor?" Brookwood girls would have said, "Sure, if you can point one out, wiseass." They would not have given away a genuine emotion. The girl with the smallest nose Red had ever seen just moved into his arms and they glided away.

"You dance real fine for a doctor" were the first words she said to him. "What kind of a doctor are you?" She was close, nothing held back, her body touching Red up and down.

"I mend broken hearts," he said. And she laughed, an unconscious laugh, not forced, not nervous.

"We hear names when we meet down here," she said. "I'm Lulu Patterson." She stepped away from Red, in time to the music, did a small curtsy that looked part of the dance and came back into his arms.

"I'm Stan Singer," he answered. "But everyone except my parents and my sisters when they're mad at me call me Red."

"Dr. Red," she said. "And what do you prescribe for broken hearts?"

He quickly kissed her cheek, a brief peck. "Take two of these and call me in the morning."

Lulu Patterson reacted as if she had been struck. "How rude, sir," she said, stopping dead in the middle of a beat. "You are a forward kind of boy."

"I apologize," Red blurted, rare for him. "A kiss on the cheek is polite up north."

"Well, they invented manners in the South." She turned on her heel and walked quickly back to her friends. Lulu Patterson was petite, a feisty five-foot-one. He loved the sound she made when she talked, her Texas accent adding to his feeling that he was part of a play or a movie where nothing was real and he could improvise his life, free from Boston, free from teachers. But Red did not pursue her. He wandered through the club getting drunker in self-defense and figuring how to get out of his doctor story. Then he got drunker than that figuring out how to get out of his army officer story. Finally he concluded that he had had enough to drink to say the hell with it. He wandered down into the club's locker room, and stared at trophy cases and the names of members who had won golf tournaments. "Bobby Prentis" was club champion four out of the last seven years. "I can whip Bobby Prentis's ass," Red said aloud to himself, "head to head."

"You couldn't carry his bag, Rusty," a voice said in back of him. "This locker room is off-limits to strangers, whether they're in monkey suits or jockstraps." The voice was a croak. It came from an ageless black man whose hair had turned white and who looked as if he had stepped from an ad for bourbon served only in private dining rooms. "You better get on upstairs now and dance with the ladies. This room is for golfers."

"What's your name?" Red asked him.

"My name is Toad," he said. "That's what they call me."

"And how do you know that I can't putt the eyes out of a snake?"

Toad laughed a laugh full of hee, hee, hee, as if that were the richest joke he had ever heard. "Because if you were a great golfer, I would have been warned a long time ago about you comin' here.

Nobody mentioned no rusty-top stranger. So I figure you gotta be a soldier boy."

"How do you figure that?"

"Your haircut," he said and continued laughing. "No one who didn't have to would look like that."

"Okay," Red said. "I'm a guest of Lulu Patterson's."

Toad nodded his head, understanding. "I can see that, now you say it," he said. "They always talkin' about her runnin' away from home. But then you figure that you don't just run away from Junior Patterson. Her daddy."

"Why are you telling me this, Toad? You could get fired."

"I'm telling you because you an outsider, you drunk and you a Yankee. All those people upstairs, the members from Alamo Heights, they don't give spit for us. No sense you gettin' in trouble."

Red picked up a sand wedge leaning against a locker. He took a few swings with it, got the feel.

"I wrong about one thing," Toad said, watching his swing. "Maybe you a golfer after all." Red shook the old man's hand and went back to the party.

"Shoot," said Lulu Patterson. "I'm not gonna be Fiesta Queen. I'm too young. I'm too short. We need a statuesque Fiesta Queen." All of her girlfriends gathered around her, assuring Lulu Patterson that she was just right for the biggest thing in San Antonio's year, Queen of Fiesta, a weeklong celebration each spring of the city's history. The highlight was the elaborate floats that ambled down the San Antonio River reflecting the glory of the past. The Fiesta Queen could be chosen from anywhere in the state, and for its young women the honor was tantamount to being First Lady, Miss America and Wonder Woman all rolled into one lucky package. The Fiesta Queen was made for life. No one in Texas ever forgot her. She would be almost as big as Doak Walker or Kyle Rote. Lulu had all the prerequisites for the title. Her daddy was oil-rich and a son of a bitch. Her momma served on five committees, and her family could verify that Comanches had stolen away her great-grandmother from a wagon train, a fact that was worth many social points anywhere in the Lone Star State. Lulu had graduated from St. Bridget's, where she wore the uniform proudly, navy skirt, white middy blouse, navy tie. She was a sophomore at U.T. in Austin, sorority absolutely, a Kappa Kappa who had slid down her share of drainpipes at her daddy's house to meet boys who had all played football at either University High, U.T. or Rice, the only really acceptable schools. So why did this redheaded doctor from the North make her strut the way Dekes at Texas made her strut before she learned better, before she learned that they were rude boys who couldn't wait to get back to the house and tell their brothers at Deke nothing but lies.

Red never held back on the edge of a crowd, never waited to be asked. He walked right up to her in front of all her friends. "Can we try again, Lulu Patterson?" he asked. "If you dance with me I'll give all these ladies free prescriptions."

"For what, smarty?" a blond charmer with a big drawl asked.

"For anything that'll make the hurt go away," Red said. Lulu hesitated, then bounced over to him just as the band broke into "Rock Around the Clock." Red could do that stuff. He did the dirty boogie, steps that San Antonio had never seen, with his own variations, using twirls and arm rollovers, turns, hand claps and jerky motions in two beats, up, down, twirls in intricate patterns that appeared to be one long movement. The young Texans all danced, but they couldn't keep up with Red and Lulu. Red was too drunk to worry that he had backed himself into a corner, and when Lulu said, "Come on and meet my folks," he repeated to her one of his father's favorite expressions, "In for a penny, in for a pound."

Junior Patterson had spent his life listening to no one, not his parents, his teachers, his wife or his children. He had a vision of what was right and he hewed to it, come hell or high water.

"Daddy," Lulu said, "I'd like you to meet Dr. Singer."

"You do look more like a singer than a doctor," said Junior, laughing at his own joke, which made the men around him laugh also because Junior Patterson owned much of the real estate around San Antonio and enough oil and natural gas acreage in the Panhandle to make things happen his way. "The military enriches our lives in this town," he said. "Protects us, spends money. Honorable profession."

"I'm not making a career of it, sir," Red said. "Just passing through. Doing my duty and on to civilian patients."

"A money-maker, right, boy?" Red was ready for an end to the interview before too much probing. The last question didn't need an answer, just a smile and a nod. Red slid away, and the music helped. He felt so right about one conclusion: people were sharper in the North; he could put one over on the world coming from Boston or New York. He found himself dancing alone as he glided away from Junior Patterson, a throbbing in his head that warned him he was crossing the line. But when Red Singer crossed the line at twenty-one years old he didn't really give a damn.

"He's a doctor like I'm Milton fucking Berle," said Junior Patterson to his friends. "Run a check on the sumbitch." Someone was always around to take a note on whatever Junior demanded.

"I don't think Daddy likes you," Lulu said to Red. "But don't worry. I've always really liked the boys of which he disapproves."

Red never heard anyone talk like that. "You want to come out with me for a ride?" he asked. "We'll do the rounds at the hospital. I'll teach you how to do a tracheotomy. Three fingers up from the sternal notch."

"You can't leave a party where they're discussin' the Fiesta Queen," Lulu said. "But I do want to see you again. I think it's forbidden fruit."

Red had always tried to make sexual points by being original. "How can you be so crude?" friends would ask him.

"I get my face slapped a lot," he would say. "But I get laid a lot, too." It was a lie so far. Red shook her hand and wiggled his third finger into the middle of her palm. This he knew from high school was a signal for "Do you want to do it?" Lulu just giggled as if it were a very odd way to shake hands. "I'll call you," he said. "Where?"

She took a ballpoint pen from the bartender and wrote her number on the back of his right hand. "Don't wash," she warned. "I'll be lost forever."

Red weaved out of the parking lot in the borrowed station wagon and maneuvered back to the base, his windshield wipers on to keep himself awake. The MP at the gate saluted him and waved him through, assuming anyone in a dinner jacket had to be an officer.

Saturday night in the barracks was the usual: a poker game in the latrine, a blanket over a foot locker for a table, several guys spit-shining their boots and their low quarters, several troopers reading on their bunks, two men drunk and disorderly, laughter, voices raised, some anger, some peacemaking, soldiers at rest. Red skipped into the barracks singing falsetto, imitating the black singer Billy Williams: "Got a date with an angel, got to meet her at seven. Got a date with an angel, and I'm on my way to heaven."

"We're trying to sleep, Singer," somebody groused.

"You sing like I fart," Richie Gwinn said. Richie was almond-colored, in Texas to play ball, to do his short army stint before joining the Dodgers spring training camp. They had hit the country bars along Commerce Street together many times, gotten drunk together on the tour of the Pearl Brewery. Red pitched batting practice to him on afternoons off at the Trinity College campus. Richie Gwinn had the bunk next to Red. He was reading *Sporting News,* looking for his name. Red hung his tuxedo carefully on a hanger and put it on the clothing bar in back of his bunk. "You think I can take a date to the Officers' Club, Richie? You think I can get away with anything?"

"You can't get away with shit," Richie said. "You want to throw change-ups to a weak hitter, the U.S. military? Bad move. They'll hit you out of the park. When you start feeling you can get away with anything, you're going to get your ass handed to you on a plate."

"You don't make the big leagues with a conservative attitude," Red snorted. He crawled into his bunk as carefully as he could, trying not to disturb the tightly made, tucked-in sheets and blanket. This made making it in the morning a cinch. Red had the wicked whirly-beds. The barracks spun around. His head throbbed as he forced himself to stare at one spot in the darkness until he could pass out.

"We don't have to go to the Officers' Club, Stanley," Lulu Patterson said to Red. "We can go to any of Daddy's real clubs. Honestly. Daddy says army pay just stinks. We can sign Daddy's name at the club."

"Where I come from," Red said, "the man pays for the woman. *He* entertains her, not the girl's Daddy. The guy. Besides, fifty cents a drink is almost free. Steak dinners for a buck and a half." Red had picked her up at her Alamo Heights house, a rambling imitation French château very close to its neighbors on both sides who also lived in large houses with relatively small lots, impeccably groomed and watered by Mexican crews for cheap money. No shortage of labor. Oil-rich in God's country was the thing to be.

"How come you were waiting outside for me?" Red asked. "I thought Southern girls kept their dates cooling their heels while their parents grilled them about their intentions and how they were going to make a living."

"Silly," Lulu said. "We're independent girls down here. And this isn't the South. It's the Southwest." They ordered whiskey sours, and Red didn't recognize one face in the Officers' Club.

Basic training had taught him a lesson: always look as if you belong everywhere and no one will ever question you. Walk swiftly with purpose, as if you have a destination, and act as if you know exactly what you're doing. It didn't hurt either if you carried a clipboard. Red was testing his theory. No one asked him for an ID at the door. Who would ever walk into an Officers' Club, bold as his polished buckle, who wasn't an officer? He had taken on several beers before he had picked up Lulu. But he had no doubt that he had the balls for anything. Brass balls, he thought. "No Brasso, no passo," as the Puerto Ricans used to say in basic training. Besides, there were the bets with Richie Gwinn and several others in the barracks. Worth the gamble. Red was in Texas for only two more months. Long enough to explain to Lulu if things really worked out between them, short enough to be gone forever if they didn't.

"Let's get down to it," Red said. "South, Southwest, North. What difference does it make? I want something strange out of life. I'm not intent to be just a lieutenant or just a doctor." Red was talking very fast, leaning across a table for two, his hands grasping and stroking one of hers. "I need a lot of companionship because I'm putting my boat into uncharted seas. Two more whiskey sours," he called to a waitress sliding by. "For a half a buck a pop," he thought, "take as much aboard as you can. Jesus." He caught himself. "*Sailing*! Why am I thinking sailing? I hate boats." He pressed on with Lulu, who had never refused a

drink in her life, going back to barbecues at age twelve when her
daddy let her shoot skeet after she had sipped two gin-fizz coolers
through a straw.

"I haven't got a clue what you-all are talking about," Lulu
said. "But I guess I like to hear it."

"We haven't kissed yet," Red said, after throwing down half
of his drink. "I believe that along with saving the lepers, curing
cancer and preventing babies, kissing within a half an hour of
meeting someone special is the way life should be."

"You talk like Rudolph Vaselino," Lulu said to him, "and you
look like, like some kind of weird lawn ornament." She immediately covered his hands with her free one. "I didn't mean anything bad," she said very soft. "I wouldn't be here unless I
thought that looks were only skin-deep. Don't you believe that,
too? I can kiss in the first half hour."

Red, believing that he floated in a bubble of immunity because
he came from Brookwood, Massachusetts, reached for Lulu Patterson, knocked over the Fiesta ware bowl of peanuts between
them, pulled her close in the Officers' Club of Fort Sam Houston
and put her delicious and unusual nose into his mouth and
sucked on it as if it were her tongue.

Before Red had a chance to switch to her tongue, two MP's
came up on either side of him. "ID please, sir," they both said,
polite as only MP's can be when they're leaning on you.

"Soldier," Red said, nodding to the MP on his left. "You're
insulting a lady."

"You boys are talking to a doctor," Lulu snapped, rubbing a
paper napkin over her nose.

"Can we see your ID, sir?" the MP's repeated. Red, thinking
that the jig might be up, went through the motions anyway,
indignantly patting his pockets for his lost wallet. "Jesus, I must
have left it in the OR," he said smiling reassurance at them.
"What's the trouble anyway, trooper, something missing in the
bandage count?"

"If you could get to your feet, sir, and accompany us. We don't
want any trouble, sir."

Red tried serious while gulping his whiskey sour between
pitches. "You're going to get yourself in a heap of trouble, son.
The surgeon general is going to fry your ass if I have to go back

to the hospital for that ID. How about I bring it by in the morning? Just let us finish in peace." Red was gripping his chair now, holding it as if it would suddenly orbit him out of the Officers' Club and into his safe bunk in the barracks. Red started to sweat as the MP's, no sweat at all, lifted him, still in his chair, and carried him out into the warm San Antonio night. They carried him right up to his commanding officer, who was leaning against the hood of a green Fleetwood Cadillac. Sitting on the hood of the car was Junior Patterson.

"Now, nothin' ethnic," Red's C.O. was saying to Junior. "We got a lot of his people at Fort Sam." Red was carried in his chair and set down right in front of the Cadillac with the biggest fins in the Southwest. Junior Patterson jumped down from his perch and yelled into Red's face, "My daughter, you prick of misery. My daughter. They're going to throw your sorry ass so far in the brig they'll have to feed you by slingshot."

Junior Patterson lunged at Red, but the MP's jumped between them. By this time Lulu was out of the club and grabbing onto her father's arm. "Now, honey," Junior said, "this poor excuse for a human bein' is a *private*. He's not a officer; he's not a doctor. He ain't nothin' but a piece of human waste."

"Daddy," Lulu pleaded, her little nose twitching adorably, "I don't care. He's strange."

His commanding officer looked down at Red. "What was the point, Singer?"

Red looked up at him. "Heads will roll for this, Captain," Red said. "Heads will roll."

The cameras rolled, and Red Singer, on the side of the set, watched and sucked it all up, remembering everything. It had taken him a year to get a job with a film company, and once he had a foot in the door even as a best boy, a gofer, no one was ever going to pry him out. After his discharge from the army, Red hitchhiked to Los Angeles with his mustered-out money and his plane ticket to Boston in his wallet. It took him two days and five rides, and on the last ride the truck driver dropped him downtown in Los Angeles. He had spent only $6 on hamburgers and Cokes. The phone call he made from a booth on the street was to the first listing under Synagogues in the Yellow Pages.

"Where can I live cheap?" he asked into the phone. "Where are there nice Jewish people, a safe neighborhood?" Whoever answered gave suggestions, and he bumbled his way, some rides, a lot of walking, to New Hampshire Avenue, one block west of Vermont, the old Jewish section of Los Angeles, located between Hollywood and downtown. If he cashed in his ticket he would have almost $700. He rented two rooms in a small apartment for $160 a month, furnished with the giveaways of years of pitiful tenants. The first meal Red ate in this new hometown was in a deli around the corner from his apartment. He sat at the counter and read *Variety* and the *Hollywood Reporter* cover to cover, knowing that the job for him would jump out of the ads.

"You don't get jobs out of advertisements, young man," the counterman with a New York accent said to him. "I did fifty-seven pictures, and I ought to know."

"I don't know anyone out here," Red said. "The only place I know is this deli."

"Well, you're a lucky boy," the counterman said. "You know why you came out here? I'll tell you why you came here. It's the three cherries."

"The three cherries?"

"Don't repeat everything I say. Where did you grow up? A slot machine. Apples, oranges, cherries. The three cherries come up, you get the jackpot. That's why everyone comes out here. When I came out I hung around near the lots. Paramount especially. I was a busboy where the producers and directors came for lunch and dinner, the Brown Derby in Hollywood. You noodge people. Keep noodging. Sooner or later you get a job. You don't want to walk here. First thing, you get a car. You're dead as Kelsey's nuts in Los Angeles without a car. Then you get in your car and you hang out where there are people."

"I don't have a sweater tight enough for Schwab's drugstore," Red said.

"A wise guy," said the counterman. "This is good."

Red got off his stool, leaving the trade papers behind. "Thanks for the advice. I'll be back," he said. "I appreciate it."

"By the way," the counterman said, "you a character actor? Like me?"

"Are you kidding?" Red said. "When I'm a producer, I'll hire you. Then you can tell everyone that you've been in eighty pictures."

"Above the line," the counterman mumbled to himself, "a true wise guy."

Red began noodging people immediately. He put $100 down on a candy-apple-painted, secondhand Austin-Healey Sprite and drove it away, owing the balance of $1,500 to a local savings and loan that seemed as if it would loan money to a kangaroo if the animal would provide a pen out of its pouch. In the next weeks Red caddied at private country clubs and noodged his employers, if they were in the movie business, for jobs. He did the same waiting on tables, parking cars and selling ice cream from a truck at the beach, losing most of the jobs for being too pushy or mouthing off to his boss. Noodging people daily. Red soon discovered softball and marijuana.

There were no dating bars yet in the early 1960s. The pill and the sexual revolution were really several years away. Out-of-work actors and actresses hung out where food was cheap and conversation plentiful: coffeehouses, bongo parties in Venice in fall-down apartments near the beach, softball games at public parks in Hollywood. If Red were driving around Brooklyn in his candy-apple-painted Sprite with the top down, his red hair only slightly contrasting with the paint, people would ask, "Who's that asshole?" In West Los Angeles he was building a character. Everyone who saw Red remembered him. They wondered briefly what he was about. But they remembered. This quality could get him by any receptionist, just as his father years ago could get into any potential customer's office by giving all the secretaries Tootsie Rolls. Several waiters he worked with at one restaurant, all aspiring actors, told Red about a softball game they played on Saturday mornings at a Hollywood playground. "You can stay in bed and watch cartoons and get depressed about your life," they told him, "or come over and get depressed with all of us."

"I'm a great ballplayer," Red gushed, and they insisted he come, hoping he'd fall on his ass. That Saturday on the playground's dirt base paths, green wooden bleachers, concrete bubblers and sunshine, Red hit a triple and a home run in his first two at-bats. After that, they gave him the ball and he was the pitcher, mixing super speed with eephus balls that took forever to come down and curves that broke in or out. The players were young men and women in their late teens and early twenties, some married, most not. They were all new arrivals to Los Angeles, seeking each other for warmth and approval while they beat on the gates of the movie studios. Red was the ugliest of them all, not the most profane. That title belonged to several of the New Yorkers, Brooklyn-born, to whom the words "fuck" and "cocksucker" were as normal as "thank you" and "please" were to other human beings. But they all got used to each other, and they all shared poverty. Games ended after seven innings, and they sat in a circle of small groups talking about their lives, their talents, their script ideas, their frustrations. Someone always had joints, and someone always brought music: guitars, bongos, occasionally even a clarinet or a sax. "Look, Stanley," one of the New York guys said to him, a boy from Flatbush Avenue with looks like Tony Curtis and tattoos on his biceps, one of a Corvette, the other of Popeye. "You're never going to act because of your complexion and your nose. Let's face it, right? What you're gonna be is an agent. Then you can get all of us jobs, right? Take ten percent; what do we give a shit? You're made to be an agent." Taking tokes around the circle, drinking Frascati sold in baskets marked "Special for ninety-nine cents," flamenco playing softly on a small guitar, it sounded great to Red Singer. For weeks thereafter he made the rounds of agents' offices. No matter what he tried, everyone was out of town, in meetings, not hiring or too busy. One agent finally saw him after Red waited in a hall outside the men's room until the man emerged from his office. Red followed him in and took an adjoining urinal, giving his pitch in a hurry. The agent turned his head. "I'll give you the best piece of advice you're ever going to get in your life," he said in a hoarse voice, hoarse presumably from making so many deals for his clients. "This business is a killer. Go back to wherever you came from and go into something real, a bank, a dry-goods store. Your generation doesn't want to bust its ass. Use your brain. This is a killer. I don't have time to piss, much less let you in the door." A week later, wearing a Superman costume he had rented on Hollywood Boulevard, Red rolled over the top of a booth at Scandia and landed almost in the lap of Richard Richards, the dean of agents in Los Angeles, a man who always wore an ascot, suits cut in the English manner and shoes that tied rather than slipped on. Richards was having lunch with a client, a homosexual leading man, a tough guy who liked to chew wooden matchsticks on camera and throw baddies through swinging saloon doors onto dirt streets. "I just wanted to warn you," Red announced. "Don't order the chili." Since Red had run into the restaurant already costumed and dived immediately over the banquette, waiters, car parkers and maître d's were hot on his trail.

"Scandia does not serve chili, young man," the agent said calmly, the way he imagined an Englishman would react.

"That's why you need me," Red said triumphantly. "To provide what you're missing in life, to be your outside guide."

"Right," the agent said. "*Outside*."

"Wait a minute, Dick," the star said. "This kid is a hot shit. What's under the costume, kid?"

"A man of steel, cowboy," Red answered.

"Have some gravlax, kid," the star said. And when the stars spoke in those days, the agents listened, even if they did wear ascots and shoes that tied.

Red started in the mail room at the Richards Agency for $100 a week, plus any tips he received from clients to whom he delivered contracts, flowers, love letters or gifts from fans that came to the office. "I'm giving you a job with reservations," Richard Richards said to him. "I'm a dignified man in a business that is anything but. Dignity is the hallmark of the Richards Agency. I want my young agents to dress as if they went to the Wharton School at the University of Pennsylvania. Tweeds and you do the numbers, tweeds and you do the numbers. That's the ticket." Red dressed in a tweed jacket over blue jeans and motorcycle boots. Sometimes he wore a red ascot. He moved to an apartment off Laurel Canyon, a place for lovers of Hollywood and jazz, of Jack Kerouac and beatnik poets, and he knew he had found his home.

CHAPTER TWELVE

O

Duke's Game

Francis Hennessey would forever be "Duke," but, by age twenty-one, no one knew or remembered that it had been a nickname given him by his father, a chip off the old "Big Duke" block. After graduation from MIT with his degree in civil engineering and a .365 senior-year batting average, Duke moved home to his parents' house. Big Duke always faked punches at his son whenever he came home from work, affectionately swinging at his boy, expecting Little Duke to block, cover up, counterpunch. It was their ritual from the time young Francis could learn to hold up his little hands. They went to see *On the Waterfront* together the week Duke had moved home. After they put the car away they sparred on the front lawn. "I coulda been a contenda," his father muttered, taking roundhouse swings at Duke's head and missing by a mile. They had a beer together, sitting in the backyard on aluminum folding chairs. "The president of The Edison went to MIT," Big Duke said. "All the years I worked it seemed like a magic thing to me, something on the moon. When I'd come watch you play ball there, talk to your coach, they seemed like kids from anyplace, the neighborhood, you know? Not from the moon. I had hoped you'd invent rockets, or even be head of The Edison yourself someday."

"I want to build things, Dad. Skyscrapers, cities."

"That sounds like money to me. Not respect. The world looks up to inventors and scientists. They get everyone's respect."

"Everybody is going to sit up and take notice of what I build. Even you, Dad. I'm going to build you and Mom the greatest house you could think of."

His father tilted back on his aluminum chair and looked at the stars. "This is the house I like, kid. It's all paid for."

There is that inevitable time in the relationship between fathers and sons when the son knows that the father may be a fool. The two can go at it hammer and tongs, years of frustration on both sides erupting, or it can be a quiet revolution, a sadness that gets no one anything or anywhere. "Time for me to turn in, Dad." Little Duke crushed his beer can in his hand and took it into the house. His father stayed in his seat. He, too, crushed his beer can flat and just let it sit on his lap. "Don't get married," he thought. "When you're fucking twenty-one years old. Your whole life ahead of you."

When Duke and the former Rita Cronin burst out of St. Ignatius Church into the daylight after their wedding, Duke felt better than at any time in his life, including the time he scored against Waltham in his freshman year in high school. He felt clean. Duke was good at making decisions, and once they were made he never looked back. He wanted his home base secure. He knew the value of a catcher who ran the ball club, the rock from which everyone could take strength. You don't go from MIT to the pros, Duke knew. So you found a cure for cancer, or a shortcut to the planets, or you made a shit-pile of money. He had made up his mind to pull the lever on multiple-choice-question three. He still had a crew cut on his wedding day, which was a Saturday in August, a date chosen by Rita and her mother primarily so that Rita would look tan in her wedding pictures. The date also ensured that many of Duke's friends would be off on jobs or trips or in the service by the middle of that summer. He didn't care about that. There was so much family on both sides of the aisle, they alone would fill St. Ignatius. His father was Duke's best man, and the ushers were assorted brothers-in-law and fellow ballplayers over the years from MIT and high school who force-fed Duke a six-pack of Carling's Black Label before the ceremony and kidded him about birth control and being gentle and not forgetting them if he needed any help. There was a High Mass and communion for all who could take it, and one of Rita's sisters sang "Ave Maria" and Rita had eight bridesmaids all tanned themselves, who, when they came down the aisle, were said to look like something right out of the Ice Capades. Waiting for Rita to come to the altar, Duke's gaze swept the church and lit on a stained-glass window he must have seen a million times when he was growing up. It was Christ punishing the moneylenders, a vengeful Christ, and he wondered briefly about the riches he wanted to pursue, then shook his head as he used to when he wanted to concentrate on the pitch. He had nothing to feel guilty about. He never shanked a golf shot. He was only protecting his friends or whoever had hit the car. Protecting your friends was honorable.

Duke was determined to hit the deck running. He was exempt from service, 4F due to old football injuries. Now he had marriage out of the way, a job with a construction firm at $7,000 a year, an apartment in Somerville near Harvard Square and a tan, lovely wife who was taught by her mother and grandmother to knit and mend socks and cook the foods that his own mother had been taught to cook. They had received a papal blessing direct from Rome. Father Cornelius X. Looney had taken them aside after the wedding rehearsal and told them the news. It had been arranged by Rita's father, Joe Cronin, who ran Brookwood Ice and Coal Company and was a big giver in the parish. "I'll keep it for you," Father Looney had said, tapping the cylinder that held the blessing, a container much like those used to mail calendars. "You come see me after the blessed honeymoon. Lucky children of Christ to be going to Bermuda. Lots of God's sun in Bermuda, God's water. Think of that, children, and love God." They promised, and Rita squeezed Duke's hand. They were so lucky. The reception was held at the Château Grande, and the horns on most of the cars blew the entire way from the church. All the police on special detail at the intersections held traffic for the Hennessey/Cronin guests. Didn't they remember Duke Hennessey? All-scholastic in two sports and a hero who had saved a man's life? The Château Grande was out on the main road to Worcester, a highway eventually leading to New York and lined with fried-chicken take-out stands, miniature golf courses, bowladromes and motels. The Château had fake battlements, a moat (a dry trench dug around the building filled with trash that blew in from the highway), a drawbridge that could never be raised and a staff dressed like British beefeaters. The Château existed as a function center servicing conventions, meetings, parties and weddings. Everyone said that Joey Cronin knew how to do things right.

Duke hated to dance. He only cared to be the center of attention when there was a crowd in the stands and they were anonymous, blank color to him, group noise. But he danced with Rita and told her she looked beautiful. And he danced briefly with his mother and Mrs. Cronin, who had so much lacquer sprayed on her hair that you could have used it as a breadboard without cracking the surface. She smelled like a refinished piece of furniture. But she kept her distance like a proper mother-in-law, and Duke's father cut in after a short time, giving his son a wink, letting him know that he understood. Duke couldn't wait to get away from the reception. He saw two of his aunts complaining about their table location and his sister-in-law trying to sing "Mother at Your Feet I'm Kneeling" when the band went on break. His sister-in-law wanted to be a nun, but she had sipped enough New York State champagne to listen to people who told her that her rendition of "Ave Maria" at the ceremony showed more talent than Kate Smith singing "When the Moon Comes Over the Mountain."

When the time came, there were dressing rooms off the main ballroom where Rita and Duke went with their various bridesmaids and ushers to change into traveling clothes. A hot rod from high school days, a chopped and channeled Ford Deuce Coupe owned by one of Duke's MIT buddies, waited outside to take them to the airport. "If any one of you guys," Duke threatened, "tries fucking around in any way, you're dead. This day doesn't need any shit from you." He knew MIT pranks. Nothing happened until the hot rod was started. Red-and-yellow-colored smoke billowed from beneath the hood. Whistles and duck calls soon followed; then came the noise of booming cannons. A tape recorder had been connected to the electrical system and smoke bombs to the accelerator linkage. Easy stuff. Duke smiled and hugged Rita. He had gotten off easily, and he slowly rolled out of the Château Grande's parking lot amidst showers of rice and paper rose petals, unaware of the banner that had just spilled out over the car's trunk that read, "When better honeymoons are made, Tech men will make them." Rita pushed on the horn, which went, "Arrooooghhh, arrooooghhh," and they were off into life, never suspecting that all of their travel clothes in both their suitcases had been padlocked together with dozens of small combination locks.

When Duke and Rita returned from Bermuda, they moved into an apartment in Somerville near the trolley tracks that ran from Cambridge and eventually into Boston. They paid $125 a month for a two-bedroom in a building that contained mostly elderly people with a scattering of graduate students who could not or would not get school housing. Duke had a job as an office engineer for Tucci Construction, a builder of large projects like school dormitories, office buildings and hospitals. Joe Tucci had been in the army with Big Duke Hennessey, had seen him fight. It was easy to give his son summer jobs when Little Duke was in college, jobs swinging a pick, laying tar, eventually surveying, fixing locations, laying out corners, checking elevations for the pouring of concrete, making sure walls were true. "This is not a favor, Young Hennessey," Tucci told him. "You doing me a favor. Whenever I can hire talent, I can build the best buildings inna world. You can go far with Tucci, Francis," he said. "But you gotta know I got sons. You know what I mean?" Duke started at $7,000 a year in a time when $10,000 seemed a fortune. New lawyers started in the biggest law firms at $6,500; bank trainees began at $130 a week; hospital interns basically starved. Duke would come home from work and grab a beer from the icebox, just like his father. "Baby," he would say to Rita, who usually spent the day with her mother, "we got a leg up on everybody. When I went to college I knew I couldn't compete as a pure scientist so I had to look down the line. What could I do? Now I know that grad school is a waste of my time. Did Tucci go to grad school? He probably finished the seventh grade. Do I need the six-month army? Or three years getting seasick on some tub? We got a head start on all my friends."

"We got each other," Rita said. "And we got apple pie tonight."

"You made apple pie?"

"Me and mother, this afta."

Duke hugged his wife. "Don't you love fuckin' whenever we want?"

"*Francis.*"

"Marriage is great," Duke said. "Fuckin' before the apple pie, after the apple pie. During it if we want."

"Francis," Rita said, softer this time. Smiling.

One night during dinner several weeks later Duke said, "I've got to go out for a while."

"Where to?" Rita asked.

"Those Tucci boys. The old man's great, but the kids are a pain in the ass. Time we started looking around for a stake." Duke had been working on a project in Cambridge, an addition to a dormitory at Harvard Law School. Every day at lunchtime, which began exactly at noon according to union rules, he and his crew would walk to a sub shop to take out sandwiches and Cokes. The guys with lunch boxes would go with them, buying drinks, candy bars, chips. Then they'd go to a small park when it was sunny, eat, swap stories, watch the girls go by. Every day for two weeks Duke had noticed a rooming house next to the sub shop with a For Sale sign stuck onto the glass of the front door. Walking by after work, he saw a young man carrying books, heading into the house. "You live here?" Duke asked.

"This is Paradise Acres" was the response. "Who wouldn't love it?"

"How many tenants?"

"I'm not really sure. Seems like a lot of people. I go to law school, but you can ask Mrs. Scanlan. She owns it, lives first floor."

"You want a room, we're all full," the woman told Duke. "I have steadies, law students. No trouble. No rough stuff. No beer swilling."

"How much do you want for the building?" Duke asked. "I was a student. I'm just married a few months. We're going to have a fine Catholic family, and my name is Francis Hennessey."

"You look like a rough carpenter to me."

"We all have to start somewhere, Mrs. Scanlan."

She rubbed her chin, which had several long white hairs jutting out from it. "When I talk money, I have a drop of tea," she said.

"Sugar and milk." Duke worked his blarney on Mrs. Scanlan, and a day later he worked sports stories at MIT on a banker in Harvard Square, the first banker he had ever met in his life.

"How come you went to MIT, Francis?" the banker, Mr. Wallace, asked him. "I mean it's not odd you went there. But it's odd you're not blowing up things in a laboratory, you know what I mean?"

"The truth, Mr. Wallace, is that my father's boss went there. It's all I heard when I grew up. And I was good in math and sciences."

"Will you be good enough in math to make payments on time? You know you have no money, no collateral. You tell me your father doesn't know about this and would not be in a position to guarantee any note of yours. You tell me you had a tryout with the White Sox?"

"I probably could have played, maybe Double-A."

The banker waited for more.

Duke stood up and paced. He could never sit still, and he sensed the banker was on his side. If he could nudge him over the line. "I got married," Duke said. "Made a decision to get on with it. I couldn't be Yogi or Roy Campanella so why prolong the agony; why keep putting on the pads to play Double-A ball?"

"What's your hurry?"

"My hurry, Mr. Wallace, is years of being on scholarship, being Irish and poor. Two of those things I can change. Let me tell you, it's a great advantage to be Irish and smart."

"Sit down, Francis," Mr. Wallace said, "and I'll let you in on a few facts of life."

The banker loaned Duke $27,000, and Duke bought Mrs. Scanlan's rooming house for $27,500, with five hundred of his own money, plus a few dollars in fees to a friend's father who was an attorney. What Duke didn't figure was the work. The rent from the roomers would cover interest, amortization and taxes and, if he were right, the Harvard Square area real estate would boom in the years ahead. Duke figured that more and more in America, education was becoming a right, not a privilege, and housing for more and more students would become a significant need. Mrs. Scanlan had provided sheets and towels to the tenants. She took out the trash; she mediated arguments, dispensed advice to the lovelorn. She made gallons of tea. The Sunday after the passing of papers on the house, Duke took his parents and Rita out for a ride in his father's green Dodge, leaving his own VW bug in his folks' driveway. Every Sunday after church they alternated dinner at the respective in-laws. "I've got a surprise for you," Duke said. When they got to the boardinghouse he stopped the car, got everyone out and stood his family on the sidewalk, indicating the house as if it were the Lincoln Memorial. "This is it," he announced.

"This is what?" said his father.

"This is the beginning of my empire," Duke said proudly. At that moment the front door almost burst off its hinges as three young men in fits of laughter all tried to get onto the porch at the same time.

Duke went bananas. "Hey," he yelled, running up the front stairs. "What the hell you guys think you're doin'? Front doors cost a fortune." The young men stopped short, looking in surprise at Duke. "You don't live here," one of them said.

"I own this place, asshole," yelled Duke, then turned and shrugged at his family. "Sorry, Ma."

Duke thought he knew what marriage meant from watching his own parents. It meant bringing home a paycheck, teaching your kids to box and play ball, teasing your wife and making your family the center of your life. His father worked for The Edison, talked about and admired his boss, went with buddies to ball games, to bowl. Once in a blue moon he took his wife to a movie. Sundays they went to church. There was one bathroom in the house; they all took turns and respected one another. What Duke never knew about and could never bring himself to think about was the possibility of his parents having sex. He couldn't think of his mother ever doing it. In his own case, Duke thought he had an obligation to make love to Rita every night. Until he bought his rooming house, that's exactly what they did. The Hennesseys had a routine the way every married couple has a routine. Duke would tickle Rita's belly with his fingertips. Then he'd play with her pubic hair and move his fingers to her inner thighs. She would shiver with anticipation and honesty, a good person but with a secret wish that there was a spotlight that would illuminate only Duke's penis. She loved to see it when it was stiff, the uncircumcised glans looking like statues she had studied in ancient art courses at Sacred Heart, the nuns talking about "the sanctity of the marble." She thought then about the uncircumcised penises. In the mornings she learned she could peek beneath the covers and see him hard, always before he woke up. Was he dreaming about her? She stopped his hands one night after he bought the boardinghouse. "No," she said.

"No?" he mumbled, intent on his tickling her.

"No," Rita said. "I'm being a maid. My mother's a maid for you, too. We're going over to the house, take out other people's trash, clean up, take the calls from plumbers, people you owe money. You've got a job like a regular guy. Why can't you just stay on your day job?"

Duke rolled over on his back and stared at the ceiling. He was already starting to put on weight, no longer in a sports training season, and he was snacking between meals with both hands: peanuts, Mounds bars, Jordan Almonds.

"I'm a worker, Rita," he said quietly. "I want things for us our families never had."

"But I'm bein' a maid in two houses."

"You're my wife," he said, grabbing again for the inside of her thighs. "Who do you think's going to be on easy street when these things start to pay off? You. You're going to have maids for every room of the house. This is for you, baby." All Rita knew was that all Duke talked about was the goddamn boardinghouse, and she liked it a lot better when she was cheering for him in high school football. She let him in finally, loving to have her man and wondering if it were any kind of sin not to tell him she was pregnant. She couldn't tell him when all he was interested in was the goddamn boardinghouse.

All through the winter and the spring Duke collected rents, did the bookkeeping, provided maintenance. He painted every pipe in the basement shiny black so they would be uniform and show no rust. Every cent he collected he brought over to his banker.

"Mr. Wallace," Duke said one day in late May, "I met every payment on time, right?"

"That's why I took a chance on you, Francis. I knew you'd be reliable."

"Then why is it ruining my life? We're having a baby. I'm working ten hours a day on the construction, and at night I'm at the Cambridge house fixing up, repairing things, painting. I get calls at home at all hours, and a week ago I had to buy a hot-water heater that I couldn't afford. If it ever needs a new roof I'll have to go into bankruptcy."

The banker looked at the big young man whose face, even with its bulk, retained the look of the baby, a merry face, expressive. "I was going to be president of Chase Manhattan," Wallace said to Hennessey. "That was my ambition when I was young. I worked long hours, and it threatened my family life, my family that I loved. So I'm a vice president here, senior loan officer and the most I can lend anyone for anything is three hundred thousand dollars. You feel like what you've bitten off is ruining your life? You have to decide how badly you want something and what you're willing to do for it."

Duke stood up and stuck out his hand. "You're a wonderful guy, Mr. Wallace."

The banker took Duke's hand. "Call me Bill, Mr. Hennessey," he said. "From now on, call me Bill."

It seemed to Duke that he was working harder than when he was at MIT but without the saving grace of the fraternity. Once in a while he would take off early Sunday morning to play touch football in the MIT League against other fraternities. It gave him the opportunity to be physical, to take out his frustrations by banging around other young men who only had to get studying out of their systems, not business and marriage and fatherhood. After the games he would check the rooming house, knocking on each door, asking if everything were in order, enough hot water, enough heat, adequate pest control, the personal touch. He wanted his rooming house to have the hallmarks of quality and service, even if it killed him. One Sunday afternoon, when Duke arrived home after having been gone all day, Rita was sitting in the kitchen with her mother. "Francis," Rita said. "Do you know what love really means?"

"For Christ sakes, Rita," Duke said. "Sorry, Mrs. Cronin, but I got to say this is private."

"You want me to leave?"

"Look," he said. "I'm exhausted. It's Sunday. I haven't looked at a paper, watched the TV, gone to a movie in weeks."

"And what have *I* done, gone to the prom every night?" Rita asked.

Mrs. Cronin had flashes of herself twenty-five years earlier. Her mother would stick her two cents in, going at it hammer and tongs when she and Mr. Cronin argued. But they all lived in the same house in Dorchester. Three generations. She was a modern woman. "A nice visit, darling," she said to her daughter. "You two kiss and make up. Marriage can be a trial, but Mother of God, it's better than anything else He's given us." When they were alone Duke and Rita glared at each other, Duke draining a Budweiser in three long swallows. He stared at her tummy, believing he could see it stretching the material of her dress. That was his baby in there, his white hope. Rita lit a cigarette. Without saying anything Duke got down on the floor of the living room in the football lineman's three-point stance, balanced to move at the snap of the ball. "What are you doing?" Rita started to say. She didn't have a chance to finish as her husband raced across the floor and encircled her with his arms and tenderly pushed her back until she was lying on the couch. "You remember all the times I drove you by the white house on the hill?"

"Yeah. Careful, don't push my stomach."

"We're going to raise our babies there. You'll be in clover, honey. That's why I'm busting my nuts."

"I just want you around more. I love you, you big moose."

"It's going to be worth it," he promised. "Here. Just slip these things off."

"I'm glad you're apologizing," she said. "Be careful of the baby. Don't push too hard. Just hold me, Francis." Duke tried to blot out thoughts of the rooming house, how paint was flaking off the ceilings, how one toilet in one apartment kept backing up, how to get rid of a tenant who kept smoking in bed.

Duke walked into the Shamrock Bar after work on the day the Russians first orbited a man in space, April 12, 1961. He knew that several of his MIT friends and at least two professors who taught him were involved in the U.S. space effort. The Shamrock was a workingman's bar on the Cambridge-Somerville line. Most of the guys on the big construction jobs in and around Harvard Square dropped in after work for gossip, a few pops, listened to the jukebox, went home or stayed to play some games, get half shit-faced, the usual week. Duke as a site manager always wanted to get down in the dirt with his workers. He thought that benevolent dictatorship was the best form of government, and he believed he could get much more out of his troops with sugar than vinegar. So far, his boss had told him, his crews were the most productive of any in the company's history. They were on time, on line, with fewer makeovers or teardowns. The teams had loyalty to the company and to Duke. After a year of ownership, the boardinghouse was slightly better than breaking even. Duke had a small slush fund for contingencies that would pay for the inevitable broken window or busted sink. In addition he had a tenant, a law student from Pakistan who, in exchange for reduced rent, did the odd chores formerly done by Duke himself or by Rita. Hennessey was the father of a little girl, Shauna, who was so small Duke couldn't believe she was real. He told everyone she was a doll he had won knocking cups off the ears of the Walking Charlie game at Paragon Park at the beach amusements. If it wasn't for the fucking Russians he would be a happy man. "Black Label, Jerry," he said to the bartender, meaning a Carling's beer, not the Scotch whiskey. "Fucking Russians, ya know?"

"Hey, we got Black Label, right? It ain't all bad and don't worry, Jack's tough. PT 109, right? He ain't gonna take any shit." The guys at the bar agreed, raising their glasses, a quick toast to Kennedy. Duke's men gathered round him, standing at the bar, swapping stories of the day. "It's great," Duke thought. "These guys wouldn't know MIT from a hole in the ground. But they're mine." The news flashed black and white from the television above the stacked whiskey bottles, the sound on low until the sports came on. "Turn it up," said Duke. The picture of the cosmonaut Yuri Gagarin faded into the reporting from Israel of the trial of Adolf Eichmann, the Nazi plucked from hiding in Argentina and brought to justice in the Jewish state. The coverage showed Eichmann in the courtroom, surrounded by the specially built glass cage. No one could get at him; he couldn't get at anyone. A group of men stood near Duke and his crew. They were painters, dressed in spattered overalls, spattered hats and work boots stained white by their job. They were all drunk and only on their first drinks. Duke was thinking about Rosenberg and Red Singer as he watched Eichmann. He was also thinking MIT thoughts, processes that he was trained to absorb: How do the Nazis ever destroy six million people? What were the logistics? Tough to conceive of six million particles of matter much less six million souls, flesh and blood.

"How many of the fuckers did he miss?" came the voice of a painter, loud, over everyone else's. Duke again thought of Rosenberg and Singer. But he sipped his beer and said nothing. The coverage of Eichmann droned on, and the painter continued to his friends, who nodded, laughed. "Kaminsky, that Jew prick, should see this," he said. "Still owes us for that job up in Revere; the world would be better off." There was a jukebox, a big old Seeburg next to the door of the bar. Duke walked over to it, got to one side and pushed it along until it completely covered the entrance. "Hey," yelled the bartender. Duke walked over to the group of painters. "I'm a Jew, you cocksucker," he said, giving the man time to prepare himself. Then Duke hit him in the throat with his fist, missing the point of his chin, but probably doing even more damage. The painter dropped to the floor as if his windpipe had been snapped in two. Duke backed up, standing against the jukebox, waiting for the others. His construction crew pushed and pulled with the painters for a few strained minutes. Then the bar fell silent. An old electrician who had worked for the Tucci brothers on their construction jobs for years said, over the silence, "You're no Jew, Hennessey." Duke said nothing. But he tried to push the jukebox back into place and couldn't budge it. Several of the men moved it back against the wall, one of them putting in a quarter for three songs, the set starting with "Big Bad John" by Jimmy Dean.

Later that night, after celebrating with Rita and relishing the lamb chops he now thought he could afford, Duke put in a call to Red Singer in California. By that time he had consumed the better part of a six-pack of Carling's.

"The star's residence," Red answered in his familiar nasal bite.

"I saved your life today, Stanley," Duke said.

"Hey, Little Duke," Red said, full of cheer over the miles. "How did you do that?"

"I killed a shit-eating dog." It was an old joke between them, and they bantered a while, catching up on their lives. They hung up promising to keep in touch. "Where did that come from?" Rita asked. "So out of the blue."

"I needed to hear his voice," Duke said, and he went to stare down at his child in sleep. (When he walked in the door Rita said, "I was worried about you. I've already put Shauna down, so you missed her. And Mr. Wallace has called you twice, says you should call him at home.")

"Oh, Jesus," Duke said. "He's going to call the loan. Why would he call the loan?"

He called his banker, feeling that he was being punished for losing control. He had to learn to grow up. "Mr. Wallace," Duke said. "Bill. You called me?"

"Are you sitting down?" the banker said.

"Give it to me between the eyes. I can take it."

"You referred a call to me from Harvard? Building and Grounds Department? You said, 'Fishing expedition, speak to them for me,' right? Well, they called. And guess what? They want your rooming house. They want to buy it for Harvard Housing. Thirty-nine thousand dollars." Duke had paid twenty-seven, or rather the bank had advanced twenty-seven.

"Are you there, Francis?"

Duke thought for several moments. "I guess I'm going to be looking for a new rooming house," he said. "Where has this been all my life?"

CHAPTER THIRTEEN

O

Freddie's Game

Freddie Temple was smoking what he and his friends called a stogie, a fifty-cent Leavitt & Peirce cake-box cigar. He was in Paris sitting on a sidewalk in Pigalle at two o'clock in the morning waiting for friends to emerge from a whorehouse. Freddie had not gone into the whorehouse because he thought he was in love with a girl thousands of miles away in a summer camp in Fairlee, Vermont. Marley Damon was a perfect girl for Freddie. Did it sound silly that she was blond and tall and played field hockey and sailed and her parents belonged to the same clubs as Freddie's parents? Freddie thought it was just right because whoever was going to be his wife should complement him perfectly. She should not be someone to whom he had to explain everything new, explain everyone old. He would have too much to do in his career to take the time to familiarize a wife with his life of the last twenty-one years. He wanted to go into the whorehouse. But he forced himself to be virtuous, thinking of classic jazz records, summoning up theme songs to make the time go by. An elderly man stopped next to Freddie. He was dressed in a well-tailored gray suit with a tattersall vest and carried a walking stick. "You are ill, Monsieur?" he asked.

"I'm American," Freddie answered. "Je suis américain."

"Ah, that explains it," the dapper man said in careful English. "You are also perhaps, pissed?"

Freddie laughed at him, knowing that pissed is what the English called drunk. He was pissed. "I'm waiting for mes amis," he said, pointing in back of himself to the apartment building.

"Ah," the older man smiled. "You are pissed, and pouf as well?"

It's an old fairy, thought Freddie. And he looked away, sucking on his stogie. The man lingered, and Freddie felt he had to justify his manhood. The French could understand love.

"If you want to know," he said slowly, thinking like so many Americans that foreigners could understand English if one spoke slowly, "I have a girl at home. We're almost engaged, engagez-vous, comprendez? Fides, compris? I couldn't go in there and be true to her."

The man looked down sadly. "I am married over fifty years," he said. "Every week since I am married," he paused, "except for the war, I go to such places." He indicated the whorehouse. "A man needs the companionship of women outside of the home. It's one of the secrets of a happy life." He tapped the brim of his hat the way Maurice Chevalier might have and proceeded, with a light step, to enter the building behind them. Freddie smoked his stogie down to a butt and sat thinking for several minutes. He had felt wonderfully romantic the entire evening and was looking forward to onion soup gratiné and red wine at Les Halles with his friends as the sun came up. Would Hemingway be sitting on a curb while his friends were with women? he asked himself. Would Hemingway be faithful to a girl thousands of miles away? Would Dizzy Gillespie? Freddie flipped the cigar butt into the street and, also with a light step, entered the building behind him.

A year later, Freddie was still in Europe, this time in the uniform of an ensign of the United States Navy. He had reported after his return from the grand summer tour to Officer Candidate School in Newport, Rhode Island, for, as he wrote his father, "four months of hell and harassment." Because he had gone to Harvard and the navy screening turned up the possibility that he might have a brain, his first assignment was to the School of Naval Justice, again in Newport, where he was trained to be an assistant legal officer. Everyone who ever taught or commanded Freddie in the navy thought, "By God. He should be the poster boy for the service." Because he looked the part and never screwed up, Temple got the plum assignments without resentment from others. He was nice to people. And he looked so damn good. His first assignment after school and his commission as ensign was to the pride of the fleet, the aircraft carrier *Constellation,* for her maiden voyage to the Mediterranean. The *Constellation* was a heavy combatant, assigned to the Sixth Fleet, and the showboat of that duty area. The ship was the jumping-off place for officers who were to become admirals. It was for high navy rollers who knew nothing about the sea, a place where they served a brief time before being kicked upstairs. The only officers on board who had any continuity were the ensigns and the jg's, junior grade people.

"What am I doing here, Mr. Temple?" a benevolent captain who had come aboard off Gibraltar said when Freddie was delegated to show him around the ship.

"You're being effective, sir, until such time as you become Chief of Naval Operations."

"I like that, son," laughed the captain. "Men not getting too horny at sea, are they?"

About half his time in the service, Freddie was deployed with the ship in the seas of the Med: the Aegean and the Marmara. Whenever the *Constellation* was in port, which was often, Freddie was the foreign claims officer, a job that ranked in his mind almost as high as if he were golf pro to the fleet. During these times the navy billeted him, at their cost, in the best hotels in the best cities: Barcelona, Naples, Rome, Istanbul, Palermo. "What's a foreign claims officer?" he asked when first assigned the duty.

"When two drunken marines don't like the music in a nightclub," he was told, "and they break every instrument, some over people's heads, the locals tend to complain. The foreign claims officer pays off the locals and gets them to waive criminal charges. He gets our boys out of the jails, back on duty and sobered up to break heads in other ports. Since you always get called in the middle of the night on these things, best to be in a hotel and not on the ship." With his feet up on one of the biggest beds he had ever seen, Freddie luxuriated at the Victoria Hotel in Barcelona. He was reading a letter from Marley Damon, from whom he heard each week. She was at Smith. "Counting the days," she wrote, "until I can really see if your hair has gotten blonder than mine. The sun bursting off the Mediterranean can't really be the same sun we so seldom see in Northampton, Massachusetts, home of the plaid skirt, the circle pin and the children from Amherst and Williams and Dartmouth who really are children, not a man like my sailor-boy at sea with his long legs and hair blonder than mine: Thine, Marley." He was true to her in his soul, would be true to her. Did he miss

Marley? He missed her. But he really missed the *idea* of Marley Damon, a complementary image of himself, something he needed to complete an equation, to complete a look. He wrote back to her, stories of characters on the ship, descriptions of brawls, cities, attitudes, letters to save, tied up with a ribbon. The phone rang as he was thinking about the Spanish Civil War he would have fought, about Hemingway and *For Whom the Bell Tolls*. There was a church in Barcelona bombed in that war and never reconstructed, preserved as a shell, a memorial. "Mr. Temple," he answered.

"The shit has hit the fan, sir. I'm down in the lobby." It was Cataldo, Freddie's driver from the Shore Patrol, a tough kid from Paterson, New Jersey, who could scrounge whiskey in a dry town, women in a monastery, spare parts to whatever you needed. Freddie was lost in thoughts of Hemingway. "War?" he thought incredulously. "It can't be war."

"What is it, Cataldo?"

"Can't be too bad," he thought. "It's the middle of the afternoon."

"Rogers ran the Jeep through a market. Wiped out about fifty thousand melons. And I think he killed an old guy. The cops who are dressed like Halloween are keeping a mob away who want to nail Rogers to a cross."

Rogers was one of the Shore Patrol, a mean man who loved to beat on heads with his billy club. He was useful breaking up fights or in intimidating the innocent. Temple didn't like him but admitted the effectiveness of his role. As Cataldo often pointed out, "Shore Patrol ain't Harvard, sir. No disrespect."

"How did this happen, Cataldo?" Freddie asked.

"He's an angry son of a bitch, sir. That, plus he was shit-faced."

"In the afternoon?"

"You better get down here, Mr. Temple, before Rogers buys the farm."

Temple buttoned the last buttons on his uniform and raced down the main stairs of the hotel to the lobby. Heart pounding, suddenly all he could think about was a screech of brakes and the crash at Brookwood Municipal. He would hang Rogers up by his balls for getting in an accident, for reminding him of his past.

Cataldo got them to the scene just as Spanish policemen were dragging the American sailor through an angry crowd who were spitting on Rogers, cursing him. "Block their vehicle," Freddie commanded. Cataldo complied, laying the Jeep right in the path of the Spanish police. "Lean on the horn," he said, "and don't let up until I take off my hat." Freddie jumped out and climbed onto the hood of his car. Everyone stopped as the horn blared and Freddie held his arms out as if he were some tall, military Christ, dressed in immaculate whites and demanding attention. He took off his hat. His close-cropped hair, bleached almost white from the Mediterranean sun, framed his face as if it were a painted badge of the elect, a gift to the crowd from heaven. "Amigos," Freddie yelled, and continued in slow Spanish, the words forcefully spoken. "Spain and the U.S.A. have been friends and allies. Do I look like the kind of person who would do harm to a friend? This man is our problem to take care of; he is our problem to punish. I speak for the government of the United States. My name is Frederick Myles Fahnstock Temple, Ensign of the United States Navy. We shall pay for all damages, pay until you forgive. Pay," he yelled once more. Then he jumped off the hood and led Rogers away, putting him into the back of the vehicle. Then he folded himself in, next to the sailor, who looked as relieved as if he had been pulled from the fiery furnace.

"Thanks," he said. "You saved my ass, Mr. Temple. So cool I couldn't believe . . ."

Temple interrupted him fiercely: "You're going to wish they had torn you apart, Rogers, before I get through with you."

"He's shitting me, Cataldo, right?" the sailor said. Cataldo said nothing, knowing that there are times you don't fuck with an officer, even an ensign. As they drove down General Franco Boulevard, Freddie was trying to guess what kind of a fine they'd have to pay for taking the life of an old man. Probably not as much as driving on the wrong side of Route 128 in Boston, he decided.

Marley came over for her spring break, a trip, she assured her father, that would be totally chaperoned by navy wives. "For God sakes, Daddy," she argued, "everything they do is based on rules a hundred years old. I'll be safer than if we were skiing at Stowe. And the trust will pay for it. I mean the trust is there for this. Isn't that its purpose?" She beat him down. Mr. Damon could never resist his daughter, even though he had the good sense to know that giving her over to the navy was the same as feeding her to the sharks. Hadn't he been on a destroyer himself? When it counted?

Marley checked into the Carlton in Cannes and spoke French to everyone. Then she shopped, even before she saw her room.

"I'm downstairs in the lobby," Freddie announced. She had resisted having him pick her up, although he wanted to make a military fuss, showing her that slavery still existed and that he had vehicles and bodies at his disposal. "This is love," Marley thought when she let Freddie into her room. Big open windows looked out onto the *plage* and the sea below. The wind blew the curtains, the wind with a smell, it seemed to Marley, unlike any she had smelled in America. She thought, "Even the air speaks French," and she walked slowly, not quickly, into Freddie's arms. He immediately began, after one long kiss, to touch her breasts, to reach for her thighs, forcefully, not tenderly at all. "Stop, Frederick," she said, stepping away from him. "This isn't what I had in mind." Then she said, "Darling," as if it were an afterthought. Freddie had been at sea surrounded by men. He was particularly friendly with the aviators, who had the feeling that, once the ten-mile limit was crossed, all bets were off. He was shocked at first that the married fliers acted exactly the same as the bachelors. They chased nurses, embassy hostesses in foreign ports and whores wherever they found them. Especially shocking to Freddie was their attitude about their wives at home, most of them back in Virginia. One drunken pilot told him as they watched the sun come up in Naples after an all-nighter, "Sure I miss home. But Nancy gets it regular from one of the dentists on base. I don't know this for sure. But I've got a pretty good hunch because he used to screw two of the squadron guys' wives and she suddenly got lots of cleaning appointments. What the hell, Temple. That's our motto really, what the hell."

Freddie and Marley had never made love. Heavy petting is as far as they had gotten. "Spiritual touching" is what she had written in her diary after the closest of their close calls.

"I'm sorry, Marls," Freddie said. "I just haven't seen you in so long."

She was wearing a navy blue skirt and a white short-sleeve cashmere sweater, and she smiled at him. "Go slow," she said. "Tendresse." She took his hands and placed them on her breasts. "Lentement," she said softly. "Lentement." She hadn't meant it to happen in the afternoon, not when she could see everything, when he could see everything. But when Freddie took it slowly, she came apart and could not stop until he was inside her easy, easy, easy, and then all the way. "It's so perfect," she kept saying to herself. "We were meant to be perfect." They both believed it, watching themselves in the tall dresser mirror, which Freddie dragged over to the foot of the bed when they had finished. "You're blonder than me," she said, watching their images, getting comfortable with seeing him naked next to her. Freddie was thinking the same thing, but he said nothing, only pulled Marley closer to him, cuddling her, while keeping his eyes and their bodies visible in the glass.

Freddie had accumulated leave time for her arrival, and they wandered the Riviera in a navy vehicle, getting used to each other. Sitting in a café one afternoon in St. Paul de Vence, they smoked and sipped wine, they held hands, each dressed in white ducks and long-sleeved white shirts with the sleeves rolled up.

"Excuse me," a middle-aged gentleman said, interrupting their conversation. He was dressed in a dark three-piece pin-striped suit of European cut rather than English, the waist pinched. "My name is Levinsohn," the stranger said. "I'm not being rude, but I get so enthusiastic when I see people this happy." He spoke in mannered English. He had a small mustache fastidiously clipped. Marley and Fred were not bored with each other. But often travelers welcome the intrusion of a new face, the new voice. They asked him to sit down, to share a glass of wine. They wanted a stranger to be their new mirror, like the mirror at the end of their bed in Cannes. Levinsohn told them he was a diamond merchant from Antwerp. He owned a small villa in St. Paul de Vence, where he visited each spring and part of the summer. Typically, he told them, he would stroll to the town center every day when he was in residence, looking for beauty in objects great and small. When he heard that Freddie was in the navy he was delighted. "I, too," he said, "sailed ships. For Belgium." He did not elaborate on this. But he made it clear he would never be satisfied until they came to his villa for a tour and a swim in his pool. It was easy. They were warm from the sun, slightly high from the wine. They had swimsuits with them in their car, and the villa was less than a mile from the café.

Levinsohn gave them a tour of the house, three bedrooms, living room, dining area, study and kitchen, a white-stuccoed jewel with red-tiled roof looking down over green and brown farms and beyond to the sea. Every inch of the wall space in the house was covered with paintings. Marley kept poking Freddie. "My God, look at that." There were Picassos and Braques, Mirós, Arps, several Renoirs. "This is a museum. Where did you ever find these?"

"During and right after the war," he said, "there were opportunities." He shrugged.

"I'll show you more after you swim." He remained in his suit and tie, and he bustled around, getting them towels, serving them gin and tonics while they floated in his pool lined with tiles he claimed were from Pompeii.

"Why don't you come swim with us?" Marley asked their host.

"I keep this recreation for my friends," he answered, rubbing a perfectly sliced lime wedge around the rim of her glass. "Somewhere a nanny of mine said that exercise and showing off one's body would be something for others, never for me. I feel comfortable in my clothes." Levinsohn kept bringing them drinks and scampering into his house to tote out objets d'art to display. He brought out jeweled daggers from the Crusades, small jade horses from Mesopotamia, a Degas dancer. The more they exclaimed, the more he brought, as if parading his splendors would keep them at the villa forever. "You must stay for dinner," he insisted.

Freddie and Marley were feeling immortal. They loved each other. They were beautiful. They were having treasures paraded in front of them beyond anything they could have imagined. Of course they stayed for dinner, dressing as Levinsohn insisted, still in their all-white costumes of the day. Gin and tonics had been replaced by a succession of wines. Several servants materialized at sunset to serve them and to cook them dinner while the merchant told stories of his collection, tales of bribes and thefts and murders in the name of fear and greed. They watched the sea swallow the sun from a Persian couch on the terrace. On either end of the couch sat bronze greyhounds by Rodin. Rice-stuffed grape leaves with olives preceded thinly sliced veal and lemon, accompanied by wines from nearby vineyards, fruity and lingering in their aroma and taste.

"You will, of course, spend the night," Levinsohn said matter-of-factly during dinner, something not to be disputed.

Freddie was for driving back to town, going to a hotel. "We can't," he said. "You've been much too kind already."

Marley was caught in the dream. Nudging Freddie she said, "We couldn't put you out. What if we go to the hotel and you be our guest for breakfast?"

"Unheard of at my table," their host said. "We have coffee and brandy. I will tell you a few more stories and show you the biggest surprise of all." Levinsohn had changed to a dinner jacket of raw silk. He wore patent-leather pumps. His teeth, and he smiled constantly, seemed like polished collectibles, ivory billiard balls, as if he had bid on them at auction. By the first brandy, Freddie would have agreed to anything just to keep from driving. He and Marley felt as if they were floating, as if the evening were not happening. But both sensed that they couldn't measure up to Levinsohn's intellectual demands. As the evening wore on, they realized they were struggling to keep up with his level of knowledge. Levinsohn spoke five languages, had many graduate degrees, friends everywhere. He had experienced war and seen death, had accumulated a fortune, told them of deceit, intrigue, all the dark sides. Freddie's head throbbed. He couldn't focus. That's when Levinsohn brought out the jewels. He spilled them from a green velvet bag onto the Persian couch: diamonds, emeralds, sapphires. But especially emeralds of all sizes, green monsters up to ten carats. He had talked of emerald country during dinner, of châteaus he had visited where the jewels were given as mementos of the weekend. He talked of Marley's coloring, how the green stones were best suited for her fingers or for setting off her throat, pinned with gold at her bodice. As the moonlight seemed to focus on the couch, it also caught Levinsohn's smile as he held an emerald up to Marley's throat and said, "A stone is yours if I may watch you make love." Freddie reacted immediately. He jumped up and began to pull Marley to her feet. She resisted and put her finger to her lips.

"I don't wish to insult you," the Belgian went on quietly. "You won't even know I'm there. I've seen many things."

Drunk, and seeming to float outside of what was happening, Freddie wandered with them to a guest bedroom. They never turned on a light. He and Marley left their clothes on the floor where they were dropped. They never knew what Levinsohn did. They made love and they made noise and they began with one sheet over them which they kicked away and eventually Freddie passed out after having the room swirl for what seemed a long time. When he awoke in the morning with a brandy mouth and a head that seemed as if it needed to be punctured for relief, there was no one else in the room. No one else in the bed. In panic he first checked for his wallet and his military ID. "Marley," he yelled then, into the hushed morning. She was swimming laps in the pool, naked as a spoiled contessa. He watched her for a minute, partly in wonder, partly in exasperation. He yelled at her again, and she heard, stopping her strong kick. She swam to the marble end of the pool. "Jesus Christ, Marls," he said. "You scared me when you weren't there. I feel like shit."

"We've got to get married now," she said quietly. "After last night we have to get married. It's the only way." Freddie bent down and took her hands in his. "I love you," he said. "You know that."

"I mean we have to get married now. This week. Before I go back."

Freddie looked around. "Where is Levinsohn?"

"I haven't seen anyone. I don't want to. But we have to talk about last night. The only way I can justify this is for us to seal it forever."

"I know it was weird," he responded. "But isn't that reaction a little dramatic? Aren't you hung over like mad?"

Levinsohn walked out of the house carrying a tray, café au lait for three and fresh croissants. He was dressed in a navy double-breasted suit with regimental white-and-blue-striped tie. His black shoes, of English cut, glistened with buffing. "Did you say 'famished'?"

Freddie, without any drinks in him, didn't know what to say. Sunlight was not mysterious or sexy. It was too real. So he broke off a piece of croissant and took a cup of coffee. Marley looked away, embarrassed, and pushed off, gliding toward the far end of the pool. "Indelicate of me," Levinsohn said. "There are robes in your bath." He went back to the house.

Freddie fetched a robe and a big towel and returned outside, feeling all the while that the dapper man was watching from somewhere unseen. The Belgian joined them as they sat sipping from their cups, faces turned up to the morning. "Open the little dish," Levinsohn said. A butter dish was covered by a silver cover. Freddie thought it probably contained jam, and he couldn't stand the idea of jam. "Open," Levinsohn said to Marley. She lifted the cover to reveal a perfect two-carat emerald sitting in a tiny edged lettuce leaf.

"I can't," said Marley. But she did. She put it in the pocket of her robe, looked at Levinsohn for a long moment, then said, "Thank you. It's beautiful." She walked away, leaving the two men.

"A mysterious race, women," the collector said. "You and I could not begin to make any comment that would be appropriate."

"I think good-bye would be a good beginning," Freddie said, sounding to himself just like his father, just like Boston. During the night their clothes had been washed, pressed and laid out as if they were garments spun of gold. They drove away from the villa, their host standing in the terra-cotta-tile area in front, holding a small statue of a Roman boy, rubbing its head, planning his morning.

"I'm serious, Frederick," Marley said. He reached over and took her hand. She looked so beautiful. What could be more romantic than being married on the Riviera, he decided. So many of his friends got married right after graduation.

"So they sailed away and were married one day by the turkey who lived on the hill," she singsonged.

"Are you all right, Marls?" Freddie asked, worried about her mood swings. They had been driving through the hills, the sun sparkling off the Mediterranean far below, the air blowing in through the open windows smelling like the heaviest spring in Boston, smelling, Marley thought, like outdoor poetry classes at Smith. "Let's stop for some bread and cheese. And some wine," she said. They stopped in the next village and sat outside at a café. They were high by the second glass of wine.

"You want to do it?" Freddie asked. "Let's do it. I'm game. They'll talk about it at home forever."

"I don't care about a big wedding," Marley said. "All I know is that I never want to leave you. Screw Mummy. What she wants is all for the wrong reasons." They finished two carafes of wine, settled up and walked to the village church, a whitewashed medieval building with a bell tower whose shadow dominated the square the way that faith dominated France. They assured a sleepy priest that they were Catholic. They repeated their vows in French with two grizzled men from the dozen who spent their days in the church's shadow, as witnesses, as parents, as best man. "Je t'aime, mon amour," Marley whispered as they kissed, and the witnesses grinned their toothless grins and the priest was pleased because it was a day when no revenue usually came in. God was good all around.

No one could believe it when Freddie came back to the ship. The officers' mess gave him a party that even the captain attended. The married fliers were particularly happy to have another companion.

"This is fabulous, Temple, you sucker." They surrounded him, pounding him on the back. "Now you can fool around when it's *really* fun. When you're married. Just like us." They toasted him and sang dirty songs, limericks from their college days.

After the navy, Wall Street was the place for Freddie Temple. His father had arranged interviews with old friends who were senior partners of several investment houses. They had been club mates of George Temple's, club brothers of Freddie's. He was offered a position at each of the firms where he interviewed. He and Marley were remarried by the Damon family minister in Bridgehampton with a massive reception later under yellow-and-white-striped tents at the Maidstone Club. Flowers were placed strategically in sand traps to honor the occasion. The golf committee, for the Temple reception day only, waived the strict rules of golf and allowed any player caught in the hazard to move the flowers without penalty. One player objected to the decorations and filed a protest, but he had not been invited to the reception and his petition was dismissed with "Sour grapes."

Freddie took the job offer from Borden, Kimball, an establishment firm on Wall Street that would pay him $200 a week to "learn investments, stocks and bonds, to enable you to give sober longterm advice to private clients." That's how the senior partner, Standish "Sandy" Borden, defined Freddie's job to him. "We'll pay you through your six-month training period, then for another six months to get you up to speed. With your background you should be doing yourself *and* us proud. You have 'partner' written all over yourself, young man."

Freddie and Marley lived in a two-bedroom apartment on East 52nd Street between First and Second avenues, a building with a doorman, working fireplaces, small baths, and Pullman kitchens. The rent was $350 a month. Fred studied for his broker's exams, joined the Harvard and the Knickerbocker clubs. Marley, already in the Junior League, immediately began to volunteer at the Metropolitan Museum and thought of keeping up her French with night classes. She had the emerald made into a cocktail ring by her mother's jeweler. The Temples thought it was from her grandmother. The Damons thought it was a generous gift from her husband's family. The families seldom spoke and, at any rate, would never speak of material things.

Freddie's training was not formalized. It was on-the-job, several weeks in various departments, learning from the people who were already doing the work.

"So what's your speciality?" the sleek-haired young man said to Freddie as they sat side by side stapling research reports. When there was nothing constructive for the trainees to do they would be shuttled back and forth to areas that needed scut work done. Most hot young men would bitch about that, but Freddie was determined. If they wanted him to do stapling or collating, he would be the best they ever had.

"Rich people," Freddie said. "I'm going to manage their money."

"A stockbroker," the sleek-haired young man said.

Freddie took his tone as disdainful. "And what are you doing in a stockbroker's office if you're not going to be a stockbroker?"

The young man began stapling triple time, banging the stapler in a frenzy. "I'm going where the real money is," he said. "Institutional sales: mutual funds, banks, insurance companies. Why sell your uncle a hundred shares of General Motors when you could sell some fund a hundred thousand shares? Same effort, hundred times the commission. I'm Chip Weld, by the way." Chip was wired, confident, a tennis and squash player who had gone to Williams.

"I know where I'm going," Freddie replied.

"The hell you do, boy," Weld replied, getting up. "Come with me." Led by the enthusiastic Weld, Freddie went into Borden, Kimball's main boardroom, where fifty or sixty customers sat, cheek by jowl, watching the electronic ticker tape flash by, dialing clients on the phones, swapping stock gossip, entering orders. All the brokers, many of them elderly, were in suits. Scattered around the enormous room were the firm's customers, pointing out bargains to each other, quietly urging on their favorites, like horses. There was no wasted motion in the room, an orderly place to watch one's money. "A good place to die," said Weld. "Do you want to spend your life bumping up against some old fart in arm garters who's going to let you in on some story about Penn Central bonds maturing in the year two thousand?"

"I don't intend," Freddie said, "to be here for long. The point in my working is to eventually run the firm. God's in his Heaven, right?"

Weld laughed uproariously at this. "You went to Harvard. Well, on the road to running the firm, you might as well have a little fun." They walked through swinging doors into a room filled with terminals, where profane men in shirt sleeves screamed into phones and at each other. They spilled black coffee in paper cups over the desks, threw spitballs, paper planes, tossed ballpoint pens at the ceiling, where they stuck like Bic stalactites. "And I've got news for you," Weld said after they had watched for several minutes. "The route to running the firm is always more visible from places of action. Or are you just another pretty face?"

A well-planned life didn't roll over at one glimpse of an institutional trading desk. At home, over the next several weeks, Freddie made phone calls to family and friends of the family. He had lunches and a few dinners with college classmates in banking, the law, investments.

"Marls," he announced to his wife when his research was through, "I'm not going to handle individual accounts, the retail business. Everything in my background tells me I should be an institutional broker."

She kissed him. "Daddy says that will mean less sailing and more golf."

In his first full year as an institutional salesman, Freddie's gross commissions were almost $150,000, of which he received twenty percent, plus expenses, which were considerable because he was out with clients, on average, four nights a week. Clients at banks and mutual funds and investment advisers who gave business to Freddie's firm demanded entertainment much more than they demanded research in exchange for their orders. In his second full year of selling Freddie made his breakthrough.

"Tim Shannon," the man yelled over the crowd noise, sticking his hand across several bodies.

"Jim?" Freddie yelled back.

"*Tim*," the man roared. "Timmy with a T. Like tit." They had met at a Rangers-Bruins game at Madison Square Garden. Tim Shannon was the assistant head trader at Cobblestone Management, a mutual-funds complex responsible for investing almost $2 billion in assets. "What I'm looking for," Shannon yelled, "is one of them cigars." Freddie had taken two traders from other funds to dinner and the game. They were feeling no pain when they arrived during the second period, and the cheroots were stuck in the corners of their mouths. Freddie switched seats with one of his clients and settled next to Shannon. He handed him a Garcia Vega and offered his own cigar snipper, the antique silver one from Dunhill. Shannon snipped off the cigar tip, rolled his tongue around, wetting the end, and lit up. "Know how I heard about you?" he asked.

"No," Freddie said.

"I heard from the crowd that you got great taste in clubs and restaurants and that you're an Ivy guy like the rest of your salesmen. But the crowd also says that you don't shit on the Irish, and then, when you give out a story, you back it up."

"We don't cover you as a firm?"

"Some dipshit from Princeton sends over research with his name stamped on the cover in orange. Thinks that's how you get business on the Street." Shannon blew a thick cloud of smoke. "We all know what the truth is, right?"

Freddie blew his own smoke stream. "May the road rise to meet you," he said to Shannon.

"Fuckin' A," said the trader, slapping Freddie on his gray flannel knee.

A week later, Freddie's boss shook his hand. "I've got news for you, chief." He called everyone chief, an annoying habit that usually put him in control of the situation. "I've taken McFarren off the Cobblestone account and put you on. You know why?"

"The trader called you and said what great taste in cigars I have?"

"Not only that, chief. He sent over a give-up check for twenty-five big ones. Your credit."

"Twenty-five thousand?"

Freddie called Shannon immediately to thank him for the commission.

"I'm partial to '21'," the trader said. "I like the bar and the turkey hash and I'm free tomorrow night." Freddie was exultant. "I've got the leprechaun by the coattails," he yelled to the trading room.

"It's better if you get him by the balls," a trader yelled back, giving Freddie the high sign. And Freddie was off to the races.

CHAPTER FOURTEEN

O

Friday, November 22, 1963.

Freddie Temple was standing at the trading desk when the news shot across the Dow Jones wires. "Jesus Christ," people said. "Kennedy's been shot." Immediately the phones were jammed, boards lit up. Freddie's biggest client called. "What can we short?" he yelled. Freddie told him very quietly, "They've closed trading. The markets are shut down. I'll speak to you." He hung up, shocked that anyone could be that big a cocksucker. Freddie didn't think, "What's happening to my money?" He thought, "What's happening to my country?" Marley checked in from her mother's apartment. "I'm coming home," Freddie told her.

Dickie Rosenberg called just before he walked out of the office. "I'm in New York," he said. "One drink. The Oak Bar at The Plaza."

"Will they play The Game, do you think?" Freddie asked. Harvard-Yale football was the next day. Friends were converging on New Haven from all over the country to tailgate, to celebrate. After all, didn't Harvard own America now? Jack Kennedy in the White House?

"Play The Game?" Dickie questioned. "I don't know if there's going to be a *tomorrow*, let alone the game."

"I told Marley I was coming home."

"One drink."

They met at the Oak Bar, which was hushed and dark. Everyone in New York had gone home to watch television. The bartenders played a portable radio and mixed drinks for a change with heavy, generous hands: a day to get drunk. "One quickie," Freddie said. "I told Marley I'd be home." They ordered Bloody Marys.

"To Jack Kennedy," Dickie said.

"I didn't even vote for him," said Freddie. "My first election. I voted for Nixon. My father said that the Democrats ruined America. He said that practically the first thing he ever said to me when I was a kid." They clinked glasses.

"I voted for him," Dickie said. "For Kennedy. I think I'd vote for anyone if they went to Harvard. Maybe not Nixon. Nixon couldn't get into Harvard." They laughed awkwardly, Freddie nervous about the time.

"I think we should call Red and Hennessey," Dickie said.

"Jesus, I haven't thought about them in a long time."

"You know why I'm thinking about them now?"

Temple shook his head.

"Because of Sullivan. The guy who got killed maybe could have been President. Maybe the Kennedy thing is just like what happened to us only nobody ever knew about it. What if he ran for President? He was running for Congress. Kennedy started in Congress."

"For Christ's sakes, Rosie. You had to bring this up today? We didn't kill the guy. It was an accident. How the hell can you even think of this when the President's been assassinated?"

"You'd be amazed how often I think about it."

"We were kids," Temple said. Reluctantly, Freddie let himself be led downstairs to the pay phones.

Red was in his apartment watching the coverage. "The world came to a fucking end," he said. "It makes what you want to do for a living seem like nothing. I can't believe it. I'll tell you though. When I got the news all I could think of was Sullivan the congressman. We gunned him down with a fucking golf ball."

"Say hello to Temple," Dickie said, giving Freddie the phone.

"Hello, Stanley. You a star yet?"

"This is no shit, glamour-puss," Red said. "I was at a party last night, Tony Curtis, Grace Kelly, Burt Lancaster. Hey, I brushed the tits of Jayne Mansfield. Walked right by and brushed them."

"You sound like the old Stanley to me."

"It's an act today, pal. Those fucking Texans. I was there. Crazy. Life is cheap. An old Mexican used to yell, 'I found the body.' Every day."

They called Duke Hennessey and got Rita. "He couldn't stand it," she told them. "He said he had to get out. It's unbelievable, isn't it? What's going to happen to all of us?"

Duke drove his car around Brookwood, going slowly by the high school, then on to the Hathaway School and around to the tennis courts in the back. Everywhere on the town's roads he saw little children, happy to be let out of classes early but somber also and a little frightened because, at almost every house, mothers would come running out to the sidewalks, hugging them, then pulling them violently into the safety of their homes, as if some monster were loose in the neighborhoods.

Duke drove into the parking lot at Brookwood Municipal golf course. It was November chilly, half a dozen cars huddled in one section of the lot, as if they could stay warmer that way. "There are always people who will play golf in any weather," Duke thought. He walked to where he and his friends had hit the wedge shots long ago, and he believed he could see the skid marks where the car had gone off the road. He took a swing, holding an imaginary club. "It couldn't be me," he thought. Too smooth. Duke looked away, off to the hill overlooking the golf course. The pillars of the white house still supported the arched curves of the front roof, still looked as if the person who owned it was the King of the Mountain. Duke took another swing with his imaginary wedge and walked slowly to his car.

CHAPTER FIFTEEN

O

Boxing Night, February 1968

It was billed as Boxing Night at the Harvard Club, three amateur fights of three rounds each, the card provided by a local promoter, the proceeds going to charity. Cocktails and dinner preceded the bouts, dinner served at tables draped in white cloths. The tables fanned out in circles surrounding the ring, which was set up in the middle of the main ballroom underneath the massive crystal chandelier donated by the Foster clan, who had refused to leave it in the big house in Beverly Farms after they sold the house to the Armenian church. Duke did the organizing for the black-tie evening after Red Singer called and told him he was coming east to visit his parents. Duke then called Temple, who he knew would smell business. Then he called Rosenberg. "How would you like to go to black-tie Boxing Night at the Harvard Club, Rosie?"

"Are you inviting me?"

"Well," Duke said, "I want you to come. And I'm also asking to use your membership. We'll pay you back."

"We'll?"

"Yeah. Red and Temple are coming. And a couple of my partners. Prospective partners, if that's okay."

"Remember car buddies from high school? Guys we kept around because they had wheels and would drive us?"

"Dickie," Duke said. "A night out with the guys. If you don't want to do it, Temple can always find someone."

"Why take us along if you're doing it for business?"

"It's a reunion, dummy. Why look for a reason? Besides, I've got a surprise for everyone. And, as they say in the real estate business, 'If you can't sell rotten fish to your friends, who can you sell it to?' "

"I'll have to delay a trip to New York."

What Dickie didn't say was that his wife, Adrienne, couldn't understand whenever pleasure was put before business. She got that from her father, and she made it very clear to her husband that she was going to push him until he got what they both deserved. Nights out were okay for her dad. She knew that when he was away from the house with cronies at P. J. Clarke's and Madison Square Garden, it was for the greater good of getting the order.

At the Harvard Club, each of them felt very much like a big man, dressed in black tie, eyeing each other, circling as if they were rivals for the same woman.

Duke was large, two hundred and twenty-five pounds, bigger than he had ever been in his life. His father had begun to call him "Diamond Jim" after "Diamond Jim" Brady, the big shooter from the turn of the century, noted for his bay window. Duke didn't like criticism from his father. The Victorians could glorify bulk, equating it with riches. Big Duke Hennessey was equating his son's pursuit of wealth with being a fat slob. Duke and Rita had three children by 1968. Shauna was followed by Francis II and two years later by their little girl, Peggy. "Call me 'King' now," Duke said to the others. "Every hundred pounds is going to be worth a million bucks."

"Lover-lips is losing his hair," Red Singer said, motioning as if he were going to muss the carefully combed Rosenberg. Dickie slapped his hands away. "Don't fuck with my hair."

After he and Adrienne had been married, they lived in Cambridge in a duplex apartment on the Charles River, several blocks from Harvard Square. He fought with his father every day about the direction of the maternity business. Adrienne pushed him every night to move to New York and work with her father. Dickie was losing his hair, and their first child was on the way. Compensation for the family struggle was that the business paid him $50,000 a year and he drove a blue Mercedes-Benz 250SL leased for him by the company.

Freddie Temple was the only one of them wearing a black formal vest instead of a cummerbund. He wore a gold watch chain across the front from which dangled a small eighteen-karat charm, a pig. The chain had been his grandfather's. Freddie's blond hair hung down almost to his shoulders, hair so floppy that he had to shake his head periodically to move it away from his eyes. He smiled at the others. "Good to see you," he said. "Great to see you." He was still out, on average, three nights a week, entertaining in pursuit of commission business.

Red Singer danced around all of them, flicking comments, kissing their cheeks, the first man they knew who kissed other men on the cheeks. Red was Hollywood, they thought, thick hair cut like Prince Valiant, now the color of leather seats in a Ferrari. Freddie asked if he had it dyed.

Red liked that just fine. "Brookwood was perfect," he told them. "If you want to be small-towners, hick-town mentality, out to a movie and pizza or Chink's on a Saturday night. Typical that you guys dump on me. I'm giving American people what they need to get up and live an ordinary life. I'm giving them romance, adventure and Saturday nights out. I'm keeping people's minds off their troubles."

"I, I, I, me, me, me. Let's get a drink," Duke said. It was his party, his idea.

The main floor of the club was filled with men in black tie who were pumped up, out with the guys, all dressed up, drinks on the way, cigars to follow. Stag. Harvard Club members invited customers. It was a perfect night to score points with clients, down and dirty.

Dickie Rosenberg was thirty-one years old. His friends were the same age. Thirty-one was the time for preening, for comparing paychecks and titles, even if everyone was bluffing. People didn't show up for Boxing Night at that age if they weren't making it or about to make it. Two full bars were set up in the first-floor reception area that emptied into the great hall where dinner and the fights were to be served up. People were four deep at both bars, drinking hard stuff, Scotch, bourbon, gin and tonics, vodka on the rocks. Beer was an after-dinner drink with this crowd; beer would tamp everything down.

Dickie was uncomfortable until he was on his second vodka. Adrienne had objected to his dressing up to go out on an evening where only men were allowed. She didn't object to boxing; her father took her to fights at St. Nicholas' Arena and the Garden when she was a little girl. She was used to being in the company of men. Her father gave her a portfolio of stocks when she was twenty-one, and she used her money to move herself in the right directions. "I'd like to dress up," she had said. "See your old friends. If it comes to that, I can get as drunk as they can."

"Adrie, you want to be the only woman out of a couple of hundred people?"

"Of course I do. Can you think of anything better? It's obviously you who can't handle this. Not me."

"It's wonderful," Dickie said. "We're pouring thousands of troops and millions of dollars into Vietnam and we refuse to do what it takes to win it. Civil rights marches are going on everywhere. The college kids are going crazy. And your nose is out of joint because I'm having one stinking night with the boys."

"Richard, I've got news for you," she said. "I can't do anything about Vietnam. But striking a blow about bullshit; I can start that in my own home."

"Damned if I do; damned if I don't," her husband said. "I'm in the Feinberg box, the box your family puts everyone in."

"Go and have a good time with the boys, darling."

"I'm too young for this," Dickie said. "Every Sunday night I grew up listening to Jack Benny, Phil Harris and Alice Faye. This is like that. And I laughed at it."

"Damned if you do, and damned if you don't," Adrienne repeated.

The foursome got their drinks and moved to the outskirts of the crowd. Red gave it to them. "I knew it," he said. "I knew that when you guys were ten, that you'd have to get married to get laid. I predicted it. I've been taking out actresses for the last four years, gorgeous kids right off the bus from Omaha, Waco, Texas, and I'm an agent. Know what that means? It means I'm a dictator, a king. You know what the sexual revolution really means? Of course you don't; you've got to be an agent to know what it really means."

"Give us some names," said Duke.

"Names wouldn't mean anything to you guys. You'd recognize them by picture, a girl from 'Star Trek,' a girl from 'Peyton Place.' I'm dating a kid now just missed the lead in The Graduate. The stars of tomorrow; that's Red Singer's specialty."

"Referring to yourself in the third person now," Dickie said. "Caesar. Louis the Fourteenth. Stanley Singer, Emperor of the Tufts University Pimps."

"Still living in the past, Rosenberg?" Red countered. "Remember famous feats of ass-kissing? Remember your hair? I look around this room and I see a lot of people making twenty-five grand, maybe a few making forty, fifty tops. That's not making money, for Christ's sake. Every day of the year I drive a Porsche with two fucking tops. I nibble so much pussy, nineteen-, twenty-year-olds, for breakfast, lunch and dinner it's a regular health diet. I see contracts with Cary Grant, Chuck Heston, Kim Novak, and I'm working on my first deal to produce my own feature. Don't tell anyone. All this and I don't have to put on a tie, much less a tuxedo." Red *was* leasing the Porsche. It was costing him more a month than the rental of his house in Laurel Canyon. He did know a lot of bartenders by name. And they knew him. And he knew the names and credits of every director, producer, actor and agent in the business. He was working with weirdos who lived on Mounds bars and Fritos on his script ideas while fucking a thirty-nine-year-old with two kids who lived around the corner from Musso & Frank's in Hollywood in a bungalow right out of *The Day of the Locust*. He had thirty credit cards (Husky Oil to Visa) on which he paid $10 each every month.

Freddie Temple drank martinis straight up at the beginning of each evening, just as his father did. "Très sec," his father told barmen wherever he traveled. "Très sec" is what George Temple told himself as he shook his nightly offering at home in the silver shaker with his college final club emblem, the shaker signed by all the ushers at his wedding. Wherever Freddie was, he thought about writing business, upping his gross commissions. "Stanley," he said. "Do you have an account with a brokerage firm? Or better yet, if I come out to visit you in Sodom, what do you say to introducing me to people who need financial assistance? Your friends use the banks for financing; they can get me into the bankers who swing. My clients are making fortunes in the stock market, and there's no one better plugged into New York than your oldest friend."

"My oldest friend, Freddie?" Red laughed. "Your parents told you in the third grade never to bring me back to your house, that I was a bad influence."

"So now you're a star," Freddie said. "My old man hasn't been right since he bet a thousand dollars on Thomas Dewey." He shook off the offer of a cigar from Red. "You never smoke stogies until after dinner, Red. You want to make me think my parents were right?"

Freddie Temple was pumped up. He didn't need the martini, but he drank it as routine, like reading the *Wall Street Journal* and the *Times* in the morning. At 11:00 A.M. that day he had been standing next to the trading desk in his office, watching the tape action on Pan American. Bobby Dillard, his biggest client, manager of Ivory Growth Fund, wanted him on the phone. The night before they had been in a bar on Second Avenue until two-fifteen talking about the Bermuda races, the golf courses of Pinehurst, North Carolina, and the mystery that their paths had never crossed before they began working on the Street. Freddie had picked up the tab.

"I'm still drunk," Dillard said. "My girl is bringing in Marys in a paper cup for lunch. Thanks a lot."

Freddie brought it back to earth. "Remember what we said about the airlines?"

"I never forget what anyone says about numbers," Bobby countered. "If you're sober, I want you to sell one million Pan American, limit twenty."

"I'll be back," Freddie said, slamming the phone down and almost simultaneously yelling at his head trader, "Tommy, got a million Pan Am for sale, twenty or better, Ivory Growth."

"Jesus," the trader yelled back. "Where the hell have you been? Bluhdorn is *buying* a million, we're working it now."

"Bluhdorn." Freddie thought. "Who runs Gulf and Western? Is buying it? A genius is buying and I'm on the wrong side?"

"Hold the order," Freddie screamed. "*No* sell order." Frantically he called his customer. "Bobby," he yelled into the mouthpiece, "Bluhdorn is buying a million Pan Am."

"Then for Christ's sakes," his client yelled back. "Cancel sell a million Pan Am, and *buy* a fucking million. Buy it, *buy*." The stock moved up two and a half points on the subsequent frenzy.

"You did a great American thing today, my boy," his customer told Freddie after the bell closed the trading day. "Quick thinking. You can expect to do a lot of business with the people from Ivory."

Freddie exulted. Points, he thought. Points with everyone. And gross commissions better than seventy grand for a two-minute piece of luck. Fat City all the way.

"I've got a guest coming," Duke informed them as they swapped stories amidst the din of cocktails. "Just wanted to warn you. He's a guy going to be very important to me, maybe important to all of you if he keeps moving where he seems to be moving."

"Who could you find, Duke," Red said, "who could possibly help me out unless it's some MIT professor figured out a way to turn shit into money."

"How about the President of the United States?"

"I think Lyndon's got too much on his mind these days," Dickie said. "Unless a couple of Republican senators are on the dance card tonight."

"I'm bringing 'Sleek' Sullivan. He's late."

They stared at each other.

"He's the brother of the guy . . ." Dickie said, letting the sentence hang.

"I don't need this, Francis," Freddie said, slipping into his best Boston North Shore accent, which implied that he wouldn't muddy his boots in anything other than good polo-pony doo-doo.

"Who the fuck is Sleek Sullivan?" asked Red. "Some guy from Whiskey Point in Brookwood?"

"Don't you read the papers, Stan?" Duke asked. "He's the congressman from Cambridge who's fighting Johnson on the war. Picture's been in *Time, Newsweek.*"

"I read *Variety* and the *Hollywood Reporter*," said Red.

"He's the brother of the Sullivan who got killed years ago in an automobile accident. We need to spell it out for you?" Dickie asked.

"Don't you guys understand anything?" Duke asked. "He's a U.S. congressman. He's a few years older than us, meaning *young*, career ahead of him, good-looking, access to dough. I don't care what you do with your lives, you've got to have the juice, be connected. Here's another thing for you people who haven't been to church lately. You ever hear of redemption?"

"If you're Jewish," said Rosenberg, "they call it guilt."

Freddie shook his head. "This is living in the past," he said. "We're in our thirties. I've got bench marks: at least fifty thousand a year by thirty, a hundred thousand by thirty-five. I don't have time to dwell on what was or wasn't."

"These are Democrats?" someone stage-whispered in back of them, a clear sound, cutting through the rattle of glasses and conversation. Sleek Sullivan could make himself heard in a crowd; his voice carried to the back of any house. He had been given his nickname when he was a schoolboy hockey player, given it by a Boston sportswriter who pinned labels on everyone. In Sleek's case, it stuck, mainly because he wanted it to stick, knew it was a name to carry through life.

"These are good guys, Sleek," Duke said. "You can make converts out of the heathen."

"The only true heathens," Sullivan said, "are my aides, now strung out around the lobby in their working clothes, business suits, put out with me for going to the fights. But I like fights, gentlemen, ever since Gillette first put them on television Friday nights. My aides mostly went to Harvard, which also puts them out because they don't see many Harvard types tonight. They see boys out on the town, and my guys don't like leisure time. They don't understand that you do business at the ringside. Are you buying me a beer?"

Duke introduced them one by one. Sleek Sullivan looked at them closely. He was forty years old, blue-black straight hair parted almost in the middle, cut long but not mod. He was running for senator and looking for money. Everyone else at the Harvard Club that night was looking for money. Duke stuck to Sullivan during cocktails, and Red commented, "Like shit sticks to flies." They all went into dinner, sitting together at a table two rows removed from ringside. "I can't believe that Singer looks so good with long hair," Dickie thought. "Covers his ears. These guys are doing things, and I'm the schmuck. I'm signing for the evening that seems to belong to other people, and then I've got to chase them for the dough." He felt that he should be further along at his age. He also knew that self-pity was the biggest sin.

"You don't want your chowder, Rosie," Duke was saying to him, "I'll take it. Look for some clams. None in mine."

"You want my salad, too?"

"What are you pissed off for? You should be ecstatic, out for a night free and easy."

Freddie found he knew many people, and he table-hopped, shaking hands, catching up on who was working where, who was making what.

"You're a cool one," Red said to Hennessey. "What's this guy doing for you, bribing the housing commissions? You never told him anything about us, did you? You're not laying anything on us, Duke. The game we played is history."

"You think I'd fuck us up, Stanley? Wake up. Sleek Sullivan is on his way. I'm helping him raise money. We live in a town where you have to get involved. I'm going to build offices, skyscrapers. You don't just go out and make that shit up. You need friends who can grease things for you."

Sullivan worked the room as well, comfortable in a sporting crowd that was loosey-goosey. He saw several of the Patriots players, a few of the Red Sox, off season now, uncomfortable in rented tuxedos, blue ruffled shirts, but used to accepting freebies from businessmen who felt wonderful around athletes.

Dinner was roast beef and Yorkshire pudding. Bottles of red wine were placed in the middle of every table, which seated ten. Sleek Sullivan sat between Duke and Rosenberg. "You belong to Brookwood Country Club?" Sullivan said to Dickie. "What's your handicap?"

"Before I got married I could play, played a lot. Maybe I was a fourteen. Now I've got to be over twenty. The game takes all day, and I can't be out there six, seven hours."

"Duke tells me you come from an old manufacturing family. Brookwood always struck me as a generous membership. They're always involved in causes, political and otherwise."

"It's a Jewish club," Dickie said to him. "One Italian member. But he was there before we took over, and he wouldn't leave. It would make us look prejudiced."

"Do I look stupid?" Sullivan joked. "The Karps and the Cohans are big supporters of mine. But they're a little old for golf with me. I mean, they can pop the ball fifty, sixty yards. But it's not golf, know what I mean? I'd love to play the course. You can get an Irishman through the gates?"

Dickie hesitated a moment. "Sure. We can play sometime."

"I'm not shy," Sullivan said. "You can't be shy in politics."

"I'm in the garment business," Dickie said. "You've got to learn early to ask for the order."

"Good then. I'd like to get your support. I'm running on my

position that we pull out of Vietnam; I don't know how you feel about that."

Singer, seated nearby, reacted to this: "We should get the hell out and get this country back together."

"You say that," Temple said, "because you live in a dream world out in L.A. with all those pinko Commie fags."

"I was in the army, Temple," Singer said. "A total waste of my time and the government's money."

"If we're not willing to do what it takes to win it," Dickie said, "it's not worth one American life. I think we all would have gone," he added, "but we were about three years too old. I would have gone, no question."

"Rock and roll kids," Sleek Sullivan said. "The lucky generation. Too young for Korea, too old for Vietnam."

"Gentlemen . . . the first fight of the evening," the ring announcer said, bellowing into his hand microphone. Cigar smoke floated above the ring, all around the hall, drifting up toward the great chandelier. Waitresses, older women, mothers and grandmothers, used to serving Harvard Club audiences at banquets, musical evenings and travelogues, took beer and Scotch orders from loud men who wanted booze with their bets and their sport.

"Two boys from Fall River," the announcer called. "Reuben Gonzalez in white trunks, one hundred forty-seven pounds, winner of twenty-two fights, seventeen by knockout. Gonzalez. In black trunks, weighing one hundred forty-five pounds, Irish Bob Murphy, undefeated in nineteen fights. Murphy."

"Middleweights," Sleek Sullivan said. "Look how skinny the Murphy is. I like him though."

"You take him?" Temple said. "Fifty bucks. I'll take the spic; he's a hungry kid."

Sullivan smiled at Temple as if he'd love to teach him a lesson. His smile was the one he reserved for WASPs who didn't know any better. "Men who run for senator don't bet on sporting contests."

The Murphy beat the hell out of the Puerto Rican kid, while the onlookers roared and hooted and puffed their cigars harder and threw money into the middle of their tables, covering bets. They slapped each other on the back and roared harder when sweat and blood from the ring showered the men sitting closest to the action.

"Jesus," Dickie said. "It's nothing like you see on television. It's brutal."

"You should see the cockfights in Tijuana," Red said between whoops of excitement. "They fight till one of them dies."

Sullivan nudged Duke, who was sitting calmly, taking it in. "You like this?"

"I like any contest," Duke said. "Like you against the field for senator. Like me against the zoning people and the banks to put up my office building."

"You know how the game is played, Francis. Don't be so itchy."

"Like Temple said, I've got my own timetable."

"Trains are seldom on time," said Sleek Sullivan as the Murphy tagged the Puerto Rican in the throat and the ref stepped in to stop the fight. "Except when Mussolini ran them." The crowd was on its feet, cheering. Many men stood on their chairs, approving the results with their clapping and whistling. Others who backed the Puerto Rican yelled "Foul" and "In the tank." There were more bouts, with the fighters a little bigger and more experienced each time.

"I remember your father was a fighter," Temple said to Duke. "I bet he never fought for this kind of audience." Duke looked around. He saw lawyers and stockbrokers, insurance agents, box manufacturers, bankers and advertising men.

"My father called the ringside people 'swells.' He loved to get blood and sweat on the swells, watch them duck and cover up, people disgusted with what it looked like close up."

"Everything looks that way close up," Sullivan said, hearing them. "I understand that. That's what I know. That's why I'm going to be United States senator from Massachusetts."

"This guy is worse than you in high school when you were running for class president. You were the transparent man," Red whispered to Rosenberg as the second fight got under way and the waitresses hustled in more beer, the tabletops now loaded with empties, the ashtrays overflowing with butts.

"Red, you don't have to be jealous anymore. You're this big-time success in Hollywood, beating them off with a stick."

"You know the Ugly Duckling, Rosie?" Red said. "That was

me in Brookwood. No shit. I knew there was something out there for me. I'm a swan. And all the time it was waiting for me in California."

"I hate the business I'm in, Red. I can't stand being under my father's thumb. We're in our thirties, and I feel like things are passing me by."

"You thought you were the ass-man," Singer said as the fight raged in front of them, a black light heavyweight and another big Irish kid, beefy, with skin that exploded in red blotches whenever he was hit. Dickie looked over at Hennessey, who was in his element, Red, who seemed ready to throw himself into the ring, and Temple, who was taking it in, interested in a clinical way, a chance to gamble. But Temple looked equally interested in the perfect ash of his cigar. "I bet *he* hit the shank," Dickie thought. "I always figured the way he ran off that he shanked the wedge that killed Sullivan's brother. Would Duke rat on us? Never," Dickie decided. "Would Duke give him one of us? No point." Dickie tried to get involved in the fight, but he kept thinking about his father, his career, his hair. "What thoughts," he decided, "for a former ass-man."

"Why did I come tonight?" Freddie thought. "Why did Hennessey bring the politician to bust our stones? What the hell does he want from us? I didn't hit the shot. It was dark. One million shares of Pan Am I can move in a few minutes. I can reach Bernie Cornfeld in Geneva; he takes my calls. Christ, the statute of limitations ran out on the accident years ago." He pulled a small notebook from his dinner jacket's side pocket and wrote down Sullivan's name and the name of the fighters and the bout on which they bet.

Duke was facing the ring. He looked back over his shoulder at his friends as if reading their thoughts. He made the sign of the cross in their direction as the crowd screamed for redemption of their own. Red left his seat and hugged Hennessey. "I'm bringing this to L.A.," he said into Duke's ear. "Black-tie boxing. It's a natural."

The crowd stood and cheered for the last round of the last fight, not wanting it to end because going home meant explanations and excuses for why they longed to be sixteen again. A no-win exercise. Avoiding the exiting fighters, a table of celebrants ducked under the ropes and cavorted around the ring. Several men jumped on each other, wrestling on the canvas floor. A few others sparred playfully, pulling punches, swinging roundhouse swings that missed by miles. All of them eventually held their arms above their heads in victory poses and left the ring like the pros they wished they were.

"It was too noisy to talk," Duke said as the men headed for their cars. "What about a quiet one for the road?"

"I've got to go home," Rosenberg said.

"Be a man, Rosie," Red said to him. "For Christ's sake." They were in the parking lot of the Harvard Club. The east wind was cutting through them. Coats were no protection. Dickie thought of Adrienne at home. Dickie knew that she viewed his sports — tennis, squash, golf — as innocent. She viewed his few evenings out on anything other than sales calls as frivolous. "You're in another generation from my dad, Richard," she would say. "You don't know how to do it like they do. They do their deals out on the town."

Dickie heard himself saying to the others, "No one calls me pussy-whipped. One quiet one for the road." Duke had a Mercury Colony Park station wagon, a monster he bought second-hand on the cheap from a dealer in Brookwood who used to sponsor Park League baseball. The others left their cars in the Harvard Club lot. They all piled into the wagon, including Sleek Sullivan, who claimed to have wanted to mix it up in the ring at the close of the evening's activities. Sullivan seemed sober, although he had lifted a glass steadily all through dinner and the fights. He smiled a lot, looking over people's shoulders for the next voter. But he would bore into you, looking right into your eyes as if he wanted to hold your mortgage. It made people defer to him, to want to please him. They were afraid that if they didn't, he would tell them what they didn't want to hear.

"Where are we going?" Red asked.

"Thought we'd hear some jazz, an after-hours joint," Duke said.

Dickie saw that they had just passed Symphony Hall on Massachusetts Avenue. "You're not going to Roxbury, are you? This isn't the fifties where everyone was nice to you. Want to get our ass in a sling?"

"Everything is cool," Duke said. "A couple of guys there work for me."

"Daddy Cool Breeze," said Red. "I left my shades in L.A."

"Remember we'd go to the One O'Clock Club on school vacations?" Freddie said. "Remember when we went with that whore to her apartment and we watched Red?" He turned to Sleek. "While he was screwing her he kept singing, 'You'll wonder where the yellow went, when you brush your teeth with Pepsodent.' I'll never forget it."

They all laughed, and then they were driving through quiet city streets. There stood old stone apartment houses, storefront varieties, liquor stores and taverns. Black faces peered out of the tavern windows, black people hurried to shelter along winter streets. Duke skidded the wagon into a spot marked Tow Zone and led them to a deserted store that had a chipped painted sign in the window: Five and Dime. Under it in smaller painted letters it said, "Buy from Grey and Skip Away." Dickie could feel things slipping away from him. Should he call Adrie? "Don't you have to check in with Rita?" he asked Duke.

"Look, pal," Duke said. "Way back in high school when we started dating I set the precedent. I told her, 'Don't expect me when I'm with the boys. I got business, I got exams, I got our future to connect. I love you all the time. But if we're gonna have the white house on the hill, don't expect me when I'm out with the boys. You can't set precedent when you're in the fifth inning." Duke knocked on the locked door. Several minutes went by, then it opened a crack. "I'm a friend of Chester's," Duke said.

"What's his favorite food?" a voice came back.

"Beef Wellington," Duke answered. The door swung in and they were hustled inside, across what looked like the department in a hardware store that sold small items for the home in the 1930s, doorknobs, brass faucets, parts of toilets, sixty-watt bulbs. The black man who admitted them was dressed in a brown velvet suit with wide lapels. Half a dozen gold chains hung against his chest, and his Afro looked as if he were growing a tightly curled tower of hair, an apartment house for small animals. "You the backup band?" he said to them. "We ain't had much waltz music lately."

"We're just here for the good times," Red piped in. The man stopped before another door. "Good times starts with bread," he said. "Ten bucks to see behind the next door." Dickie could see that Sleek Sullivan was eager to introduce himself. But he kept his mouth shut. They paid the ten, and their guide led them to the club. Freddie would swear it was John Coltrane on tenor sax who blasted them as they came into a room that sounded to him like Eddie Condon's in the Village in the middle 1950s. There were several tables of white men with dates, the men looking as though they had just hijacked a convoy of Seagram's trucks. They were stretching their suits, and they were loud, talking through the jazz, ignoring the women who were ornaments in short dresses, beehive hairdos, white lipstick and eyeliner, laughing over Seven and Sevens, nervous together over drinking out of glasses that might not be clean. Everyone else in the room was black, and it wasn't Dickie's imagination that told him that his party better be connected.

"Hennessey, Tennessee Tootles His Flute." A man came up to them and touched Duke's hand.

"Power to the people, motherfuck," Duke answered, and the man laughed from deep in his belly. The man ignored current style. His hair was slicked back like Sugar Ray Robinson's, and he, too, was in dinner jacket, black tie, although the jacket was purple satin.

"Chester," Duke said proudly, "I'd like you to meet my friends." They shook all around.

"What you doin' with the children?" Chester said to Sleek Sullivan.

"They're my campaign managers, volunteers of the future," the politician said.

Chester Grey, through various straw corporations, was a major Cambridge landlord, owner of more than thirty triple-decker houses, tenements and apartment buildings. Duke had found him by accident, chasing a deal near Harvard Square, and negotiated eventually with the man himself, who was amused by Duke's street talk and persistence. Grey led them to a table, stayed long enough to let the crowd know they were untouchable and moved away on a sea of jazz to make sure everything in his room was smooth. They ordered beer while "Take the 'A' Train" pierced the darkened room and Sullivan excused himself for the men's room and to look for faces that might eventually make their way to the polls.

"I want you guys to kick in for Sleek's campaign," Duke said right after Sullivan left. "You can do yourselves nothing but good, in the heart and in the wallet. Believe it. He's going to be the next senator and Bobby Kennedy is going to be President. If we're on board early it will help us all."

"What is this, blackmail?" Temple said. "I can't stand Bobby Kennedy. He wants to give the country away. Besides, if you don't know a Republican when you see one . . ."

"All I see is an asshole," Hennessey said, "who doesn't know how to hedge his bets."

"I have to reach in my pocket because you want to cut deals?" Temple said. "What if I never saw you again? Would it change my life?"

"Yes, pretty boy," Duke said. "It would change your life. You'd always wonder if you could measure up to the guys on the other side of the tracks. There's something in you that can't dog it. Your curse is that you've got to know. When we were kids what did you want more than anything?"

"To fuck Judy Hirshberg," Red said.

"The white house on the hill," Dickie added.

"A three handicap," Temple remembered.

"Right," Duke said. "Are you going to roll over and play dead? Isn't one of the points of life to lord it over your friends? King of the Mountain?"

"You always were too honest for your own good," Rosenberg said. "What's all that have to do with our getting in bed with Sullivan?"

"It has everything to do with it. I can spot a winner. He can plug me in all over this town. You think I was going to take out trash and collect rents and coins from fucking washing machines in basements for the rest of my life? I'm going to build buildings, cities. This is how you do it, scratching people's backs, them scratching yours."

"That's your dream," Red said. "When we said we'd all fuck Judy Hirshberg in the seventh grade what we really wanted was to fuck *anyone*. You guys dream about it. I'll make movies about it."

Freddie Temple was drinking his beer and smiling through the conversation. "I made over a hundred thousand last year. You boys are like a bunch of old women. You can say what you want, and then I'll say two words: 'New York.' It's the only place where making it means anything at all."

"Don't be an asshole, Freddie," Duke said. Temple shrugged, still smiling.

"Smile, Freddie," Rosenberg said. "What if you hadn't had a trust fund?"

"Look who's talking, Mr. Horatio Alger himself," Red said. "You're an aging ex-playboy," Red said. "And you're the only one working in a family business. That doesn't count."

"Did you morons ever read *Henry IV*?" Dickie held up his hands. "Don't give me wiseass answers. I know you never read *Henry IV*. I'm telling you this so you won't talk behind my back about how I flamed out in high school." He hated to be defensive, but he blustered on. "The King's son, Prince Hal, leads a wild life with Falstaff. No one thinks he'll be anything but a playboy. But he repudiates Falstaff, indeed he always said he could shake off his bad companions and become a true king."

"*Indeed?*" Hennessey said.

"*Repudiates?*" Singer mocked.

"I don't get it, Rosie," Temple said. "But it sounds good over jazz."

"You're the assholes, you guys," Rosenberg fumed, too mad to be cautious. Running on. "You want to put your money where your mouths are? How about this?" He reached. "We have a golf match every five years and we compare our lives. We put a thousand bucks apiece in the first pot. The most successful of us keeps the money. Then we up the ante to five thousand for the next meeting and match. Either you put up the dough or you drop out. If you drop out you'll always know you're the supreme loser. Then each contest we increase the stakes by five G's. By age fifty we're playing for fifteen grand apiece. By then we'll see who's got it or not. Family business means nothing. Mine is a horseshit one-man show now, and I'm either going to quit or hit a home run with it."

"We play every five years?" Temple asked.

"We get to bet on the golf also?" Red asked.

"Laying off your losses already?" Duke said.

"Okay, then," Dickie said. "If you're in, we won't have to hear any more crap about how we're measuring up. Talk is cheap."

"Sticks and stones," said Red. "A thousand in the pot and golf matches every five years."

"If we survive five years," Temple said. "Fucking hippies. Fucking Vietnam." The band was finishing "Lullaby of Birdland," and then the piano player took over, doing a fair imitation of Ahmad Jamal.

"Remember Marian McPartland at the Hickory House?" Temple asked. "I don't know why I'm thinking about that. Maybe every time I went to see her I was ossified."

"You're not ossified," Dickie said, feeling back in control. "You're trying to change the subject. Another part of the contest is that if you don't show up for the match you forfeit the money to the others. You owe it anyway."

"The last time we made a pact like this was about Sullivan's brother," Red said.

"Irony and pity," Rosenberg muttered.

"What's that?" Hennessey said.

"Doesn't matter," answered Rosenberg.

"Look at that guy," Red said, pointing at Sullivan, who was stopping at tables, introducing himself, sticking out his hand. Several women dressed to the nines asked him to sit with them. Hennessey's table watched as Sullivan pulled up a chair, motioned to a waiter for drinks all around, began telling stories that made the women laugh, while they gave each other looks over the laughter, looks in which Sullivan did not share. "He must have not come to these joints in high school," Red said.

"He'll wonder where the yellow went," Dickie said. "Let's get some paper, get this down before some people chicken out." Their waitress provided a needle from her purse. For the second time in their lives they pricked their fingers and signed on a napkin over the dots of blood.

"This is a nail-their-balls-to-the-ground contract," Duke said. "What we've always wanted to do to each other."

"Speak for yourself, Hennessey," Temple said. "How are we really going to judge, short of bringing tax returns, 1040s?"

"How do I know you're a WASP?" Duke answered. "It's one of those things we'll know."

They all signed the agreement, a napkin embossed "Grey's Hardware Store." Only Rosenberg had any doubts about who would win. The only thing he really knew for sure was that he *would* get his balls nailed to the ground on the golf course.

"You boys want some company, all dressed up and nowhere to go?" a woman asked. She reminded Dickie of Dorothy Dandridge, the star of the movie *Carmen Jones* in the middle 1950s.

"We love company," Red said. "Any more at home like you?"

"Wait a minute," Duke interrupted. He jumped to his feet and quickly headed over to where a tall black man stood behind Sleek Sullivan's chair. The man placed his hands on Sullivan's shoulders, pushing down with force as the congressman tried to rise. The women at his table backed their chairs away and watched, the way people circle around an accident, not too close. "You've been stopping at every table talking about Martin Luther King," the big man spoke down to the top of Sullivan's head. "What the fuck do you know about Martin Luther King? You're probably too dumb to really know about jazz. And you're certainly too dumb to be sitting with our women. No matter that you look like some mothafuckin' waiter at the Ritz."

"Easy, pal," Duke said. "Why don't you just let him up and we'll take him back to our table, sit and listen to the music." Chester Grey slid up to them, the kind of man you never saw coming, a man who would appear at the first signs of trouble or the first signs of money. "Now, Judge," he said quietly to the big black man. "This little fellow you're leaning on is a congressman down in Washington. And there is some saying he could go a lot farther than that. I'm sure he was just making nice with the ladies and trying to get a few votes. This is democracy, Judge."

"I think he tryin' to get laid, taking the name of Martin Luther King in vain . . ."

Sleek, once the pressure on his shoulders had been removed,

jumped up, outraged. "I know Dr. King," he shouted. "I've talked with him, pressed the flesh, felt the dream."

"That's a wet dream for *you*, honk," the man called Judge said with no smile on his face. "Don't tell me about no Kennedy neither. You can just forget about coming down to eat where I shit." Judge crooked his finger at the ladies at the table, and they moved away with the big black man. None of them looked at each other. They just left.

"I better walk with you boys to your car, Mr. Hennessey," Chester Grey said. "I don't know what riled up the Judge. But he the kind of man likes to wait outside."

"What happened, Sleek?" Duke asked.

"Well." Sullivan smiled. "I asked them for their vote. Then I suppose I said something about coming over and sitting with us, buying them some drinks. Maybe I said something about rides home and that we were all God's children."

"Time to go," said Duke.

"No one wanted to hear that I had shaken the hand of Martin Luther King."

"You've got to do more than shake a hand, shake a hand," Chester Grey said.

"I knew it was a mistake coming down here," Dickie said. "They don't want us. It's not like the old days. Then you felt racy, but safe."

"It's better now," Red replied. "All the cards on the table. The way life should be. This is America with everyone expressing themselves. It's natural now. You can protest; you can really stand for what you believe."

"Oh bullshit, Stanley," Temple said. "You're just swallowing what you hear in Hollywood. The cities are coming apart; the country is torn up. This is freedom carried to its illogical extreme. No one is man enough to say *no* to anything."

"Okay," Red said. "Okay. No more beers."

"Right," Dickie said. "We're leaving. Each of us owes eight bucks."

"Jesus," Freddie said. "You should come in the investment business. You're going to be so successful, how about taking the tab?"

Chester Grey saw them off in Duke's Colony Park wagon. The

Judge stepped from the shadows and stood next to the club owner. "Should have let me teach the mothafuckers something, Chester."

"Soon enough you teach 'em your way. For a while I'll teach 'em mine."

Duke cruised away, leaving no rubber. He never exited anywhere in a hurry.

"Let me take that big spook back into the ring," Sullivan cursed. "Show me a man who can't face me in the face."

"Congressman," Hennessey soothed him, reaching out an arm to pat him on the shoulder. "You could have taken him. But what would it prove?"

"Yeah," Red yelled out, "with an M16 and a grenade launcher."

"That's the whole thing," Sleek Sullivan said. "Fucking Vietnam anyway."

Freddie wanted to shut it all out. He rolled down his window to get some winter air on his face after the long evening. " 'Dear John,' " he said out of nowhere, the words to the popular song during the Korean War. " 'I was overseas in battle when the postman came to me, he handed me a letter I was happy as I could be . . .' " They all joined in. " 'Dear John, Oh, how I hate to write . . . Dear John, I must let you know tonight that my love for you has died, it's like grass upon the lawn, for tonight I wed another . . . Dear John.' " They sang on the ride back to their cars, Red because he knew the lyrics to everything, Dickie because he was sick of talking, Duke to keep himself awake and the candidate, Sleek Sullivan, because wasn't he on top of the world and wasn't he old enough to remember when war seemed like fun?

CHAPTER SIXTEEN

O

First Match: 1973

Even though it was for the golf match and, coincidentally, for Red's bachelor party, they were all writing off the trip to Los Angeles as a business expense. The planes brought them separately to California. It gave them time to prepare as they gazed down on rivers and lakes, farmland and mountains that made them all feel both trivial and exalted, poetry of flying cross-country.

Dickie had upgraded his ticket at the last minute. Red was meeting him, and he wanted to let him know that he could afford first cabin. He took full advantage of drinks in first-class: gin and tonics, wine, Grand Marnier with the hot-fudge sundae for dessert. "Do I look like a man in control of his life?" he asked the stewardess. "Do I look like a wonk?"

The stewardess didn't understand anything he said. But he looked rich to her, saying whatever he said in his wide-lapel suit, wide polka-dot tie. So she stayed to pour him extra drinks, hoping to profit from any good advice, knowing that college for her was the first-class section of airplanes.

Dickie and Adrienne had moved from Boston to Scarsdale, New York, to a house with a small swimming pool. Her father had put up most of the down payment, a bargain they had struck because of Dickie's ambivalence about New York. Denim had changed their lives in the beginning of the 1970s, and it was the excuse Adrienne needed to push for the move. It was she who lobbied her husband to consider maternity jeans for the looser atmosphere of the new age in which she believed. "We've intellectual freedom now," she argued. "How about the comfort of our bodies? Look good, feel good. Hang out with your baby."

"Hang out with your baby" became the motto in their advertisements, on their letterhead, on billboards along the Mass Turnpike and leading into the city from the airports of New York. Jeans were jeans, but every pregnant woman in America suddenly wanted the label "Hang Out with Your Baby." The Rosenbergs' company sold five hundred thousand pair the first year of production. This necessitated beefing up New York operations, giving Adrienne the leverage she needed to get them, with their own new baby Oakleigh, to pack up for Scarsdale.

"Oakleigh Rosenberg?" Dickie's father said. "What kind of a name is that for a Jewish boy? Of course The Countess would probably approve. But that's your mother's side."

"O is for Grandma's dad. *Oscar* Baer. *O*."

"If you only went to Wharton instead of Harvard . . . whatever you picked up in Cambridge warped your mind."

"Adrienne is as Jewish as you can get, Dad. *She* loves the name."

Adrienne's father hit the roof when he heard it. "Oakleigh Rosenberg," Slapsie Maxie exploded. "They'll laugh me out of Clarke's. Hi, boys, my grandson's name is Oakleigh Rosenberg. Better you should name him Pinkus Pinocchio Rosenberg. How about Abraham Lincoln Rosenberg? Better Mickey Mantle Rosenberg, at least with that name they don't laugh me out of Clarke's."

"It's a new era, Daddy," Adrienne said to her father. "You got used to taking a daughter to the Garden; you'll get used to Oakleigh."

"What's wrong with Max?" he said seriously. "Maybe the next one is for me, and I suppose I won't care what you name him as long as my grandson is no sissy and as long as he's got it here." He pointed his index finger to his heart. "And here," he said even louder, moving his finger to his ample belly. "The guts."

Dickie wore a business suit when he landed in Los Angeles, remembering what his father had always told him, "You are *never* not doing business. When you travel, you forever keep next season's line in your mind. Who knows who you sit next to? And you must always dress like you don't need it, but you must want to increase the volume."

Red Singer was wearing bell-bottom faded jeans and a jean jacket covered with embroidery over a black T-shirt with the motto "Save the pubic areas" written in white. He had thought the expression up himself.

"Baby-cakes," he greeted Dickie at the top of his voice, not caring that he was stared at by all the people waiting for their luggage. Red kissed him on the lips. Dickie rubbed it off violently and broke away. "For Christ's sake, Stanley. I come from the East . . ."

"I'm just glad to see you, smoothy. Bring your money?"

"I brought a picture of my kid, how about that?"

"Anyone can have kids, Rosie."

"Red. So hot to trot. You've got to calm down a little. I've been flying for six hours."

"When you see my film you'll forget about your flight. When you meet my bride you'll flip." They carried the bags, suitcase and golf clubs, to Singer's red '56 Thunderbird, which sat in the sun, its hardtop off, looking like a hymn to rock 'n' roll. "You like?"

"It's beautiful. When did you buy it?"

"Who buys? You don't buy out here. It's leased." Red took him on a tour, on the freeways at eighty miles an hour, slower as he showed him Malibu, Topanga Canyon, Venice beach. "Don't kid yourself, my friend," Singer said. "It's beautiful, warm, the incredible flowers and vegetables. But eighty percent of the guys here came out for the pussy. And they all want to be in front of the camera, agents, managers, producers. Everyone." Red drove him along Mulholland Drive. "This is the road to the studio," he explained. "Remember when Jack Benny used to joke about taking girls parking on Mulholland Drive? Look down. That's the valley, San Fernando. You want to work there, not live there." Singer whipped them around curves, driving like a racer. Dickie leaned forward, trying to keep his carefully combed hair from uncovering the thinning spots. At home he was selling the shit out of denim maternity jeans, but Red was anxious to go three up before they ever got to the first tee. He slowed down coming into Hollywood, pointing out Grauman's Chinese Theater and where the stars were embedded in the Hollywood Boulevard sidewalks. "This is grubsville," Red said. "Like lower Washington Street in Boston where the strip joints are, where you get pizza late at night, hard stares and hookers."

Dickie changed the subject. "Are you getting married for money or for love? You used to say that we were all schmucks for loving our wives."

"My dad told me it's just as easy to fall in love with a rich one," Red answered. "He taught me everything he ever learned selling on the road, that the road was life. I'll let you be the judge when you meet Lindalee. She's up at Pink House now."

Dickie started to laugh. "*Everybody's* dad told them to marry a rich one."

"What's so fucking funny?"

"I've got a kid named Oakleigh. You've now got a fiancée named Lindalee; you've got a name for your house."

"You ever been to Bermuda?"

"Not yet," Dickie admitted.

"Every fucking house in Bermuda has a name: Swan's Nest, Heron's Leap. Every shack, rich or poor. I live in a pink stucco house; I gave it a name. Lindalee comes from Mississippi, home of the world's most beautiful women. That's the kind of thing they name people down there. When in Rome, right?"

Dickie was still laughing. "You lease your house, too?"

Red smiled as well. "The bank owns my house. I put about nothing down, maybe a grand."

Dickie was thinking that he had never seen anyplace as beautiful except for sections of Europe when he was younger, when he knew he really belonged in the Lost Generation after World War I. They drove down Sunset Boulevard past the Beverly Hills Hotel. "That's where you're staying," Red told him. "A place designed to make you feel insecure because you'll think everyone you see there has more money than you. Remember, though, they'll think the same about you. Let's visit Pink House; we'll check you in later."

"The hotel was pink," Dickie said, looking back at its towers, the royal palms bending on the lawns.

"Pink, pink, you stink," Red said. "Remember that?"

"Black, black," Dickie responded. "No takesies back."

"Before we get to the house," Red asked, "how's your life, Rosie?"

"I can't talk about my life at your house?"

"Of course you can. But women don't understand the childhoods of the guys. You know. It doesn't mean anything to them. I'm going to war every day out here. I can't let Lindalee know I'm going to fucking war. How do you think I got her? By being on top every minute, being the winner. No serious shit for Lindalee."

"Marriage is serious, Stanley. You're gonna kid yourself if you think you can keep it light when you're married. The Kennedys get all their bills sent to a central office. The bills get paid, and the Kennedys never see any of it. You and me, we're not there yet. You have a bad day, and the bill from Bonwit Teller comes, you may hit the roof. And it's one woman, you know? One woman, supposedly for life. Not the lover boy struttin' down the hallways of Brookwood High in your letter sweater."

"You telling me you might as well write me a check for a grand?"

"This has got nothing to do with how well we're doing. I could probably buy and sell you five times. Maybe marriage in Los Angeles is different than Boston and New York. But maybe you're shitting yourself."

"I love her, Rosie. If you smile, I'll kill you. I've got to have Lindalee. As for the grand, maybe Duke and Temple come in with all the cards, what do you think?"

"I think you asked me about my life and I never gave you an answer. I still drive a Mercedes 250."

"No convertible? No coupe?"

"Fuck you. My wife drives a Town and Country station wagon. We stay at the Waldorf when market seasons are on. We stay at the Regency when we go to the theater. We vacation in Barbados, and we rent a house for August in Chatham. You can lease things all you want. But we *own* the business, and nothing works like owning the business. Temple doesn't own his business. Duke is Duke. He's hungry, but . . ."

"You're going to say, no Yiddisher kop." Red tapped his head. "Don't kid yourself. I always thought Hennessey had some Jewish blood. Plus he's hungry. Hungry means everything."

Red had turned up onto Beverly Glen and gunned the Thunderbird, darting past other cars all the way up the winding road. Pink House was on a side street halfway up the Glen, a two-story stucco dwelling that their fathers would have called a bungalow. "I was an agent when I moved here," Red announced. "Kissing ass in a thousand different colors. When *Pounce* is released it's going to be Brentwood or Bel Air, maybe Holmby Hills. No more of these canyons where you drive home thinking Charlie Manson lives next door and you pull in the driveway and there's a coyote staring back at you. A coyote probably with fucking rabies. Lindalee likes Bel Air. Says it reminds her of Mississippi. So don't queer my act."

The path to the house was lined with earthenware pots in which orchids grew.

Red called, "Oh, Delicious? The man with designer samples -is here." Sounds of James Brown flooded the house. Red began singing over the music. He knew every lyric.

A voice, soft, but dead clear through the song said, "If I knew your friend dressed so good, I would have gone with you to the airport." Lindalee Hoffman walked down the narrow front stairs. If she had come to Hollywood in the thirties or forties her studio would have changed her name to something European: French or Spanish, Linda LaFlamme or Linda L'amor. One producer who saw her first screen test yelled out, "Lindalee Lingerie." Dickie thought that there had been no one in high school like Lindalee. No one in college. No one during the time when all he wanted was a blond debutante, when he was drunkenly writing free verse about fucking his way into the Social Register. Lindalee was everyone's idea of a pinup or a *Playboy* centerfold. She was an inch shy of six feet, two inches taller than Red. Her hair was Marilyn blond, Mamie Van Doren blond, and she was bursting out of a gray and white seersucker sunsuit, a large version of an outfit in which a little girl might be dressed. She wore no makeup or lipstick. Her voice and accent, even though acting lessons had layered them over, were unmistakably Deep South. "Y'all went to Harvard," she said, moving to shake his hand. "I used to go to William Faulkner's house on New Year's Eve when I was little. With my daddy. Mr. Faulkner used to tell us ghost stories on New Year's Eve. I'm pleased to meet an educated friend of Stanley's." Dickie was pleased to kiss her on the cheek, on both cheeks. Totally charmed, he said, "I'm in love for the first time," the line he had used for years.

"Lover-lips," Red laughed. "You're such a schmuck." Red hugged them both. "We'll have some champagne and then drive you to the hotel. Lindalee and I drink only champagne."

Temple usually went to the Caribbean in February. This year he promised Marley Barbados in March, a longer trip than in the past, to make up for this weekend without her in California. He made the promise not through guilt but as a matter-of-fact response to a change in their routine. He didn't want any of the others blowing the whistle on the accident long ago. He was going west as insurance, he told himself, even though it would cost him a thousand dollars. With Wall Street's current stream of consolidations and bankruptcies there was no way he would win the pool. Triple screwed, he thought, since I'll never beat Singer or Hennessey on the golf course. Temple had never paid much attention to the running of his firm's business. He was an institutional salesman. He entertained, he took the orders, he pocketed the commissions. He was a partner in the firm. It was an honor at his age. He thought that if you sold a product well, the business would take care of itself. Freddie watched the land of America go by from thirty thousand feet. How many golf courses and swimming pools was he flying over? How many rich people? Why was he in a business that seemed to be going out of business?

Even in the Depression, his grandfather had maids and a chauffeur. And he was in investments. Freddie found it difficult to comprehend the chaos on Wall Street, to realize that retail customers would order two hundred shares of General Motors and get shipped five hundred shares of General Electric or get shipped nothing at all and then call the SEC or their lawyers. He wasn't really aware that Wall Street firms couldn't handle the paperwork load, that they were drowning under the volume of activity in the late 1960s, everyone choking on the frenzy to get in on the action. The Street was moving the merchandise, but no one was minding the store. All the beans were counted by hand, and the hands could not keep up with the trading volume. Stock exchanges began closing an hour early, then two hours early to catch up. Then they were closing one day a week.

On the plane Fred couldn't shake memories of his lunch with Borden, Kimball's senior partner at the Racquet Club. Sandy Borden had hired Freddie, trained him in the business. Borden ordered a Bombay gin martini straight up, with an olive. Not until he took an approving sip, shut his eyes and inhaled slightly did he look directly at Temple, toasting him by raising his glass. "Frederick, we shat the bed."

"For Christ's sake, Mr. Borden, I did three hundred fifty thousand gross last year. My department did nothing but business."

"Everyone did nothing but business," the senior partner said. "But everyone spent, and no one figured out costs. With all the volume we had only red ink. The Exchange stepped in this morning. We are below their capital requirements. As a matter of fact, we're basically out of business. If the company's worth anything it's furniture and fixtures and a few of the hunting prints in the partners' dining room."

"But," Freddie said, "we're a hundred years old." Sandy Borden smiled. "Look around you," he said. "Everyone in this room voted for Richard Nixon. He's not our kind of man, but we all voted for him. He couldn't get into this club if he were shot in here from a cannon. The times are out of joint. Pretty soon we won't even have an oyster bar." Freddie couldn't talk. He had to think about this. When he was growing up he heard about a friend of his grandfather's who had shot himself. He had stuck his custom Purdey into his mouth when his firm went bankrupt. He had killed himself, Freddie was told, because he couldn't stand the silence he thought he felt when he walked into his club. He couldn't stand the disgrace of the bankrupt. "What are you going to do?" Freddie said. He somehow didn't think the business failure would apply to him. He was doing fine. He was too young.

"We'll probably merge out, make the best deal we can under the circumstances, pick up the pieces."

"What about the name?" Freddie said.

The senior partner sipped his martini, thought about sweetbreads for lunch and shook his head. "I'm not sure you understand, Frederick," he said. "The club of Wall Street is finished. It's over. Do you know anything at all about the new Jews?"

Freddie laughed to himself about that line as he got up to stretch his long legs one more time before the final approach to LAX.

"You're going to Los Angeles with the firm falling apart to go to a bachelor party? We are supposed to be in Mad River this weekend." Marley made her lips as thin as possible when she said this.

"I made a promise long ago," Freddie said. "What I say I'm going to do, I honor that commitment. You can dump on it, but that's what St. Luke's taught me.

Marley laughed. "I stopped believing that when I was sixteen. My field hockey coach asked me to bend over and touch my toes in the locker room to 'test my flexibility.' I was facing away from her at the time, and I took her seriously until I felt the hand on my bum."

"We can go to Mad River for the rest of our lives. We can go to Chamonix. Anywhere. It has to do with honor."

She looked at her husband. It was winter on Park Avenue, where they lived on the eleventh floor in a fine building near the corner of 72nd Street. They had two children, Myles in the Buckley School ("Buckley bums suck their thumbs") and the baby, Brett, with an au pair in her own room the way it should be. Marley didn't want to know about businesses folding. "Honor?" she said to her husband. "Honor is on the East Coast. God knows what's in Los Angeles."

Freddie was going to work for the new Jews, which his old senior partner meant to mean anyone who was not a Lehman or Oppenheim or Loeb or Baruch. Freddie had been recruited by Irving "Ace" Cohen, a bridge life master at thirty, connoisseur of racehorses, American Impressionists and Cuban cigars. Ace Cohen had been chosen by the New York Stock Exchange to take over the failed businesses of three old-line concerns that couldn't make the transition to days when volume on the Exchange exceeded fifty million shares. The surviving firm that Cohen ran was Peterson, Pyle. An old name. "These assholes just barely got used to television when the computer came along," Cohen told him, chomping on an unlit Garcia Vega. "What did you lose in the firm, seventy-five, a hundred grand? No more than that?"

"It was bitter," Freddie said, "at the end, everyone pointing fingers. It used to be special to be a partner in a Wall Street investment firm."

"And you always made money, right?" Cohen said. "An institutional profit center. The guys watching the cash registers took you down the tubes, right? You kept selling all the way until the last day?"

"I've got relationships. They kept coming through."

"I'll be honest with you, Freddie," Cohen said. "Institutional salesmen are a dime a dozen: bring the analyst to lunch, memorize someone else's research reports and spew the shit back. Get the tickets to the Knicks, to Forest Hills, the Yankees. But you can give us a certain legitimacy." All the time Cohen talked to Temple, he concentrated on his Quotron machine, eyes flicking only occasionally to Freddie's face. Cohen was a trader. He needed to know prices all the time. But he never forgot what you said or what he said to you. "I want you," he said, "to get into places we could never get into: the Cabot banks, the big life insurance companies, the old school-tie pension plans. The Street is coming down around our ears, and we want to be there to pick up the pieces. We want to go by Merrill Lynch like a shot in the next five years." He flicked an intercom switch next to his Quotron. "Buy fifty thousand Caterpillar tractor at a quarter," he said without moving his eyes from the screen. He watched the ticker tape for several minutes, not speaking. Then, satisfied, he swung his glance around, relit his cigar and leaned his head directly at Freddie. "Well. You want to be a revolutionary, take a lot of stock in this company? Or you want to stay a Gentile, lower your handicap at the Maidstone Club, wear pink and green and be an asshole all your life?"

"We do almost no business out here," Freddie thought as his plane flew over the Rocky Mountains. "One office in L.A., one in San Francisco but small." He had checked the small leather-bound book that listed all the members of his undergraduate club at Harvard, their addresses and occupations. There were a lot of brothers on the West Coast, many well connected. Brothers took care of brothers. The bonus was that he counted on Red Singer introducing him into the movie studios. Ace Cohen made everyone want to work their butts off for him. He'd be amazed when Freddie brought movie clients into Peterson, Pyle. The collapse of his old firm shook Temple's faith in the natural order and in his certainty that he led the charmed life. He had pondered not going to Los Angeles at all, giving business excuses, sending a check for a thousand with good luck to all of them. But he couldn't do it. The same way he could never have protested the Vietnam War or married someone of whom his parents did not approve. Years ago, if an Ace Cohen had considered him an asshole, he would have passed it off to jealousy. Now he thought he could see the future. If a new era was dawning in Wall Street, he could afford to blow a thousand to his old friends, knowing he'd get it back tenfold down the road. Besides, shouldn't they all be clients? Chuck Colson had said, "Get them by the balls, and their hearts and minds will follow."

He had never been to California. One boy he remembered

from St. Luke's School had come from San Francisco and was rumored to have been from old family money, Mexican land grant money. The boy had been skinny and homesick and had left after third-form year. Schoolboys had called him "Goldrush," and for some reason he had hated the name. He came out swinging whenever it was thrown at him. So he was called it all the time. Freddie's house master said, "They hate nicknames in California." And Freddie had believed that.

He went directly from the airport to the Beverly Hills Hotel when he landed. After checking in, he went to the Polo Lounge and ordered a Mount Gay rum and tonic, which is what he drank whenever he went from someplace cold to someplace warm. And he looked around. In the Polo Lounge in March he wore loafers with no socks. The crowd looked to him like the crowd in the Oak Bar at the Plaza in New York, only without neckties. He instinctively realized a basic truth about Los Angeles: if you show up for the game in a Brooks Brothers suit and tie, the customer will be eighty percent in your pocket. He finished his drink and walked around the pool, unconsciously sucked into the fantasy that everyone adopts when checking into the Beverly Hills Hotel, that he was a producer with a hot property. Freddie knew that he looked like he had come to L.A. carrying a bag full of money. A front man. Once he came to grips with that, he could call Red Singer.

Duke Hennessey, at two hundred forty pounds, owned the back of the plane, blowing off nervous energy. He talked to people, wandered the aisles, bobbed his head in greeting. He asked strangers if they were on vacation or business. He had one Bloody Mary after they took off from Boston. But Duke didn't need alcohol. He discovered that as he had gotten older his moods would swing erratically. When business went well he was euphoric. When events or his lenders or his lawyers didn't move as quickly as he wished he would throw chairs against the walls. Then he would become despondent. He would grab snacks between huge meals followed late at night by as much as a quart of ice cream. He wore his hair long but just recently began blowing it dry with Rita's dryer. When he played sports in school he assumed he would win, he felt he had control, over events and over his body. He made a vow on the plane, determined to get back near two hundred pounds. In the last month he had assembled his first major parcel of property in Boston, a granite building erected in the 1930s housing several small law firms, two accountants and a travel agent. Duke had personally raised over a million dollars for Sleek Sullivan's victorious Senate campaign, putting the bite on everyone from MIT classmates and professors to ballplaying friends from the old Cape Cod League to other real estate developers who had their own fish to fry. In return, Sullivan had dropped a few words in the right places, made a few phone calls if only to say that Hennessey was okay, that you didn't have to worry about Hennessey. The building cost a quarter of a million. Duke had already lined up a bank to go into a renovated ground floor. His interest rate would stay fixed, but he could write off this interest and depreciation while raising all the rents. It was his biggest deal so far, and he knew it would be worth, in time, over a million to him.

"You grew up in a neighborhood, in Boston," Duke said to a stewardess he had picked because he could tell she was Irish. "Most of your friends had parents with the mother Italian and the father Irish or the other way around. You thought that flying was the only way to break out of the neighborhood, and your best girlfriend from home is now a nurse."

"How'd you know that?" she said. "I don't believe it." She was careful after that. She saw the wedding band. But he gave her a short lecture on how she could own her own apartment and how little she could put down and where to go for a mortgage and what communities in Boston to shop for real estate bargains. She thought the big man was adorable, and she moved Duke and his carry-on luggage through the curtain into first class. "Breaking away from home is only a first step," Duke told her when she brought him a second Bloody, this one for free. "Next, you have to go after what you want. And you have to ask for it."

"Is that for real?" she said, pointing at the ring on his left hand, believing that there was nothing for nothing in this life.

"It's for real." Duke smiled.

"We Irish have to stick together," she said. It was something, Duke thought, that Rita would have said years ago. He took a cab to the hotel, marveling at what grew in California, the trees and flowers and ground cover. But what he marveled at most was that all the cars were so clean. He counted eight Rolls-Royces along the way. He had never seen a Rolls in Boston except in an auto show. It was a typical March at home, Duke thought, miserable and raw, snow followed by bitter cold and days of unrelenting gray, with winds whipping off Boston Harbor like wet towels snapping in your face. Growing up with that, Duke thought, it must be the same in March everywhere. He could conceive of making $10 million. But he couldn't conceive of a place that didn't punish you in the winter. When he arrived at the Beverly Hills Hotel he started to have the sinking feeling that told him Red Singer wasn't so dumb after all. He began to think that maybe his million-dollar building in Copley Square wasn't such a big deal. He forced himself to think about catching a key game in high school against a team where everyone looked like a ringer. All PG's and six-foot-five. Take charge of the game, he used to tell himself. They're only a fucking bunch of mackerel snappers, just like us. He also did this at MIT. It was his mantra. And after he thought about it for a while, he was ready to play.

They all met that night at Pink House, where, Duke said, "Stanley unveiled the beauty queen." Lindalee had changed into black silk evening pants and a long white cotton blouse with puffy sleeves. She wore her long hair piled up on top of her head. "You do your hair up for entertaining," she explained. "That's what they told us way back at the All-States." The boys just stared while Red stayed close to his fiancée, every so often hugging her, kissing her, making sure they knew she was all his.

It was strained for a while, like any reunion. "First you got to know," Red said, "there are, at any one time out here, at least ten thousand scripts or projects floating around. Maybe even a lot of them are good, could be good movies, maybe even profitable movies. But there are only five people who count in the entire business. Ten people at the absolute outside maximum. Everyone else is giving themselves hand jobs. What I mean by really counting is people who can make whatever movies they wanna make. It's always been a dictatorship. But every fucking cabdriver with a script thinks he can be the dictator." While Red talked, his arm around Lindalee, all the others thought one thing: "How the hell did a guy like Singer get a girl like this?"

"I know y'all are tired," Lindalee said, "from your trip and all. So I made a batch of tacos, which is the best food to eat when your insides are all jumbled from flying."

"Where'd you get tacos in Mississippi?" Dickie asked.

"Silly," Lindalee replied. "When you travel all over in contests you get to eat the home food. We went to Texas tons of times because they got some of the best contests. Lots of tacos and refried beans. Chicken-fried steak. Nothing, of course, as good as Delta food, but I got kind of partial to tacos. Look good in a plate, you can arrange 'em nice, put stuff around 'em."

"You're not going to find a woman like this in America" — Red beamed — "who can ink a contract for twenty-five big ones in a James Bond where she gets bumped off during the credits, who can twirl flaming batons and cook you a meal to break your heart built around corn mush."

"And my Stanley's got better hair than Sean Connery," she said.

The other guys were on a distant planet. They looked at each other. Red grinned from behind Lindalee and slowly raised his middle finger. He was even developing a drawl.

The next day was Saturday. Red had told them his bachelor party was being produced the way all great parties should be. They were to check out of the hotel, take their golf clubs and luggage to the main entrance at 3:00 P.M., the Beverly Hills having no problem with late checkouts in March. They all slept late and eventually met at the pool, laughing when they each showed up wearing sunglasses. "Hollywood bohos," Duke called them before he climbed up onto the diving board and did a giant cannonball, splashing people pretending to read scripts and others who shrank from water anywhere on their bodies unless it were specially treated. "I saw Ted Williams last time at bat," Hennessey said, reaching for something grand to compare this with. "This is nothing compared with that."

"It's just a lot like the Riviera," Freddie said. "Ever been to the Eden Roc, Rosie?"

Rosenberg was covering himself with Bain de Soleil, knowing that he always equated being tanned with being successful.

"Let's say I drove by it," Dickie said. "On the Riviera I never spent more than $2.50 a night. In nineteen fifty-nine my father wasn't exactly stuffing hundred-dollar bills in my pants."

"My heart pumps piss for you," Hennessey said. "I'll organize a benefit for the Rosenbergs."

"Forget when we were kids," Dickie flared. "We never had as much money as you thought we did. I had to work just like you. We all caddied. You want to compare hardships?"

Freddie saw too many people on telephones plugged in next to their beach chairs. He signaled for one himself. He called his office, apologizing, with his hand cupped over the mouthpiece, to his friends. "It's a business that never stops. You have to know the numbers all the time. It's obsessive." Freddie still looked as he had in his twenties, slim-waisted, no laugh or frown lines, his madras bathing trunks the same kind he wore on his college spring breaks in Bermuda or on Christmas jaunts with his parents in Montego Bay.

"I'll be sorry if I call home," Duke said, "because people on the other end of the line love to give out bad news, make you feel shitty you're away."

"I feel the same," Dickie said. "I've been married for years. Whenever I'd be on the road and call up Adrie, there's always that strain, you can feel it. Your different days get in the way between you."

"This is incredible," Duke said, pointing with a swizzle stick to several young women in bikinis and high-heeled mules parading around the pool, looking for spots in which to settle. "Where's this been all my life?"

"The sexual revolution," Dickie said. "And what are we doing? We're all married. The pill for us only means we're not having more children."

"Rita won't take the pill. Vatican roulette or frenchies."

"Christ, I haven't heard that word in years. Drugstores still sell safes?" Dickie joked.

"No, asshole. I got 'em saved from high school. A gross lasts forever when you've been married as long as me."

Freddie cradled the phone under his chin. "Buy the Penn Central," he said. "The real estate alone is worth a hundred bucks a share. That's what my people tell me." He lit a cigar. Two women in bikinis watched Freddie.

Duke and Rosenberg instinctively sucked in their stomachs and wondered if they looked at all like movie producers. Dickie felt a little embarrassed being with Duke, who wore a small gold cross on a chain around his neck. Temple hung up on New York. "When in Rome," he said, handing Duke his cigar. He did a graceful dive into the pool, where the only other occupant was an overweight man intently doing laps, dog paddling between meals to please a young friend on a chaise eating cheese and popping grapes. "Where's this been all my life?" repeated Duke, and Dickie silently agreed.

The limousine picked them up at three o'clock. A man jumped out of the backseat, a short man, perhaps five-foot-five, with long brown hair pulled back in a ponytail and muscles bulging out of a pink T-shirt, muscles that said weight lifting. "I'm Romeo," he said. "I'm Stanley's partner, if he hasn't already told you, and I'm producing his bachelor party." He formally shook everyone's hand and ushered them into the back of the stretch. As they took off, Romeo talked nonstop. "I'm not used to dealing with civilians," he said. "So put the brakes on if you find yourselves losing me. First of all a little Mary Jane." He lit up a joint, closely rolled, that he took from a pounded silver cigarette box. "Victorian," he added. "Got my name on it. Gift from The Stars. My rock group. You know The Stars? Crazy cocksuckers, but platinum early in the game, and I'm along for the ride. I found them, produce them, give them allowances, spoon-feed the crazy fucks."

"Where does Singer come in?" Duke asked.

"I figure the redhead is headed platinum also," Romeo said. "And he appears not to give a shit, which helps out here." He passed around the silver box. He handed a joint to Dickie. "Smoke 'em if you got 'em," Romeo laughed. "You light up. Take a toke. Pass it on. This is how you make friends, get into show biz. Dope got *me* into show business," Romeo explained. "I couldn't take school, but I love music and I could weave a web when I was high. People believe me, don't ask me why, and big balls didn't hurt. Made a million when I was twenty-seven years old, pissed on Brooklyn, thank you very much, America, and came to the land of angels, where it is the dream of the three cherries that keeps you going. Stanley Singer stole twenty-five hundred dollars somewhere two years ago to option a book about a businessman with a social conscience who has a secret life as a terrorist. Why the fuck not? His thing out here was do a favor for everyone he met so that everyone would owe *him* someday. Not so dumb. With the book optioned, he took most of his agenting money to keep a young writer on the script, two hundred twenty-five a week and all the malted-milk balls the kid could pop. Red's agency found me in Chicago. The boss knew that one of the independents wanted into the music business, had good instincts, knew that sooner or later I'd want Hollywood, showed me the script, which I dug. It was a natural. Next thing I know, Stanley and I are sitting with that prick Pokross, head of Entire Artists, at your very hotel eating chicken salad with grapes, drinking white wine, and he makes us a deal, one hundred K producer's fee plus six points of the net profit of the picture. Every point in *Easy Rider* was worth one million dollars, a lot of fucking malted-milk balls and a lot of shit." He pointed to the cigarette case.

Duke and Rosenberg were giggling. Temple smiled a smile at Romeo as if the man were his long-lost best friend. "Where's the party?" he asked.

Romeo thought they were stupid. "Where else do you have a bachelor party if you're throwing it for the biggest above-the-line success story since Thalberg? . . . Vegas."

They stayed at the Tides, the hotel's name having to do with fortune rather than the desert. Ten men were part of the bachelor party, including the three Easterners. "A test of your marriages," Red predicted. "And a send-off for mine. You guys probably had a private room at Locke-Ober's or some fleabag and a stripper with stretch marks and a forty-five recording of 'Teach Me Tonight.' Schmucks. Tonight for me is good-bye to freedom. Tomorrow we tee it up before you guys present the checks. No hills, long course, lot of sand. Rosenberg will be in more bunkers than Eva Braun." They had a two-bedroom suite with a living room connecting, a room the size of a 1940s starter house in Connecticut. Red was sharing a bedroom with Temple. Used to Las Vegas, Singer had ordered a masseur to the room shortly after their arrival. Temple watched. "So what do you think?" Red said as the masseur, dressed in shorts and gray basketball jersey, rubbed in silence.

"Lots of funny mirrors," Freddie said. "Like an amusement park."

"Do you think life is like fucking Brookwood in nineteen fifty? Rosenberg and I never knew *anyone* outside the town. Hennessey had relatives, cops and firemen, maybe they lived two towns away. A trip for them was the next parish, for Christ's sake. My father saw more of the world than anyone I knew. And he saw New York City, if he was lucky, mostly upstate New York, New England. Tupper Lake, New York, was like fucking Venice or Madrid for all we knew."

"I've fished near Tupper Lake, Red. It's nothing like Venice."

Red turned his head to look at Temple. "You'll never make movies, Freddie."

"No, but think about it," Temple said. "Where do you think the money's going to come from to make pictures? It's going to come from Wall Street. You can dump on the money men. But they're going to own you, and you're going to have to kiss butt every step of the way."

"Ah, but in between butt kissing, I get massages."

"I wouldn't let another guy rub me," Hennessey said to Rosenberg in their room. "I don't know what it is. A trainer could tape me up years ago, no problem. But having another guy's hands on me just grabs me the wrong way."

"My father always got massages," Dickie said. "Called them rubdowns. I thought of them as something for rich fat men, that somehow they were related to making them feel skinnier."

"Rosie, I think you're the kind of guy who's going to go for rubdowns someday."

"How do you figure?"

"You never in your life want Red Singer to go one up." Duke rummaged in his suitcase and took out a cut-down broom handle. He tossed a plastic Wiffle ball to Rosenberg. "Pitch a few to me in the living room," he said. "Won't break anything. Swinging a bat warms me up for the match tomorrow. And I want you to swear to your handicap if I'm gonna give you all those strokes."

"Want me to sign the card in blood?"

Duke looked at him for a moment without speaking. "Just pitch me the ball and duck. Throw as hard as you want."

In a private function room at the Tides, waiters who had seen it all hustled about with chafing dishes, bowls of shrimp and oysters. The room was ringed with floor-to-ceiling mirrors that reflected the color of the carpeting, floors and trim — Chinese red. The waiters brought the guests drinks on lacquered trays from a small bar set up in one corner. A long table stood in the middle of the room. On it sat ten place settings. Romeo had arranged everything and stood surveying the room as if approving a set. He was dressed in a white linen suit with extra-wide lapels over a maroon silk shirt opened to the waist. A gold lion medallion hung on a chain around his neck.

"You're a Leo," Hennessey said to him.

"You got a good eye," Romeo responded, tuned to anyone not kissing the hem of his garment. No one was going to fuck around with him. Hadn't he grown up on Flatbush Avenue and made a million by the time he was twenty-seven? He didn't trust people who were not in the business. They probably never even laid eyes on *Variety*, let alone *Cash Box*. Why did Singer even bother with these people unless they had markers out on him. If Red were paying off their markers in Vegas, maybe he wanted Romeo to get the strangers laid or something. "Drink, sir?" a waiter interrupted. "Just bring me a Stoli on the rocks with an orange peel," Romeo said. "Every ten minutes bring me another until I tell you to stop."

Freddie, Duke and Dickie wore ties. They were the only ones who did. The five other men were all friends of Red's from Los Angeles, all in the movie business. There was Lulu Sample, the writer of *Pounce*, who Red claimed lived on malted-milk balls but who seemed to be taking other nourishment that evening in the shape of fried wonton and an occasional little red pill that he kept in a tin box labeled Altoids. He was overweight, in his late twenties, dressed in blue jeans, work shirt and a madras jacket that was two sizes too large. His clothes looked as if they were pulled from a bin in a thrift shop somewhere around 1952.

A young director was there, a man who had escaped his New Jersey roots, learned to make commercials in New York and longed for sunshine, somewhat like Ratso Rizzo in *Midnight Cowboy*. His name had been George Goldberg, but he had changed it officially to Godard Goldberg after his hero, the director of *Breathless*. He looked like a young Zero Mostel. Every conversation he had with anyone related only to how his life matched some movie in the past. "You'd look just like Ramon Navarro if your hair were a little fuller, same lips," he said when he met Dickie Rosenberg.

Red introduced them to Manny Gates. "You're going to love Manny Gates," Red had told them at Pink House. "He's got the dream job, art director. He's just like us, like he grew up in Brookwood. Same small town."

"You goin' limp on us, Red?" Hennessey had asked.

"This guy was one of the hottest creative advertising guys in New York. Wanted to make movies. But don't we all, darling?" The others hooted, particularly Rosenberg, whom Red had called phony for years.

"An art director," Red explained, "is someone who makes films look the way they do. The art director gets the branding irons, the buckwagon, the animals, gives it the look of a Western. Only trouble with the job is that it's below the line. Dog shit, if you want to stand up and be counted by the people who count. Above the line, in the credits, are producer, director and stars." Manny Gates drank martinis before dinner in a long-stemmed glass and kept rearranging chairs, repositioning ashtrays and bottles on the bar, fussing with things and kissing Red on his cheeks.

The last two guests were actors, as Red described them, "ultimate hot shits," who lived up in the Canyons, played flamenco guitars and cursed anyone who gave them jobs. Jimbo Nails was the leading man, the romantic lead who knew he was different because he thought he had a brain and did the *New York Times* crossword puzzle with a red ballpoint pen every Sunday night after he ate a bagel with guava jelly and did two perfect lines of Cartagena blow. Jimbo's smile said volumes, encompassed a room, established him as all-knowing, someone you wanted to have at your table. Jimbo had a smile that sucked you in. His buddy was the comedian, second banana to Jimbo, his gofer. His name was now Jonathan Wild, and he had trouble remembering when he was ever anyone or anything else. Most of the time he limped around as if he were a combination of Rigoletto and the Hunchback of Notre Dame. He was crude, constantly advancing his own cause like every other shrewd fool in history. For a while during cocktails, the two groups were separate, circling each other like boys and girls at an eighth-grade cellar party. Red finally grabbed Hennessey by the arm and pulled him over to Godard Goldberg. Red pushed the two men together. "Look, assholes," he said in a loud voice so that everyone stopped talking. "This is my send-off. I wanted my oldest friends in the world and my newest friends to be here. You don't have to fall in love with anyone but me. But let's mix it up." Red, drinking Mexican beer from a glass filled with ice and smoking dope, gave thumbnail sketches of his friends for each other, flattering, exaggerating, making it personal. "Dickie Rosenberg," he said, "doesn't know whether he's a Hebe or a *sheygets*. That's a Gentile for you heathens. Don't count him out. He'll hang back, hang back, hang back, then stick it to you. Don't be fooled by this guy. He's like someone, one minute he's clacking the clacker, next minute he owns the studio." About Jimbo Nails he said, "Jimbo would fuck a snake if he could hold it down. This is a compliment. He either has the greatest smile in the world or one constant gas pain. He's got to win an Oscar because he gives the impression that he doesn't give a shit. The truth is, he cares more than anyone." At this point

Jimbo started whipping shrimp at Singer's head, some of the shrimp dipped in cocktail sauce. But it stopped Red's monologue. Then Romeo, acting as master of ceremonies, opened the sliding doors of their private room to admit a little man in tuxedo and blue ruffled shirt who carried in a tape recorder. With a flourish, the man pressed "On." Out came their top twenty songs of 1955, and Red jumped to his feet. They all got up, ten of them dancing the steps they learned when they started to dance, high school forever in the patterns they would repeat all of their lives. "Rock Around the Clock," "Black Denim Trousers," "Hearts of Stone" by the Charms, "Boom Boom Boomerang" by the DeCastro Sisters, "Ling Ting Tong" by the Five Keys. The waiters watched and smiled, most of them, in their twenties, younger than the guests. The music was strange to them and the guests old guys, not with it.

"So what do you guys do?" the actors asked the men from the East. "I mean, *we* split wherever we came from before, and we none of us ever wants to look back. Our lives didn't start until we crossed the border to Los Angeles County."

"I'm a clothing manufacturer," Dickie said.

"You mean we can get free suits?"

"He makes maternity dresses," Duke explained. The two actors burst into laughter. "Far out, amigo," the jester said, patting his own tummy. "You look like an actor," they said to Temple. "Peter O'Toole in *Lawrence of Arabia.*"

"He is an actor," Duke said. "He's a stockbroker."

"No shit," Jimbo Nails said. "What's hot?"

"We're in the market," the jester said. "But we trust guys from California. Nothing personal. We can put together some money if you got something really hot."

"I like you," Goldberg the director said to Duke, as the men seemed to drift together into one group near the bar. "You're like a producer. No insult. In the best sense only. You know what everyone is doing: you keep them segmented, in line. What are you?"

"I'm in real estate," Duke said. "Big projects, office buildings, office parks, apartments." No one else heard him say this. But he would be doing those projects one day. He could hear himself mouthing the words, and he hated himself for wanting to play up to Red's asshole friends.

The director was suddenly bored. He didn't want Duke in real estate, he wanted him to be a fabulous character, someone he could put in one of his films. Anyone who wasn't in the business didn't understand life. The only thing he knew about real estate was that every three or four months someone had to find him a new house to rent. He didn't deal with bills or checkbooks. When he was in Los Angeles he would search out some lover, some believer with whom to stay.

The music continued to play as the waiters brought in dinner, mounds of Chinese food the way they loved it in Vegas: Jewish Cantonese, brown sauce over everything, egg rolls, spareribs, pork strips, Chicago chow mein, sweet and sour chicken, crispy noodles, shrimp with lobster sauce, pork fried rice. The food was served at the table with pitchers of Budweiser, Red's favorite beer since he had been thirteen years old. They piled it on and turned their attention to Singer. He toasted them all. "I used to borrow, borrow, borrow, right, Rosie? Borrow to share one order of egg rolls. Then I had to pay it back within a few days or else someone would hold me down in the playground, give me a pink tummy, a hundred noogies. And I'd always pay it back. Everyone paid things back when you were a kid. Now, bring in the food, open bar. I don't even know where I am. My sergeant in basic training used to say that I'd wind up behind bars. Well, if this is jail," he went on, "there's an old joke: Rastus is walking down the railroad tracks, and his mother, looking out the window, sees him and says, 'Rastus, Rastus. You come in here, right this minute. That train's gonna roar by and suck you right off.' Well, Rastus looks at his mother and yells back at her, 'Come onnn, train.' I've said this before, my wonderful friends. Lou Gehrig said, 'I'm the luckiest man on the face of the earth.' What more can I say?" That's when the actors put the bowl of fried rice on top of Red's head and Hennessey started whipping egg rolls at the actors, yelling, "You haven't known him long enough to do that," as Shirley and Lee sang above the bash, "Come on, Baby, Let the Good Times Roll." Red was about to run amuck with the chow mein when he was restrained by Romeo, who reminded him that he was going over budget and that he better save something for the big scenes. Temple banged on a glass with a spoon for attention. "It's an Eastern custom," he said, standing with a glass in his hand, "to toast whatever the occasion. This being a solemn, almost holy celebration, I thought I'd tell an appropriately serious tale concerning Stanley Singer." Freddie paused, then began: "These two cocksuckers . . ." Freddie had used this ploy dozens of times, always surprising people that those words would come out of his mouth. The words changed people's perception of him. It made people wonder if they had him wrong. "I've known Stanley since he was ten years old, and I've never held it against him that he was a square peg in a round hole, estranged, depraved, perverted, an ugly kid who got kicked out of every class, school and friend's house he ever entered. Funny that he's been so loyal to the past. There's a school in the East, a prep school where the motto is 'Dare to be true.' I always thought of Stanley when I heard that motto. I hope we can be as true to him." Freddie held his glass aloft, holding it toward Red. The others stood also, reaching their glasses toward Singer. Then Rosenberg tapped on his glass with a spoon. "I suppose this is a time for honesty," he said.

"That'll be a first," Red yelled.

"I just want to say a few things about marriage," Dickie said. "Marriage is not like a hand job at B.C. night school, where we used to go parking."

"Boring," Temple yelled at him.

Maybe it was the jet lag, the morning at the Beverly Hills Hotel, the hop to Vegas, the booze, the pitchers of beer, but Dickie felt equipped to preach, felt that he was the only person who really knew. "Red Singer has been looking for love all his life."

"Bullshit," Red yelled.

"Weddings and funerals, times for honesty," Dickie went on, realizing that he was very drunk. "We thought Stanley was going to have to pay for it all his life, and now it seems that Lindalee is actually going to marry him for his money." The others applauded. "But I want to wish him the deepest, darkest wish. That he truly be loved."

"To love," Jimbo Nails yelled, throwing his glass into a fake fireplace set at one end of the room. Jonathan Wild threw his glass also. Then they all did, into the fake fireplace made of plastic bricks. Most of the glasses didn't even break, and Jimbo went around collecting the unbroken ones, whipping them again and again until they cracked. "Bad luck," he called, "unless we get 'em all."

Romeo signaled for quiet. "What does a future Hollywood mogul deserve for his bachelor party? First of all, he deserves a blindfold. Blindman's buff." He produced a silk paisley scarf from inside his jacket. Then he tied the scarf around Singer's eyes. "Now he deserves a surprise," Romeo said, pushing on Red's shoulders until he sat down. Romeo opened the door to their private room and admitted three women dressed as cheerleaders in bobby socks, short pleated skirts, sweaters with the letters BHS. The costumes were orchestrated by Manny Gates, the art director who knew how important the look was. The music was punched on again, the tape playing the Beach Boys' "Be True to Your School." Romeo made sure that the mix of women was blond, brunette, and redheaded. The lights were lowered by rheostat. One of the girls pulled off Red's blindfold as the music played on, while another sat in his lap and a third pulled her sweater up and rubbed her breasts right in his nose. "I'm getting married *every* month," Red yelled, moving in to kiss a nipple. "My father told me that America was a wonderful country." Looking at Hennessey, he went on, "You're the only guy I ever knew who really had a cheerleader."

"Careful," Duke's looks said. You didn't mess with Rita Cronin's name. Red sat and grinned, the way men grin self-consciously when they have been given the surprise of a belly dancer's services or a strip-o-gram. Dickie was watching the women and thinking about Adrienne, that she would be thinking divorce if she could see him. "You're goddamn right I believe in prosecuting the *thought*," she had once said during an argument. He believed her.

"Dirty boogie," Dickie yelled at Red. The bridegroom obliged by jumping to his feet. " 'Gee' by the Crows," Red yelled, and Romeo obliged, his tape having worked up all of Red's favorites. No one else danced with the cheerleaders, as Singer led them in a drunken striptease. The real cheerleaders were the other men. Hennessey loved to watch; Temple wanted to participate; Rosenberg never wanted to be part of the crowd, would have loved to have seen pictures of the party when he was alone. The women got into it. They were young enough to remember real cheerleaders. One of them had been a cheerleader in Pennsylvania, a true football state, and she felt far superior to the other two girls. Not so many years before she could touch her heels to her ponytail when she leaped. For three years she was on the varsity squad. Goldberg the director hovered around the dance urging Red on. "Do it to them, Stanley." He was framing the scene with his hands, seeing how it played from different angles. The Hollywood people were active, into it; the Easterners hung back as if they hadn't known the others long enough. The women were naked except for their socks and sneakers. Red was naked also. The two actors were eager to do the same, but Romeo restrained them. Red was nuzzling and pinching and grabbing and kissing whatever he could grab. "You think he's going to do it?" Hennessey asked Rosenberg. "He shouldn't do it even if he's drunk if he's really getting married."

"I like Lindalee," Dickie said.

"I just couldn't believe her," Duke answered. "That she would be interested in Singer. Would you fuck one of them? You ever been unfaithful?"

"Would *you*? Have you?"

One of the cheerleaders stood up and signaled with her hands the way Milton Berle used to do on television, asking for applause. "Beyond here it's a new deal," she announced. "We can do girls and boys, girls and girls, girls and waiters if you want, but it'll be extra because the waiters will get fired." Everyone began yelling his choice. Romeo said, "It's the bridegroom's call." Red had been busy trying to get two cheerleaders to play Choosing-up-sides with his penis as a baseball bat. "You just go hand over hand until you reach the top," he was explaining, making them laugh, the girls who had seen it all.

"What do you say, Stan?" Romeo asked him. "You want them going down on each other? Offer them to your friends?" Red sat up in the middle of the men who had circled around the show, Red sprawled in the midst of the three cheerleaders, Red tumescent and un-self-conscious.

"He's the kind of guy they need for skin flicks," the director mentioned to the actors. "A natural."

Singer sat up and looked around. "You think I want nine assholes holding it over my head that I'd screwed some strange stuff right before I got married? This business is tough enough without blackmail."

"But we're your friends," said Romeo. "Whatever you do with us is sacred."

Red laughed. "That's why I think I'll stop it now. Mr. Control.

Roll the clips, Romeo. Girls, you want to stay, stay. You want to go, thanks for the memories."

Dickie was impressed. He couldn't believe that Red could switch gears so quickly, and he didn't want the cheerleaders to leave. But Dickie would not be the one to ask them to stay.

A screen was moved in on wheels at the far end of the room. Red still sat naked on the floor, already absorbed in what was coming. Two of the girls dressed and left, getting no nibbles from the other guests. The one who had been a real cheerleader in Pennsylvania never gave up on a group. She put her uniform back on and stayed, curious, not hard-bitten enough yet to realize that you had to cut your losses. The lights were cut and a projector clicked on, filling the screen with images. The clips from *Pounce* ran for ten minutes. Charles Bronson's on-screen daughter is killed by drug dealers, and he wants revenge. That was the hook for the movie, but it did not star Charles Bronson. Too expensive. It starred people who jumped off the screen at you, people all discovered in the Saturday softball games of Hollywood, buddies looking for the breakthrough. Jimbo Nails's smile filled the screen, chase scenes topped *The French Connection*, shoot-outs blew away *High Noon*, love scenes gave you a hard-on underneath your popcorn box. The lights came up into silence. Then the actors and the art director started to clap, slowly at first, rhythmically. Then everyone joined in. Red got to his feet, still naked, and made the sign of the cross, blessing them as if they were the apostles and he the Hollywood Messiah. Rosenberg, Temple and Hennessey stood together, amazed that they liked what they saw. "The prick will make a million out of this," Hennessey said. Red could feel it washing over him. He felt as if he could go naked into the casino and it wouldn't matter. Later on in his room, Singer paid the cheerleader something over a hundred dollars to get into his bed. He wasn't sure what he had paid because he grabbed a bunch of bills, twenties and tens, and gave them to her, cupped in both his hands. He thought of what they said about him in college, that he would screw a snake if he could hold it down. Just what they also said about Jimbo. Well, he never would be screwing a cheerleader if he hadn't gotten drunk. He would be faithful to Lindalee. He could be faithful. But he wasn't married yet. "Come on, lover boy," the cheerleader said to him. "Beat 'em, bust 'em, that's our custom, go, lover boy, go," she chanted.

"A little less noise, you guys," Freddie Temple called over to them in the darkness of the bedroom. Temple had asked the cheerleader if she could bring over a friend. "Believe it or not, I like to work with friends," she had told Freddie. "It's like double dates from the good old days when I'd give it away free. Well, maybe for hoagies and beers. Somewhere back there though, I got smart. You want anything special? You know, or do you trust my taste?"

"I like *you*," Temple replied.

"We can do that," she said, squeezing Freddie's arm. "We can do almost anything. Except backdoor. I think that's dirty." Freddie accepted the cheerleader's friend, a tall brunette with a beehive hairdo. She had come to Vegas with an ice show and remained to do chorus work and have an occasional "good time" for money and tuck away memories of big spenders to laugh about with her girlfriends.

Freddie had never really thought about being unfaithful to Marley. He had grown up in an atmosphere of betrayal and divorce where parents routinely fooled around. Yet everyone remained cordial, ex-wives and ex-husbands. No one ever seemed to move away except to different houses in the summers. The fact was that the chorus girl was someone he paid for sex. He felt this was not a real betrayal of his wife. The opportunity came to take a whore; he took her. He loved his wife. There was no question of love in Las Vegas. The girls called to each other, joked around, delivered champagne to the two beds. They passed around a joint and eventually passed around each other. "We'll have fun, fun, fun, till our daddy takes the T-bird away," Red sang, and Freddie sang, too, hating his singing voice, always off-key. This was much better than having a stripper come to a private room at Locke-Ober's in Boston while the boys in black tie drank stingers and smoked stogies.

Hennessey and Rosenberg lay in their respective king-size beds, not sleeping. "Red said he'd buy me a blow job," Duke was saying. "Told me that eatin' ain't cheatin'. I admit I thought about it. What do you do? Everybody thinks about other women. You ever fool around? It's ironic. You were supposed to be the big man with women. Tonight you just stood there."

"Of course I think about it, Francis. But you think I'm going to jump in a circle of crazy drunk people and go at it? Go home with the clap, fuck up my career and my life for a piece of ass?"

"Who would know? We're three thousand miles from home. It's not stopping *those* guys." In the darkness he jerked his head toward the next room.

"Those guys are different," Dickie said. They fell silent, each trying to sleep, each straining to hear sounds from the next room.

"I'm glad you didn't get laid," Duke said at last. "You're not all bad like everyone says."

Rosenberg wished he were home, wished he had gotten laid. "Remember what you used to say?" Dickie asked quietly. "If ifs and buts were candy and nuts, we'd all have a helluva Christmas."

"What do we play for?" Singer said on the first tee. He had the same swing he used when he was thirteen. They all could see the boy in the swing. It was true about all of them. Their swings were like fingerprints.

The desert course was flat and long with numerous sand traps and man-made lakes to make it challenging.

"I don't have time to play anymore," Red said. "So you guys will be giving me plenty of strokes." He was loosening up below the first tee, swinging freely, his swing looking grooved.

"I suck," Dickie said. "I always sucked, and if I spend fifty thousand on lessons I'll *never* give you strokes."

"Just tell us about last night," Duke said, "and I'll give you a stroke a hole, even on the par threes."

"You had a glass against the wall." Red grinned. "You could have come in. I would have let you watch."

Duke blushed. "Fuck you, Singer. You're gonna burn in hell."

Temple didn't want any questions about the night before. Time for golf, time to stay within himself. He swung his driver. "Turn the shoulders," he told himself. "Square them to the target; watch the club head strike the ball; finish high."

"Okay," Red said. "I'm flipping a tee." He tossed a red tee into the air. It came down pointing to Temple. "It's you and me," Red said. "We'll play three matches of six holes each. We change partners after six holes, so the front side is three holes, the back side three. Fate, you swinger, you. Fate." He laughed, digging Freddie in the side with his elbow.

"Handicaps," Dickie said. "No way are we playing all even." They argued over this, finally agreeing that Rosenberg and Temple would get strokes on all the par-five holes and on the four most difficult par fours. "This is only for old-time's sake," Duke pointed out. "This is sight unseen. We haven't played together in twenty years. You might have gotten good."

"Some things change," Red snorted. "But never the way you swing a golf club."

Rosenberg had been thinking the same thing since breakfast, thinking about the day long ago when the congressman was killed. "Okay. I'll say it," Rosenberg announced. "We're all afraid to say it. You're all thinking it."

"Just hit, Rosie," Temple said. "No philosophy on the first tee."

"I just don't think we've played since Sullivan was killed."

"Just play golf," Temple said. "Odd or even?" He held out one hand, which held a golf ball.

"Odd," Hennessey said. Temple opened his hand, showing a Maxfli ball with a number three stamped on it. "Your honor," he said.

Dickie stood on the tee, trying to concentrate on muscle memory, the way he knew a swing should look. Years of experience, back slowly, left arm straight, hesitate at the top, come down in the same rhythm as the backswing. He went back beautifully, then lunged at the ball, couldn't wait to hit it. The shot duck-hooked to the left, not even traveling twenty yards, until it rolled between several palm trees and almost into a pond on the adjoining fairway. "Is it in?" Dickie asked.

"The question of the ages," Red answered. "Is it in?"

"Take a mulligan," Duke offered, a chance to hit it again with no penalty, the custom often repeated by weekend golfers playing friendly rounds.

"Bullshit," Red called. "No mulligans. Play 'em as they lay."

"I'm gonna nail your ass to the ground, Singer," Duke promised, knowing that Red was trying to itch him into screwing up his shot. He hadn't hit a golf ball in years, but his childhood groove came back to him and his drive soared straight off the tee, avoided the traps across the fairway at the one-hundred-eighty-yard mark and rolled to a halt two hundred twenty yards out, dead center. "That's my partner," Dickie called. "A-plus."

They were playing a $2 Nassau, $2 for the winners of the

front side, $2 for the back and $2 for the winners of the overall match. No one had mentioned the thousand apiece, but Rosenberg had thought about it the entire weekend, felt it slipping away.

"Rosenberg killed the congressman," Red whispered to Freddie. "No doubt about it. See what kind of shot he hits when he's under pressure? Tee it up."

"No. You be captain, Stanley. You're the bridegroom."

"No problem," Red said, and, with his smooth, effortless swing, he moved into the ball. The first hole was heavily bunkered, a four-hundred-yard par four with a slight dogleg to the left. Red split the fairway, and, with some draw on the ball, his shot turned the corner and rolled thirty yards beyond Hennessey's, where it would be an easy seven iron to the pin. They all applauded the shot. Freddie Temple hit his drive a mile in the air but only about fifty yards out. "Got under it," Duke said. "Dipped those knees. Scooped it."

"Teed it too high," Dickie said.

"Everybody's an expert," Red said as they got into their carts. "It was an EA. Elephant's ass. High and smelly."

Duke and Dickie drove together to Rosenberg's shot. "Just relax and be smooth. Just make a good swing. Let the club head do the work." Duke encouraged him the way a good captain should. Dickie's ball was close, but it had not gone into the pond. He made a smooth swing with a three wood from a good lie, and the ball soared over some palms and was back on the first fairway. "That's it," Duke exulted. "Just swing easy, great shot." They bounced in the cart after their balls. Duke hit his second, a five iron, to the back of the large two-tiered green and faced a long putt back to the flag, set on the first tier. After he hit the approach he told Rosenberg, "I'm ready to go home. Enough of this shit. I can't be away from the business."

"I feel guilty that I'm away, seems like false pretenses," Dickie responded.

"Well," Duke said, grabbing his putter, "like the old punchline, 'Fuck it, it's only a hobby.' One more day, we're home."

"I didn't do it, Francis."

"Yeah. Well, it doesn't matter what happened. Sleek Sullivan's gonna be President, so maybe it was all for the good."

"There's no way we'll ever have another President like Jack Kennedy, from Massachusetts. Sleek Sullivan didn't even go to Harvard, for starters. And he hasn't got a father who can buy West Virginia."

"I don't know the word 'never,' " Duke said. "If you're a winner when you're three years old, you're always a winner. Let's go eat 'em up. Keep your head down. Forget shit you can't do anything about."

"Now you got a stroke here," Red encouraged Temple. "Just don't try to hit it too hard. You want to kill everything."

"That's Wall Street. It's how I work. Kill everything."

"Save it for the girls. You're all fucked out after last night. You're overhitting today. That's why the ball's not going anywhere." Temple already lay three and was not yet on the green. Singer had hit his second a few yards off the apron and ran his chip to within two feet of the cup.

"You got any business for me out here?" Temple asked, waiting for the others. "All your friends must be in the market."

"How about a trade-off?" Red answered. "Someday you're going to raise me millions of dollars to make movies, whether you know it or not. Until then, sure, I got friends in the market. Put this one in the hole and you'll meet a few."

"I want to meet a few I don't have to pay a hundred an hour."

"Fucking, getting fucked." Red laughed. "What's the difference?"

"You know the difference, Stanley." Temple's wedge went way past the pin and off the green.

"Next hole, partner," Red said. "I got the four."

Hennessey made five, missing his putt for par. Rosenberg rolled a long putt within six inches and tapped in for a bogey five, net four with his stroke. "No blood." Dickie smiled.

"No shit," Red countered. He was annoyed that Rosenberg halved him and realized that what he really wanted was to shut him down, to take as much of his money as he could. But Duke pumped his partner up. Dickie parred the next hole, a par five, giving him a net birdie and putting his team one up. He had sunk a fifteen-footer to do it. Duke put his tee shot on the third, a par three surrounded on three sides by a man-made lake, within seven feet of the cup. The hole was one hundred and forty yards long. He hit a high eight iron that stopped almost immediately. No one else hit the green. And although Red made a three, Hennessey calmly stroked the ball into the back of the cup for a birdie, then did a little dance of triumph. "Two up, you losers," he cried. "One unit in the jar." His team had won the front side of the first match, worth $2.

Temple tried to destroy every shot, to prove he could hit it farther than anyone else. His drives sprayed long right or long left. His approaches did the same. He played with emotion, strange for him. He swore each time he mishit, and, with the next chance, he would swing even more mightily with the same disastrous results. "Long and wrong," Duke would say after each bad shot. "Long and wrong." Singer kept his team in it, playing almost perfect golf. He halved Duke's par on four, halved Dickie's bogey, net four, on the fifth. The sixth hole was another par four, three hundred and eighty yards. But from the back tees, which they were playing, one's drive had to carry almost two hundred yards over water, where a fountain, every twenty seconds, shot towers of spray toward the sky, another block to concentration and timing. You could play it safe hitting way to the right. But it would take another two perfect shots to get home, which probably would mean double bogey. Duke made it over but sliced to the right, making his second a long hit to a green bunkered on all sides. Dickie hit his drive straight at the longest section of water. "Get legs," his partner yelled. "Go, go, go," yelled Rosenberg. It plunked with a small splash just short of the bank. "Once a little hitter, always a little hitter," Red said. "I could fart the thing across."

Freddie topped his drive. It rolled into the pond, although he had taken a bigger swing than Casey at the Bat. They laughed, and the fountain of spray rose to the sky, mocking his efforts. "Doesn't two bucks mean anything to you?" Red asked, wagging his bottom, anticipating his shot. Then he concentrated, paused over the ball, hesitating for a long moment. He took his driver back slowly, slowly and, with perfect rhythm, whipped his hands through the ball, hearing the click of solid contact, one of the great sounds in life. Red's drive ripped over the water and moved left as if controlled by radio, bouncing along the fairway, pulled, it seemed, by the magnet of the green. It left him with less than one hundred and forty yards. The foursome ahead of them, putting on the green, saw the drive finish and applauded. "Must be one of the club pros," they agreed and moved on. Red's easy par won the sixth *and* the back side for his team. But Duke and Dickie had won the first match, one up.

"Now I'm warmed up," Temple promised Rosenberg, his new partner for the next six holes.

"Freddie," Dickie said. "I didn't say anything this morning. But I'm not casting the first stone or being judgmental."

"So?"

They walked together from the carts to the seventh tee. "So hookers for Christ's sake. I mean Red's always been an animal, but Frederick Myles Fahnstock Temple?"

"Let me tell you something, partner. Number one, it's *my* business. What are you, a priest? My philosophy is that falling in love is the sin. What's the big deal? Are you some kind of prude all of a sudden? Beating Hennessey and Singer in the match is a much bigger deal than last night."

"I just wouldn't screw a whore while I was married."

"I told you in college, Rosie. You're hopelessly middle-class." They were hopelessly outclassed, despite their strokes, for the next six holes. Against Hennessey and Singer, the best they could manage was two halved holes.

"The two Harvard guys," Singer laughed to Hennessey. "We used to say it was a fairy school. The truth is, your edge is gone if you're born rich."

"Hey. Temple never could play golf. At least he's attacking the ball," Duke replied.

"Yeah. I know what you mean. Rosenberg's changed more than any of us. He's lost it. If he ever had it."

"Don't start feeling sorry for him. There's six bucks at stake." Their team took all three units, front side, back side, the match. Temple wasn't stupid enough to want to press when they were down two holes, a press being a separate match for another unit. He knew when to cut his losses in the investment business. "Two high handicaps can never beat two low handicaps unless one of the highs is a sandbagger," Temple said. "I hope you guys meet lots of sandbaggers someday."

"My mother told me," Duke replied, "never play poker with

a guy named Doc. Never eat in a restaurant called Mom's. What's the rest of that shit?"

"It doesn't matter," Singer said. "Now is the real battle. The Jews versus the Goys. First the golf. Then we match IQ's."

"In a battle of wits, Stanley," Temple said, "you're completely unarmed." Temple had first told him that line in the seventh grade.

The last six holes included two par threes and one long par five, the finishing hole, almost six hundred yards. Length was almost its only problem, a straightaway hole, built for tourists who enjoyed beating the hell out of the ball with only a fairway crossing a deep bunker guarding the green. They played the first three holes all even and talked about children. "You going to have kids, Stanley?" Duke asked him, right before Singer's three-foot putt on the second hole. "Redheaded little fucks with a Southern accent?"

Singer just dug in over the putt, paid no attention to his opponent and calmly stroked it in. Then he looked up. "No," he said. "I'm going to have beautiful little blond children with Jewish brains who like grits."

"The new master race," Dickie added. "We're one up." But they lost the third, making the front side even. They sat in their carts, side by side at the sixteenth tee, waiting for the foursome ahead to tee off, businessmen on a convention, name tags on their golf shirts. By midmorning it was almost ninety degrees, dry as always, but with no wind. Waiting in the carts, they put their faces up to the sun for the moment, happy to be away from everything but golf. "Thirty-six years old," Duke said. "When my father was thirty-six, the only traveling he had ever done was to war."

"My father only traveled with sample bags," Red said. "Until now. Florida with my mother, two weeks in a hotel, proud to see the Red Sox train at Sarasota for a day. His biggest thrill in a lifetime." Rosenberg and Temple said nothing. Their parents traveled all the time.

"You can hit, Dickie," Duke said. "They're fifty yards down the fairway."

"One thing," Red told Rosenberg. "You're looping at the top of your backswing, so you can't come into the ball with any power. Stop at the top. Then get those hands in early; get 'em popping. Stop at the top, then pop at the ball."

"Why didn't you tell me earlier?"

"You're my partner now, you schmuck."

Dickie paid attention and hit his best drive of the day, straight down the middle and much longer than he believed possible. Red topped his drive, stopping thirty yards short of Rosenberg. But their drives were academic, as Hennessey parred the hole, and their opponents, without strokes, could manage no better than bogey.

The seventeenth was a short par three, one hundred and twenty yards. But it was all carry, over a lake, with more water in back of the green. This required a precise shot, a nine iron or a wedge. You couldn't be long, and you couldn't be short. Temple hit his wedge to the back of the green, his best shot of the day. Hennessey and Rosenberg both went into the water, Duke over the green, Dickie very short, a high nine iron that never had the legs. "Now for the money player," Red announced. He concentrated, took several practice swings, then smoothly swung his wedge. The ball flew in a high arc, moving slightly right to left, and landed with a soft thud, stopping virtually where it hit, less than a foot from the hole. "Give it to me?" he asked. They made him tap it in, which he did before Temple putted.

"There, you pricks," Red said. "Good sports would have given me the putt. If you sink this, Temple, I'll kiss your butt in Bullock's window in Westwood at high noon." Freddie was short with his putt by ten feet. "Jesus," Duke fumed. "How could you be short? Never up, never in, right?"

"Sorry, partner," Temple said. "I choked."

"Jesus," Duke said again. "One more hole for all the marbles. Think positive. Think the ball into the hole."

They drove in their carts to the par-five last hole. The afternoon sun still baked the desert course. They had detoured frequently and picked up beers from the refreshment stand near the ninth. Red, wanting to let out some shaft, pumped up by his birdie, hit a long hook into the adjoining fairway. Rosenberg drove short but straight. Both their opponents stayed in the fairway, in good position. As the game proceeded, everyone but Dickie moved his ball along. Duke and Singer were almost over in three, but stayed on the back edge of the green. Temple was ten yards short. Dickie had hit his second pretty well up the right side, topped his third only forty yards and hit a five iron into the middle of the deep trap guarding the front of the green. "Just close your eyes," Hennessey said. "A Hail Mary."

Temple skulled his wedge over the green.

"You got a stroke, for Christ's sake," Hennessey yelled at him. "What are you, a Zionist?" Freddie slammed his wedge into the ground, burying it in the soft earth. "Shit," he said. "I haven't done a thing the whole day."

"Guilt," said Singer.

"Bullshit," said Temple. "You want to raise the ante for a second eighteen?"

"Touchy, touchy," Red said. "Come on, Rosie, show 'em what you're made of."

Rosenberg dug himself into the sand trap, his heels planted. "Hit an inch behind the ball," he told himself. "Don't stop the club. Follow through." He screened everything out but the ball, forcing himself to concentrate. Back slowly, he lunged down, awkward, so anxious to hit he almost fell forward, a terrible swing. But his wedge took just enough sand, flicked the ball up over the lip of the trap, struck the flag right at its base and screwed itself down, right into the cup for a five, net birdie. Rosenberg jumped up and down in the trap, cheering his own shot. Singer jumped in with him, hugged his partner, kissed him. Hennessey walked over and picked the ball out of the hole. "Rake the fucking trap," he said. "We still got two tries for the tie." Temple made a great chip that stopped only several inches away. Duke putted for the birdie from the back edge, determined not to be short. His putt broke wide, long enough, but not even close. It was over. "I'd rather win a buck on the golf course than do a million-dollar deal," Duke said after they all shook hands. "Why is that?"

"Because it's you against the world," Red answered. "And it's you against yourself. No other sport gives you that." Dickie agreed and felt that with the sand wedge he had turned around his life. He knew that all weekend there had been vibrations from his friends thinking, "Poor Dickie." But if you hole out from a trap to win a match on the eighteenth, no one can ever count you out. It means you can hole out in life. Dickie believed in signs. They paid up in beers and loose change at the clubhouse bar. Red grabbed a cigar box used to shake dice, a gamble for who would pay the bill. "Okay," he said, "let's put checks or cash in the box." They had agreed beforehand to bring their thousand apiece to the course. He took four blank scorecards and passed out pencils. "Each of us writes the name of the guy who's most successful on a card and sticks it in the box. The bartender reads the names and destroys the cards so we don't see the handwriting."

"And the criteria again?" Temple asked.

"Don't be such an asshole," Duke said. "Anybody knows successful when they see it. *Criteria.*"

"It's just that successful out here is not necessarily successful back east."

"What about ties?" Dickie asked.

"Then we argue about it and vote again," Singer answered. "Write it down." They wrote and brought the box to the bar. The bartender's name tag said Zeno. He was tall, with long blond hair that he wore pulled back and tied with colored elastics. "You Italian, Zeno?" Hennessey asked.

"Nope," the bartender said. "I'm the only Swiss bartender in Las Vegas."

"Do us a favor, Zeno," Hennessey said. "Shake up the box, open it up, pull the cards and read the four names written on 'em out loud."

"Any particular order?" asked the Swiss bartender.

"As you grab them."

They sat on bar stools, and the bartender did as he was told. "Singer," the Swiss read the first card. Red whooped, pounding the bar.

"Okay, that's *your* vote," Hennessey said to him.

"Temple," the bartender announced.

"Only Temple would vote for Temple," Red yelled. Freddie just smiled, admitting nothing.

"Singer," the Swiss repeated.

"Let me see that," Duke said, grabbing for the scorecard. The bartender, as instructed, ripped it up and threw it in the trash. He read the last card. "Singer," again. Three to one. "Oh, you are beautiful guys." Red hugged the other three. "And honest? Like you wouldn't believe."

"It's a wedding present," Hennessey said. "We know you need the money."

"Wouldn't give a Hebe a break, would you, Freddie?" Red said. "How about being a man now and making it unanimous?"

"I didn't vote for myself, Stanley," Temple said.

Rosenberg thought that Red deserved it. He was making the biggest splash. But he also believed in the magic sand wedge. He'd make a splash when the stakes were much bigger. Give Red the little victory.

"What about the money?" the bartender asked.

"The money is mine," Singer said, taking the cigar box, scooping out the cash and the checks. He tossed the bartender a twenty. "Here, Zeno," he said. "Buy yourself a fondue."

They left the clubhouse and walked the short distance to the hotel. Getting to the elevators they had to walk through a small room lined with slot machines and two roulette wheels. Roulette wheels were in action twenty-four hours a day. Red stopped. "One roll," he said to the others. He put all his cash and the checks on red. "Four thousand," he announced to the croupier. "One roll." They watched as the wheel spun around, the steel ball flipped in by the croupier counterclockwise, just like in a marble shooting contest. "I sweated blood for that grand," Hennessey said. "And you're gonna piss it away on one roll?"

"I'm surprised at you, Duke," Singer answered, his eyes zeroing in on the spinning wheel. "You're borrowing the bank's money; you're gambling on yourself every day. When you're hot, you push it. It's a rule of life." The wheel slowed. The ball skidded from slot to slot, seemed to park in twenty-six black and, with one more skip, found home on sixteen — red. The croupier pushed stacks of chips over to Singer. The redhead waved his hand. "Cash me in — except for this." He tossed the croupier a hundred-dollar chip.

"High roller," Temple said. "I figured you'd be serving time for armed robbery by now."

"We'll give you the small change any day," Duke said. "Wait until nineteen seventy-eight."

"That's what they say about the Red Sox," Singer answered.

"Eat your hearts out." They walked in his wake as he skipped through the casino.

"If Rita knew about the grand, she'd kill me," Hennessey said.

"If Adrie knew about any of this, it's divorce," Dickie said.

"You guys are pussies," Temple said. "In five years it's mine." He walked quickly to catch up with Singer.

"I still chipped in from the trap," Rosenberg said to Duke.

"I'm proud of you, Rosie," Duke said. "You can't beat dumb-ass luck." Duke patted Rosenberg's balding head.

Red and Lindalee sat in a booth in Chasen's, Red eating cheese toast, Lindalee sipping Campari and soda, which she hated but which she thought was a great diet drink. "I'm glad you wanted to be alone tonight," she said.

"I want to be alone with you all the time. It's the business doesn't let me do it. Every day you gotta remind 'em that you're not dead."

She sipped. "Sometimes you can't show you're so anxious. Let everyone come to you."

"You're an actress. You're a woman. I've gotta be out there ringin' their bell."

"Did you ring their bell in Vegas?"

Red took a big bite of the toast, a house specialty.

"I came home with the bacon, didn't I?" he answered. "Against all those high school hotshots."

"*Stanley. Miss Texas*," people called, and a noisy foursome crowded around their booth, people who knew about *Pounce*, knew it sounded hot. "You're *alone*? Join us. Romeo's coming later, Nailso's coming, too."

Lindalee pinched Red under the table. Two pinches for *no*.

"Come on," they urged. "No one *chooses* to eat alone."

"You're only as good as your last dinner, right?" Lindalee said.

They were carried along with the crowd to a big table in the front of the restaurant where everyone entering or exiting could see them.

Lindalee remained cool. At intervals, during dinner, with laughter all around them, Red would hug her to him and whisper in her ear, "I really need you. I do."

CHAPTER EIGHTEEN

O

Twosomes: March 1978

It snowed the day before the Hennesseys moved into their white house on the hill overlooking the golf course. While Rita complained about the movers ruining the house with their feet full of snow and mud, Duke was out on the terrace looking over the wintry fairways.

The year before he had refused to let Rita run a fortieth birthday party for him.

Rita had recently pulled several white hairs out of Duke's head. "You're going to be prematurely gray," she told him, thinking that she would always color her own hair.

"So I'll have white hair when I sit on the top of the mountain," Duke thought. "It's the way it should be." He had paid $175,000 for the house and put down a third. Even the down payment was more than the Hennesseys or the Cronins, his wife's family, had ever seen in their lives. He was proud to carry all of them on his back, getting the relatives jobs, lending them money, standing up at their kids' christenings. Only his father got angry whenever Duke offered anything.

But what Duke was doing right then was putting other people's money into a hotel on the Boston waterfront, one of the first hotels ever built there. He had showed his father a model of the proposed structure, with a lobby designed to resemble a giant clipper ship, the kind that Boston merchants sent out to open the China trade.

"Francis," his dad said, "it's nice to build things. You probably would be in line to run the Edison Company now, if you had gone there. All my years working, I never once heard management talk about what they owe. All I hear you say is how much Prudential is lending you, how much the banks, the pension funds are lending. Never do I hear you talk about paying back."

"It doesn't matter. You don't pay back in this business, you depreciate. In a couple of years, because there'll be so much cash flow, it'll be like they turned on a money flood. Worry about me; don't worry about the lenders. And you don't have to worry about me."

"You're getting fat." The father pushed two fingers into the son's belly. "Soft."

Duke laughed, but his father did not.

"Hard underneath, Dad," his son answered. "Hard and rich." His father shook his head as if his son didn't have a clue.

The mayor and Sleek Sullivan were already sitting at a table by the window. They met for breakfast at the Ritz Grill at seven-thirty, the time when people serious about money and power met to jump-start their hearts. Only losers had breakfast at home.

The mayor was John "Whitey" Malone, Whitey when he was a child with light golden hair, Whitey since his fine hair prematurely turned that color. He made a career out of never rocking the boat and of running for office three hundred and sixty-five days a year. He ran unsuccessfully for president of his fourth-grade class at parochial school, St. Clement's, in Roslindale. He ran and lost again in fifth, sixth and seventh grades, finally wearing his classmates down in the eighth grade when they gave in and elected him. He repeated this pattern through high school, college and into life, paying dues as a state rep and then city councilor. "If Whitey Malone," the people said, "is stupid enough to keep running year after year, maybe he deserves it. Maybe we deserve him." After running for mayor four times he also wore the Boston electorate down and won by a narrow margin. In his inaugural speech, written for him by three members of Harvard's Kennedy School faculty, he said, "There are two bronze statues of James Michael Curley outside City Hall in Dock Square. My aim after I'm through as mayor of this great city is to have the people choose to replace one of those statues with one of John 'Whitey' Malone."

The maître d' led Duke Hennessey to the mayor's table. Duke was starting to live up to his nickname. He wore the largest-size camel's hair chesterfield coat that was offered at Freedman's Factory, a manufacturer that sold to Brooks Brothers and Saks Fifth Avenue. If you gave them the right name at Freedman's, they would allow you to buy from the rack for a third off retail. "Wear dark colors," Rita told him. But he thought natural camel's hair was the stuff of riches. His suit, gray herringbone, was full price from the Andover Shop in Cambridge. It was three-piece, and the vest almost covered his belt buckle. Duke drew the line at suspenders. Those were for old guys, lawyers on State Street, MIT professors who smoked pipes.

Sleek Sullivan was the junior United States senator from Massachusetts. At fifty his hair was still blue-black, styled, long and parted almost in the middle. He swam for exercise in the Senate pool because Jack Kennedy used to swim there. The disadvantage Sleek had was that he had to scrounge to build his money base; it had not been inherited. But he was shrewd at picking people, and he believed in the first law of Massachusetts politics: You scratch my back, I scratch yours. But you have to scratch mine a little harder.

"You're looking like a rich Irishman, Francis," he said to Duke. "Where'd you get the coat?"

"Freedman's," Duke said.

"When it first looked good for me in the mayor's race," Whitey said, "it was in the days the *Globe* wasn't turning over every rock in the city. I got overcoats then, suits, cases of Wild Turkey, to which I was partial, delivered like magic to my garage. Now I'm lucky I get the driveway shoveled; nothin' in the garage but tools and old tires. I can recommend the kippers."

"You've got to be shitting me," Sleek Sullivan said. Most of the time Sleek would say "kidding me," but never when he was in Boston, where it was expected he would not put on airs.

"I'm not going to teach you about protective coloration, Senator. Who am I to talk taste?"

"Jesus, Whitey, you think you're at the Ritz you have to order kippers? You ever have a kipper, Francis?"

"They have corn flakes?" Duke asked.

"You see, Whitey," Sullivan said. "This boy went to MIT. You went to English High, I believe, but were not one of the few lads who went to Harvard from that place."

"Thank God I went to Boston College," Malone said. "I was president of my class."

"We're not running for anything here, Whitey. I was merely pointing out some cultural differences."

Duke waited patiently while the two politicians danced their dance. They needed him to watch, to make sure he understood that there were procedures.

Sullivan had all his edges smoothed down. He could talk low or high, Charlestown or Beacon Hill. They ate and probed each other until Duke couldn't stand it anymore.

"Are we going to get going, gentlemen?" he asked. "Construction work starts at seven A.M. I've got two guys who are supposedly bricklayers out in the truck double-parked trying on my hard hat."

The mayor signaled a waiter for more coffee. "Martin Lomasney," he said, "used to be political boss of the old West End. World War One. He always said that in politics a word was better than a note, and a nod was better than a word."

"That's fine," Duke said, "since we're basically here for a handshake."

Malone held up his hands. "Mr. Hennessey. All I can tell you is that you've done your homework, and so far so good." Sullivan pointed to his own face and winked at Duke. Duke relaxed then, thinking that a wink at the Ritz was as good as a word. He would get his hotel. There would be several trusts established in respectable downtown law offices, trusts with anonymous names that would be the recipient of revenues from that hotel. Nothing would link the trusts to Mayor Malone or to Senator Sullivan, but someone would come around regularly to those law offices with a briefcase that eventually would be filled. "You go along to get along," Duke knew, without any politicians coaching him. There would be three hundred rooms in the hotel. Each room would cost two hundred thousand to build. He would make out like a bandit, and he hadn't paid taxes in years because of all the depreciation. No taxes, and periodically he would take a distribution from his commercial properties. Since technically the distributions represented borrowing, they were also tax-free. "Don't be a wise guy," he told himself, trying to suck in his gut after breakfast. "And try not to have partners who don't know how to nod and wink." He also tried not to think about his father as he walked out of the Ritz, looking for his double-parked truck.

Rita came out onto the terrace. "The movers want to know where to put your weights." Duke swung around, his thoughts interrupted.

"This is what's wrong with this fucking country now," he said. "No one wants to make a decision; no one takes any responsibility."

"Frank. Don't make a federal case out of it. All I want to know is where to put the dumbbells."

"You were right the first time. Weights. Down the cellar. You think if I said in the bathtub, they'd put 'em in the bathtub?"

"This is the way to act the day you get your dream house? You should be on top of the world, not snapping people's heads off." She turned to go.

He stepped quickly to head her off. "I'm sorry, baby. We *are* on top of the world." She resisted slightly, but he pulled her close, hugging her.

"Can you go a little easier, Frank, now that we've got it?"

Duke squeezed her, looking over her shoulders down onto the golf course. "Rita," he said, "now we got to pay for it."

Duke walked around his new house noticing paint chipping on the walls near the terrace, a problem with wooden houses. They had to be painted every few years. "Not cheap to paint anymore," he thought. "Moisture gets into any small space, and it spreads."

"Come in, Francis," Rita called him. "You'll catch your death. Make sure you step on the plastic runners."

"I'll be right in. I'm walkin' around."

"Dad," their son, Francis, asked, "can I run out with the car? The drugstore, just out and back?"

"What could you need we don't have here? We got a drugstore worth of drugs in this house."

"It's all in the bottom of boxes, Dad."

Duke sighed. He had heard it before, thought it all before. The kid played soccer, not football. And he went to fairy school, private school. And his friends called him "Deuce," the Second, like he arrived on the *Mayflower*. The school told Duke that his boy was dyslexic. Jesus H. Christ, you can't be dumb anymore. He remembered Barton Gold in grammar school, who had pubic hair at eleven and was six feet tall, grossly fat. "My mother says I have a gland problem," Gold used to say. Sure he had a gland problem. He was fat. Today everybody's got an excuse for everything. I got a dumb kid who plays a European game, and I'm paying for him to go to school. He's got to have the advantages, Rita says. Was Brookwood High Harlem? Or fucking Watts? Then he said his thoughts to his wife.

"It's different," she responded. "They're busing kids in from Roxbury; the average Brookwood child gets lost in the shuffle. Remember the knuck-knuck division in high school? You want Frank in the knuck-knucks?"

They ate at the kitchen table surrounded by packing boxes, dinner a chicken casserole brought over by Rita's mother.

"I could have taken out at China Garden for us," Francis the Second said.

"You'll wear a path out walking to the garage and back," his father answered, remembering well what it was like when he got his own driver's license. Before serving the casserole, Rita brought in a cold bottle of Lancers sparkling wine. It was their favorite. "To our wonderful house," Rita said.

"We have some?" the boy asked. Duke waved the comment aside. "Did a 'Deuce' have to have champagne?" They clinked glasses with each other and with the kids' mugs of ginger ale.

"I've got the better room," Peggy said to her brother. "Got its own bathroom." Peggy was fourteen, much bigger than her mother at the same age, heftier. She could hit a tennis ball as hard as a man and was moving up the ranks of New England Juniors. She never gave up when she was behind. His son, Duke figured, was like Rita's family, the Cronins, doomed to be ingratiating in life, like the Irish funeral directors in Brookwood, rubbing their hands and looking for referrals. Rita, at forty, was spreading out and fighting it. She was coloring her hair, giving it almost platinum highlights, wearing it short and perky. She played tennis three times a week at Charter Country Club, a predominantly Irish golf club catering to people who, Duke said, "couldn't wait to get into the fancy place so they could name their firstborn Huntington Houlihan."

"The bedroom ceiling has some leaks in it, Frank," Rita said. "There's fresh stain marks from the storm."

"I'll send some of the guys over, you give them a list."

The kids chatted on about tapes they wanted, concerts they had to see, the Grateful Dead, Little Feat. Duke ate his mother-in-law's casserole and let it all wash over him. Rita was concentrating on everything her children said, important to pay attention to teenagers, she knew, because they could drift away from you these days. She sent them off to study, nothing like her parents, who assumed she was doing the right thing because she was brought up in the church. Rita didn't want her daughter going to a Jesuit school for college. Not that they didn't give a fine education. Rita believed that her children should not be taught by priests and nuns. Not these days. Didn't the Kennedys go to Harvard?

Duke had tried to block out everything else except that he owned the white house. Everyone babbled around him, had babbled since they walked in on the heels of the movers, tracking snow, ice and mud into his house. He wished he could spend the first night there alone.

"What if we sat in the dining room from now on?" Rita said. "What's the sense of having a dining room if we always eat in the kitchen?"

"It's the house I wanted, honey," Duke said, "not the dining room. Christmas and Thanksgiving maybe we use the dining room."

"Christmas and Thanksgiving we go to your folks, my folks."

"I grew up eating in a kitchen. So did you. For some reason I can think in a kitchen. I can write deals on a kitchen table on the back of an envelope, on a napkin. I don't have to worry about scratching a table."

"I don't understand you sometimes, Frank," she said. "You want to make all this money. But there are things you think are too good for you."

"Like eating in the dining room."

The doorbell rang. It was Duke's parents bringing a quart of ice cream, half vanilla, half chocolate. They had been bringing ice cream for years as a special after-dinner treat. Rita took her mother-in-law on a tour of the house. Duke took his father through the cellar to see the furnace, then outside.

"We used to watch this house when we were kids," Duke said.

"It was the only house we could see when we caddied. We thought the King of the Mountain lived here."

"What do you think now?"

Duke didn't answer. They stood on the stone terrace flanked by two huge terra-cotta urns that seemed mystical to Duke. He pointed to the stars. "I know they're closer to here than they were to us caddies down there. I suppose I do feel like the King of the Mountain, getting something I've wanted since I was a kid."

His father looked up at the stars as well. "I thought I wanted to be middleweight champ. I traded the chance for security for your mother. I'm proud you bought this house."

"But I can't relax, Dad. It's not my own life anymore. It's Rita and the kids, and the Redevelopment Authority and the banks, and the goddamned people who say my buildings throw shadows on the Boston Common."

"Little Duke," his dad said, "don't you know the only thing we ever do alone is shit."

Duke laughed and faked a right hand at his father's head. The older man instinctively blocked it and stepped inside, pulling a punch to Duke's midsection. "Frank can't even box," Duke said. "Doesn't know about Graziano and Zale. They call him 'Deuce.' "

"Your mother's losing weight. Too much," Rita said later after the in-laws had gone. "She looks terrible."

"Slowing down. She's almost seventy."

"My mother's birthday is next week. You'll be away. We almost never go away, and you go to play golf with the boys. It isn't even business."

"It's been planned for five years. We've talked about it for five years."

"I don't want to fight tonight." They were still in the kitchen.

"I forgot something," Duke said. "Come on." He picked up one of the kitchen chairs and carried it through the downstairs into the front hall. He opened the front door looking out onto the circular driveway of crushed stone and placed the chair outside the door, on top of the welcome mat. "Get up there, honey," he said. Duke's back was a problem, something knocked out of place from football. Rita climbed up and Duke lifted her off, cradling her in his arms. "Welcome home, Queen of the Mountain," he said. "Beat 'em, bust 'em, that's our custom, go, Hennessey, go," she said, and he carried her into their house, careful to step on the plastic runner.

"Richard, come see this."

Dickie Rosenberg was feeling strong, a Bostonian living in New York who would never be a New Yorker, New York a hick town that jumped for fads. He could beat it. It was tougher to make it in Boston. He smoked a pipe at home and often smoked cigars at work, and he had an increasing sense that everything was coming around. It didn't matter that Adrienne had triggered the change in their lives, that she pushed him. They had moved from Scarsdale to the city just at the right time. No traumas for Oakleigh, leaving nursery school chums after he had started regular school. It was kindergarten for him at Allen-Stevenson. A club mate of Dickie's on the board and favors owed from long ago helped pull the youngster in. They lived in an apartment on Gramercy Park, one of the classic buildings with the original Otis elevator miraculously lifting them up to their third floor. They had four bedrooms and high ceilings with elaborate moldings and a small library filled with books, many of them American first editions: Wolfe, Hemingway, Faulkner. Gideon, born in 1975, rode the leather pig footstool many afternoons watching "Sesame Street" and learned to count in Spanish from the au pair who had come from Argentina. "Dress British, think Yiddish," a friend of his father's had told Dickie long ago when he got into Harvard. Their apartment looked British, or at least English countryside, lots of chintz, dark woods, ornate frames on old portraits bought on Second Avenue. And Dickie had changed his name, *their* name, to Rose. This was only partially his decision. Adrie had applauded it herself, one of her pushes.

It had started with their business and a dinner in 1976 at the "21" Club with Adrie's father, who had been a regular at "21" since the early 1950s. "Slapsie Maxie" Feinberg knew everyone at "21," from the lawyer Roy Cohn to Alan King to Dr. Bill Hitzig, the society internist, who had treated the Hiroshima survivors. "You kids are so smart," Maxie said to them at their table opposite the middle of the bar. "Cleopatra wore the same goddamned dress you're making today. A piece of cloth with four holes. What's the big deal? Besides, no one's getting pregnant today. How can you get pregnant when everyone's busy getting divorced?"

"We're not getting divorced, Maxie." (Adrienne had called her father by his first name since she was a little girl.) "How could I divorce someone who's every day getting to look more like you?"

"I'm not fat," Dickie said, not caring that this might be an insult to his father-in-law. Maxie insulted everyone, gentle ribbing, and expected, even encouraged, it in return. He didn't care for people who didn't give it back and his favorite show business people were Phil Silvers and Jack E. Leonard, people he also resembled.

"Things start with the head," Maxie said, pointing to Dickie's rapidly thinning hair, "and they work their way down the body."

"Well," Dickie said, "what do we do? The jeans sell, the sportswear moves all right. But everything's flattened out."

"Always go to the market," Maxie said. "What do your girl-friends say?" he asked his daughter.

"You know what? My friends are all working, going to work or looking for jobs."

"What do they wear to work?"

She thought for a moment. "Well, a standard suit or a blazer and skirt. They certainly don't wear Halston Ultrasuède. I suppose there's not much choice."

"What have I always told you about business?" Maxie asked.

"You always told me to focus on a simple idea and, when there were bad times, to strip away the crap and get back to basics."

"Stripping away the crap, what's wrong with the maternity game?"

"There's no growth," Adrie answered. "We're looking at a dead end."

"Let me tell you a story," her father said, waving over her shoulder at the owner of the New York Giants. "Luigi lives in a little town in the mountains of Italy. He's a tailor. After working all his life he gets a chance to take a trip to Rome. Not only does he get to Rome, he gets a private audience with the pope because of his many years of hard work and his simple purity. Well, when Luigi goes home, he's a hero. No one from the village had ever seen the pope before. They give Luigi a celebration, a big parade. The mayor gives him a medal in front of the whole town, and he says, 'Il Papa, the pope. What was he like?'

"The whole town listens, holding its breath. 'What was he like?' Luigi says. 'A forty regular.'

"That's focus," Slapsie Maxie told them. "And further," he said, "what do you do if your business is dead-ended?"

"You change the way you do business or you get another business."

"Right, Mr. Harvard boy."

"We make clothes for my friends who are all going to work and not having babies," Adrie said.

"Right again," Maxie said. "Excuse me." He got up. "Order me the burger. I got to say hello to President Nixon."

Dickie went to see his father in Palm Beach, where he spent the winters playing golf and gin rummy at the Palm Beach Country Club. David Rosenberg was semiactive in the business at seventy-two but had become much more interested in Left Bank Jerusalem politics than the hang of maternity garments. The 1960s had taken the fight out of him. That's when, he said, "America stopped dressing with any taste. At least at the Palm Beach Country Club you can see people dressed." His father still drew $75,000 a year plus a heavily padded expense account that paid for everything from his and his wife's dry cleaning to automobiles to country-club dues.

"Dad," Dickie said, "I want to sell the business, pay you out and move on."

"You can't sell the business. I own eighty percent."

"But I've been running it for almost seven years."

"It's healthy. You make a goddamned good living."

"It's going nowhere, and you know it. We're milking it dry, and someday there'll be nothing left to milk."

David Rosenberg prided himself on being an intellectual. He wasn't an old-fashioned cloakie; he was a Wharton man. He wasn't going to let himself get emotional about the younger generation. If Dickie could get him a deal that would pay him out what he was currently earning, he'd play more golf and more gin rummy and raise more money for the Combined Jewish Philanthropies. At age seventy-two why should he worry about how much denim to order, how much corduroy and whether the dye lots were uniform. "Get me a million," he told his son, "and I'll make eighty thousand tax-free. Never mind I don't get the dry cleaning paid for anymore. You'll take care of me. It's part of teaching a son right from wrong."

His father didn't even question his son about his own plans. "Not a young seventy-two," Dickie thought. *He'd* never roll over like that when the time came.

That night at "21" had planted the seed. "No more classes at the New School," Adrienne said. "No more putting up with that shit at your reunions with people asking me, 'What do you do?' We're going to make clothes for the working woman, the average woman, not Mary Wells or Joan Crawford at her Pepsi Cola board meetings."

"Is that what we're going to do?" Dickie asked. It was the winter of 1976. A week after that night Dickie walked purposefully in New York, into law firms, banks, insurance and stockbrokerage offices, calling on friends, contacts from school and business. He used to look carefully at only pregnant women, what they wore, how they walked and moved, trying to improve his own label. That week he looked at working women and talked to as many as would talk to him about what they were missing in their wardrobe. Adrienne did the same thing on her own routes. "There's no variety," she was told. "The clothes don't fit except for suits that cost a thousand dollars; I can't find anything in my size; the stuff that looks great never fits me; it's all so boring." Two hundred and fifty thousand dollars got them started, half of it from family and several friends, all equity, nothing borrowed. One of their friends who contributed was Jimmy Madow, an innovator in the shoe business who was one of the first Americans to begin manufacturing in the Far East. Taiwan, Hong Kong and South Korea. "Forget factories here," he told them. "You can't make anything in this country now. My guy in Hong Kong can find you the looms, the stitchers, the works. You'll get great quality control. You can get a hundred little yellow bodies working on one garment for half of what you pay even down south. This is the future, boys and girls, and it speaks a mile a minute and bows and scrapes and can't do enough for you, and in time they'll grind you into the ground. But by then you'll have so much money you won't give a shit."

Adrienne and Dickie kept walking the streets of New York for weeks, from Wall Street to the East Side to Lincoln Center, watching what people wore, taking endless notes. Adrienne was as tall as Dickie. In heels she took the high ground over him. While they were dating and early in their marriage, she often wore flats or casual shoes with little or no heel. She had slouched when she was a preadolescent and did so even into high school until the boys had their own growth spurt. Her father was forever after her to square her shoulders, to be taller than any boy and to be proud of it. After several years of marriage, she began emphasizing her height, always a heel on her shoe, those that gave her the longest line, sweeping, uncluttered, and her hair almost as black as a basic Chanel, worn long, slightly below her shoulders. "If you got a wife taller than you," his father-in-law told him, "it makes you go twice as fast. You want to be twice as tough as the other guy, three times as rich. Look at Billy Rose, Willie Shoemaker, Napoleon."

"I'm not short," Dickie replied.

"You got the picture, though. Twice as tough, three times as rich." One day they wandered the streets as people came home from work. They stopped for a drink, a glass of wine in a restaurant on Madison Avenue in the sixties. They sat at a window table. "Full-figure designs," Adrienne said. "I've seen two, only two, size eights in forty minutes. What I do see is hips, bottoms and thighs."

"There's no color out there," Dickie said.

"Navy, gray, charcoal. We'll give them new colors and new materials. What else?"

"No factories. We make the pieces in the Far East." Dickie ran on. "If they want the goods, the stores come to *us* in New York. No sales force making calls. We'll give them theater in New York; make it an adventure to see the styles."

"There isn't a company on Seventh Avenue that doesn't have a sales force," Adrie said.

"No other company has got *you*. They'll come to see you. I used to love to come to New York when I worked for my father. Everything I saw was bigger than life. That's what the city is to outsiders: they're intimidated by it. They hate it, but they have to have it. Like the cloakies at the trade shows with hookers."

Adrie smiled at her husband. "Now we need a name."

It was she who thought of "Hang Out with Your Baby" for the maternity business. Dickie was good with fabrics and colors, great with the hand, the feel of a garment. Adrie could sell, bite you in the thigh to get the order.

"You made me Jewish, you know," he said to her.

"That's just so much crap," Adrie said. "In New York we had

two kinds of Jews. First, there's the fake kind from the Harmonie Club, the Germans who used to have Christmas trees and Easter egg hunts for their kids and look down their noses at everyone else. Then there's the peasants like you and me, never mind Penn and Harvard. If you're from Poland or Russia, you're a peasant. You Bostonians all thought that you were descended from the Czar's Imperial Guard. We all backslide from being Jews. You. Me. I dated jocks, the bigger the hunk the better. You played the role. But we always come back to being Jews."

"You let me name Oakleigh."

"What the hell. I rationalized that. He'll have to fight his own battles. I didn't make you Jewish. You just got strong enough, or hurt enough, to accept it."

"The name of the company," Dickie suddenly said, "should be Adrienne Rose." There were flower arrangements near the entrance to the restaurant. Dickie got up and pulled a pink rose from the bunch and laid it down in front of his wife.

"Adrienne Rose. Sounds like a country and western singer."

"Bullshit. It sounds like a winner to me."

"Well, maybe better than Adrienne Rosenberg."

"Pardon me. It's a big step up from Adrienne Feinberg."

She laughed. "Testy," she said. "Everyone dumps on their own family until someone else dares say something. How often did you wish you had a name that wasn't so obviously Jewish?"

"Only a hundred thousand times."

"Well, I got news for you. Cary Grant was Archie Leach, right? God knows what half the designers in New York used to be. You think Hattie Carnegie was Hattie Carnegie?"

"*Now* you like the name."

She picked up the rose, sniffing it. "I like it so much I think we can give our kids an enormous advantage, a brand name so they can never be branded."

"Like you said. They'll have to fight their own battles. I never really thought about changing my name."

"That's a lie. I'll bet you did. You know Irving Wallace? In the sixties his kid changes his own family name back to Wallechinsky. Looking for roots. You think Wallechinsky was an improvement? I say let sleeping Wallaces lie."

"I guess I thought about it. The name. Sure I did, especially when they started to call me 'The Rose' in college. My father is practically Orthodox by now. He'll be wild if we do it."

"Shakespeare said, 'What's in a name?' "

"Yeah, but Shakespeare didn't live in Palm Beach, and he wasn't a pillar of Temple Shalom."

"Adrienne Rose," Adrie said, rolling it around on her tongue like a Good & Plenty.

"How about 'A dress is a piece of goods with four holes — unless it's an Adrienne Rose.' "

"Have I told you lately that I love you?" Adrie said, using an old line of Dickie's, a line he took from the song.

"Do we have to change our lives every few years to get you to say that?"

"Just our names, darling. How about Oakleigh Rose? Sounds like a producer or a designer."

"It doesn't sound like a left fielder for the Red Sox. It actually sounds like a fag."

They left the restaurant on a one-syllable high.

"Richard, come see this," Adrie repeated.

"So it's a khaki full skirt," he said, watching her shake it out.

"It's a color for fall: 'On safari.' It's okay to bring the jungle into the workplace."

"Is this all the mail?" Dickie asked, flipping through bills and advertisements. "Doesn't anyone write letters anymore? The last time I got letters was in the army. Maybe I got one letter from you when we were dating. One letter. How can anyone look back at the great romances of history if there's no letters to read? My father's right. It is the decline and fall of Western civilization. But of course let us have 'the jungle in the workplace' before it's over."

"While you're having cosmic thoughts, we're selling thirty million dollars' worth of goods."

"Adrienne Rose, always focused, eye on the ball."

"I threw out all the junk mail, including a campaign plea from Sleek Sullivan. We don't need to contribute to a Massachusetts politician. It's enough we spread it all over New York."

"Look, Adrienne. We're not a New York manufacturer. Our business is all over America. We *have* to spread it around, Republicans, Democrats. We make everything in the Far East. We don't want Congress fucking up our deals. Sullivan is a key guy for us. I know you resent Boston for some mysterious reason."

"I could care less about Boston. I just don't understand why the past has such a hold on your gonads."

"It does for everyone," Dickie said. "Gonads or not, better a Sullivan as President and owning us than a President who doesn't know us from a hole in the ground."

"Everyone knows Adrienne Rose," she answered, resting her case.

"Well, queen of all you survey, time to get dressed. Dinner with the retailers."

She scoffed. "Retailers know nothing. All they know is they buy it from us for five dollars, sell it for twelve and the manufacturers take everything back they don't sell because they're afraid the stores won't do business with them."

"Except for us."

"Yes," she said. "Except for us. Want to zip me up? Do all the hooks."

"I'm in the business, remember?"

It was a working night during a working week, and they were home by eleven. Separately they looked in on their sleeping children. Dickie sat on the edge of his son's bed. There were kids who still called him Rosenberg at school. But it would be okay. People would forget. Oakleigh was dark like his father with a large nose from his mother's side. But he was smart. "You can tell what a kid has in the brain department early," Dickie thought. "The kid read like a whiz at three," he remembered. "Cereal boxes, warning labels, anything. I never believed I'd have a son who was a New Yorker." He kissed his own hand and pressed it to the boy's head. Later, Dickie lay on his back, knowing he couldn't fall asleep that way but not wanting to turn on either side, toward or away from Adrienne. After dinner at Lutèce they had left the people from Saks and Neiman's and gone to the apartment of Herbert Hastings, the hottest new designer of haute couture. "I like you two," Hastings had told them, "because you're going to make scads of money and invite me to wonderful things. Plus we shall never compete. I have fools for clients. You have workers for clients, you have dreamers. Don't ever quote me." He gave them cocaine, the first time they had ever tried it. Dickie thought a good martini vastly superior to cocaine in the high department. He lay on his back because Adrie kept snuffling. He couldn't stand his wife's snuffling and thought further about what a good idea older generations of married people had sleeping in separate bedrooms. Finally he rolled over toward Adrie and felt himself growing hard as he pressed against her bottom. "Stop snuffling," he whispered, running his hand over her hips, starting to play with the hairs of her crotch. She woke up with a snore. "Jesus," she hissed. "What the hell are you doing?"

"What the hell do you think I'm doing? Coke must make you horny."

She was annoyed. "You're about an hour too late. Go to sleep." He rolled over, away from her, annoyed and almost instantly soft. Soon he began to giggle to himself, thinking the rag trade's watchwords, "You're only as good as your last line," and listened to Adrienne Rose snuffle in her sleep. He began to get hard again and giggled some more, thinking of lines from high school: "It was a small wash so I did it by hand."

Freddie was feeling his oats. Since May Day 1975, when brokerage commissions became competitive and the monopoly of fixed rates set by the New York Stock Exchange ended, the fun went out of institutional business for him. "We have to be price-conscious, Freddie," his clients told him. "We can't justify paying full rates. You're going to have to come down."

He still entertained clients at least three nights a week, still went to Madison Square Garden and Yankee Stadium, still went to Christ Cella and Le Cygne, still had the hot ticket to Broadway and the entry code to the madam next to the Dakota, where all the girls said they had gone to Vassar, Sarah Lawrence or Bennett. But all his clients ended up talking about the cost of trading, to which Freddie responded as St. Luke's School had taught him to respond: "It's so tacky." The Irish traders and portfolio managers who were his clients would respond, "That doesn't work in the real world, Freddie. Only cents-per-share works. Pass the hollandaise. And I'll have another St. Pauli Girl."

He was feeling his oats because of something his father always called "a sea change." Having drinks one night with the old man who came to New York periodically to play court tennis at the

Racquet Club and swap stories at the Knickerbocker, Freddie asked him for advice, something he had almost never done in his life. They clinked glasses. "Cheers, Frederick."

"Cheers, Dad." Freddie told him about the institutional gravy train getting derailed. "It's an insult to do business for pennies a share. I'm not a discount store. It *is* tacky. Standards are going to hell."

"You sound like me." His father laughed. "Just ask yourself one question. What do you do best?"

Fred thought for a moment. They both sipped their drinks, small narrow sips of gin.

"I can sell. And I know an extraordinary range of people."

His father dipped his tongue in the gin. He said, "Bring together the people you know and charge them a fee."

That week Freddie had lunch with a classmate from St. Luke's who was a partner at Lehman Brothers. "What the hell do you do?" Freddie asked.

"I sell companies to other companies. Mostly the companies come to us wanting to sell or wanting to buy."

"Do you ever create the need? I mean go to Pepsi, for example, and suggest they buy Canada Dry?"

"We don't market actually. We have relationships. People know us; they seek us out."

"How do they structure the fees?"

"Five, four, three, two, one. Five percent for the first million, four percent for the second million, etcetera — the Lehman formula."

"Everybody's a gentleman?"

"Everybody's a gentleman. But remember, Lehman Brothers believes in small offices and big houses."

Freddie Temple believed in big offices *and* big houses. He liked Gucci loafers with no socks in the wintertime.

A week later, Temple went in to see his boss, Ace Cohen. "Should I resign," he said, "or are you going to give me half a million dollars to gear up an investment banking division?"

"What's investment banking?" asked Cohen, to whom trading was a way of life. If you weren't a trader, you were an asshole. "About half a million," he said. "Where do you get that figure? Why not twenty?"

"Don't negotiate with me," Freddie said. "Everyone's negotiating with me. I've gone to my last Yankees game with the Irish traders. If I'm going to be a hooker, I want to be on Park Avenue, not in Brooklyn. If I hear one more fucking story about opening up the hydrants on Flatbush Avenue as a kid, I'm going back to Boston."

"It doesn't cost anything to listen."

Ace heard Freddie and spit out the tip of another cigar, chewing on the end without lighting it. "I know what corporate finance is, for Christ's sake. It's full of people that watch for the bosses to leave at six o'clock and then bug out."

"We can't just do what we like in this business," Freddie said. "You hired me for these very reasons. You're a cynic. The public doesn't give a rat's ass about the stock market anymore. The institutions are beating our brains out on price. Where's the money going to come from? Let me hire a couple of hotshots. We'll do old-fashioned financing, build up the relationships."

"Shit. I got relationships up the yingyang," Ace said. "I remember in sixty-five buying half a million Syntex and getting stuck with it for two hours. It would have busted us, but I gutsed it out. Laid it off on Jerry Tsai at Fidelity. Made half a point, and he never knew I fucked him. I don't want Peterson, Pyle in goddamn meetings all the time. Investment banking is meetings. I want Peterson, Pyle in action." He furiously chewed his cigar. "Aahhh, fuck it," Ace finally said. "It probably feels right. The big question is, Are you the guy to do it? Doing trades is different from pulling a company apart. You're not going to go through the stock guide with a red pencil figuring out price earnings ratios. You're going to do financing, drafting prospectuses by hand, living at the printers until four-thirty in the morning. This ain't fun and games."

"How do you know so much about investment banking?"

"Because I always stuck my *ponim*, my face, into everything on Wall Street and came up with what I like best. You can't eat delicatessen and be in investment banking. But it doesn't mean I don't know how to do it. You can fuck blondes and brunettes and redheads, but if you want to really make money you got to concentrate on who you want to fuck the most."

Ace gave Freddie free rein to snake people from other places, firms like First Boston, Merrill, Dillon Read, promising them better money, but also stock options in the newly public Peterson, Pyle, Inc., enough options to make them rich in a hot stock market. They would also make bonuses based on the deals they brought in.

Freddie shoved Peterson, Pyle into investment banking, and it cost a lot less than half a million because in the 1970s no one came out of business school onto Wall Street except true rebels or contrarians. Wall Street was dead in the '70s. But Wall Street is always dead the way vampires are dead, waiting for blood to wake them up.

Freddie Temple at forty-one looked exactly as he had at thirty-one. If anything, he looked better. In addition to squash several times a week, he had begun to run. He ran in Central Park early in the morning. Or he ran downtown before evenings of business, down on the docks by the Battery and out by the Statue of Liberty, times of peace for him, times when he assembled deals in his head.

"You're late," Marley said, when Freddie came in the door. "I know you don't think the Metcalfs matter, but she's a Mellon cousin and they have at least two Braques and a Corot in the master bedroom. And they invite people they like out to their ranch in Jackson Hole."

"Frank Metcalf is a fat fool. If Bankers Trust didn't send him a check every month, he'd be sifting through Dempsey dumpsters looking for a veal chop. He was in the second boat at Groton, and he'll never be any better than that in his life. These people don't get it."

"Jesus, that sounds like a direct quote from Ace Cohen. For the last ten years every hero of yours was Irish or Italian. Now every hero is from *Our Crowd*."

"Ace Cohen is far from *Our Crowd*."

"Well," Marley said, "leave it to you to know the difference."

Freddie refused to be sucked into a pissing contest.

"Where is Myles?" he asked.

"Myles is at a birthday party. Brett is at a birthday party."

"Those kids go to more parties than we do. Brett told me the other day that she wants to hang out at Macy's when she grows up. Like the older girls at Brearley."

"This is New York, darling," Marley said. "The girls become women faster than anywhere else. Your Boston women have that arrested development. Ever notice that?"

"They're deprived. They don't have a chance to hang out at Macy's."

"You think you're so superior. So judgmental."

"I just can't stand people who don't pull their weight."

"Please don't give me the Cotton Mather speech. Did you ever think you could work-ethic yourself right out of a marriage?" Freddie ignored the comment and walked to the bedroom to change his shirt for the evening.

At thirty-nine, everyone told Marley Damon Temple that she looked wonderful. She walked everywhere, played tennis three times a week at the River Club, was a docent at the Metropolitan Museum and had a married lover who met her weekly in a hired room at the Yale Club. Her lover was an attorney whose offices were on Park Avenue. His name was Bayard Grant Trent, Jr., but everyone called him B.G. B.G. was a snob, "a snob, with hats from Dobb," his Yale yearbook had said about him. He took it as a compliment. His specialty was wills and trusts. Marley speculated before their affair if he would take his pants off before he made love to her.

"I'm using this room so my wife can come to town, change in comfort to go to concerts, put her feet up. What's the point of an in-town club unless you use the facilities." This he told the assistant manager who gave him his key. "I'd like the same room, if possible, each Wednesday." He would go to the room, sit in an armchair with a book from the shelf, usually a selection of stories left by estates of various alumni to the Yale Club. Or he would bring and read wills or draft trust instruments while he waited for Marley to arrive, two rapid knocks on the door, gin and vermouth mixed in a flask from her handbag along with her own Pears soap wrapped in a scented handkerchief.

"Do you know why I'm doing this?" she asked him the first time she appeared.

"I haven't the faintest idea," B.G. responded.

"I'll be honest," she said. "I'm doing it in self-defense."

"Then it's my lucky day." He smiled, putting down the papers he was working on.

"First a drink," Marley said, reaching for a tumbler on top of the old bureau. "We'll use one glass, how's that?"

Freddie loved approval. When he was young, he thrived on good words from headmasters, coaches, teachers. As he got older, he sought it at work from clients and superiors. And all along he sought it from women. The more he was admired and praised, the more his work became renewed, as well as his belief in himself. He flirted wherever he was, in the office, at luncheon meetings with waitresses or coat-check ladies, with saleswomen in department stores, at dinner parties. If he thought he would be encouraged, he would move to hold hands under the table or rub the thigh of the woman upon whom he was moving. He didn't care about long-term attachments, he had no time for them. Freddie had brief affairs in hotel rooms, downtown, uptown, and he kept a dozen blue-wrapped packages from Tiffany's in an office desk drawer to send out as good-bye and thank-you gifts. They were identical: ceramic Tiffany gift boxes with white ceramic ribbon. The tops lifted off and the boxes could store hairpins, earrings, extra buttons, ponytail elastics. With each box his card was also identical: "Put me in there too. F."

The Metcalfs lived in an apartment on the East River at the end of 78th Street, full of antiques from generations of Metcalf travels around the world, antiques musty and dusty. There was seldom talk of business at the Metcalfs' because Fat Frank had never worked. Guests were chosen for their schools, their clubs, their sporting interests, sports of leisure: sailing boats, shooting, fly fishing. Freddie had an insurance drink before he left his apartment, a long bourbon to give him an edge. Marley courted Sally Metcalf because she was an important point woman for both the Kips Bay Boy's Club Benefit Committee and the board of the Whitney Museum, both places on Marley's wish list. Not that Marley was unconnected herself. You just never could be too sure in New York. "Have all your ducks in a row," Freddie had said to her for years, really telling himself the same thing.

As they didn't talk business at the Metcalfs', they also didn't mingle the way people mingled at the end of the 1970s. At the Metcalfs' the men talked with the men; the women with the women.

"You know," Frank Metcalf was saying, "someone actually

won the winter shoot at the club with a pump. Quite remarkable hand-to-eye coordination." Freddie rolled on the balls of his feet, impatient, looking over people's shoulders, drinking more bourbon and occasionally saying yes to a piece of cheese or bacon wrapped around a chicken liver. He noticed Marley having no problems at all talking with the women about charity benefits and the children's schools. Freddie knew everyone at the party (dinner for twelve), except one couple who had driven in from Greenwich. Malcolm and Susie Frost were younger by a few years than anyone else in the room. Susie was a cousin of the hostess and a daughter of the chairman of Douglas Foods, a Fortune 500 company based in Minneapolis. Malcolm did something for Chemical Bank but had plenty of time for games of various sorts and got along swimmingly with Fat Frank Metcalf. Freddie switched place cards before dinner and put himself next to Susie. The dining room was dark, candlelit. Freddie gave Sally Metcalf a pat on her bottom and a finger to his lips ("Shh"), knowing she would think it delicious and leave it alone.

"You went to Harvard?" Susie Frost asked Freddie at dinner. "I went to Pine Manor. But I came, left, came back. Rather a checkered college career, but it was great fun at Pine Mattress. I don't mind they called it that." She was petite, small mouth, small upturned nose, trim figure in a Bill Blass red silk dress. She had teeth as white as the ankle socks of an East Side dancing school class and a dimple in her left cheek that she told Freddie was her "come hither" dimple.

"Did you hear about the boy at a coming-out party dancing with a debutante? ' "Harvard family?" she says to him. "No," he says. "Yale family?" she says. "No," he answers. "Let's double cut," she says.' That's what the East means to me," Susie said. "Harvard or Yale."

"Where did your husband go?" Freddie asked.

"Dartmouth," she said, flashing her dimple and white teeth at him. Freddie moved his left leg so it was touching Susie's, pressing her slightly. She didn't move her own leg away. By the end of the petite marmite she admitted that she was on the board of directors of Douglas Foods and that she was her father's favorite child. By then they were holding hands under the table. During roast beef, Freddie was forcing his hand between her legs, just about reaching two fingers as far as her crotch. She was certain her father would love a visit from Freddie and Peterson, Pyle with a view to a new investment banking relationship. Sally Metcalf tinkled a small silver bell between the meat course and salad. "Now we all turn to the partner on our other side," she trilled. It didn't matter. He talked of trivia to the woman on his right while Susie Frost fondled him beneath his napkin. She had tried mightily to unzip his fly with just her right hand but gave up and was content to play a waiting game. Freddie also knew that time was on his side. The bell would tinkle again at dessert and probably many times after that for people in a potential investment banking relationship.

"I've never seen it fail," Freddie said to Marley when they were finally home in bed. "Every time you dread going somewhere, it always turns out much better than you thought it would be."

"I saw you absorbed in that rich little girl."

"She went to Pine Mattress. I'm going to get some business out of her." They lay in silence for a while, aware that the other was wideawake, the time in marriage when even a swallow was noticed by one's partner.

"You're going off to play golf with Rosenberg soon, aren't you?" Marley said finally.

"It's Rose. Richard Rose."

She laughed without mirth. "You can be so self-righteous."

"It's an obligation from the past," Freddie said. "And it's business. Those guys are all feeders to the business. And they're loyal."

"How about you, darling. Are you loyal?"

Freddie could always make love to his wife. He never had a problem in that department, and Marley never turned away from him. When all was said and done, they knew they were meant for each other.

"I don't want to hear about *Saturday Night Fever,* for Christ's sake," Red said into the phone. "I don't want to hear about *Grease.* If we could get these fucking New Yorkers out of this town, we could bring some taste back into the business." Red was talking to Harold Benjamin, who ran Crown Pictures. Benjamin came from Tulsa, Oklahoma, had gone to Columbia Business School and from there to Touche Ross, where he was assigned to their Entertainment Division. "Dumb-ass luck," Red thought. "At least Benjamin isn't a New Yorker. The New Yorkers in the business are the crudest people I've ever met. They'd tear your balls off and feed 'em to you. In a submarine sandwich. They call it a hero." Red felt that he was still a Bostonian, would forever be a Bostonian with sensitivity and a desire for order. God knows he didn't mind crude, up to a point. But the New Yorkers were pricks. He wasn't a prick. He was, if anything, too soft. Which is why, he thought, he had had a few bad years. Which is why he was talking to Harold Benjamin, who was, Red knew, also a sensitive man.

"Are you trying to tell me that you're pissed that Travolta looks like he can really dance in Brooklyn? What are you telling me?"

"Look, Harold. We're soulmates, whether you know it or not," Red said. "I've driven through Oklahoma. I was stationed in Texas. You were raised like me, little ladies and gentlemen."

"You're full of shit, Stanley," the head of Crown Pictures said. "Get a good script, and I'm not going to hear any of these speeches about New Yorkers. Some of my best friends . . ."

"He doesn't know about the Yankees and the Red Sox," Red thought. "I've got a great script, Harold. You have to read it again with new eyes, Eastern eyes."

There was silence on the other end of the phone. "If we didn't play softball together years ago, Stanley . . . You realize you're basically calling me a schmuck. You could call me a schmuck when I was a substitute left fielder. Now I run a major studio, and I believe I deserve to. How do you think what you say makes me feel?"

"You're also my friend," Red said.

"You want advice from a friend?" Benjamin said. "Nobody gives a shit about a motorcycle cop from Connecticut. Get a good script and friendship counts. By the way, you never used to put me in until the seventh inning. How do you think that made me feel?"

Red hung up and shook his head. "It's a cruel fucking town, babe," he said to Lindalee. "It's a great script. A state cop who wants to be a society boy from New Canaan, Connecticut, marries a rich girl he gives a speeding ticket to."

"Every town's a cruel town," she said. "Oxford, Mississippi, was a cruel town if you were the wrong people."

Red still wore his hair very long, but it was starting to thin slightly and the flame in it was turning down like autumn moving sadly toward snow. Lindalee still looked like Bert Parks was going to pluck her off the runway and crown her Miss America. She wore high heels with everything and clothing designed to get her instantly out of producers' waiting rooms and into their offices and minds. Red used to love the way she looked. "Jesus, Lindalee," he suddenly said, "can't you put some fucking clothes on when you get dressed?"

"How many times do I have to tell you, Stanley, that it's interesting to have people think you're something that you're not."

"What!" he said. "You think it's interesting that people know you dress like some starlet? Like some light hook?"

"You don't say that about Jill St. John."

"Oh, for Christ's sake. Jill St. John is another story. Plus she's Jewish."

"You goin' to throw that in my face? There's never been a Jewish hooker, right? You're as pure as the driven snow. I'm sorry I converted, went through all that shit." They were on the terrace of their house in Bel Air on Stone Canyon Road, the house bought within a month of the release and success of *Pounce* in 1973. The house, Red thought, was proof of his instinct and good taste, not Beverly Hills but Bel Air, gates to drive through, private police, a showplace for old-time Los Angeles money, like Brentwood. He knew nothing about San Marino. The house was a New England Colonial, a house Red felt superstitious about. It would be lucky for him. The bottom of the swimming pool was painted with the Brookwood High logo in blue and red, school colors. Red insisted on this. "Be true to your school," he had told the decorator, who had certainly had stranger requests.

Today was a Saturday. Red was dressed in tennis shorts with a pink Lacoste jersey, and he carried his racket, ready to meet three friends who didn't need a hit movie as badly as Red. He couldn't help himself. He drew back his racket instinctively. He would never hit Lindalee. "That's it," she said. "Hit a woman. A Yankee-ass trick."

"Stan the Man." The words flashed across the terrace. It was Harry Singer, the Tootsie Roll man, Red's father. He was holding a little boy's hand, a funny little boy with hair the color of a Cardinals' hat. Without saying a word, the little boy began tap dancing on the tiles of the terrace. His grandfather began to sing, "East side, west side, all around the town. The tots sing ring-around-a-rosy, London Bridge is falling down . . ." His mother ran to the boy, lifting him off the ground and squeezing him.

"Jesus, Dad," Red said. "How many times do I have to tell you, I hate New York."

His father shrugged. "It goes with the routine, Stan."

"Give Daddy a kiss," Red said, easing the boy from his mother's grasp. He kissed the child on both cheeks, on the tip of his nose. Then he placed him on the ground and held his head in his hands. "You got the talent, Valentino. Always remember, you got the talent." The little redhead, four years old, didn't skip a beat or change his expression. Put back on the ground, he began whistling "The Sidewalks of New York" and resumed his tap dancing as if he had a battery in him that hadn't run down. "A natural," Red said.

"Val," Lindalee told her son, "it's time for lunch. Your nap. Swimming lesson at three." He still hadn't said a word. But he turned and skipped toward the kitchen.

"Would he be great if they were remaking *An American in Paris*? One of the kids? 'I Got Rhythm,' right?"

"I don't know," said Harry. "I don't really see Val as a little French kid."

"Everybody's a producer," Red said. "Everybody's got a script, opinions. Everybody's in the fucking business."

"Watch your mouth," his father said.

"You tell him, Dad," Lindalee added. "Your son used to be a loving boy."

"*He* was the true natural," Harry Singer said, as if his son weren't there. The grandfather wore bell-bottom jeans with metal studs on the back pockets and a thick belt with a silver and turquoise buckle from Santa Fe. After his mother died of a stroke in 1975, Red wanted his dad in Los Angeles. Red would find him work if he had to work; family should be together. Harry lived in an apartment in Westwood. He walked the streets near the fraternity houses and rooted for every UCLA team from soccer to water polo. After a year he couldn't believe he had ever had a life outside of L.A.

Father and son embraced in the doorway, their hug feeling to both as if it was them against the world. "I've got to go down to Jangro's; do the deal," Red told him. "If I don't get this thing off the ground, I'm in the toilet. You know what I'm saying, Dad?"

"I know what you're saying. I'll stay here and play with Val, take a dunk in the pool."

Red gave his father a nudge in the ribs. "Keep your hands off Lindalee."

"You know," his father said, "I wish you wouldn't fight in front of Valentino. Your mother and I never fought in front of you kids."

"You fought plenty, Dad. You think we didn't hear everything even with doors shut? Everything's bliss on wheels when people look back."

"Your mother and I had respect . . ."

"Respect is why I'm going off to hump this script, Dad. Respect is in the gross, the numbers. That's it. Finito." He drove a new red Jaguar and raced down Stone Canyon Road blowing his horn at the parking attendants working the Bel Air Hotel as he barreled by.

At the studios, as everywhere in that narrow town, people liked to have Red around. He kidded everyone, duked everyone, remembered everyone's name: security guards, commissary people, parking attendants, best boys. Everyone who ever worked on a Stanley Singer production knew that they'd have a happy set: the best food, the best T-shirts, a family. "The trouble with you, redhead," Slim Jim Jangro told him, "is that you can't see the forest for the trees. Every little guy in the town loves your ass and you totally neglect the iron, the people who can do you some good. You want to be loved by the little people, run for mayor.

You want to make movies, you need rabbis. You know this. Why not use your *kop?*" He tapped his head.

"I have a dream."

"So did Martin Luther King, you asshole, and look where it got him. I call you an asshole with all love and respect. You know that." Slim Jim Jangro ran Paradise Pictures. An accountant and lawyer by training, he was put in place by the number crunchers who controlled the stock and who thought you ran a movie studio the way you ran Procter & Gamble. Jangro lived in Holmby Hills, near the house the Bogarts had lived in, near the Playboy Mansion. Tennis at Jangro's on Saturday was a new Hollywood institution, and you had to be competitive. No customers' games at Jangro's. After the others had left, Red found an excuse to linger.

"I'm interested in the country, Jim," Red told him, "in the world much more than local stuff. I don't have time for that." He was not going to get pissed off, not when a project was at stake. "Politics is my interest, national politics."

"I never heard you were involved."

"Sleek Sullivan is my man, senator from Massachusetts, who's gonna be President someday," Red said. "You want to check the heft of that script again. I've been close to Sleek Sullivan for years. Now I appreciate your honesty, Jim. This is constructive criticism, right?"

Slim Jim shrugged.

"Look," Red said, "I'm not going to bullshit you. Everything is personal in this town; everyone's got an ax to grind. So-and-so won't do my picture because I didn't play him on my softball team, someone else because I dated his wife long ago."

"I don't take anything *personal*. I just read the grosses. I keep the charts, like the stock market. That's what I go by."

"Just read the script, Jim. Think Pacino in this movie, Belushi as the sidekick." Red slammed two copies of his script down on the desk. Both were bound in his signature red-leather binding with dollar signs embossed on the covers in gold leaf. Slim Jim Jangro rubbed his hands over the covers. "Feels good," he said. "I like the heft." He paused. "I've got a little advice for you, Stanley. I don't want you to take it the wrong way." He leaned back and folded his fingers over his stomach. He wore a gold wedding band, but he was not married. "You want," he said, "to get involved in the community more. You're forty-something, right?"

"About," said Red.

"You should join the shul. Probably B'nai Moshe on Wilshire, or if you're Reform, Temple Israel in Brentwood is important. I know you play golf. It's time to join a club. You're not a kid anymore, and you got to understand the way business is done when you're not a kid."

"I appreciate your honesty, Jim. Are you also going to tell me that I got the wrong wife for this?"

Slim Jim cracked his knuckles. "You said it, redhead. Not me."

Red had known Slim Jim Jangro since the accountant had come to Hollywood and had audited several of Singer's movies, usually praising him for his attention to detail and to budgets. Red played things close to the vest when it came to the studio's money. He got high points for that. What the establishment didn't care for was his random mouth. "Lindalee is Jewish, Jim," said Red. "She converted."

"Nobody takes that seriously, Stanley. They wouldn't take it seriously in Shaker Heights, or Skokie, Illinois, or Scarsdale. Why the fuck would they take it seriously in Hollywood? It's time maybe to get ethnic if you want to be taken seriously. But I'll read the script. I respect you."

"We've got no marriage if I don't have movies," Red later said to his wife. "If I can't make me happy, how can I make anyone else happy?"

"You are not an actor, Stanley. You are a businessman. You think men who run rubber factories or make aluminum throw tantrums and want to get divorced every time they have a bad season?"

"Those guys have a paycheck every two weeks probably. Good times and bad. They do the same things, day in, day out."

"My daddy went bankrupt in business. He told me all the time that his guts were churning and he hoped his little girl would never know gut-churning times. But I know them, Stanley. My gut's been churning for almost two years." They were in their bedroom overlooking the pool and terrace. The house backed up against the canyon. They could hear the coyotes at night, howling against progress.

"I'm not fooling around with anyone," Red said.

"Stanley," she replied, "you fool around with *everyone*. You always did. I suppose you always will. You push it over the line, that's your problem. You push it too far."

Red sat up in bed wearing white silk pajamas with crimson piping and his initials, also in crimson, over the breast pocket. They were a gift from the leading lady of his last movie, a disaster about wild dogs who raise a baby girl, a female Tarzan. The film was hooted from the theaters.

"All my life," he said, "I felt on the outside looking in. This is no news to anyone in this town. I know. They all feel the same way. Everybody good out here was at one time a fucking reject. Think about it. Name anyone out here who was ever most likely to succeed in high school. You got to be able to bite your best friend in the ass, your banker, your lawyer."

"Your wife," Lindalee said. "Your kid."

"You know your trouble?" Red asked. "You're too fucking smart. That's why I married you. Because you look like a light hook, but you had this unbelievable IQ. You were a loner, too. Don't give me any shit that you weren't."

"So if I'm so smart, why do I stay with a loser? If you're looking for a way out, Stanley, I'm not going to make it easy on you." Lindalee was next to him in their king-size bed. She wore an extra-large white T-shirt that had the words "Slip Slidin' Away" printed in bold black on the front.

"I can still do it," Red said. "I don't have that problem."

"My daddy was very advanced for a Southerner," she said. "He told me about home and away games."

"That means okay, right?" Red took off his silk pajamas and threw them over the end of the bed. Lindalee never took off her T-shirt. She knew what her husband liked. And that night she decided she'd indulge him, the baby boy. After they had made love, cradling their heads in their hands as they lay on their backs, Lindalee asked, "You know what one of the great tests of love is?"

"Will I respect you in the morning?"

She laughed. "Stanley," she said, "I named a kid Valentino for you. I would never have done that, never, for anyone I didn't think was going to stick in the business."

Red kissed his wife's nipples and hoped he would hear the coyotes in Stone Canyon. Falling asleep, though, he kept pushing away what Jangro said about his wife and joining a temple. What kind of shit would he eat and how much? It was a mistake, he decided, to marry someone who wasn't Jewish. Valentino would never really get it; the people who counted in town had a secret joke that excluded anyone who hadn't known the inside of a shul. Fuck it, he thought, Valentino will never be in the business anyway.

○

CHAPTER NINETEEN

April 1978

"**Y**ou know why our golf has been so lousy?" Duke asked. "Because we're at the fucking crossroads."

"I agree," Red added. "Thirty wasn't the end of the world, but forty is what our fathers were when we got out of high school."

Freddie Temple said, "I kind of like it now."

"That's because you don't know the difference between shit and Shinola. I'm in a business," Red said, "where I get pushed by twenty-year-olds who busted out of high school."

"Then you can relate to that, Red," Dickie said.

"Oh, chime in, *Mister* Rose. By all means."

Dickie ignored the jab. "I'm much happier with forty than thirty. I was lost at thirty."

"Now you're farting through silk," Red said, "thanks to a brilliant wife."

"Red," Dickie said, "we've known each other since we've been ten years old. You wouldn't be acting like this if you hadn't borrowed the five grand to show up here. You're trying to get us pissed off enough to let you win it back on the golf course."

"Boys," Duke Hennessey said, "this is supposed to be fun."

They were sitting in the refreshment stand next to the ninth hole at Alligator Run Golf Club, just outside of Miami in Coral Gables. People retired to Florida for such a day, temperature in the eighties, low humidity, sky the color of Wedgwood, the wind not enough to bend a social security check if it were held out between two fingers. "God's fucking waiting room," Duke had said driving to the course from their hotel. "I see cars moving at eleven miles an hour and I pass 'em, there's nobody at the wheel."

"I know," Red added. "The people all in their seventies and

eighties, they're all three-foot-eight sitting on phone books in their cars, folks shriveled by the sun."

"*My* folks think it's the greatest," Dickie said. "Golf, pinochle and gin, cocktail parties. How bad can it be?"

"Retirement is death," Freddie said. "Life is work. I couldn't be out of the action. I'd last six months."

They had agreed to meet in Florida the first weekend in April. Duke got them the rooms at the Key Biscayne Princess Hotel owned by a developer friend. Freddie Temple arranged their golf through a client who belonged to Alligator Run, a private course peppered with ex-CEO's of Fortune 500 companies. Men who could compare war stories, liver spots and customized golf carts.

Dickie held his arms open to the sky. "How can anyone possibly complain about anything on a day like this? I mean, to be young, rich and Jewish. What more could anyone ask?"

Red spit a stream of Diet Pepsi across the table at him.

"Let's play, partner," Duke said, slapping Dickie on the back. Then he took the cigar box that lay on the table between them and shook it. He placed it down and opened it. Five dice lay in the bottom. "Twenty-seven," Duke said, handing the box to Temple. "Your roll." They all shook for lunch, low man to pay.

Singer spun a seventeen and said to the boy running the lunch counter, "Can I sign for this?"

Temple was disgusted and reached in his pocket, pulling out some bills.

"For Christ's sake, Freddie," Red said, "I'm only kidding."

Singer paid for lunch. "I even tipped the kid a finnif."

"Stanley," Freddie tried to explain, heading for their golf carts, "this is a private club. No tipping. They don't even see bills here except once a year. A hundred members. They split the costs a hundred ways, and if you can't afford it, you shouldn't be a member."

"Don't be an asshole, Freddie. Tipping is a way of life," Singer told him. "The kid didn't give it back, did he?"

"Stanley. You'll never learn."

They were playing partners, nothing fancy. Duke and Dickie against Singer and Temple. As they drove to the tenth tee, Duke and his partner were two down on the match with the front nine lost.

"I have to tell you," Hennessey said, "I feel a little funny with you having a different name. I mean, if you were my daughter, I'd have to get used to the new name if you got married. I was used to Rosenberg; Rose is a whole other story. It's like I changed my name to Henderson. Tough to get used to this being WASP."

"Look at all the movie stars, Duke. They all got their names changed. John Wayne was Marion Morrison. He got used to it. Fans never know the difference."

"Well, maybe Richard Rose can hit a golf ball better than Rosenberg ever did. *That* would be the change."

"The big change, Francis, is the numbers," Dickie said. "We're going to go public one of these days. You can own my stock."

"Everything in my life is in bricks and mortar," Hennessey answered. "My fortune is inflation; use the banks' money, the insurance company's money; pay no taxes and leverage yourself to the moon. Jimmy Carter may be a shitty President, but if you build to suit, he's making you a rich man."

"We're both in the middle of the fairway," Singer yelled at them. "You going to hit or shoot the shit?"

As they had since they were children, Hennessey and Singer played even, at nine, the low handicappers. Temple and the new Richard Rose also played even, with handicaps at twenty-four.

Going into fifteen, the Hennessey team was one hole down on the match, one up on the back side. The fifteenth was a par-four, dogleg-left, four-hundred-and-fifty-yard bitch of a hole. There was palm forest on the left and right, lining the fairway. A straight tee shot had to carry just over two hundred yards to make the corner. But if you were too ambitious, there were traps to catch the gorilla hitter. The true players went for the corner, trying to draw the ball around the bend and catch some roll to prepare for a second shot over a pond that guarded the green. It was the number one stroke hole, too many hazards to negotiate for the Sunday player, too much skill and length needed for par. Temple crushed his drive, his best of the day, but it went dead straight, rolling into one of the fairway bunkers. As the others watched, in various forms of trouble themselves, Temple nudged his ball, sitting in the sand, a few inches with his club. "What the fuck are you doing?" Hennessey said. "Now you're hitting three."

Temple looked up. "There's an obstruction. I can get relief from an obstruction."

"Not playing with anyone who knows the game you can't. You're hitting three."

"I know the sport better than you, Hennessey. Take a closer look." The three others gathered around the deep sand trap while Temple pointed with his seven iron. "Look, it's a safe, for Christ's sake. It was right up against my ball." Sure enough, a condom was stretched out in its unmistakable beige shape.

"Is it used?" Red asked. "It makes a difference if you moved your ball whether it's new or used."

"If there's a goddamned obstruction," Temple insisted, "Coke bottle, apple core, whatever, you can get relief in a trap. It's a rule. I can't hit the ball through a frenchy."

"You could fuck with one around your dick. That should be the rule: hit right through it. You've moved the ball, you're hitting three."

"That's bullshit, Duke," Singer said. "He's entitled to a drop."

"You can check that out," Hennessey said, "but he moved the ball with his club, and he didn't ask us for a ruling first."

"Because you guys don't know your ass from a hole in the ground about the rules of golf."

"You mean about gentlemen sports, right, Temple?" Dickie said.

"Fore," came several voices from back down the fairway.

"Fuck you," yelled Red, cupping his hands so he could really be heard.

"Let 'em hit, for Christ's sake," Duke said, waving the players to go through.

"Those are members," Temple said. "You said 'Fuck you' to members."

"I said, 'Good luck, you,' " Red said, "and I waved them through. I'm a fucking gentleman, even though I'm not a fucking goy."

"We better enjoy this round," Temple said, "because we'll be playing somewhere else tomorrow."

"Come on," said Dickie. "Money talks."

"And bullshit walks," Duke added. They took their argument to the rough while they waited for the next foursome to play through.

The average age of the men riding up the fairway had to be eighty. Two of them hit the ball less than a hundred and twenty yards; the other two hit right and left, into the forest, where alligators fed on brand-new balls. "Nice, not to outgrow your money," Dickie said, as they huddled in the shade out of the Florida sun.

Freddie stepped forward as the elderly foursome hit their second shots out to the corner. "Sorry to hold you up," he said. "A little ruling problem. Obstruction in the trap."

"Who are you?" a white-haired man wearing pink and green and looking like a refugee from Grosse Pointe asked.

"Fred Temple," Freddie said, "New York, Rockaway Hunt and the Maidstone Club."

"Good description," the man said, and proceeded to move his ball, using a half swing with his five wood, to the end of the corridor, from where he could see the green in the distance. None of them were anywhere near the trap where Freddie's ball rested. The elderly men all yelled too loud and waved thanks as they pressed on toward the end of what was the end of all their afternoons. Their gas carts polluting the air, they chuckled together, proud that they were still able to hit through boys they thought of as half their age.

The foursome walked back to the sand trap. "You know," Hennessey said, "if you get to move your ball in a trap, you have to take a drop, not nudge it with a club. No matter what happens you're hitting your third shot."

"Who gives a shit?" Singer said. "I'm fifty yards ahead of all of you. Forget it, Freddie."

"It's the principle of it," Temple insisted. He strode into the sand, swung much too hard with his seven iron, hit way in back of the ball. It popped out of the trap and stopped barely six feet away. Everyone backed away and said nothing. All three fought to keep from laughing. Temple crushed his next shot with the three wood, and it did manage to make the very end of the lake that guarded the green. "Put it in your pocket, Freddie," Red advised him.

"No, goddamn it. I'm playing by the rules of golf," he answered. Temple hit eleven shots by the time he got to the green. Every shot was worse than the last.

"Freddie, for Christ's sake, put the ball in your pocket," Singer said. "Don't aggravate yourself. It's a fucking golf hole. You want to make me miss the putt?"

"You want to file a protest with the USGA?" Hennessey called at them. "You can't take more than a triple bogey, Temple. You want two more geriatric foursomes to go through us? We finish at midnight?"

"Humor him," Dickie said. "You wouldn't know about being a shitty golfer. Let him putt out." Dickie put his own ball in his pocket, leaving Singer and Hennessey to fight for the win. Both of them were on the green in three, both at least twenty-five feet from the cup.

"Putt out, for Christ's sake, so we can concentrate," Duke said.

Temple made sure he took his time, to aggravate everyone. He three-putted from ten feet and snapped the putter over his knee.

"Obviously, he's not really a WASP," Singer said to the others. "You seen this much emotion in him in thirty years?"

"Not since he killed Sullivan," Dickie said. "That day he took off."

"That's funny, Rosie," Singer said. "We always thought *you* killed Sullivan."

Dickie looked right at them. "You'll never know though, will you?" he said. "Sticks and stones."

Duke waved off the moment and yelled over at Temple, "By the strict rules of golf, motherfuck, you have to putt with half a putter from now on or use any other club. You can't use anyone else's putter."

"By the beard of the prophet, she's mine," yelled Red, reminding them of the punchline of an old joke. They tried to concentrate then, Red and Hennessey, and they both missed the putt for four. Singer missed the putt coming back, however, and his team was even on the match, two down on the back side, going into sixteen.

Temple didn't talk to any of them until they were all on the eighteenth green. The match had turned after Dickie had buried his chip shot on sixteen for a birdie, the only hole he had won the entire day. They had won the back side and were one up on the match. On eighteen, Temple had been prepared to putt with a choked-down three iron, with the face held square, like a putter blade. He would write his check for $5,000 after the match, he thought, tell them all to go fuck themselves and leave for home.

The eighteenth was a short par four, three hundred and fifty yards, finishing up a hill. The drive was the key to the narrow hole guarded on the left by thick palm forest, on the right by a long pond that ran the length of the fairway. Directly in the center of the fairway, about two hundred and twenty yards out, was a single royal palm, majestic, fruit-bearing, a lighthouse for the tee shot. Occasionally some big hitter would ram his drive into its trunk, the ball caroming off crazily, sometimes into the pond. The hitter would go bananas, penalized for a straight shot.

"It's a thinking man's game," his opponents would say. "You've got to move the ball right or left or be short. Think about it."

"It's unfair. It sucks."

"Golf is fair," they'd tell him. "It's life that's unfair."

Dickie had sliced his drive into the pond. Temple shouldered his into the forest, dropped a ball and hit a lucky five iron that eventually stopped on the back edge of the green. Singer and Hennessey hit irons off the tee, both playing left and short of the giant palm. Then Singer hit a seven iron, and he hit it well. But he underestimated the incline of the hill and was at least ten yards short. Duke, the thinker, always had confidence in his fairway woods. Somewhat stymied by the palm, he hit sharply down on a ginty. The shot soared almost immediately, clearing the top of the palm by inches and, still climbing, reached its apex directly in front of the green, seemed to hover and then dropped like an eagle on a snake. Even Red applauded one of the best shots of the day.

While Temple was moving his cart around to the back of the green, the other twosome had gone ahead, excited by Duke's shot, anxious to see where his ball had landed. Temple was lying three and had a handicap stroke on the hole. He was as intent on being pissed off as any ten-year-old picked last for the sandlot game. Hennessey and Rose were concentrating on their next shots when Temple marched to the green with his two iron, prepared to putt. "What . . . is . . . that?" he exclaimed. They were the first words he had spoken since the fifteenth. Something was resting on top of his ball, and he approached cautiously. He stood above it. "Did you do this, you bastards?" The condom lay over his golf ball like a rain hat for the player who has everything.

"No hard feelings, Blondie," Duke said. "You can have a drop."

Even Temple laughed. But Hennessey proceeded to three-putt, and the match finished all even.

Dickie accused him of purposely pulling his last putt. Duke shook his head. "You better be kidding. I thought you knew me. Nickels and dimes anyway," he said. "I can afford to be generous when I pocket the twenty grand."

"Fifteen," Dickie said, "if five of it's yours."

"Hey, five saved is five earned," Duke answered. "Orientation week."

Freddie had to beg them not to leave the condom at the bottom of the cup.

"You see, guys, the whole world's trying to be like California." The four men sat in a hot tub looking up at a night filled with stars and landing lights of aircraft that blinked in the skies over Miami as if they were watching a video game.

"We've been to California, Red," Hennessey said, "the place where nobody knows anybody else. Everybody out there failed in other lives. Do you actually know a real person in California?"

"I know Lindalee."

"Yeah," Duke said. "She probably burns a cross on your lawn on . . . your, whatever it is . . ." No one else said anything. They pushed the water around, creating a tide. All their lives, they could say anything to Red. He invited it. But the code also said they couldn't say anything about Rita. "I'm sorry, man," Duke said. "I didn't mean it. The problem is, you're Red."

Red couldn't resist. They were a foot away from each other. "It's okay. I know you're sorry. Like you were sorry when Rita took on the basketball team after the Arlington game."

Duke went for him then, knowing it was his own fault, but knowing that it was expected. They churned up the water in the hot tub, Dickie and Freddie getting in the way. It splashed to a close. The effort to defend honor having been made, it soon died away. They poured more champagne from the ice bucket next to the tub and lay back into more contemplation of the sky. The tub was planted in a courtyard adjoining the beach at their hotel.

"You guys remember," Dickie asked, "when anyone new came

to school and after gym we'd be in the showers and the guy would suddenly realize that a bunch of us would be pissing on his legs and that's how the guy would be broken into the crowd?"

"You never pissed on anyone's legs, Rosie," Singer said. "You were too fucking prissy for that."

"We used to do the same thing at St. Luke's," Temple said. "Probably every high school kid in America did it."

"Rosie," Hennessey said, "I hope you're not telling us that you're pissing in the tub?"

"Who would know?" Dickie asked.

"We might turn you upside down on general principles, make you drink it up."

"Even if you didn't piss in the tub, we might do it anyway," Singer said. Dickie knew they'd do it and moved to change the subject. "Let's get with the voting. The nice thing about this year," he said, "I deserve it. And I don't need the money. When you don't need it, things always accrue to you."

"You know," Hennessey said, "I like you, Rosie. I always liked you even when everyone said you were an opportunist. I always defended you."

"That means you're going to vote for me?"

"I control two million square feet of space, for Christ's sake, in a market that's going to explode. You're living in that hick town, New York, where everybody's jerking each other off."

"But I'm the first of us who's going public. In two years we'll be on the big board. None of you can compete with that."

"We don't vote on the come," Duke said. "You got to show here and now."

"Okay," Rosie suggested. "Let's go around like we used to in the high school clubs. Good and welfare sessions, remember? Sit around and give constructive criticism."

"All the clubs were Jewish in high school," Duke said.

"I have news for you," Dickie responded. "Outside of Brookwood or New York or Beverly Hills, no one gives a shit about the Jews. Where we grew up, we didn't have a clue."

"There are Jewish members of The Golf Club, you know," Temple said. "A few guys from Harvard when we went there. I go up to see the folks, play a round, shoot some skeet."

"It's horseshit," Duke said. "The guys tell me around Boston, you got a few token Jewish members. They look good, they got money, think they're Episcopalians. They all went to Exeter, won't embarrass anyone. They marry the shiksas, some of them. If they got Jewish wives, the wives never show up there, who they going to talk to, know what I mean?"

"Sounds like someone who wants to join The Golf Club to me," Dickie said.

"Fuck you. I look down on them from my backyard," Duke answered. "Someday I'll probably pave them over, build Section Eight housing, let the boonies from Roxbury in."

"I never knew you felt that way," Temple said.

"Ahhhh!" Duke backed off. "Who gives a shit? The WASP is dead anyway."

"Not at Alligator Run he isn't," Dickie said.

"Let me tell you something," Red interrupted, grabbing the champagne bottle and refilling everyone's glass. "It's interesting. When you're in my business, you only see people in the business; you don't give a shit about the citizens, anyone else, you know what I'm saying? You're not conscious that anyone else really lives in L.A. Then one day a banker who fiddled some numbers for me in a deal with U.A. called me. He went to Stanford, grew up in Pasadena; good guy. His great-grandfather came out in the gold rush. He took me to play in a member-guest at the Los Angeles Country Club. Well, it was another world, another fucking world. Everybody I met that day owned a company. A company that either manufactured something or loaned money to the companies or insured the companies. Everybody I know in my business is either a shit-heel or about to be a shit-heel. I see *Fortune* magazine covers in the drugstore all my life, and I never once opened one up. Because it didn't have anything to do with me. That's what the L.A. Country Club was like. I swear to God, everyone there looked like they were chairman of Goodyear Tire, all with short hair. Those guys look great forever, but the wives are all a piece of shit by forty, looking like everything they smell smells bad. But they're all in control; it's all taken care of. I showed the fucks. Shot seventy-eight on my own ball first time I looked at the layout. We won a prize, but nobody got very excited. Maybe I didn't show them. You know what I'm saying?"

Dickie chimed in, mocking Red's tone. "This is a long way of saying the WASP isn't dead, you know what I'm saying, Duke? Don't say 'Fuck you.' "

"I'll say let's vote, get more champers," Temple suggested, and he clanged his glass against the empty bottle until the waiter ran to them, eager to show why he had left Havana.

"Dom Perignon," the waiter announced, swirling the bottle around in its iced tub.

"Hola, Chico, compadre," Dickie said. Again they voted, on bar chits, then gave the waiter the folded pieces of paper. "Open them and read what's written, please," Dickie said.

"Check your tip first," Red suggested. The waiter did, but he was a person who wanted to have his own business someday. He knew that busting his tail and building relationships was more important than whether he was getting more than fifteen percent. Miami would be better than Havana. He opened the first vote. "Richard Rose," he said. He pronounced it "Reechard."

"Dead giveaway, asshole," Red said. "Vote for yourself. No one else would call you Rose."

"I would," said Temple. "He wants to be Muhammad Ali, I'll call him Muhammad Ali."

"Do you think the kids Kareem Abdul-Jabbar grew up with still call him Lew?" Dickie asked.

"No," Red replied, "because Lew Alcindor was his slave name probably, like Cassius Clay was."

"Well, Dickie Rosenberg was my slave name."

They laughed, and the waiter opened the second ballot. "Duke," the waiter read.

"Hey, hey," Duke called to the night.

"Temple," the waiter said next, and the rest of them hooted.

"You don't even know what I do," Temple defended himself. "The truth is, in the next five, ten years, I can be the key to all of you. I can make all of you rich. This should give me the pot if you guys were honest with yourselves."

They nodded to the waiter, and he read the last name. "Hennessey," he said, lingering over the syllables.

"Shit," said Richard Rose. "It's not fair, and my skin feels like when I'd been left in the bath too long by my mother. Puckered." It occurred to all of them.

"Last one in's a rotten egg," Hennessey cried, and leaped from the hot tub. He ran bare-assed straight to the ocean, splashed in the surf and threw himself, in a great belly flop, into the waves. The others followed, Singer hesitating. Red bent down, naked as the rest of his friends, a small belly starting to predict his future. He made sure his room robe was there and his rope-soled canvas shoes he called his Basque country-days.

"You need bathing costumes on the beach, Señor," the serious waiter said. Red pulled a ten-dollar bill from the bottom of his shoe. "On top of the tab," Red said.

"Gracias," the serious waiter said. "For not calling me amigo," he added softly. Red was already on his way to the surf, telling himself, "I borrowed the five grand; I borrowed the ten-spot; in for a penny, in for a fucking pound." He threw himself into the waves, the water not much cooler, he thought, than the hot tub.

There were no complaints from the hotel. It was too late for beach walkers who cared anything about four naked guys in their forties. But it was a night, clouds across a big moon, that they all thought about other nights with clouds across big moons when they longed for someone to love, for someone to love them.

The foursome sat in a line on the sand, throwing stones and shells into the ocean, Duke's stones traveling the farthest.

"Only ex-catchers can throw sitting down," Dickie said.

"Because you, Rosie, threw like a girl," Red pointed out.

They were quiet, scuffling around for flat stones to toss.

"I never thought in a million years," Duke said, "that I'd be so casual about winning or losing fifteen grand."

"That's because you won," Temple said.

"Bullshit," Duke said. "Remember when we'd ask people in the drugstore for quarters so we could go to the Chink's and split a fucking egg roll?"

"We used to pull such shit," Red added. "Remember we took the subway into Boston, went down to the docks, to the Union Hall in the eighth grade, to sign on for summer work for freighters going to Europe?"

Dickie laughed. "And how the guys in the Union Hall said, 'Let's put them in a corner, make them piss their pants?' "

"And we ended up going to the Casino, watching that fat dame stripping, saying she had pussies all over her body because of her fat folds?" They were quiet again, heaving stones.

"I've got a chance to meet the President," Hennessey said.

"Talk about pussy," Temple snorted. "First the Panama Canal. What next? Carter's worse than Neville Chamberlain. What's going on today makes Richard Nixon look like Winston Churchill."

"Who's Neville Chamberlain?" Red asked.

"You're so fucking dumb, Singer," Duke said. "Chamberlain played center field for the St. Louis Browns. You guys can laugh, but I hear that Carter is a good guy. He's serious about the God stuff and what he sees for the country. Sleek Sullivan tells me Carter's okay, that I'd like him. Even though he never played American Legion ball."

Red said, "You're so full of shit it's coming out your ears."

"Jesus, Duke," Dickie said. "I take an awful lot of crap from Adrie about this whole contest. Are we ever going to be free of this? I mean, we vote you fifteen thousand, now you want the blood?"

Duke stood up. He was in front of them, between the other three and the ocean.

"I'd rather look at the water, Frank," Singer said, "than your uncircumcised dick."

Duke didn't move. "I'm going to tell Sleek Sullivan. I'm in his jersey; he's in mine. Every time I see the fucking guy I want to tell him. It'll be okay. What happened was years ago."

"Don't be an idiot, Duke," Temple said. "Go to confession. Tell God, but don't tell Sullivan. He's a senator. He can ruin us."

"He'll own us for life" was Singer's reaction.

Dickie said, "Anything you've got going with Sullivan, forget it if you tell him. He'll never trust you again. Be rational, Duke. What did you go to MIT for if not to be rational?"

Duke shook his head. "Remember when three of you couldn't take me? Okay, I got your fifteen thou, or I will have. You pricks would never stop payment on a check. I'll tell Sullivan. I mean it. But I'll give you a chance. If I can get to the hot tub before you can stop me, before you can hold me down, I'll spill my guts." Duke jumped up and started to run back toward the hotel. He ran like a rhino, big rump gathering speed, rolling with power like a pulling guard. Red caught him first, not going for the legs but jumping onto Duke's back, trying to bring him down like a Brahma bull in a rodeo. Temple went for the legs, a proper prep school tackle. He received a knee in the side of the face, but he brought Hennessey down. Dickie rolled on top, trying to pin an arm. Duke threw them all off. He had barely started to run before he was dragged again to the sand. Everyone got mad when the blood was up, like old times, pissed off, made stronger through the anger. Duke would have hurt them if he could. The others held on for dear life, knowing what would happen if they didn't hold on for dear life.

"Had enough?" Red yelled in Hennessey's face. Dickie had all his weight on Duke's right arm. Temple and Singer held, leaned on, twisted, sat on, everything they had to do until Duke let it go.

"Okay," he finally panted. "I don't tell Sullivan; you don't stop payment on the fucking checks."

"You sure?" Red asked. Duke nodded. They wouldn't let him up until he nodded. "One thing though," Duke said.

"Yeah?"

"I want to know. Did Rosenberg piss in the hot tub?"

They laughed at this, believing him.

"It's *Rose*," Dickie said, letting up the pressure on Duke's arm. "I want to show you something." He went to his own robe, which he had left at the side of the tub. He came back to the others, wearing the robe. He pulled something out of the pocket and unfolded it. "See this, Duke?" he asked. "You've never seen one before. It's a five-thousand-dollar bill. Your payoff. James Madison, the fourth president. You want it? They don't make these anymore. You want it?" They watched Dickie walk back to the tub and drop the bill into the water. "You want it bad enough," he said, "you can dry it out." He went back to the hotel.

"Poor fucking Rosenberg," Singer said.

"He doesn't realize," Hennessey said, "you play ball with politicians you see every President ever been on a bill: McKinley, Lincoln, Grover Cleveland. Cash changes hands; you see history." Duke went for the hot tub as Temple and Singer watched.

"It's Rose," Singer said, as much to the Florida sky as anything else.

"I believe it," Temple said, $5,000 poorer but ready to deal. He knew you had to spend money to make it.

○

CHAPTER TWENTY

1983: Puerto Rico, Foursomes

"I'm here," Adrienne Rose told her husband, "but it doesn't mean I have to be jumping up and down with glee about it."

"I win forty-five thousand dollars, fifteen from each guy, for a long weekend in the sun, you could be a little looser about the whole concept."

"A," she replied, "you haven't won it yet, your little contest. B, we make more money in fifteen minutes, one minute actually, if the stock goes up a quarter of a point."

Richard sighed. "Adrie, if it's all going to be such a pain in the ass for you, why the hell did you come?"

"We've been through this before, darling," she answered. "You wanted me to, and I said I'd come to stroke the bankers, to stroke Freddie Temple."

"Well, one of my many clichés, you'll be quick to point out, is that I learn something every day. One thing I'm going to teach you is that some things are beyond price. Winning a dollar on the golf course, for instance, is more satisfying than a quarter of a point up on a million shares of stock."

"That bit of information," Adrie said, "is one of the many reasons I'll never play golf." She smiled. "I know what you're thinking. You're thinking what it would be like to be divorced. You're thinking why do you need this aggravation?"

"You know what a noodge is, Adrienne?"

She laughed.

"We're like an old married couple," she said, "falling into our routines."

"We *are* an old married couple," Richard said, "only more so because we work together, which ninety-nine out of a hundred married couples never could."

"But you'll never kill the goose that lays the golden eggs, would you, darling?"

"I wouldn't even fuck the goose," he thought. But Richard would never say it. They were in a deluxe room at the Pepino Beach Hotel in Puerto Rico, about an hour out of San Juan on the northeast coast. Their room was on the beach, where spotlights, hidden in the palms, illuminated the surf at night and the trade winds annoyed the women before dinner as they walked to the restaurants clutching their hair.

There were twenty-seven holes on the golf courses of Pepino Beach, an early Robert Trent Jones design, many of whose holes were laid out along the ocean. The Bermuda grass of the fairways teed it up for the players. The golf professionals complimented everyone on every shot. A small truck cruised the holes on a constant basis, dispensing Corona or Michelob beer and everything from planter's punches to one hundred proof piña coladas, the specialty of Pepino Beach.

Adrie opened the sliders and went out onto their balcony, inhaling deeply, spreading her arms. "It's really beautiful, Richard," she said. "It's funny, but you never think of Puerto Rico as beautiful. You think of *West Side Story* or something. I'm going for a swim. We have time." She was speaking into the wind, and her husband was already on the phone to New York.

Adrienne Rose at forty-three still smoked Merits, still drank whiskey neat the way her father used to. But she sipped, never really liking it, the way she used to choke down terpine hydrate and codeine when she had the flu as a little girl. She had targeted for age forty-five: the bags under her eyes, the wrinkles on her forehead and the slight goombah, as her mother called it, under her chin. "Growing old is bullshit," she told her designers. "Every pattern you make, keep this in the front of your mind. You're thirty-four years old and you're a woman, so you have to be twice as good as any man and you're out to kick ass. Part of kicking ass is looking fresher than anyone else who gets into the elevator in your office building. That's who you're designing for."

Adrie ran as she used to run at camp, arms and legs in all directions, into the surf and dived underneath an incoming wave. She swam for a white aluminum raft, anchored fifty yards out in front of the breakwater. She hoisted herself up, shook out her hair and lay back, catching the last of the afternoon sun, happy to be alone. The owners of Pepino Beach, Canadian developers who relished privacy, cut their beach into sections separated by large barricades of stone, giving each fifty guests, in effect, their own private beach. Adrienne was alone on her section, and she almost dozed off when she sensed something in her peace. Without opening her eyes, she checked that her bathing suit was in place, pulled it up over her breasts, checked the fabric over her crotch. She opened her eyes and pushed herself onto her elbows and saw a swimmer backstroking toward the raft. She thought that she had never seen anyone backstroking anywhere but in Olympic races on TV. The swimmer backstroked all the way until he slapped one hand against the aluminum. He turned then and, like a seal, in one motion, came onto the raft. "Jesus Christ, Freddie," Adrienne said to Temple, "you scared the hell out of me. Nobody does the backstroke." He was blinded by salt until he wiped his eyes, then he beamed. "Adrienne. I had no idea you ever went into the water."

She loved that. They kissed cheeks, and she thought, "God, he smells good. There isn't a hair on his body."

"Where's Rosie?" he asked.

"Where do you think?"

"He's on the phone with New York."

She nodded. Freddie had probably just come from doing the same. "You look like you've been down here all week. We got in less than an hour ago."

"My business takes me where the money is," he said. "In the winter the money sometimes is in Palm Beach or Palm Springs or Lyford Cay, even Gstaad if I bring an interpreter. Rubs them the wrong way if they hear French with an American accent. But most of that ilk are a pain in the tail. Anyway, the tan's probably from when I took the kids to Curtain Bluff."

"Richard thinks we need to borrow twenty-five million to gear up some manufacturing in New York."

"If you shut your eyes, parts of New York are just like being in Hong Kong or Taiwan. He's probably right. Three hundred stitchers in some firetrap off Mott Street."

"I hate to borrow anything. Everyone who put up early money has been paid back twenty times. You still have your stock, don't you, Freddie?"

He looked her right in the eyes. "I never sell stock in my clients' companies. I hold on until they're not clients anymore."

"And you never lose a client." She held his eyes.

"Not if they're smart."

Adrie dangled her legs over the side of the raft. "Are you alone this weekend?"

He laughed. "I brought a flat belly," he said. "Mostly to piss off the others. Aside from the fact that I'm in love."

"Red's divorced also," she said. "But he didn't waste any time getting married again."

"Red's a romantic. He married old Hollywood, a girl who used to have birthday parties in Beverly Hills when half a circus entertained her. Cary Grant was her escort at her sweet sixteen party. It's the first thing Stanley told me about her. I'm in love with a flat belly; Stanley's in love with Sam Goldwyn, Louis B. Mayer."

Adrie eased herself off the float into the water. She held on to the raft. "What are you, the class historian?"

"Adrie," he said, "I know your father pushed for you to go with Goldman or Bear Stearns. The truth is, we got you a better deal. We got you more money. And I'm on a raft in Puerto Rico with you and you've been staring at my cock and wondering."

Adrie kicked her legs the way she had been taught at camp years ago. "I know you got us more money than Goldman offered. I care about that more than your cock, although I admit I'd like to see it. You don't think this is pushing the client-banker relationship?"

"Rosie's one of my oldest friends," Temple said. "Now he's one of my richest friends."

He moved to the edge of the raft and put his legs over Adrie's shoulders. Then he slid his bathing suit, made by native ladies in Antigua, over his thighs. Freddie never had a problem getting hard. He got hard at Harvard-Yale hockey, club initiations, bachelor parties, bridal dinners. He never had a problem screwing Marley no matter what was going on in his marriage or his life. He got divorced because they had played out the string, because his deals meant that home was a hotel. And when Bill Simon made $20 million from the Gibson Greeting buyout, the stakes went up for everyone on Wall Street. No one had time for relationships that didn't have eight figures somewhere in the sentence.

"Just a taste," she said, and stuck her tongue out, running it around the end of his penis. Then she kissed it several times, feeling Freddie's hand at the back of her head, urging her down. She pulled away then, floating several feet from the raft. "I said just a taste. I can't imagine doing that with anyone from Goldman Sachs. See you at dinner." She struck out for the beach, remembering from her camp days how important it was to keep the legs kicking hard. Freddie let her go, shrugging the bathing suit up over himself, uncomfortable as it was. Then he lay down, arms and legs stretched out, catching the last of the day's sun. "Probably not a good idea," he thought. He was thinking about the possibility of losing the business. "But we're in there too tight. I shouldn't have pushed her head. She wants everything to be her idea."

Adrienne was thinking of advertising as she swam in. "Just a taste," for her spring line 1984. Get them in for a taste, they'll buy the sweaters; they'll buy the tailored shirts with the shoulder pads. She couldn't wait to tell Richard.

The Hennesseys were hitting tennis balls with each other, Rita hitting everything flat and hard with short, educated strokes. Duke cut everything he hit, cute drop shots, lobs. And no matter where Rita put the ball, deep, short, angled, Duke caught up with it and dinked it back. "Let's play a set," he called. "I hate practice." Rita could practice all day, working on form. Duke needed games.

"First ball in," she yelled over at him and drilled her serve, bang, right on the tape, to Duke's backhand. He cut it back, putting so much backspin on it that the ball moved toward his side of the net. "Are you going to play like a man, Frank?" she said, disgusted with him.

"You dance with the guy what brung you," he said. "I can't change my game; it's a natural slice."

"Play like a man," she reiterated. They played hard with each other. They never noticed Red Singer until he applauded a forehand drive by Rita that whipped past Duke like a fastball on the corner. He could only wave at it. "Blow that man away." Red whistled and clapped. Red was in shape. He had started running in recent years. His weight was below what it was senior year in high school when he was on the track team. With the pounds he had also shed Lin-

dalee. Or she had shed him. "Let's face it," he said at the time.
"She's much too smart for me. Once I couldn't pull the wool over
her eyes it was history. Finito."

Lindalee was now a vice president in charge of production at
Paralax Films, an independent, getting to be one of the women who
counted. She still loved Red, "as you'd love a naughty child," she
said. "I'll forever have a sneaker for him. But he's so insecure, like
everyone in the business, that he'll always carry things too far. Too
eager to please, too many gimmicks in his movies. Overkill. If he
cut twenty-five percent out of everything in his life, a quarter of his
scenes, a quarter of his bullshit, he'd be one of life's big winners.
Overkill. Fun to live with for a while. Lots of presents, many hugs
and kisses. Twenty-five percent too many of those, too; a tongue
man like every guy who's Jewish." Their son, Valentino, stayed
with Lindalee. Red saw him officially every other weekend and two
weeks in the summer. But he dropped into his old house in Bel Air
almost every night to see his son, talk sports and movies with him.
"Get you a gee-tar," Red would say to his boy. "Buy you a Cadillac.
Make you a star."

Valentino was a serious child, given to computer games and
backgammon. "No Cadillacs," he would deadpan. "A Cord. A
Hispano-Suiza. A late-sixties Porsche 911."

Lindalee would grin at Red behind the boy's back. "Anything
your little heart desires, chicken," she would say. "The generation
that's going to save our ass."

"You're too smart for your own good," Red would tell her before he left.

Duke and Rita came over and hugged Singer, who was dressed
in custom-made cream-colored tennis costume, pleated shorts and
a cotton polo shirt with a Cardinal logo, red as the bird, over his
left breast. He carried two Prince rackets in their cases. "Thought
I'd hit with the pro, work on my topspin." They told one another,
like old friends, how well they all looked. "Unbelievable." Red
asked, "How long have you guys been married now? Seems like
forever."

"Almost twenty-four years," Rita said.

"Missed the whole sexual revolution," Duke added. "The only
pill Rita ever took was an aspirin."

Red thought, "I don't think they even had a date with anyone else in their entire lives." It wouldn't matter if Duke was worth fifty million. To have known one woman in his life. He shook his head, clearing the horrible thought.

"I can't wait for you guys to meet Laura," he said. "Finally I'm really happy. I mean, you know what it's like. But for me to be really happy. I never believed it was in the cards."

"What's she like?" Rita asked, sipping Gatorade she kept in a thermos jug.

"Let me answer it with a story. You guys are both Catholic; your kids are Catholic. Marriage is difficult enough without another religion getting in the way. Lindalee was a fucking tiger, excuse the language. She didn't think Judaism was strong enough. Do you believe it? It amused her. Thousands of years of history and it amused her. So Valentino doesn't know whether to shit or wind his watch about religion; you know what I'm saying?"

"Yeah," Duke responded. "Your new wife's Jewish."

"She's not only Jewish" — Red smiled at them — "she's the granddaughter of Franklin Fine Fishman. Triple F Studios, one of the moguls of Hollywood, like Goldwyn, Louis B. Mayer, Harry Cohn."

"Remember the four F's?" Duke asked.

"Find 'em, feel 'em, fuck 'em and forget 'em," Red answered. "Things you *don't* forget. Like your army serial number. Rita, I'm sorry. But I'm from Hollywood. Hollywood people swear a lot. Mostly because they came from Brooklyn and they all grew up with an inferiority complex. Almost everyone, including me, who goes into the movie business was considered a loser or a freak in high school. Now we overcompensate. Therapy taught me that. I didn't make it up."

"You are definitely a freak," Hennessey said. "Is she rich?"

"Laura? She was named after the character in the movie *Laura* with Gene Tierney, remember her? My father was in love with Gene Tierney, and so was Franklin Fine Fishman. So he insisted his granddaughter be named Laura, and he pulled the money strings, so, as Monty Python says, 'There it is.' Laura has a trust which I already looked into, and it cannot be broken. She gets the income and little pieces of the principal, diddly-squat as far as Red Singer is concerned. But she used to have birthday parties with whole circus acts, ponies, clowns, stars at the parties as escorts for the kids, Cagney, Gable. Cole Porter played 'Happy Birthday' for her one year on a white Steinway. Then he played 'The Lady Is a Tramp,' which was her favorite song when she was ten. Only Hollywood royalty could get Porter to play a Rodgers and Hart song."

"Where is she?" Rita asked.

"Every time we go anywhere, she calls her kids, two adorable kids, Ari and Sara. Then Laura takes a nap."

"You bring your money, Red?" Duke asked. "I'm not conceding anything, but Rosie's looking pretty good on paper."

"But it's character as much as money," Red answered. "Temple's getting pieces of all our action."

"As I said, I'm not conceding anything."

"Mr. Singer." One of the pros approached them, a young man who grew up in Santurce and looked like Alex Olmedo. "You got the last lesson of the day." Red kissed both Rita and Duke again, slapped the pro on the back and headed for the next court.

"Nice shirt," the pro said.

"We have a good lesson," Red told him, "I'll send you a dozen."

They watched Red go. "The last of the true hot shits," Duke said.

"Do you ever wish you were married to someone younger?" Rita asked, "or to a woman in a business?" They were walking back to their room along the beach path. The ocean was as navy blue as a uniform, with the surf pounding beyond the breakwater and the air smelling like babies. Duke rubbed her rear end as they walked. "You're my girl," he said. "These guys are a bunch of douche bags. You're a woman. You're a mother. They wouldn't know a real woman from first base."

"Adrienne Rose is a woman."

"She's a fucking man," Hennessey said. "As a woman, she can't carry your beach bag. And she never hit a tennis ball like you."

"You're threatened by her," Rita said. "You like her."

"Sure I like her. She's one of the richest women in America. But she's still a fucking man. All bottom line."

"How can you say that? It's a totally chauvinist remark."

"Oh, Jesus H. Christ," Duke said. "Trust me."

They met in the bar for drinks at seven, eager to tell each other how fabulous they looked. The bar, in a building designed to look like an old sugar mill, was one of three at the hotel. It was the smallest as well and led into what was billed as the island's only true gourmet restaurant, for which reservations and jackets for men were a necessity. The Hennesseys and the Roses lined up side by side, as if they were the parents, having marital tenure on the others. They sized each other up, singing praises, the men on their good behavior.

Laura Fishman (she had kept her maiden name) had bowed to the Farrah Fawcett look. She had a mane that looked as if it could be the logo of her grandfather's Triple F Productions, as the lion served for MGM. She tossed it constantly off her shoulders, brushed it off her face, as if the gestures gave her time to compose her words, which always had something to do with the movie business. She refused to talk about anything else. She married Red because she thought he had the potential to give the bird to the world, the way her grandfather had done. She also knew that her grandfather had settled originally in Boston after his journey as a little boy from his family's village in Poland. Laura was superstitious. She had married her first husband, a Beverly Hills stockbroker who looked like the young Tony Curtis, because Curtis had also been one of her grandfather's favorites. The marriage was doomed from the start when Franklin Fine Fishman announced at the wedding reception, "The schmuck tried to tell me that Paramount Pictures stock was cheap."

"You can make back the price of the wedding, Grandpa," the schmuck said, and he'd been in the family for only an hour.

"Anyone marries into the Fishman family is automatically on probation for five years. And *nobody* tells me what's cheap or not cheap in the business." His own son, F. F., Jr., Laura's father, was lost deep in the back lots of *his* dad's persona and ended up drowning in a fishing accident off Catalina during the energy crisis of 1973.

"Your dresses are too cheap for me" were the first words Laura said to Adrienne. "You know, inexpensive. But several of my girlfriends who go out to the Valley every day swear by them. One of them even wore one for fun to Swifty's party the night of the Awards."

"Every little bit helps," Adrie said to her, and turned immediately to greet Freddie, who walked tall into the bar with his date. The other women would all claim that Freddie's date looked young enough to be his daughter. Freddie's date was twenty-six and worked on the account side of a bubble-gum account for Ogilvy. Gabriella Hobbs was her name. "Gabby Hobbs," she said to everyone, giving a strong handshake that implied a lot of time growing up playing field hockey. Now she rode, she sailed, she played golf and tennis and had worked with Marley Temple on a New York hospital benefit. The first time they made love she said to Freddie, "My father never did this to me, if that's what you're thinking." Freddie looked down at her long legs and soft skin the color of women in travel ads for South America (her mother was from Chile).

"I'm thinking how beautiful you are and why I'm the perfect man for you."

"Why are you?"

"Because at this stage of your life you want to get into a client's Lear jet with me and have dinner in Paris. You want to go to Aspen and sail from Northeast Harbour and hear stories of Bohemia Grove and Henry Kissinger's jokes. You've got your list, and I've got mine. If you've got the most beautiful pussy I've ever seen and I've got the nicest toys you've ever seen, why shouldn't we be selfish with one another?"

"Or something like that," Gabby said. "How about a piece of bubble gum? I need something sweet." Gabby paid no attention to his speeches. But he was right, she thought. She did like all that stuff. And, she supposed, he did remind her of her father before he went broke and before AA made him sober and the most boring he had ever been in his life.

They sat in the bar at a table for eight, boy girl, boy girl, and ordered planter's punches with a splash of Myer's dark one hundred proof rum on top. Except for Adrie, who had a Perrier, and Temple, who insisted on a Bombay gin martini, straight up, with two olives. "To old friends," Dickie proposed, raising his glass.

"New friends," Temple added, looking at Gabby and Laura Fishman. "The contest," Duke and Singer said, almost in unison. They clinked.

"The nice thing about the eighties," Red added, "five years ago, ten grand was a stretch, a hardship. I admit it. Now fifteen is like what falls out of my bathrobe on the way to the shower. And the bathrobe has my crest."

"Your logo," Richard said.

Red was feeling his oats. In the last five years, two of his movies had been among the top grossers of the year, one of them about an Irish vice cop during Prohibition who falls for the flapper daughter of the Jewish king of Boston crime. That's exactly how Red described it when he pitched the idea in a story conference. One of the studio heads was leaning way back in the La-Z-Boy chair he needed for his disc problem. His eyes were closed, and his hands were crossed over his stomach. Ignoring Red's pitch he had said, "I see two helicopters." Red jumped up and hit the lever on the La-Z-Boy, flipping the studio head out of the chair into the middle of his coffee table and the bowl of chopped liver and Triscuits that sat there for his pleasure. "Fuck you and the horse you rode in on," Red screamed. "I'm taking this script to Columbia where they appreciate making a buck." Red had the reputation as a screamer, someone who could clear the room with his ravings. It was nothing new in Hollywood, and by this time he was dating Laura Fishman, so he felt comfortable pulling the lever on the La-Z-Boy. Red was getting package power, the ability to match directors with bankable stars and present them, together with a screenwriter, to the money sources, who could always find the millions for bragging rights to the next *Godfather*, the next *Rocky* series, even the next *Sound of Music*.

Red banged on his glass with a silver pen, given to him long ago by the production crew of *Pounce*. "Everything goes back to the schoolyard," he said. "All my movie ideas. All Duke's ambitions. He's even got the white house we all wanted. Dickie's need for money also goes back, so he basically could tell his father to shove it. Don't say no, Rosie, I was in therapy long enough to understand these things. It's in Temple's pulling the strings also because he thinks he was born to do it. My toast is to all of us, things of beauty, pieces of work, and," he added, "to the women who support us, put up with us, and give precious meaning to us," he paused, "wherever they may be." He went around the table, kissing cheeks, tops of heads, and said, "Now everyone cross your arms in front of you and hold hands with your neighbors."

"I always had the feeling, Red," Hennessey said, "that you would turn into a pinko Commie fag, and you've never disappointed me."

"Just do it, Duke. Don't try to be a fucking marine all your life. For someone who was 4F you give a good imitation."

They joined hands. "We're lucky to be friends," Red intoned. "Healthy and prosperous together. The top of our games. May the Lord keep blessing the hard workers. And, particularly, all of us."

Then he told them to kiss each person to the right and the left.

Dickie sang the song he remembered from camp dances. "Friends, friends, friends, we will always be, whether together in dark stormy weather, Camp Wah Hoo Wah will keep us together." People in the bar watched the ritual and laughed, thinking that the group was part of an insurance convention or stockbrokers who had won a sales contest.

"Was that a Hollywood routine?" Temple asked Red. "The hand holding?"

Red laughed. "Christ, no. At least I learned it from a con man in Rancho Santa Fe who used to close his deals by doing it in restaurants with potential investors. He thought it gained him credibility by being semireligious. I lost twenty-five grand with him in some bogus tungsten mine in Nevada. Strategic metals. We needed tungsten in the arms race. But I don't know if there ever really was a mine."

"Do the movie, darling," Laura told him. "Don't give the plot away. Register it with the Writers Guild."

"Laura thinks everyone's going to steal my ideas," he said.

"I grew up in Hollywood, dollface," she said. "Your friends should always be a little richer than you, so they got to worry about you fucking them, not the other way around." She signaled for another round, and the maître d' made his appearance, making sure he came to the person who looked as if he had twenties folded in his fingers. "Your table is ready, Mr. Singer. Any time you wish to go in, sir." Red looked at them in triumph as the maître d' hugged menus to his chest. "We're ready to roll, Ricky," Red said. "I call you Ricky because I know you used to be married to Lucille Ball."

Adrie asked, "If he were black, would you call him Bojangles? Ricky Ricardo was Cuban." They were at two tables for four pushed together and covered with fresh white cloths.

"Let me tell you something, sweetheart," Red held forth. "When Sam Goldwyn was at the height of his powers in Hollywood, he wanted to buy rights to a book about lesbians that was a best-seller at the time and that he hadn't read. 'Buy it,' he told his junior producers. There was censorship at the time; movies about homosexuals were forbidden. 'You can't buy that book, Mr. Sam,' Goldwyn was told. 'It's about two lesbians.'

" 'Don't vorry about it,' Goldwyn said. 'In the movie ve'll make 'em *Americans.*' " Everyone laughed except Laura.

"My father used to tell that story," she said. "He hated Sam Goldwyn."

"The point is," Red went on, "you can say anything about anyone in my business. You can call anyone anything and somehow make them love it. That guy loves being called Ricky, I guarantee it."

Rita wanted to head off any trouble. "Why don't we go around the table and briefly tell each other about our children. Get that subject out of the way."

"I can get that out of the way faster than anyone," Fred's date said. "I've never even had an abortion." Before planter's punches, Gabby was nervous about being with Freddie's friends, who seemed so much older than he. After several drinks she wanted them to know how much maturity she brought to the table.

"Well," Adrienne Rose said, "I used to have a friend at school from Texas whose mother, my friend claimed, used to drink too much. Her mother'd get up on a table and say in a loud voice, 'Why is it that the neatest parents have the shittiest kids?' "

"Well, I think I'm the best parent in California," Laura said. "Not just with my two but with Valentino also, who can be a handful. Thank God none of you have to play the stepmother role, it's the toughest thing to do in the country, except for getting a script off the ground. In L.A. the stepmother is always the bitch to the old wife because the new wife gets the gravy, picks up the pieces of the old wife's mess, doesn't have the hassles, whatever."

Richard chimed in, "Lindalee seems to be doing pretty well in her own right." He had liked Red's first wife.

"Oh, Lindalee has been banging her way from Sunset to the Valley for so long she doesn't know which way is up," Laura said. "It's so obvious that she'll marry for money. But she better do it soon since everything she's making is going down the toilet."

"Stir it up, Rosie," Red said. "I appreciate it." He glared at Dickie.

"Can we talk sports now," Duke asked. "Or religion?"

"We're all big people in the nineteen eighties," Richard went on. "Just because someone's not here anymore doesn't mean they have to be expunged from the records. They're not dead if they're divorced. If Adrie and I were divorced, I'd be civilized enough to talk about her good points, if the moment arose."

"Darling," Adrie said, "that is so civilized of you, especially since you'd be either dead or broke if we weren't together."

"Well, let's talk about *your wife*" — Laura turned to Freddie — "since I'll probably never meet her."

"She's still using her walker," Gabby shot back, "and being treated for Alzheimer's."

"Remember encounter groups?" Adrie asked. "This is having great possibilities."

Freddie looked at his date. "A gentleman doesn't comment on those not present, especially dear departed ones. Henry Ford said, 'Never complain, never explain.' Just for a time in our lives there was no one like Marley. I'm sure she would say the same about me." He smiled slightly as he said this, and Gabby squeezed his cheek. "Could you love a face like this?" she asked.

"I may be sick," Dickie and Red said almost simultaneously as Hennessey made gagging noises and pointed his finger into his mouth.

"Grow up, Frank," Rita said to her husband. But she was laughing as she said it.

"It's amazing, really," Gabby noticed. "You guys have been friends longer than I've been alive. You dump on each other, you can say anything to each other. Despite what Freddie says, he talks about all of you when you're not around."

"That's because we're his meal ticket," Hennessey said. "He makes a living off of every one of us, and we're too dumb to even ask for a discount."

"Speak for yourself, Duke," Dickie said. "We get Temple cheap."

"Well, he raised almost a hundred million for me running those syndications in low-cost housing, those Section Eights. He got his pound of flesh. But I'm not putting his feet to the fire for an eighth of a point. He's entitled."

"What am I, a *pisher?*" asked Red. "I only got twenty million for Cardinal Productions. But Temple's lawyers made sure that no one could read the frigging prospectus. I couldn't read it except for the part that guaranteed my compensation even if none of the movies in the syndication ever made a penny."

"And accounting procedures will make sure that none of them ever do," Dickie said.

"Hey, fuck you, Rosie. You're jealous of my perks."

"I know. Your kids can have elephants brought to their birthday parties, and you can charge it off as production expenses to one of the films."

"Yeah," Red shot back. "And you can probably build a weekend house in Connecticut, entertain buyers and store managers and pack the whole thing into Adrienne Rose's books."

"We wouldn't do that, Stanley. We're a public company."

"Sure," Red said, "and I donate my salary to the PLO."

"Sounds like we should be drinking a toast to America," Duke said, lifting his glass.

"You mean to Ronald Reagan," Temple said, "who has made all this possible."

"What an asshole," Laura said. "He was a joke in Hollywood years ago, my grandfather said, and he's a bigger joke now. My grandfather and Joe Kennedy were as close as *this*. Now Stanley and I turn out the stars for Sleek Sullivan and in eighty-eight Stanley Singer and Laura Fine Fishman will be eating Irish salmon at the White House."

"Sullivan's cute," Adrie said. "Let's face it. We all know him. My father says he sounds like a Communist. 'The mild and meek will vote for Sleek.' All the rhymes in his ads. They want him to sound like Jesus Christ."

"It's Jesus H. Christ, remember?" Duke said. "Got to get the titles right. I'm glad we got politics into this."

"Still leaves religion to go," Dickie added.

"I like you guys," Gabby said. "Always something to offend everyone."

By the middle of dinner, drinks had eliminated any shyness and Singer had ordered champagne to make sure no one sagged in midevening, not with the casino waiting next door.

"Do you believe," Gabby said, before coffee and dessert, which only Hennessey ordered, "that when I go on weekend parties to the Hamptons or even to Greenwich, that we play charades? Most of my friends in advertising are killers at charades."

"You're not thinking," Laura asked, "that when there's gambling around, you'd play parlor games after dinner?"

"Games stir people up," Gabby insisted.

"That's why we're going to the casino," Freddie Temple said, steering Gabby up from her chair. "How about this," he said to the others. "We each start with a thousand. At midnight we cash in. Low man buys golf balls for everyone tomorrow. After midnight you're free to roll what you like."

"Let's do it," Duke agreed, and the men headed to the small casino next to the dining room: three roulette wheels, three blackjack games, two craps tables, no slot machines, no chemin de fer, no alcohol. If you wanted to drink, a lounge was just outside the casino enclosure. The women headed for the powder room. "You think we'd see some fur fly, we stayed at the table?" Duke said to Dickie as they waited for the ladies.

"I think that Singer will probably have ten wives at the rate he's going."

"She's got a great set of blue blades between those legs. Rita's been kicking me under the table for two hours. Think she's ready to go back to Boston?"

"Adrienne won't leave until she draws some blood."

Red was oblivious. "You guys joining me where the action

is?" he asked. "Or are you just going to bet red and black like the true pussies you are?"

"I play blackjack, you asswipe," Duke said to him. "I went to MIT, remember?"

"All I remember," Red answered, "was you over at my fraternity, beating your meat."

"Do you think at every important juncture of history," Freddie asked, "women were taking leaks in the john?"

"They don't take leaks in there, you schmuck," Red said, "they redo their faces. Women won't sit on toilet seats outside their homes."

"I'm shocked at such male chauvinist remarks," Dickie said. "And I'm going to report everything you say."

"I bet you will, Rosie," Duke said. "I bet you tell Adrienne every little thing."

"Wouldn't you," Freddie said, "for a company doing half a billion?"

"Shit. He's got to pay taxes though," Duke said. "Don't pay taxes in real estate."

"In the movie business" — Red tapped his head — "they cook the books like they write the scripts. They make it up. But whatever we do, by God we've all been players, all of us."

"Amen, brother," Hennessey echoed.

"Fuckin' A," Red affirmed, and ran to hug his wife, who emerged first from the ladies' room, rifling through her purse.

"I need moola, baby-cakes," she said. "I need a line if we're going to roll those bones." Laura used language the way she remembered her grandfather using language, thinking that all of life occurred on soundstages and back lots.

In the casino they broke in different directions. Duke and Rita went directly to blackjack. Richard took a seat at a roulette table. Red, Adrienne and Laura hurried to craps. True gamblers only went to the craps tables. Freddie and Gabby would drift, play a little of everything, watch a little, look to skim something from every game. Dickie took a thousand dollars in chips. He had agreed to it. His preference would have been one hundred, make small bets, make it last. He gambled every day on the next season, on hemlines, pads in shoulders, the price of the dollar versus the yen, the cost of labor in Hong Kong. There was something calm, not desperate at all, about $5 down on red or a low number or even the raciness of double zero. It meant nothing to Richard. It was mindless, good therapy while he waited for the ball to drop.

Red took his position opposite the croupier, placing small bets until someone rolled a winner twice in a row. Then he raised the stakes, betting with the shooter, trusting his gut about the person rolling and doubling up on the come, urging the shooter. "Come on, Mendy," he cheered a man who looked like a shoe manufacturer on a long weekend with a honey. "Go, you Mendy. Hum, babe." Mendy was what his father always called anybody in the shoe business. Mendy rolled a seven. Both Red and Laura urged him on as if they were rooting in Dodger Stadium, until everyone at the table was cheering his run. Mendy was sweating. He pushed his sleeves up and rubbed the dice in his palms between rolls, his honey pushing the croupier after each pass not to miscount the chips as they kept letting it ride. Mendy kept the dice for almost ten minutes, attracting a crowd the way dice tables always do, people on their tiptoes to watch the show. Temple and Gabby drifted over, Rita with them. Rita reminded Gabby of mothers of her friends. She felt protective of Rita, felt badly that she might somehow be mauled by the other, more racy women. Gabby felt she could hold her own against Laura Fine Fishman. Adrienne Rose she wanted to impress. If she could pitch this account, it meant out of bubble gum forever.

Duke was oblivious, counting the cards, rolling up tens and twenties at blackjack, attracting a little notice from the pit boss roaming the casino but not enough to lean on. They changed dealers at Duke's table. "Usually the counters are those scruffy fucking kids," the pit boss said.

"Sí," said the first dealer. "Hippies with the computers in packs they wear on their backs, all their clothes filthy."

"We let him win a few thousand, then give him a speech. Comp the drinks at the bar; he's with a party. The redhead will give back twice what the fat one makes."

Richard Rose played it safe, watching the wheel. Every time red came up three times in a row, he'd put $50 on black. If red came up again, he'd double up on black, $100. The modest system kept him alive at the table and allowed him to concentrate on the women, on what they wore, looking for ideas, trends they hadn't spotted. He felt he worked seven days a week, wherever he was, and that his eye was great. "Wearable and salable." Those were the hallmarks of Adrienne Rose.

Mendy finally crapped out, snake eyes after the run of his life. He was sweating from the emotion, grinning with the applause. Red yelled at him from across the table, "All this, Mendy, and you had to be with your wife?" Mendy laughed. He understood what Red was talking about. Adrie had been betting with the house for the last half of the shooter's run. Her father had always bet with the house, and she had upped the ante by a half on every roll, calmly watching, not getting excited, taking her chips in big stacks when the dice passed to the next player. She doubled up against the shooter when Laura's turn came and won big when Red's wife rolled a three and immediately after threw eleven, giving back most of what Red had parlayed on Mendy.

Laura watched the croupier push stacks of chips toward Adrienne. "You're betting against me?" she asked. "I'm not playing at a table where friends bet against me. What the hell kind of friend are you?"

Adrie was cool. "It's only a game. The guys play against each other on the golf course."

"That's sports," Laura almost spat at her. And she dragged Red from the table over to one of the wheels. She pounded her handbag down in front of her and demanded, "A thousand in twenty-dollar chips. Can't even get a goddamned drink in this pissant joint." Adrie stayed in her place, shrugging at the people around her and going back to small bets against the house.

Duke was up big when the pit boss tapped him on the shoulder. "Just want to tell you, Señor, that drinks in the lounge will be complimentary tonight."

"Hit me," Duke said to the dealer, and received a six. "Again," he said, and received a seven. He held up a hand: "Enough." He flipped over his hole card, an eight, and was paid off. He swiveled around in his chair. "Do you usually interrupt your guests in the middle of a deal? You might do it to the wrong person someday, much as I appreciate free drinks."

"We would go broke with guests like you."

Duke got up from his chair and bumped his stomach against

the pit boss. They looked like an umpire and a manager in a beef about a close call. "I'm not greedy," Duke said. "Whatever I do at blackjack wouldn't be a pee hole in the snow to either of us. I was enjoying myself, and I'm not anymore. Maybe you better check who your players really are before you piss them off." Duke didn't make scenes over diddly-squat things. It was why he could shrug off failures in business and why he could play the game of golf. He never replayed holes in his mind, holes that he should have birdied or parred. You had to bury your disasters. If you dwelled on them, you were dead yourself. "This place is a bustout," he told Temple. "I'm going to bed."

"You're taking the ball and going home?" Temple asked. "You're the one who was counting cards and you're sore?"

"I'm going to take a hit and an insult because I got a good memory? Be serious." They walked over to where everyone but Adrie was now playing roulette. Duke ran a finger down Rita's back. "I'm going to bed," he said.

"I'm up almost thirty dollars," she answered. "How can I quit now?" She turned around.

"Keep playing then," Duke said. "Only fourteen thousand, nine hundred and seventy dollars to go and you'll make up what I'll probably be giving Rosenberg tomorrow."

"It's Rose," she whispered at him. Duke lifted his wife off her seat and brought her very close to him. "Let me tell you something. Nothing ever changes. I run my finger down your back, all I think of is feeling your bra underneath, the same thing I thought when we were sixteen. And once a Rosenberg, always a Rosenberg. Same like I'm a Mick and you're a Mick and millions of dollars, thousands of fucking tennis lessons ain't ever going to change that."

Rita dealt with his soapbox by ignoring it. She turned around in her chair and bet the low numbers as Duke stomped off to bed before he gave in to the temptation to start something. The man stood alone by the casino doors as Duke approached. The pit boss rubbed his nose deliberately, a nose marked by chicken pox scars. Duke stopped and flipped him a hundred-dollar chip. "Here," he said. "Fill up one of the holes." And he walked on.

"You nothin', man," the pit boss hissed at him. "We made the phone calls. You nothin'." Duke laughed on his way out to the soft night. For some reason he thought of one of his heroes, William Zeckendorf, the man who developed Century City in L.A., Society Hill in Philadelphia, Mile High Center in Denver. "I'd rather be alive at eighteen percent," Zeckendorf said, "than dead at twelve percent." Duke was alive, and the banks were his best friends.

Red sported the biggest cigar in the casino, a Monte Cristo Number Four from Davidoff in St. James. Laura insisted that Red smoke her father's favorite, and he was hip as he pushed chips all over the felt with Laura at least one step ahead of him.

"Les jeux sont faits," Freddie announced as the wheel spun and Gabby giggled and it made so much more sense than craps, which seemed serious and which nobody seemed to understand except disgusting people. Freddie kept taking her out to the bar to drink champagne. "Champagne breaks," he told her. "Get used to them."

"That's kind of horseshit, isn't it, Frederick?" But he believed in champagne breaks, as he believed in moonlight swims, and he pushed her to move in that direction, with no interest in inviting the others to join them.

Richard methodically kept track of where the ball fell, marking in one of his small leather notebooks that Adrienne inevitably gave him for Hanukkah: low number, red, even. Adrie wandered over and stood behind her husband's chair. "I'd rub your head for luck, darling," she said, "but I'm up about twenty-six hundred and I don't want to jinx anything unless my rubbing could grow hair."

"Let's be discreet about rubbing," Dickie said. "I'm almost finished here." The roulette wheel was spinning and the croupier was waving away final bets as the ball jumped to its own conclusion. That's when Laura put a thousand on number six. The croupier shook his head and motioned to her, "No bets, too late." Laura shoved the chips back onto the number as the ball twitched its last twitch into the six slot. "Pays thirty-five times," she yelled. Muscle, always dressed in black tie, descends swiftly in casinos. "Tell him who we are," Laura yelled at Red as the action in the room focused on her. Only the seasoned gamblers motioned for the dealers to continue, for the croupiers to pass the dice. They knew that emotion was death for the true player.

"Let's calm down, sweetheart," Red said, trying to put Laura behind him. "We'll get this straightened out." Dickie and Temple got up from their seats and stood with Singer. The croupier kept shrugging and spouting Spanish a mile a minute to the muscle and the pit bosses, who were being very smooth with Red. "Señor," the boss explained, "Luis is a top croupier. The rules of the casino are stricter than the rules of life. And the government of Puerto Rico watches us like hawks. It is clear it was no bet. What can I do?"

"You can tell him to give me the thirty-five grand and we'll call it no hard feelings," Laura yelled at the top of her voice. "This wouldn't happen at Tahoe or Vegas."

"Why don't we take a break?" Dickie said. "Have a nightcap."

They ushered each other out of the casino, moving as a group like a piece being removed from a puzzle. Freddie took Laura's arm as they went to the bar. She had never really known a WASP in her life, and she took Freddie as a sedative, as if he had been sent by the U.N. as a mediator from a neutral country. "It's the principle of the thing," she told him. "I don't give a shit about the thirty-five grand. Sorry. I don't usually swear." She was a lady for Temple, and she calmed down. Singer needed to score points all the more. He had to nick the hotel for concessions, and when they sat in the bar and faced each other, guests and management, like negotiators at the Paris peace talks, Red got free golf and a dozen balls for everyone as well. Laura apologized for raising her voice, although she made mental notes to dump on Pepino Beach Hotel to money guys she knew in Beverly Hills who lived to stick it in people's ears, guys who could launch hostile buyouts, guys who always gave her daddy seven-figure lines of credit. In her father's study was a needlepoint sampler on the wall given to her grandfather by Laurence Olivier. It said, "Revenge is a dish best eaten cold."

"I wish I could have met the old man," Adrienne Rose said to Dickie when they were back in their room.

"She'll go through Red like shit through a goose," he said.

"I don't know," Adrie answered. "There's an aspect of him that is endearing. I can see where that would make him attractive, like a wicked child."

"We used to say he was a wild hose out of control."

"I'm sure you all would have been flattered by that description."

"The boys are the boys. You should know that better than anyone."

"All I can tell you is that meeting someone with a daddy thing like Laura makes me feel that she's my evil twin and that I'll never get out of therapy."

"I told you this a million times. If you grew up in New York, therapy is like your hump. You're all Quasimodos in New York. Besides, it's a grandfather thing with her."

"You still love me?" she asked, opening the book she was reading.

"I loved you from the minute you played 'Porgy' in P. J. Clarke's and I was drunk and went in to cut the ice block in the urinal down with pee. Nina Simone sang the song."

"That's what I still love about you, Richard. How you want to even turn taking a leak into something romantic."

"Fuck me," Laura commanded in the room dark as the alleys of San Juan. Red tried hard. He put as many as three fingers into her. He put his tongue inside her and tickled her clitoris. She manipulated him, teasing his scrotum with her fingertips. She put him into her mouth and licked the underside of his penis. He would stay hard for several seconds and then lose it. "I can't fuck you," he finally said, "when I'm ordered to do it. You think I'm a goddamned money-making screwing machine."

"You used to be."

"I used to be the fastest human in Brookwood; I used to hot-wire cars in high school; I used to be lots of things."

"Are you telling me you'll never be a money-making screwing machine again?"

"The only thing I could do if I was ordered to would be to go into combat."

"Okay," Laura said. "Then fuck me."

He tried his damndest for another twenty minutes, wondering all the time how he was going to pull a happy ending out of the script he had written himself into.

"Jesus Christ," Laura finally said. "If you can't fuck on vacation, when can you fuck?"

"That's what's wrong with you, baby," Red told the darkness. "You think this is a vacation. You think this is a movie."

They stood on the first tee, a benign straightaway three-hundred-yard par four with no problems except deep traps to the left and right of the green: a convention-hotel first hole, make everyone feel good. They waited for the foursome ahead to hit their second shots. "You guys hear about the man," Red asked, "who had trouble fucking his wife? So he went to his doctor, who told him that a pill was just developed that gave you an instant hard-on, which would last for exactly an hour. The guy was desperate, and he begged for the pill, which the doctor gave him, and the guy gobbled it right there. Bang, his pecker went into orbit, at least eight inches, just like a steel bar. He raced home, his pecker rubbing against his belly button and rushed into his house expecting to find his wife. But only the maid was home, who tells him that his wife is out shopping, but expected soon. He's got forty-five minutes of his incredible hard-on left, and he paces for another fifteen, twenty minutes. Then, with only fifteen minutes of erection remaining, he calls the doctor in a panic. 'Doctor,' he says, 'I've got fifteen minutes of hard-on and my wife's shopping; only me and the maid are home.'

" 'Well,' the doctor says, 'fuck the maid.'

"The husband was indignant. 'For fucking the maid,' the man says, 'I don't need a pill.' "

The others cracked up. "Whose idea was it," Red said when they stopped laughing, "to take the women along?"

"It was probably your idea," Hennessey said, "to show us what a Hollywood hot shit you are."

"Well," Singer said, "whosever idea it was, it was a lousy one. It's like four bad blind dates."

"Hey, Stanley," Duke said, "you've always treated your wives like dates anyway."

"And you never had a date in your life," Red snapped. "You married the first girl you saw in the sandbox. You didn't give her a fucking engagement ring. You gave her a pail and shovel."

Duke laughed. "Touchy Stanley. We never see you touchy."

"Remember Christmas vacations, in the seventh or eighth grades," Dickie said, looking down the fairway. "It felt like this, free and easy, nothing to do but play hockey, fool around, safe and warm, watch Jackie Gleason on the TV."

"You feel that way," Temple said, "because we're rich, we've made it."

"But would you trade it all for a real golf swing?" Duke asked.

"I can *buy* a golf swing," Temple said, "on the fees I get from Irish developers."

"Tee it up, rich boys," Red said. "By the way, if I *owe* a million, does that make me a millionaire?"

"I don't care how rich you think you are, Singer," Duke said, "if I tip you upside down, I know I won't find a dollar seventy-five cash."

They all sported new clubs except Hennessey, who had an assemblage of what he called his lucky sticks, leftovers from years past, his favorite MacGregor Tourney sand wedge, a Bulls Eye putter a caddie had given him, a ginty whose shaft he had replaced. His only concession to the high-tech game was a Taylor Made metal driver Rita gave him for Christmas. He bitched about the sound it made when he hit the ball. "Sounds like those metal bats the kids use in Little League, clunk. Balls were meant to be hit with wood." But he punished his drives with the metal club. And he was superstitious about not returning Christmas presents.

They teed off into bright sunshine and drove their carts recklessly, like teenagers mad to burn rubber. They had decided to play Jews and Gentiles, Singer and Rose versus Temple and Hennessey.

"A gay designer gave me a key chain a few years ago," Dickie said. "It's a flat brass rectangle with the word 'cut' stenciled on one side. He told me that he'd go to gay bars and throw the key chain on a table. It was an advertisement for his preference: circumcised cocks, *cut* versus *uncut*. Today it's the cuts versus the uncuts."

"Nothing like the authority of a million shares of something to make you a fucking expert about everything," Red said. "Just like a doctor."

"That's no way to speak to your partner. I *am* an expert."

"Okay, maven," Red said. "Win me some dough."

They played loose for a $5 Nassau, the best they had ever played together. Temple and Rose made several pars and never went over double bogey. Singer and Hennessey moved the ball well, chipped and putted as if they played at home four times a week. At the end of nine there was no blood except for the unit ($5) Red made for birdieing the eighth and the unit Duke earned for a sandy (getting up and down in two from a trap) on the third. They stopped for drinks and hotdogs at the turn. "My kid, Valentino, can already outdrive me," Red bragged. "He's got a swing, I swear to God looks just like Johnny Miller."

"I thought we had a rule," Duke said. "We don't talk about our kids on the golf course."

"We never had a rule like that," Red answered.

"What do you want to aggravate yourself for?" Dickie said. "We're playing great."

"My kid doesn't aggravate me," said Red. "He's a star."

"You're full of shit," Duke told him. "All kids aggravate their parents."

"Maybe yours do," Red insisted. "You want to change the subject? We get bratwurst at our club, bratwurst and three kinds of mustard. These taste like Fenway Franks. And when we get finished with the bratwurst, they cook extra and put it into lentil soup. That's what I call a club. Classy."

"This tastes good to me," Temple said. "I haven't had one of these in years."

"You wouldn't know a good hotdog if it bit you in the ass." Red laughed. "All you know is roast beef and Yorkshire pudding."

"And prime pussy," Duke added. "Don't forget about that."

"What's it like," Dickie asked, "to make love to younger women?"

"I have to tell you," Freddie answered, "with Gabriella I get a headache every time after we do it. She carries aspirin with her. For me. I guess it's just more intense doing it with youngbloods."

Their golf went downhill from there. Only Richard Rose hit the ball straight on ten and eleven, and he told Red his secret as they drove up the twelfth fairway.

"I imagine I'm a robot and the swing is automatic. Really.

Adrie hired a TM teacher a few years ago. I called him the two-million-dollar monk. Haven't you noticed how calm I've been? I'm swinging within myself, not lunging or overhitting."

Red snorted. "Everyone who plays this sport is a sicko. If Hennessey hears that you're going to a Buddhist pro, he'll destroy your game."

"My guy's not a pro, for Christ's sake. He teaches transcendental meditation."

"Oh. A golf cult. Why not shave your head and play in those robes, put little bells on your fingers?"

"Let me tell you something," Dickie said, "I run a public company doing *half a billion* in volume. If we make a profit and the stock goes up, I can wear a dress and a red ball stuck at the end of my nose. And I wouldn't be doing that if anyone fucked me on price, even golf pros."

"I'm voting for you," Red said. "Don't panic."

On the tee at the next hole, Rose was taking practice swings, eyes half shut, visualizing the spot his ball would land, left center of the fairway. The others started to chant, "Hari Krishna, Krishna, Krishna . . . You're an asshole, Hari Krishna." When he teed off, Dickie hit the ball as if he were chopping wood, producing a shot that rolled along the ground for almost twenty yards. The others were gleeful. "That's what happens when you pretend you're not Jewish," Red told him. "You can't shut off your mind. You want to be a Gentile, you can have a two handicap. But you wouldn't trade twenty mil for it, you know what I'm saying?"

Hennessey and Temple agreed on almost everything as they rode back and forth to their shots. "Everybody I know," Temple was saying, "complains about one thing — taxes. There were hundreds of millions of dollars of tax-sheltered investments last year, and the field is going bananas: drilling rigs, barges, low-income housing, garden apartments, historic preservation, leasing deals, venture partnerships, you name it. You structure a deal, a hotel, I don't care, we give them one-for-one write-offs and tell them that in three or four years we sell the hotel. They get the write-offs and eventually a long-term capital gain. We turn ordinary income into long-term gains. You give us any deal, we'll sell it. The public wants product; we want product. You can make yourself thirty percent, your markup plus management fees. It's unbelievable."

"As it happens, I've been talking with my banks about another waterfront hotel."

"Who needs the banks? You can bring in ten thousand limited partners who all kick in five grand and think they're half-assed rich. Give them a write-off, promise the upside and they'll all think they're Trammell Crow, Eddie DeBartelo, big men."

"I never liked partners," Duke said, "but I'll think about it."

"Look at Rosie, flailing away." Temple pointed. "He's been waiting to kick our butts for all these years. I hate to give him fifteen thousand."

"I suppose we could have raised the golf stakes, taken it back out here."

"Right," Temple said, "and see Singer get hot, birdie three in a row or something and we're out thirty grand, not fifteen."

"Your first loss is your best loss." Duke laughed.

"At least we've all got the fifteen K. Who'd have believed it?"

"Bullshit, Temple," Duke said. "You had it when you were thirteen."

"My father told me, 'Never count anyone else's money. You'll always be wrong.' Hey," Temple yelled suddenly and, putting his foot down hard on the pedal, raced his cart over to where Richard Rose stood in the rough.

"You can't move your ball in the rough," he said, still yelling, as if he had caught someone stealing a hubcap off his car.

"I'm not moving the ball," Dickie said. "It was in a god-damned hole. You think I'm going to cheat you for a five-dollar Nassau?" Temple backed off, and the thought flashed over him that he was Adrienne Rose's investment banker. If one of his major clients wanted to use his foot mashie in the rough, well, he could swallow that. He also remembered the condom in the sand trap.

"You counting another stroke?" said Hennessey, who did not collect any fees from Rose. Singer walked over to them. "My partner doesn't improve his lie in the rough. It was casual water. You get a drop from casual water." The temperature was ninety-three. It hadn't rained in two weeks, and the grass was stiff and dry as dead cornstalks. "Look at this," Rose said. He stuck his seven iron into a patch next to where his ball lay. "It's a hole made by some animal. There's no penalty for moving from a mole hole. Is this the U.S. Open?" He was staring at Temple.

"Sorry," said Freddie. "I couldn't see that hole from where I was."

Duke laughed at both of them. "What goes around comes around," Duke said. "You take the best lie you possibly can. Tee it up in the grass if you want, you'll still hit the shittiest shot of the day." While they watched, Rose pushed his ball on top of a tuft of grass, sitting well up, almost as if it were on a tee. The pin was about a hundred and twenty yards away, and he took an eight iron, knowing that many of his irons he hit fat, not far enough. He dipped his knees on the downswing, trying to help the ball along and ended up scooping his shot. The ball went "poop," straight up in the air, traveling only about twenty yards. "Cheatsies-provesies," Duke said.

"Forget it, partner," from Red. "I'm on in two." They drove to the green.

"I would never move the ball, Red," Dickie said. "How long have we known each other?"

"Forget it. I can't believe how pissed he seemed. I've almost never seen Freddie with a temper. Probably didn't sleep last night."

Rose said nothing. But his heart raced, and he was short of breath. The adrenaline surged.

"Not too smart, chief," Duke said to Freddie. "You'll kill the golden goose for a five-dollar Nassau."

"We were two down. I didn't need anyone nicking a stroke on us."

"Well," Duke answered, "as the punchline to the old joke says, 'Fuck it, it's only a hobby.' "

They finished the match two down to Singer and Rose and lost a total of only one unit, $5 apiece, not counting side bets. They shook hands on the fringe of the eighteenth hole and went to have a drink on the clubhouse terrace, which overlooked the finishing hole, a picture par three whose green was set in the middle of an artificial lake, a hundred and ninety yards from the back tees. It was the number one stroke hole, rated the most difficult of the course.

Richard Rose had signed for the piña coladas. It was the least he could do. They sipped their drinks, frosty cold. After the hours in the sun, despite the canopies over their carts, the first drinks brought a rush, an instant high. They all felt it, were warmed by it. Duke held up his glass. "There's no debate this year, Rosie. We can't lie or fake it. I think I'm going to be worth a hundred million, *more* in a couple of years. I'll control five million square feet of office space, four hotels, malls, office parks built to suit major tenants. By the time we play again, it'll be no contest. But this year I'll give it to you, a million shares times twenty or so, plus you draw what, five hundred grand, plus the perks, good luck to you and the Red Sox. For a bald-headed devious prick, you deserve the pool."

"Wait a minute," Temple said. "The contest is much more than money. It's who's doing the best *at the time,* who's most successful, not just in money terms."

"Spoken like a man who's never won," Red said.

"Let me tell you something. William Simon, right? He was secretary of the treasury under Gerry Ford. He parlayed something like a *hundred thousand* of cash into over *twenty million.* He bought Gibson Greetings, borrowed almost completely to do it, and for collateral pledged the assets of Gibson, a company he didn't even own yet. Then, after he's in control, he takes Gibson public, pays back the banks and he's got equity of more than twenty million, no personal debt."

"So that's what you're going to do next, Freddie?" Richard asked.

"America is a wonderful country," Duke added, "and Simon isn't even Jewish."

"He for sure isn't a harp," Red piped in.

"I'm not so sure of that," Freddie said. "But isn't that the greatest story you ever heard? I see the future, and it's going to be me."

"Look," Dickie said suddenly, pointing to the eighteenth green. Someone had hit a shot that just barely cleared the water, bounced on the light fringe and rolled to a stop a foot from the cup. "An FM," Hennessey said.

"A fucking miracle," Singer agreed.

"Somebody must have had Chi Chi over for a guest," Temple

said, squinting into the sun, trying to see who was walking the narrow bridge built to cross the water from tee to green. The sun backlit a golfer dressed all in white, polo shirt, duck pants, leather Foot-Joys. His arms were held high over his head with an iron in his right hand like a sword held up in victory. The light shimmered around him as if he were the only golfer in the world, the rest of his foursome lingering in back of him, their pastel clothes a cheap imitation of the man striding ahead toward his birdie tap-in. It seemed such a glorious act to the men drinking their piña coladas, to have that look, to have hit the perfect shot.

"Jesus," Temple said, "it's Sleek Sullivan."

"Could have fooled me," Hennessey added. "I thought it might have been the Savior himself." He paused. "Although Jesus probably would have holed out the tee shot." Hennessey put two fingers in his mouth and whistled. He made motions for the senator to join them. They gave Sullivan the chair facing the island green.

"Best shot I ever hit in my life," Sleek said, ordering a rum and tonic. "Always drink whatever the local drink is, people notice it, good for everybody. God shed His grace on thee," he toasted them, a prayer and a line from "America the Beautiful." He had proposed in the Senate to make that song the national anthem. Sleek kept rolling, trying to wrap everyone in his arms. "Francis," he said to Hennessey, "what an ideal setting for a member of my finance committee to relax in while dreaming up new lists of contributors." Sullivan's smile seemed to say that he knew things you didn't know. Not that he smelled something bad but that he understood what your particular price was. He knew about the contest. "Is this it?" he asked. "As the old joke says, 'Tonight's the night?' You paying each other obscene amounts of money when it could be going for charity. Or better yet, to improve the quality of public life."

"Are you following us around, Senator, or are we following you around?" Red asked.

Sullivan took a long gulp of his rum and tonic. "Well, I'll tell you, Mr. Singer. I'm down here at the kind invitation of the governor of this island because he thinks I may be the key to making Puerto Rico the fifty-first state. In return, I get to see some of his golf courses, some of his people, get my game in shape for the season, try to hit the ball as good as my colleague, Senator Quayle."

"How are you seeing things these days?" Freddie asked.

"I'm seeing a lot of people smacking their lips because they think they're going to be making a shit-pile of money in the next few years. You know the motto on the New Hampshire license plates, 'Live Free or Die'? Well, the President has a neon sign in his brain that flashes that word 'free' every two seconds, and it means leave everyone alone to fuck their neighbor, no controls, no limits on anything."

"Americans never liked limits," Freddie interrupted.

"You're on Wall Street," Sullivan said. "No one knows anything on Wall Street except how to mark up the fees. Come eighty-eight and the American people will be choking on the so-called freedom of Ronald Reagan. When they finish throwing up what that senile fool is serving, we are going to be there with Alka-Seltzer, Pepto-Bismol, hair of the dog, whatever it takes."

"*We* meaning *you* in '88?" Freddie pressed.

"What do you think you've been contributing to all these years, a fund to put Sullivan on the Armed Services Committee?"

"What about someone like Bill Bradley?" Dickie asked.

"Bradley's heard too many dribbles. He's still a Rhodes scholar, not a politician. The people need politicians. It's funny," Sleek said. "My brother was unique. He was a tail hound, something I always worshipped about him. But he was smart. He told me when I was a squirt, that there was a line I should always remember, a line that explained all human behavior. The line is 'Men are fools, and women are crazy.' My father had money, which gave him a pulpit, and it must have been *his* line, but I never heard Dad say it. My brother John Paul drummed it into my head. Said if I used it right, I could have what I wanted. If J.P. hadn't been killed, I'd be carrying his jock. I've been to confession many times over the thought that I was lucky that John Paul Sullivan was killed in that accident. It'll probably make me President of the United States. As a matter of fact, J.P.

was killed out your way. Brookwood. I think I should have a plaque put down to commemorate the site. A historic place, right? Plant a tree? How about it? 'Great brother dies, inspiring greatness in others.' " He lifted his glass. "God shed His grace on thee," he said again. The others looked at each other, lifted their own glasses and drank.

"Nothing like stickin' up for your family," Duke said.

"If your mother and father had a fight," Red quipped, "who would you stick up for?"

"Old joke," Dickie said.

"I'd stick up for my father," Red answered his own quip. "He stuck it up for me."

The others tossed ice cubes at Red.

"Make a note," Sullivan yelled over at his playing partners, who watched him carefully from a nearby table. "Memorial for J.P." Then, to the foursome: "What do you say we go another nine? Can't quit on a birdie."

"What about your guys?" Hennessey asked, nodding at them.

"They're happy to take a rest, believe me. And I'm sick of looking for their balls in the rough, palm fronds dropping all over the place. Don't want to get hit in the head."

"A fivesome's too slow," Temple said.

"It's only fair," Red suggested. "Rosie won the bet this year. We get to play with the senator. Rosie can play with the girls on the beach, play backgammon with Adrienne Rose."

"Good idea, Stanley," Hennessey said. "Rosie doesn't play, it makes sure the senator doesn't get hit with a palm frond."

"You know, Senator," Dickie said, "even back in high school, you know what they'd do to me? I'd be in the shower after gym, my eyes all full of soap. Suddenly I'd feel something warm on my leg when the shower water was pointed all on my head. I'd whip around, and there would be Hennessey and Singer peeing on my leg. I don't mind not playing with you. I've got to Federal Express these checks to my bank." He stood up, and Sullivan stood with him, sticking out his hand. Sleek's three partners stood up at their own table.

"One of life's great satisfactions," Sullivan said, "is seeing old friends prospering, doing so well. America is a great country."

"Ahhh, but is it good for the Jews?" Red asked, the old litany of the ghetto. Sleek seemed surprised by the words.

"Forget it, Senator," Hennessey reassured him. "Red's father always used to say that, and Red's been saying it all his life. I didn't understand it then. And I still don't understand it."

Richard Rose shook hands and headed back to the hotel. He turned once to watch the others moving away toward the first tee. Sullivan, in his white costume, still seemed to catch the light. He walked in front of Dickie's three friends, sure that they were following him, sure that money always drew a crowd.

Richard found Adrie lying on their small beach. She was covered with an oily sun lotion and wore a yellow bikini that she had bought in St. Barts.

"Too much sun, they're saying now, is no good for you," Dickie said down at her. She was lying on her back with tiny plastic cups stuck over her eyes. Without moving she said, "It's a bunch of crap. It's all in the genes, whether you take the sun well or not. My father died of a heart attack, but he was brown as a goddamned berry. Never even peeled." Dickie considered that and said, "I won the fifteen thousand."

"Great. Now you owe me seventy-five hundred. What charity can we give it to? How about a stained-glass window at the temple, with our parents' names on it?"

"Can we weave King Solomon and the Maccabees into it, too?"

Adrie chuckled.

"Sleek Sullivan's here. We had a drink with him, and he went out with the guys to hit a few."

"He'd take a bite out of your heart if you gave him half a chance."

"He's running for President in eighty-eight." Dickie sat down in the sand next to his wife.

She rolled over onto her stomach. "I hope you talked to him about import quotas."

"He birdied the last hole. It wasn't exactly the right time to bring up business."

"Richard," she said into the sand, "always ask for the fucking order." She reached around and untied the top of her bikini.

Dickie took off his shoes. He got up and walked to the water's edge, looking for flat stones to throw into the surf and thinking that Senator Sullivan was glad his brother had been killed: "He wants to plant him a goddamn tree."

To clear the thought, Dickie totaled up his net worth in his mind, skipped a stone into the water, felt the sun full on his balding brow and knew he would have another chance to ask for the order.

○

CHAPTER TWENTY-ONE

Home Hole, 1988:
Brookwood

"So, the Crash happened. What do you think?" Singer asked. "Is the world coming to an end?"

"Women have to buy clothes; people want to go to the movies," Dickie answered.

"But women can go to discounters, and everybody can rent a movie for ninety-nine cents. I wouldn't let down to anybody but you, Rosie, but I have to tell you that hitting fifty sucks; I don't care how many people come to a fucking surprise party." They were alone in the back of a stretch limousine that had just left the side entrance of the Ritz-Carlton Hotel in Boston. They wore black tie, Richard Rose with black formal pumps, Red Singer with crimson hightop sneakers. They had flown in that day for Freddie Temple's fiftieth birthday dinner, to be held at The Golf Club in Brookwood. "Plus my back hurts," Red added. "I've had arthroscopy on my knee, rotator cuff problems and I can't pee into the pot from the doorway of the john like I used to."

"Someone told me," Dickie said, "that after you're forty years old, if you wake up without an ache or a pain, you're dead."

Red laughed. "That's good. Right also. But I'm glad we're going out tonight while it's still light. I want to see the old places, everywhere people disapproved of me."

They had come to Boston alone, without their wives, and they were to play golf the next day. Both women, Adrie and Laura, tolerated the match, but preferred not to waste their time in a city that one claimed was the "asshole of fashion" and the other claimed was to L.A. what "Arabs were to Jews."

"You want to share a suite?" Dickie had asked when they made plans weeks before.

"Separate rooms," Red insisted. "You always have to believe you're going to get lucky. It's why I've kept a blanket and a six-pack in the trunk of my car since I've been sixteen."

They drove with rush-hour traffic, the sun still bright at five-thirty on a Friday, people tapping their dashboards in time to music, ready for a spring weekend. "It's interesting about the passing of time," Dickie said. "You say fifty sucks."

"It's the back nine, baby."

"Somewhat, I agree with you. But I had my twenty-fifth reunion at Harvard, and it was the first time in everybody's lives that anyone seemed to admit failure or tough times. At forty-six, it was suddenly okay to be honest. Lots of people resist reunions because they think it's when doctors and lawyers pat themselves on the backs, but by the twenty-fifth we've all taken whacks, we've all had tragedies."

"Except you, Rosie. You dance between the raindrops. You're the only guy in the East I know who's in the Forbes Four Hundred."

"Yeah. But barely. And that dubious honor doesn't stop heart attacks or make cancer go away."

"Give me a fucking break."

Dickie was used to making pronouncements. His wealth meant that he held forth. He was honored by charities naming him Man of the Year. The media sought his opinions. He always had an answer, a quotable quote. When the Crash of October '87 took Adrienne Rose's stock from forty-two to twenty-eight in a morning, he immediately announced to Dow Jones a million-share buy-back of their own company's shares. He saw the Crash as the aberration of a moment, a blip in the long progress upward in the Dow Jones and in consumer spending. Richard Rose also believed the media, which had been unstintingly full of praise for the couple's management of the business. The revolution that put millions of women in the workplace would never stop. And those women trusted Adrienne Rose. He would have a hundred-dollar stock. He would be up there with Sam Walton, Warren Buffett, John Kluge — a billionaire. This would be the last golf contest, called off forever because Dickie Rosenberg made the others suck hind tit forever.

Red had the driver go by way of Commonwealth Avenue, the

wide thoroughfare starting at the Public Garden in Back Bay, with its statues of men famous in Massachusetts history, from Leif Eriksson to Admiral Samuel Eliot Morison, perched on his rock, gazing out to sea. "Jesus," Red said, "I love to see the trees in bloom on Comm Ave. The magnolias come out the end of April, right after the marathon. When the trees come out, I think about one thing."

"Baseball."

"Right. When it's finally okay to throw, when it's warm enough so you don't toss your arm out."

"Let's go by the Hathaway playground before we pick Duke up."

"Let's pick him up first; he'd appreciate it."

"He probably goes there all the time," Dickie said. "Why do you think he never left Boston? He's probably still hitting fungoes there with Billy Shea."

"You wouldn't dare say that to his face."

"Well, don't you tell him I said it."

They drove along, by Fenway Park, by the package store that sold beer to underagers with fake ID's, by Brookwood High, by B.C. night school, what they called the reservoir where everyone took dates parking. They eventually drove along the road that paralleled the Brookwood Municipal golf course, the road to Duke Hennessey's house.

"Sullivan's going to be President because of *us,*" Red said. "You have no idea how often I think about this road."

Dickie shook his head, waved his hand, willing the idea away. "Did you ever argue in college late at night," Dickie asked, "about whether Judaism was a race or a religion?"

"I never thought about anything in college except getting out of college or chasing something. Oh, I thought about having so much money that nothing people always beat on me about would matter, like grades and being a good boy, all the asshole things."

"So what do you tell your son?"

"Naturally I tell him that all the asshole things matter and that if he wants to see how not to run a life, follow the example of his old man. All that shit. I also tell him that movies are everything and TV is nothing."

The driver parked in Duke's circular driveway, and they got out to walk around. Duke joined them on the terrace overlooking the golf course. The three men had already celebrated their own fiftieth birthdays. Freddie Temple was almost a year younger, entering kindergarten early because of his size and his father's desire to get his son's life underway. There were still players pulling handcarts on the fairways below. "Very few caddies anymore," Duke said. "My kid never did it. Beneath him. None of these kids went to work, and of course it's our fault. Or the mother's fault. Our generation has the most spoiled children in history. Sometimes I walk down in the woods, pick up lost balls."

"Don't worry," Red answered. "Drive through the UCLA campus. All you see is Oriental faces. They're going to bust their asses and own America."

"The new Jews," Dickie agreed.

"If there *were* caddies," Duke asked, "what's your guess they make today?"

"Caddies at Pebble Beach, I can tell you, make about thirty dollars a bag per round."

"Thirty fucking dollars," Duke sighed. "What'd we get? Two, two-fifty a loop? With a buck tip if we were lucky."

"I could always make more," Red reminded them, "putting for dimes."

"Once a hustler, Red . . ." Duke said. He had gone completely white now, with a mane that reminded people of Tip O'Neill. No diet he tried worked for long because every time he added a million square feet of commercial space to his growing empire, he added fifteen pounds for the worries. He now controlled over seven million square feet of space and weighed almost two hundred and eighty. His favorite afternoon snack was either a Mounds bar or an Almond Joy ("Sometimes you feel like a nut, sometimes you don't"). He was taking pills to control his blood pressure. Every time he exercised, the occasional tennis or squash game, he could play for fifteen minutes and then was forced to lie down, puffing and wheezing. Everyone from Rita, to Duke's doctor, to the men he knew on high steel thought he was going to go up in a puff of smoke.

"Jesus, I'd like to see you and Marvin Davis in the same ring," Red said. "You got to watch yourself, Francis."

"You know it's a bunch of crap. Jim Fixx, the runner? No one could have been in better shape, dropped dead of a heart attack. He was thin as a rail."

"Every fat man in America uses him as an excuse," Red said.

Dickie was watching the golfers. "We could go anywhere tomorrow," he said. "You really feel like standing in line to play Brookwood like all the weekend warriors?"

"Look," Red said. "We all got a million things we got to do, places we got to be. I know. You used to be conceited, but now you're a great guy."

"Are you paranoid, Stanley? I'm only complaining that it'll take us seven hours to play tomorrow if we play the public course."

"You don't want to go back to the scene of the crime," Duke said.

"What do you want me to do, punch you in the mouth? Kick you in the crotch? You want to play King of the Mountain again, roll around on the ground? How long does it take before we let each other up?"

"You know the answer to that, bubbala," Red laughed at him.

"Never," Hennessey said. "Let's take a ride." He put his arm around Dickie, hugging him.

"Cheer up, Rosie," Red echoed. "We love you. We just don't want you shitting us. Or shitting yourself either."

Rita came outside, kissed the new arrivals and packed them into the back of the limo. She lived as her mother lived, knowing she knew better than anyone in the family. She ran the big house on the hill no differently than her mother ran the triple-decker where Rita had grown up. Everyone knew where he or she stood, from Midnight Mass on Christmas Eve to Sunday night pizza in front of "60 Minutes." Duke knew that there was a refuge at home where everything made sense, where he could wrap it around himself like a homemade afghan.

"I can't believe we've known Rita since freshman year in high school," Dickie said. "She looks fabulous." Which is what everybody says to everybody even if they're dying of cancer.

Duke accepted it, knowing he had a better deal than any of them. "Let's drive down to the school," he said. The driver took them to the rear of the Hathaway School, to the tennis courts. A few kids hit balls to each other, and there was a half-court basketball game in progress, two on two, using one aluminum backboard still connected to the steel pole that had been there when they all went to the school.

"Come on," said Singer, getting out of the car. "See if we can shoot a few hoops, one game of horse or something."

"That's why you wore sneakers," Duke said. They walked down the stairs to the courts and, as they arrived, all games ceased.

"We didn't do anything, Mister," one of the kids bouncing a basketball called to them.

"They think we're the mob," Dickie said, "moving in on the territory, the mustaches."

"Hey," Red called, "no problem. We used to go here. Just like to take a few shots. For old times' sake. Just ten minutes with the ball." The kid shrugged and whipped the ball at Red's chest, wise guy, quick pass. Red caught it easily and went behind his back to Hennessey. "Here you go, Cooz," he said, as Duke fired up a jump shot at the basket, getting at least two inches off the ground. The shot swished, never touching the backboard or rim. The kids watched with amusement as the three men tried a variety of shots and roared when Duke passed to Dickie, who wasn't looking, and the ball bounced off his head, almost knocking him down. "That's it for me," he announced. "I don't want to go to this thing all filthy, never mind with a concussion." He walked back to the limo, his pumps scuffed, rubbing his head. Red and Duke finished off the game, Duke winning with a hook shot that Red could not duplicate, and they gave the ball back to its owner. "You learn anything from watching the old pros?" Singer asked.

"Yeah," one kid ventured. "I learned that I should probably dial 911 when I see the old pros coming."

They laughed. "You're a smart kid," Red said. "They always had smart kids in Brookwood."

"Like your shoes, man," another one said.

"He's just one of the boys," Duke told them, and they walked away to the car, each thinking how old the old farts used to seem to them, any old fart over the age of sixteen.

"Honest to God," Hennessey admitted as they drove, "I look forward to the weekend where I'm supposed to forget about seven million square feet for a few hours. But you never forget."

"Tough problem," Red said sarcastically, "especially when it's pumping out about thirty-five dollars for much of those feet. My heart bleeds. And I know Boston's got the hottest real estate market in the country. You don't know from tough business until you know the movie business."

Red blinked his eyes, a nervous habit he was fighting to control. Why the fuck did he blink his eyes, he thought, when he had it made? Temple had raised $200 million for Red's Cardinal Productions for the financing of twenty-five movies. They promised a rate of return to investors of twelve to fourteen percent over the life of the limited partnership. Temple took a $5 million fee for structuring the deal, plus continuing management fees, and Red had the cheapest financing possible and years of production guaranteed. He remembered being in the audience at a rented Westwood movie house, seated with Temple and several of Freddie's flunkies in double-breasted suits from Paul Stuart and Dunhill. It was a Saturday morning. Red had rounded up the stars of Cardinal's latest hit about flappers in the 1920s. They were onstage doing the Charleston before coming down and mixing with the audience, all potential investors in Tinsel Town I, the name of Freddie's partnership. The movie was to be shown after the Charleston and after a presentation by two stockbrokers who had hired the theater and were soliciting orders for the deal. One of the stockbrokers stood onstage in front of the screen.

"Look," he said to the audience, "I'm not telling you you're going to double or triple your money here. What you *will* get is a minimum of eight percent, in a quarterly check, comparable to a money fund or high-grade bond. The upside with this fabulous concept is, after Cardinal recoups its marketing and production costs, *you share in the profits.* You actually can *all* be producers. We'll go on the sets; we'll meet the stars; we'll have receptions in their homes. Incredibly, you can even put your two-thousand-dollar IRA contribution into the partnerships and earn the interest tax-free."

"Watch this," Red whispered to Temple. "I thought it up this morning."

The stockbroker held up and displayed a red T-shirt with the Cardinal logo. "Red Singer had these made for every one of you, along with Tinsel Town partnership pens and tote bags. All this and *the man* himself," the stockbroker excitedly added, and started to chant, "Red, Red, Red," in a low murmur that built to a cheer.

Soon the audience joined in, clapping and cheering as well. "Red, Red, Red." Singer stood on his chair then, facing the audience, waving them on as Freddie Temple kept calculating the fees in his head.

As they drove into the gates of The Golf Club, Dickie felt the old tug: if he lived in Boston, would he ever be a member here? He and Adrie had been on missions to Israel, had met prime ministers, had visited kibbutzes, had prayed in front of the Wailing Wall. He had been honored in the past by both the UJA and Israel Bonds as Man of the Year. How different his life would have been, years ago, if he had married Julia Hepburn. His fantasy woman still had long blond hair, upturned nose and pumped her elbows when she danced.

"This is like a set for a seedy British movie. The clubhouse needs a paint job" was Red's reaction. "The whole side is peeling. We'll probably have ham salad for dinner, stuffed eggs for appetizers. Well, maybe we'll go to Chinatown afterwards, they stay open late, have Scotch in teacups, boneless spareribs."

"It's funny," Duke said. "All the time we caddied and the wire fences separated Brookwood Muni from this joint and Temple from us. Now he's the guy controls the spigot for all of us, my syndications, your underwritings. Everybody dumps on the WASP, and he laughs all the way to the bank."

"And he's not even married," Red added.

"And he looks the way he looked twenty years ago," Dickie said.

"So why wouldn't any of us trade with him?" Duke asked.

"Probably because he's a dumb goy." Red laughed. "Who else would give a stag fiftieth birthday party?"

"I even had to have the bust-outs, Rita's family, at mine," Duke said. The limo moved around the gravel driveway and deposited them at the front door.

"Look at that." Red pointed to a sign over an adjoining door a dozen feet from the club's main entrance that was covered by a pink-and-white-striped awning. The wooden sign spelled out "Ladies' Entrance." It was faded with time and weather.

"Adrie would love that," Dickie said. "Apartheid lives." They fidgeted a little, watching the employees take down the flag from the flagpole that stood on the grass of the turnaround. They adjusted their ties, not wanting to be early, wondering who else would be there.

"It's showtime," Singer announced, and, on springy steps in his red hightop sneakers, he led them into The Golf Club. They were directed to the Hunt Room on the second floor, a room painted in the green of Jaguar cars and covered with prints depicting English fox hunts of the nineteenth century. Looking as if he were made for any role acted by Richard Chamberlain, Freddie Temple leaned against a marble fireplace mantel, martini straight up, in one hand. Next to him stood the only woman in the room, a younger female mirror image of Freddie, his daughter, Brett. She was dressed in a short black Christian Lacroix, and her hair, blond as Sweden, hung to her shoulders. The three men quickly crossed the room to them. "Happy birthday, Blondie," Duke said, squeezing Freddie's hand.

"Is the portrait growing old in the closet?" Dickie asked. They all had met Brett at one time or another. She worked at Peterson, Pyle as an investor banker under her father and had done so since she graduated from Harvard Business School. Her brother, Myles, lived in Boulder, Colorado. He had dropped out of Lake Forest College (Last Fucking Chance) and followed the Grateful Dead until he made his peace in Boulder, doing odd jobs and wondering what Jerry Garcia was *really* like. He thought of his father much more than his father thought of him. But he couldn't focus on Freddie as anything more than Mr. Right with highly polished shoes, who disapproved of everything. His sister sent him money on a regular basis. She greeted them with a cool hand but gave in to Red's embrace, knowing that no deals in L.A. were complete without kissing. Most of the suits she wore to work were from Adrienne Rose. She said she was glad to see her father's three old friends and they should not hesitate to ask her if they were missing anything they wanted.

Dickie said to her, "We were told this was a stag fiftieth. I suppose you're not going to condone anyone coming out of a cake."

"Au contraire, Mr. Rose," she said. "I'm Daddy's hostess. But anything goes as far as I'm concerned. He insisted I be here tonight, and I insisted that it not be a damper on anything. If you've been around the edges of New York in the last few years, if you've seen Henry Kravis and his ilk in action, you can handle girls coming out of cakes."

"I'm sure that's true" is all Dickie could think of to say, impressed. The three men nudged each other with their elbows. "If you ever need a job . . ." Duke said.

"Call us," Red added.

They left father and daughter to receive greetings from other friends moving in to wish them well. The three stayed together for a time, got their drinks at the bar, looked for familiar faces, then fanned out to take their chances. Ace Cohen, the chairman of Freddie's firm, was there, blowing smoke rings. There were several rivals of Freddie's from other "silk stocking" firms, old Harvard and St. Luke's School classmates, a few men who had served with him in the navy. Sleek Sullivan was there, an announced candidate for President. Sullivan worked the room as if it were *his* fiftieth.

"You're the spittin' image of Pat Riley from the Lakers, Senator," Hennessey told him.

"Singer actually introduced us in L.A.," Sleek answered. "I told him I was much better looking after he pointed out the resemblance." The senator limited himself to one Bushmills a night. Everyone seemed to want to be near him, and he gave the impression he was theirs. But he was no one's and remained pursued.

Dickie nursed a drink and stayed apart from the crowd. There were almost forty men in the room for cocktails, and a black man played quiet jazz on a grand piano, jazz that Temple remembered from years back in New York at the Embers and Birdland. An older man using a cane walked slowly up to Dickie. "Mr. Temple." Dickie knew him, but hadn't seen him in years, knew he must be in his late seventies. "Still standing as if he had a three iron stuck up his tail," Dickie thought. "Young Rosenberg," the senior Temple said, "see you in the papers all the time and you know what I think? I think your fathers had great character to have you all caddie when you were boys. You meet my granddaughter? It's a different world today. I'll live to see a colored President, no doubt. And he probably won't be any worse than Carter or Roosevelt. Country's too goddamn big to govern anyway."

"Well, the future President's probably in this room."

Mr. Temple shook his head. "Our junior senator? There's no body to the man. Ambition in a silk suit. I never liked Frederick playing with you boys years ago, but I thought it a good education for him before he went away to school, teach him to know who'd try to claw ahead of him years later. But you all have the same stuff in you. Must have been the bomb, as a lot of people said." Dickie realized that Freddie's father was drunk, still handsome, and drunk. Ace Cohen joined them, chomping his cigar. "Looking good, Richard," he said. "Mr. Temple," he added, "send your check in yet to the UJA?" Ace Cohen could always clear a room. But he raised more money for Jewish charities than almost anyone else in New York, and he was never shy about asking. "Never mind." He patted Freddie's father on the back and turned to Rose. "I heard you and Adrienne are going to open your own stores."

"You heard right."

"My only comment, and nobody asked me, but you're an important client. Every time I stray from what I do best, I get my ass handed to me."

"You're a trader, Ace, not a manufacturer. I don't even see that you're in a real business. Freddie thinks it's a good idea."

"Freddie thinks trees grow to the sky."

"Well, after the Crash of eighty-seven, everything dropped dead for a week; time stood still, no one bought a skirt or a blouse in America. Then," Dickie went on, "wonder of wonders, life continued. Our stock recovered ten points in two weeks, customers came back. Just a pee hole in the snows of history."

"Nothing like that," Mr. Temple said, "ever happens without more to come later on. The big message in that crash was to get your debt down. I've told that to Frederick. Get out of debt. He thinks I'm an old fart, but he always comes to Boston when shad roe is in season. Nice to see you so prosperous, Rosenberg. It's because you were a caddie." He moved on to the next group, leaning on the cane that had been his father's.

"Probably got the gout," Ace Cohen said. "All those guys suffer from gout. Too many sauces and the sauce."

"These mergers and LBO's going to go on forever?" Dickie asked. "One thing Mr. Temple said I agree with. I don't like all this debt. All these youngbloods in fancy wrappings telling everybody, a billion here, a billion there, do it, no problem. Cash flow will bail everyone out. These bankers never worked in handbags or ran a maternity business. What happens if the economy turns down and the borrowers miss payments? Freddie always talks the deal, never, is it good for the business."

"And you're going into your own retail outlets?"

"But we can generate all we need internally."

Ace chomped his cigar. "My grandfather was right," Ace said. "In America the streets *are* paved with gold. You make your deals. All I care about is that my positions show a profit at the end of the day. Easy to keep score; you don't have to go to meetings, and you can send out for deli at lunch."

Freddie was the ringmaster all through cocktails, and Brett never left his side. They touched base with every group, brought people together, introduced them, flattered, smiled and moved on. "My wife will be pissed when she finds out there was another woman here," a man said, a man Freddie had taken private through a $200 million LBO.

"Don't be ridiculous," Temple reacted. "Brett is one of the boys. Aren't you, darling?"

" 'Bottom Line Brett' they call me," she said. The client beamed and felt lucky to be invited. He wouldn't tell his wife anyway. Men moved clockwise, counterclockwise; everyone there worked the room, looking for signs that said the next guy was richer than they.

Freddie tapped on an empty glass with a spoon, getting everyone's attention. "Greetings to all," he said. "I can't tell you what it means to have friends assembled to meet other friends. This isn't a speech. But as my old-time buddy Red Singer would say, 'The sooner we get dinner, the sooner I can open my presents.' " There was a pile of packages on a table at one end of the room. They were all wrapped in serious paper, metallic colors, gold and silver. Dinner was served in the club's original banquet hall, the walls crowded with photographs of the place in its early years, scenes of men golfing, playing tennis, bowling on the green, racing coach and fours. A moose head hung over the mantel of the stone fireplace, one eye gouged out in a prank after the 1927 Harvard-Yale game. Dickie, Red and Hennessey sat together at a table for six with Sleek Sullivan, Ace Cohen and Freddie's lawyer, an aristocratic New Yorker named Pantaleoni who looked so secure, as if he could get anyone to agree to anything. Matchbooks were scattered across each table, green with yellow lettering stating: "It's So Nifty, Fred Is Fifty." It was the last of the smoking crowd, a third of the men with cigars, several with cigarettes, these being the cheaters, puffing greedily, never allowed to do it at home or in restaurants. It was a self-satisfied group in black tie, men who felt that anything under a hundred million net worth was an odd lot, even though most of them had considerably less than that figure. They had high hopes.

Freddie sat with his father and daughter at a small head table in front of the fireplace, a spot that looked out over the other tables. "I've been to a thousand dinners in this room," Freddie's father said. "Bachelor parties, bridal dinners, dinners before cotillions. Never seen a stranger crowd. All my friends, for instance, would wear their fathers' waistcoats. I see several cummerbunds and matching ties, for God's sake. Ties that clip on." Freddie and Brett just laughed and signaled for the drinks waiter.

"The best dinners," Ace Cohen said to his table mates, "are dinners where everybody leaves with something in his pocket for tomorrow, an idea, a pledge."

"Good," Sleek Sullivan said. "I'll give you an idea; you give me a pledge. You know Cuomo is not going to run this year. I can win New York; I skipped down Fifth Avenue on St. Paddy's Day. They thought I was from Ozone Park in Brooklyn. I felt love."

"There's no love in New York, Senator," Red answered. "What you felt was the long johns you got to wear in the parade in March. Never confuse applause in New York City with love."

"Red's just pissed that there are people in the world cruder than him," Hennessey stated.

"There's lots of love in New York," Dickie said. "New York is one of the most romantic places in the world. But it's always young love that eventually goes back to Minneapolis or Memphis or Boston. It doesn't stay long in New York, unless it's love of something other than your fellow creatures."

"You guys don't know what you're talking about," Ace said, "because you're not New Yorkers. You never see the city. Weddings at the Temple of Dendūr with Saul Steinberg and the Tisches ain't my New York. It ain't real New Yorkers' New York. Although I'll admit *my* New York is gobblin' Chinese at two in the morning in the back of the limo taking you home from a meeting on Broad Street after you've pitched a fucking German bank and won the account."

"Well," said Sleek, "we can still talk religion and politics. The night is young." The piano played on as the mussel soup was served. The player did Freddie's favorites, ranging from Cole Porter through some Gilbert and Sullivan. Sleek finished his soup quickly, got up and table-hopped, introducing himself, although everyone knew who he was. He knew his job was to seduce the fat cats, the Brahmins from the Reagan camp, from the Bush crowd. His people were positioning him as the "New Warrior," someone who hadn't fought in World War II or Vietnam but would only fight new battles: crime, pollution, greed.

"Would you take a Cabinet position?" Dickie asked Hennessey. "You discovered him, after all."

"It's like baseball," Duke answered. "I'm in the sixth inning. I got ten million in tax-frees stuck in a box, and I got two million in treasuries keeping them company. They're all in Rita's name. But it don't make any difference because she's signed onto paper and I'm signed onto paper, too. And if it gets hairy, we can all say adios to everything."

"Boy," Red said, "for Friday night at a party, you're enough to depress a hard-on. You got ten million in tax-frees. I got hundreds of thousands of shares of over-the-counter shit. I paid nine, ten, eleven for and now it's all fifty cents to a buck a share. Play money, so what the fuck?"

"But you've got Cardinal," Dickie pointed out. "You could sell out to MCA, Paramount. What about Sony?"

"Let's face it," Singer said. "We all punch up the calculator every day, jot the numbers down. What am I worth? Bang, bang, the numbers come up on the little screen. I couldn't have a bigger house, bigger cars, bigger boat — whatever — if I had twice, three times as much dough. How many fucking rooms can I live in?"

"But there's always something, isn't there, Stanley?" Hennessey asked. "The big white house, the three handicap?"

"Getting into Judy Hirshberg's pants," Red added for him.

"Let's enjoy it while we're healthy," Dickie agreed, telling the waitress, "one small piece," as she served the fillet. "No hollandaise on my asparagus."

The first toasts started with the entrée. "I always thought that Freddie was adopted," said a man who had been his classmate at St. Luke's School. "No harm intended to the Temples." He bowed to Freddie's father. "But Freddie never acted the way he looked. He forever sponsored the underdog, the strange kid. And the strange kids, the underdogs, always turned out to be the Shah's nephew or the South American dictator's son." Everyone applauded. "I'm flattered to be invited tonight, especially since I inherited my money. I'm proud to be on the A team." Everyone clapped some more, got to their feet and lifted their glasses in Freddie's direction.

"What a load of shit," Hennessey said. But he stood as well and drank it down with the rest. "You got a toast?" he asked Dickie, really asking all of them at the table. "No way am I making a fool of myself with speeches. I go to benefits, the baseball writers' dinner in the winter, stuff for the cardinal, anything for the mayor because it's business. I write the checks, put the arm on various people, leave the public bullshit to the comedians among us."

"What about when your daughter gets married?" Red asked.

"I'll leave the toast to the bandleader."

More speeches went on through dinner, mostly clients praising Freddie's ability to make them rich. "I thought LBO was a goddamn railroad," one of them said, "until I learned the gospel of borrowing when someone else has to pay it back. America is a wonderful place, and Fred Temple and I will be brothers for another fifty years." Freddie himself got to his feet during the strawberries with zabaglione.

"You all may find this hard to believe, but my daughter, Brett, pushed for this evening. I would have gladly passed on any celebration of the beginning of the slide into decay."

"Boo, hiss." The guests gave him the raspberry.

"But there is one big reason I'm glad we're having this party. I wanted a time capsule guest list of friends. I'll explain that," Freddie said. "A time capsule seals in the best of a society so that ages later people can gaze upon what was special in earlier days. You represent the best, the most innovative in the business life of this country. There is almost one of everything entrepreneurial in this room. And it's *you* I'm celebrating, not my birthday. It's all of you."

Duke and Red Singer made rude faces at one another.

Dickie thought of Adrie. She had given him a small dinner for his own fiftieth with friends and family at the Four Seasons. "Saul Steinberg can take a planeload to Venice to celebrate," she had said. "What we do, we do as Adrienne Rose does, with understatement and taste."

"New York is a pep rally for money now. Even Boston's Golf Club has taken on a different cast of characters." He laughed to himself. "I could probably get in here in a second now. What did Groucho say? Any club that would have me I wouldn't think of joining."

Brett was on her feet, adoring her daddy, signaling for the lights to be put down. Waiters wheeled in the cake with fifty candles. "One for each deal," Brett said. They sang "Happy Birthday," and almost everyone in the room thought about being fifty, measured his net worth against how many years he had left before he couldn't get preferred seating at Le Cirque, couldn't get recognition at the Four Seasons or Spago or the Palm in Aspen. Or until he couldn't get it up at all. Everyone thought of that.

Sleek Sullivan waited until the singing died down and rapped on his glass. "I've known Fred Temple since the days," he said, "when he tried to sell me a few shares of stock. 'Anything to get the ball rolling,' Fred used to say. I told him I'd buy an idea that *he* bought himself and I wanted to see the confirmation slip that proved he owned it. I also said at the time, I'd buy *if* he got three other people to donate something for my congressional race. He did it. I did it. And we've been doing for each other ever since. One of the first laws of politics: Do it for each other. You may think it's do it *to* each other, but that's wrong."

"Can you see him with his finger on the red atomic button?" Singer whispered to Hennessey.

"You said that about everybody who's run for President since Truman," Duke said.

"Hey, I'm producing the inaugural if he wins. I'll be sneaking the bimbos in the side door. Into the Lincoln Bedroom. I've got a role."

"Don't be an asshole, Red," Duke hissed at him.

"So," Sleek was finishing his toast, "I'd like to lift a glass to a true friend, someone who gives real meaning to the term WASP, to Fred Temple. With *A Stiff Peter*." Everyone hooted, especially Brett. As her dad said, "one of the boys." Mr. Temple pulled himself to his feet and said a few words about his son, really an excuse to tell the joke he was famous for telling at club dinners for more than fifty years. He told it with a bad French accent, "The Tale of Pierre La France, the Great French Aviateur," the joke that finished with the punchline "When Pierre goes down, he goes down in flames." He basked in the attention he knew he'd receive. His son rose to shake his hand. Anything else would be overstepping the bounds of good taste.

"He thinks it's *his* birthday," Hennessey said, applauding nonetheless with the rest of them.

"No one left in Hollywood could play the part," Red commented. "Maybe Michael Caine in another twenty years, but he wouldn't look as good. It's that *look*, Rosie, you'd kill for that look, right? Mr. Rose, the *sheygets*? Are you ready for tomorrow? We're playing the skins game."

The piano player broke into "For He's a Jolly Good Fellow." Everyone joined in, everyone basking in the feeling that they all were gentlemen and that the singing would be followed by cigars and brandy. Indeed, waitresses passed humidors, and brandy was brought around on silver trays. And the men crowded near the piano and sang songs they loved, going back to World War I ("Over There") and the summer camps of their youth ("Goodbye My Coney Island Baby").

"You know," Sleek said to Hennessey, "about an hour is the limit a politician gets to stay at any function anywhere in his career. Only an hour for anything."

"You'd rather develop commercial property? And how about sleep? I've got news for you. *No one* in this room gets much sleep. I'd take No Doz at MIT cramming for exams. All I wanted was to get out of school so I could sleep. I'm lucky, I get three hours a night." He laughed. "Something I always wondered about. When does the President of the United States have time to take a shit?"

"I'll let you know in a year," Sullivan answered. "And while we're on the subject, somehow I keep thinking of a hundred thousand dollars. Is that a dream or what?"

"Well, it's funny you mention that, Senator. I happen to have fifty employees. And all of them have spouses. Wonder of wonders, they've all kicked in a thou apiece for your presidential aspirations."

"It's not just my aspirations, Duke. I would hope it's the country's as well. What about when? Not that I'm pushy."

"We're teeing off early tomorrow morning. I could bring the checks with me. We could have the drop after we finish."

"I've known you many a year, and all that time you never let anyone in. Not *really* in. I suppose I object to that term, 'the drop.' "

"Senator, all my employees chip in a grand. Their husbands or wives chip in a grand. Ninety percent of them don't have the grand, much less the two. I issued two-thousand-dollar bonuses for each of them. They cough it up and I hand them over in a big manila envelope. Do I have to make confession at the same time?"

Sleek clapped him on the shoulder. "One more song." He pushed his way to the piano player and made a request. Sleek sang "My Wild Irish Rose" in a tenor good enough to charm any press corps. And as he sang, he made eye contact frequently with Mr. Temple. Freddie's father gave back the stare, perhaps conceding him the government, but telling the senator that he'd never have the club.

"It's too bad they don't make nice little movies anymore," Red said. "Too bad the blockbuster is everything. What a sweet little scene. You're lucky, Rosie. You're about the only one of us who doesn't have to kiss someone's ass to be king."

"Me and Mr. Temple," Dickie agreed, as Sullivan reached for the high note to finish off his song.

"No strippers, no one coming out of the cake. No blue flicks,"

Freddie said, as people were leaving. "Looks like fifty is the beginning of the big slide."

"No after-hours joints," Hennessey added.

"We can still do that if you want." Red was ready. "We can do it all if you want. Like my bachelor party."

"It's boring, I know," Temple said. "But doing the deals is a bachelor party. Just think, somewhere in the world now, someone's signing papers. It's eight o'clock in L.A.; all the players are still at work."

"It's for twenty grand tomorrow, birthday boy," Hennessey said.

"What a present that will be," Freddie announced. "I'm coming to tee it up."

"Good night, Daddy." Brett squeezed his arm. "It was a great party." He watched her walk swiftly through the room and onto the landing at the top of the grand staircase. Sleek Sullivan had been waiting there. She didn't take his arm, but Freddie saw him guide her by the elbow to the stairs and down.

"I never got to tell 'Wee Geordie' in my Scots accent," his father complained. "I only got to tell 'Pierre La France, the Great French Aviateur.' No one has time for the finer things in life anymore." Father and son saw everyone off into the spring night, the piano player finishing with "Goodnight, Sweetheart," which made Freddie's father feel that at least *someone* remembered the good old days.

The threesome sang "Sh-Boom" in the back of the limousine at the top of their voices and only stopped in exhaustion when they could no longer remember any of the words except the mindless chorus.

"Just think," Dickie said, "if we were born a few years later, we'd be singing 'Hey Jude' instead of 'Sh-Boom.' "

"I don't give a shit what anybody says," Red added, "there is nothing in history to compare to making out to rhythm and blues songs. Old-fashioned rhythm and blues, while you're parked by the reservoir at B.C. night school, trying to get someone to move into the backseat."

"Remember how we hated singing class in the seventh grade?" Dickie asked.

Hennessey remembered. " 'Daffodils,' for Christ's sake."

"For It's Up wi' the Bonnets of Bonny Dundee," Dickie crooned.

"I like that one," Red said. "All us Hebes singing 'Bonny Dundee.' "

They were in Duke's driveway. "Five years goes by so fast," he said. "I never really thought these matches would go after the first time. I've known you guys forty fucking years, and the best thing I can say about it is that you're the only schmucks I could ever sing 'Sh-Boom' with."

"Write if you get work," Red called out of the car window.

"And hang by your thumbs," Dickie added, the old lines from "Bob and Ray," which started in Boston. Duke called after them, standing in his dinner jacket in front of the white house on the hill, "I get front-seat window forever, assholes."

They were quiet for a long time, their eyes shut driving through the old neighborhoods. "When we grew up," Dickie finally said, "we knew everybody in Brookwood and maybe a dozen people in the next town. That was our life. Everybody married from within that circle and stayed. Now everything is so fragmented."

"We had dinner every Friday night at my grandmother's," Red answered. "Chicken."

"So did we."

After a while Red spoke. "I hate to play golf hung over, particularly knowing I've got to hand over twenty thousand to the goy. You got any interest going to the Combat Zone or Chinatown?"

"I've got a late date," Dickie answered.

Singer woke up immediately. "You prick," he yelled. "I thought this was a buddy movie, not a fuck-your-buddy movie. You're going to leave me alone? With nothing to do?"

"It's just an old friend. God knows when I'll be in Boston again."

"Can I have sloppy seconds?"

"Grow up, Stanley, for Christ's sake."

"No, it's fine. I'll be fine. Watch an old movie, order a fucking omelet from room service."

"The old Red would have duked the bell captain, ordered up a hooker."

"At the *Ritz*? What do you think I am?" They laughed, but Red had already made up his mind to drop Dickie at the hotel and keep the car. He could drive around, scout locations, never let it appear that he had nothing better to do than go to sleep.

Julia Hepburn was waiting in the upstairs lounge at the Ritz. When Dickie walked in, he saw her immediately. She was seated against the far wall. She wore a large black picture hat as if that, and her position in the room, would guard her from scandal. "*Mister Rose*, I assume," she said. And he knew she had rehearsed a thousand opening lines. "I practically haven't seen you since I was running naked down the main street of Concord." It was awkward kissing her cheek because of her hat.

"Who are you?" he asked. "Mata Hari?"

"You're the married one. I assume I'm protecting you."

"I could have asked you to meet me in my room."

"I don't go to gentlemen's hotel rooms at midnight." They stared at each other.

"Shall we start again?" Dickie asked. "How about the hat?" She took it off and shook out her hair, a blond perm, ringlets that flirted, a Rapunzel who was now probably a sustainer of the Junior League. Dickie saw her as she was in his youth/her youth, his green light at the end of the dock. "You look beautiful," he said, really meaning you *looked* beautiful.

"And you look rich. I know you lost all that beautiful hair. Somehow I felt that you had to be bald to make clothes for women. What's Seventh Avenue without bald men? But you still have that sexy mouth. I can't wear your clothes, I'm afraid, because I don't work for Merrill Lynch. Sweaters and skirts are quite enough for my shop. 'Creations,' it's called. You'll laugh. Not very grand. Silk flowers, gift wrappings. Every year it gets Best of Boston. Small town, I know. Would our children have been bald?"

"Probably not our daughters. And anyway, you inherit from your mother's side."

Julia ordered a stinger. Dickie held up two fingers. In for a penny, he thought. "God," he said, "you still drink stingers. I haven't even *thought* about stingers in years."

"You forget. Concord, Mass, is still heavy-duty cirrhosis country. We can still punish ourselves, leave the fads to others." Her face was lined, but still strong. Age had tightened her features. She looked as if she spent much time out of doors skiing, hiking, climbing mountains. But in New Hampshire or Maine. Nothing out west. He thought of the boy he was that had wanted her so badly. Now even stingers couldn't bring him back to that. They talked of parents and marriages and children. When he had kissed her cheek, she gave off a smell that was not perfume. An essence of the earth was all he could think of. Peat moss? Her age? The brandy? He'd wanted to see Julia, wanted a mad time. She had married a Boston lawyer and divorced when she was certain he cared more about his Civil War memorabilia and his trout flies than he did about her.

"We always sparred," Dickie said. "There was always that tension."

"That's because there was the sex or the hope of sex. Now I find men of your age talk about it, probably think about it. But don't do a lot about it. It's in the abstract, like studying Plato or Aristotle."

"Men of my age," Dickie repeated. "I don't suppose we're headed ultimately to my room the way we're getting along."

"She'll get along better with me," Red Singer's voice said in back of Dickie. "I'm much more interesting." He stared at Julia. "You're perfect for something. What is it? Can you act?"

"My name's Hepburn."

Dickie was relieved. It was a mistake to meet Julia. Now he could sucker the old redhead into the deal.

"We don't have anybody like you anymore. Maybe Meryl, but that's it." Red pulled up a chair without being asked. Julia noted his dinner jacket, his red hightops. "I remember you," he went on. "Rosie always kept us away from you. Have you two been having it off all these years?"

"Jesus, Stanley," Dickie said. "What did you do, visit England once, pick up some expressions?"

"I've been there on the Concorde *twenty* times, maybe thirty. The doorman at Claridge's calls me Red."

"I'll bet he does," Dickie answered.

"Men haven't fought over me in years," Julia said. "How bloody marvelous."

"Does the doorman at Claridge's call you Jules?" Dickie asked.

"You have no right to be hostile," she said. "You're married."

He recalled the old illogical Julia, whom he had chased so far. "All we're doing is having stingers." He turned to Singer. "Did you miss me, Stanley?"

"Let's put it this way. I hate to think you're having more fun than me."

"Now don't be all pus-sy, Richard," she said, just as she used to say it to make him be a good boy. "I've loved Mr. Singer's movies, and how many times do we get a chance to learn something new?"

"Julie Christie used to drive me crazy when she wore her hair like you," Singer said. That was it for Dickie. He stood up.

"Julia, it was nice to see you again. I'm sorry I got you here under false pretenses."

"Don't go, Richard. I'm sorry."

"It's no game if you go, Rosie." Singer put his feet up on a coffee table. Dickie kissed her again on the cheek, smelling the same musty smell, not at all like years ago when he thought she smelled like baby powder. He put his middle finger under Singer's nose.

"Don't go away mad," Red said.

"Just go away," Dickie answered automatically, and walked to the elevators, thinking that Adrie was probably still up watching David Letterman. He wondered how it was possible to be worth more than a hundred million dollars and still feel like a schmuck.

"All my life I've wanted to bird-dog you, Rosie." With their golf clubs in the trunk, Singer and Rose rode in the limo to Brookwood Municipal golf club, the Muni. Duke had pulled strings at the town hall to get them a tee time. They did not have to wait in line, dropping a ball with the starter, until their foursome was called. Not like the other players at public courses, the dawn patrol. Dickie didn't say anything.

"You mad at me? I wasn't going to stay until you got pissed off."

"I don't care what you did. You did me a favor. You can't go home again."

"What's that supposed to mean?"

"You're the moviemaker, pardon me, the filmmaker. Figure it out."

Red stared out the window. "You know the definition of eternity?" Red asked. "It's the time between when you come and when she goes home." He laughed. "You have breakfast?"

Dickie just shook his head, yes.

"Come on," Red pushed, "you're dying to ask, aren't you? Well, we played mind-fuck for about an hour and I gave it my best shot. But she turned me down. Told me that she always felt vulnerable for Jewish men and she'd like to see me again and that you were a prick."

"I'm a prick?" Dickie spoke for the first time. "She said that?"

"Actually, she said you were a shit, not for just last night, but forever. Guess she really knows you."

"Women . . ." Dickie said.

"Smart, aren't they?"

Duke was up early hitting range balls with a wedge off the front lawn into the deep woods below his house. He felt a bubble across his chest. Not a pain, more a flash of indigestion. He stopped swinging for a minute, and it went away. He had had several of those feelings in the last few weeks, not like a pain at all. "I know it's sausages," he thought. "These goddamn words I never heard of when I was a kid: cholesterol, dyslexia. Strep, for Christ's sake. Nobody gets a cold anymore, got to get tested for strep." He thought about having his name and Rita's on so much paper that if things went bad the banks could take away everything down to his solid-brass American Legion baseball medal. No old-timer in real estate would have signed his name to anything. Only thing they could give then was due diligence, good faith and hard work. Things were fuzzy around the edges. The Bank of New England was throwing money at anyone who walked in the door, and said he needed $5 million for condos in East Fucking Overshoe. And they were buying other banks for two and a half, three times book value. That's like saying fifty grand for a Dick Stuart baseball card. And he was going to play golf and probably give up another $20,000 to Temple, not to mention the hundred K to Sullivan after the match. All this and he couldn't even digest sausages for breakfast. He hit a sweet wedge with a little draw on it.

Freddie finished one hundred sit-ups on the same rug in his old room where he had done sit-ups in his youth. "I shouldn't be here this weekend," he thought. "I've got to get my arms around the fund." He was raising half a billion dollars for a leveraged buyout fund, and, once raised, it would make him for life, give him his own leverage to do any deal, anywhere in the world. Bill Simon was moving on the Pacific Rim. That was the future. Maybe he'd take a house in L.A. or San Francisco, spend half his time there. He had been irritated by the straw rug on his bedroom floor. It rubbed against the mole he had on his lower back near the top of his left buttock. He had had the mole as long as he could remember. Lately, when he wore a jock to play squash, it rubbed against the mole, making it sore. He felt it, and it hurt to the touch, felt hot. He promised to put a Band-Aid over it after his shower. He joined his father for breakfast, which he ate in the dining room, even though there was no more cook, no more maid. Fred's mother had died several years before of lung cancer, a vicious smoker until the end. "Damn the torpedoes," she had said, "get me a Lark." His father was eating shredded wheat with a sliced banana, what he always ate on Saturday mornings. "Dad," Freddie said, "there's nothing in the house to eat. And when's the last time you had it cleaned?"

"You can forget about any goddamn nursing home."

"You don't need a nursing home. You need someone in here on a regular basis, cooking, helping you. You got ten thousand Exxon and all those other stocks and bonds and the trust. And this house. Brookwood's the hottest real estate market in the area."

"I reinvest the dividends. And I want to die in this house. I don't want any of the *new* people to have it, glitz it up."

"It's probably worth three or four million."

"It's the principle of the thing."

"Well, I can have shredded wheat, I guess. How come there's no more bananas?"

"I buy them one at a time."

Freddie thought he'd like to have the family house, plunk it down in Southampton. *He* would glitz it up. Bostonians just never would care for whatever New Yorkers did. He knew there were still bumper stickers in Boston that said, "Honk If You Hate Bucky Dent."

"What would you think," Freddie asked his father, feeling perverse, "about putting half a million into my LBO fund?"

His father snorted. "About like I feel about buying a second banana."

"This one's for you, Dickie," Red announced as they waited on the first tee to hit. "Saul Goldberg wanted more than anything else to be a member of a fancy all-Gentile club. He moved to another city, had his face reconstructed, his nose done, changed his name to Samuel Morgan. Then he moved back, met the right people. Finally he got into the fancy Gentile club and no one suspected it was old Saul Goldberg. Finally he's invited to play in his first foursome. He steps up on the first tee, takes perfect practice swings and duck hooks his drive twenty yards into a flower bed. 'Oy vey,' he shouts out unconsciously, then looks around quickly at his partners. 'Whatever *that* means.' "

"I always loved that." Dickie laughed. It was a perfect spring morning, the dew almost faded from the fairways, robin's song accompanying the whack of golf balls, the low engine noise of mowers, hoots from the distant triumph of a big drive, a long successful putt.

"Okay," Duke said, "action like the big boys today. Skins game. We start the first hole at five dollars a man. Whoever wins the hole, outright, he collects the fivers. Two tie, we all tie and the next hole we play for ten bucks apiece. No one wins, the third hole is carried over for fifteen bucks. I say we do the first six holes at five dollars per, the next six at ten and the last six at twenty bucks."

"This could be some serious change," Dickie said.

"You're getting to be such an old lady," Red snorted.

"I just don't gamble," he replied. "A two-dollar Nassau is fine for me."

"Play it this way today," Duke urged. "King of the Mountain."

"King of the Mountain," Freddie added.

They kidded with the starter and asked him if he knew Hartigan, their old caddie master. The starter told them that Hartigan had been fired years ago, caught breaking and entering houses in Brookwood with his two sons, boosting TVs and stereos.

"You can't make up what really happens in life," Red observed. "Did you ever think that if we did today what we did in my cellar years ago, we'd probably be indicted for rape?" They had all thought about that. And they continued to think about it as they hit their tee shots on the first hole, a par three, one hundred and sixty yards from the blue markers. Only Freddie hit it straight, his five iron stopping on the fringe of the green.

"Birthday boy, the iceman," Hennessey said, his own shot having sliced into the woods. "Don't you have any sense of guilt? Doesn't anything bother you? All I could think of in Red's cellar was that I was breaking training. That, and being unfaithful to Rita, whose tits at the time I had barely touched."

"I feel guilty," Freddie said, "but not about things I can't control." Duke looked at him, noticed his white half socks that barely rose above his shoes. Duke thought only girls wore socks like that, girls who wanted to get tan ankles. He strode off down the hill toward the woods. His caddie had already disappeared on the hunt for Duke's ball.

"I've forgotten what it's like to walk on golf courses," Dickie said to Singer as they moved to their own balls, both left of the green. "Guys I know in New York, who run their own companies, take pride in how fast they can play eighteen holes, how they can race around in a cart in under three hours, out in time to spend a few more hours in the office."

Red nodded. "In the business," he said, "that's not our problem. We can take six hours a round. In carts yet. But everybody's got a phone and the schmoozing takes longer than the hitting. The only people who can really play the game in L.A. are the people out of work."

"What about you?"

"I schmooze, I hit. I schmooze, I hit. But I can always win by a stroke when I have to. You know what I'm saying? God gave it to me. Look at the robin. Look at him holding his head up, cocked. You know why? Listening for worms. I learned that making some fucking nature movie years ago. You learn things on location, Rosie. Good for your gin game, too." Their balls were lying next to each other. They both had to hit over a large trap guarding the green and then try to stop their balls fast. The pin was on their side, and it was a shot Dickie had no clue about. So he said, "What are we going to do about Sleek Sullivan?"

"Let me hit this first." Red skulled his shot to the right, ending up farther from the green than he was in the first place. "Don't ever do that again" — Red glared — "or I'll rip your face off."

Dickie flinched and hit his own shot right into the middle of the trap.

"You deserve it," Red told him.

Duke lost his ball in the woods, eventually getting onto the green and making a five. So did Singer. Rose picked up. Temple messed up his chip and made four, winning the first skin, five dollars from each of the others. The caddies handed them drivers for the next hole and scurried down the second fairway to watch for the shots. "Just like us," Hennessey said. "Little hustlers. Helping out the family, making a few bucks. They probably putt for quarters now, not dimes, lie around in the grass hoping some day they'll own the big white house on the hill."

"Are you going to become a whiskey priest, Duke?" Red asked. "Next thing I know you're going to be sobbing and singing 'Too-ra-loo-ra-loo-ral.' "

"Red's just all pissed off," Dickie said, "because I asked him what we're going to do about Sleek Sullivan?"

"What you did was make me shank my shot," Red said.

Temple was surprised. "What do you mean 'do about Sullivan'? He's a senator. If he becomes President, we're along for the ride. If he loses, so what? In this state, you're senator for life. It's a win, win for us. Now, are you going to dick around or are you going to play golf?"

"You better be a little nicer to us," Red said. "Customer golf. We who giveth can also taketh away."

"Today, baby," Temple said, "you're going to give till it hurts. Hit away." They hit their drives.

Three of them played the first five holes feeling frozen in time. All except Freddie, who felt he was in one of those unconscious modes that pro golfers think about when everything is automatic, confidence, perfect rhythm. The zone. He felt that about his life now, like a Hovercraft, buzzing along the surface, no sweat. *Tempo.* He thought of a song as he took long strides to his ball: "I Got Sixpence, Jolly Jolly Sixpence, I Got Sixpence to Last Me All My Life . . . And I've got no wife — I'm free."

"The others all went away," Duke thought. "They have no center to their lives, and I'm still balanced the way I was behind the plate." He shook his head and attacked his second shot on the par-five sixth hole, sending a three wood screaming down the fairway over a pond and onto the green, twenty feet from an eagle. Pumped up, protecting his homeland.

"Got your ass into that one, big boy," Red said.

Red was thinking about L.A., worrying about L.A. "Do I have the ability to pull the trigger?" he asked himself. "The biggest men in Hollywood history could point the gun and pull the trigger. Zanuck. Am I a killer? Do they look at me that way?" Years ago Red had gotten a call at his office from his father. It was the middle of the morning. "From my father," he said. "I'll take it in the toilet." He heard his secretary tell two writers waiting to see him, "Red Singer? He's a killer." But every time he left L.A. he was afraid to go back, afraid no one would remember him. And Laura. Laura Fine Fishman, keeper of the flame. What was she doing while he was in Boston giving away twenty grand? He remembered what she had said when he left: "Don't worry about me. Between Guy" — the personal trainer, pronounced G-E-E — "golf lessons at Hillcrest" — tennis was passé — "lunch with les girls, old friends from Westlake, reading your scripts, I wouldn't have time or energy to fuck anyone else." Red was not reassured. But he had his new Pings with him, and he knew that if he could break eighty, the right people would always want him around. Everybody wants you around if you can break eighty.

Dickie played atrociously. He even whiffed on the seventh tee, the wind with him as he swung mightily, hoping to cut the corner on the dogleg right. Freddie had won fifteen dollars from each of them on the first six holes. Everyone else was shut out. The harder Dickie tried to play decent golf the worse he got. "I'm too smart to be any good at this," he decided. "The more boring you are, the better golfer you're going to be. I have too much imagination. We're going for a billion in sales, and I'm in Brookwood, Massachusetts, on a public course?" Dickie couldn't believe his golf was so bad. He had said to an old retailer years ago, "Can anything be worse than that?"

"Yes," the retailer said. "December." That was in the days when the only off-price store sales of the year were in February and July. The same retailer told him about the elephant for sale at one of his stores for $750: "A customer said, 'An elephant for seven hundred and fifty dollars? Are you crazy? Who would want that?'

" 'With a year's supply of hay?' the retailer asked.

" '*Now* you're talking,' said the customer." And the retailer added to Dickie, "It's *price*. The whole megillah is *price*."

Dickie and Adrienne had cut out the middle man, built a garment for $3 and sold it for $25. "I'm getting like my father," Dickie thought, "the business, all the time the business."

"This is crazy," he announced to the others, having hit his ball into the water on one of the two water holes on the course. "I can't play this game."

"You never *could* play this game, Rosie. For forty years you couldn't play this game," Red told him.

Rose thought of Adrie when he should have been thinking about keeping his head in back of the ball. Adrienne Rose. People referred to him as *Mr. Adrienne Rose*. He crunched all the numbers, but lately he couldn't get one thing out of his mind. He had been working late at the office, his usual custom. Adrie would leave first, then call in with a message, where to meet her for drinks, where dinner was to be, whether black tie or not. They went out in the city four nights a week and on weekends off to the country, a farm in Johnsonburg, Warren County, New Jersey, near Hope and Tranquility, where no one really went. But they would. Because Adrie had the eye. She had said in *Women's Wear Daily* long ago that "only eleven people in New York City dare to be original," meaning that she was one of them and she didn't know the other ten. Coming down in the elevator, Dickie was alone with a young designer who had just applied for a job.

Interviewed by Adrie, he was put on hold, not because of lack of talent but because he had grinned in all the wrong places and she didn't hire wiseasses for Adrienne Rose. Dickie stood in the back of the elevator, pressing against the wall, even though he was alone with the young man, who had smiled at him, a shit-eating grin. "Takes one to know one, Richard," he said out of the blue. All Dickie could think of was a pompous response:

"You can kiss Adrienne Rose good-bye, youngblood, if you think you'll ever work for us."

The designer held up his hands, palms open. "Hey, that's cool," he said. "But someday you'll walk down Fifth Avenue with us. You get to choose the sign you carry." Dickie pressed harder against the wall as the young man continued to grin.

Rose took a ten on the hole, thinking about the young designer.

Red said to him, "You know what an alte kacker is?"

"No," Dickie said. "I went to Harvard."

Red looked at him. "*You're* an alte kacker. An old fart. Old before your time."

They stood on the tee at the thirteenth hole after playing the previous six holes with no blood. All the money would carry over to the last six. It had accumulated so that each of the last holes was worth $20 from each man, plus the $240 total from the middle six. Ahead of them in the thirteenth fairway were four duffers wearing double-knit slacks, Budweiser golf caps, white belts with white golf shoes, a Double Cleveland. They hit the balls way right, way left and two feet up the middle. "Fore, you hackers," Duke yelled at them. But there were foursomes stacked up in front of the Budweiser group and stacked up in back of them also, the typical six-hour weekend round at public courses. They saw the group behind and the group ahead pull cans of beer from their golf bags, drink and hit, drink and hit. They didn't care if a round took eight hours. It was like being on the playground forty years ago. They could bitch and moan about the slowness of play when they got home. But they wouldn't trade it for anything.

The foursome settled down on the last six holes, concentrating on their swings. But no one made a birdie to win one. They continued to produce a series of holes where no one threw in a lucky shot to take the pot. By the time they reached the seventeenth, the shortest and easiest-rated hole on the course, they were playing for a total of $1,700, all to the man who won outright. The seventeenth was a par three, one hundred and ten yards long. The tee was on a hill looking down to the small green, guarded by deep traps in front and in back, with tall evergreens hemming in the sides of the hole like parentheses. "Remember years ago," Dickie said, "we'd throw the balls down. Closest to the pin won a dime from each."

"Easier to throw it than hit it," Duke said. "Half a wedge is a shot I always have trouble with." But Duke hit his half wedge to the back of the green, the ball stopping just on the edge of the trap. "Lucky," he said, "but probably a winner."

Dickie almost missed his shot completely, a topped nine iron that rolled down the rock-covered hill, ending up in rough grass, short of the front bunker.

"Nice hit, Alice," Red commented. Singer hit his own shot onto the green twenty feet from the pin. "Hey, hey, hey. Pay me now or pay me later." Freddie Temple took a nine iron and tried to make a smooth swing, slowing it down, concentrating on not hurrying. His practice swings were perfect. But when he swung at the ball, he couldn't help lunging, throwing his right shoulder around, forcing the ball left, deep into the evergreens. "Long and wrong," Red called.

"Come *out,*" Freddie shouted. They heard a clunk as the ball hit a tree trunk and bounded out of the woods as if tossed by a leprechaun. It bounced once onto the green, again against the pin and disappeared with a rattle into the hole. Everyone saw it, no one was looking the other way. They jumped up and down, shouting. Hennessey did a little jig; Temple waltzed around, his elbows pumping. They clapped each other on the back and engulfed Temple. None of them had ever made a hole in one. "Another FM," Duke rumbled, knowing it would cost them the $1,700 apiece. "A fucking miracle," Singer agreed.

"Not so fast," Dickie reminded them. "I've got a stroke on this hole." Dickie did have a handicap stroke. He had one on every hole, and if he buried his second shot it would be for a gross score of two, net one, a tie. Hennessey and Singer carried

Dickie down the hill, rubbed his head for luck, gave him tips about how to play the shot. "Now you're going to see a classic," Dickie said. "No lucky bounce off a tree. I'm going to run an eight iron into the jar. Lot of green to work with."

"Use a wedge," said Duke. "Soft."

Singer agreed, but Rose took an eight from his caddie, took a few practice swings and calmly stroked his shot, running it over the trap, bouncing it on the edge of the green and rolling it perfectly in a line, bango, right into the middle of the cup. "Routine bird," he said, as whistles erupted from the others. "No blood." Dickie picked the two balls out of the hole. He tossed Freddie the hole-in-one ball. "A moment of glory," Dickie said out loud.

"The title of your movie," Red said, adding, "what the fuck, Freddie, there's always the eighteenth. Par four. If you hole out from the fairway, a two should win it."

But Hennessey and Singer halved the eighteenth with pars, and they lay around in the grass near the green, smelling the spring smells, watching other golfers hit their shots. They pulled random blades of grass, held them in their lips like cigarettes, looked for four-leaf clovers. "What now?" Dickie asked. No money had been won for the last twelve holes, and the course was too crowded to wait for the first hole again.

"How about the old contest?" Red suggested. "Over the road. It's daylight. We can see if cars are coming. We wedge over the road; closest to the traffic sign wins."

"We're too old for that shit," Hennessey said.

"Bullshit. We're never too old," Red insisted. "Besides, now we all got umbrella policies."

"Wait a minute," Temple said. "We have to vote on the fifteen thousand apiece."

"What fifteen thousand?" Duke asked. "Don't you know we decided to cancel that? The stakes got too big." Temple leaped to his feet, his face red, a color his skin never took on.

"Jesus, you knew that, Freddie," Dickie added. "After the crash of eighty-seven and all, it wouldn't look right playing for that kind of money."

Freddie stood over them. "You . . . bastards."

Duke took an envelope from a zippered compartment in his golf bag. "Before you stomp off," he said, "happy birthday. We voted last night."

Temple ripped open the envelope and smiled, glowing, like Billy Budd. "After all these years," he said. "At last I won a pot. And I know enough to push it if you're a winner. Let's hit over the road."

They shouldered their own bags and headed for the grassy spot looking over the highway that ran past the clubhouse. As they walked, the black stretch limousine, its windows darkened, drove by them, stopped and backed up. A rear window snicked down, and the handsome face of Sleek Sullivan peered out at them. "Beautiful day for the ball game," he said. "Remember Jim Britt? He used to announce the Red Sox games? Remember he used to say, 'If you can't take part in the sport, be one anyway, will ya?' " He held his hand out to them. They each shook it.

"Remember Jerry O'Leary?" Duke asked. "He used to do the radio quiz show?"

"Yeah," Red said. "Sponsored by Waleeco bars. It's a 'Who am I?' Remember?"

"Remember," Dickie asked, "Hood's three-flavored ice cream?" He said it like a chant, the way vendors in the stands at Fenway Park sold it.

"Forget the trivia. Do you have any goodies from my constituency?" Sleek asked, still sitting in the limo.

"We got one more little game to play," Duke said. "Then I'll dig it out."

"We're on a short tether, Senator," a voice came out of the dark, next to Sleek. Impatient.

"It's okay," the senator said, and got out of the car. "I like little games." Sullivan wore a double-breasted Armani suit, dark gray with tasseled loafers. He did a little pirouette so they could admire him. "Like you, Freddie," Sleek said. "No socks."

"Lady-killer," Temple said.

"Armani won't play in Iowa," Dickie said.

"That's where you're wrong," Sullivan said. "What America hasn't had in a long time is a pretty face with balls. That's the package: a pretty face with balls."

"No speeches on the golf course, Senator," Duke said. "It ain't a church."

Sullivan patted Duke on the butt, on his wallet pocket. "Money talks, bullshit walks."

They moved to the grassy spot bordering the parkway. "We chip over the road," Red explained, "to that sign. It's about sixty yards." He stared at the others. "But you can't choke because you might hit a car. Closest to the sign takes the pot." Cars slowed around a curve near them and accelerated as they passed. On a warm Saturday in May the traffic was heavy, people out shopping, gawking, taking kids to McDonald's, looking at houses they would never own.

The five men watched the automobiles. "I know this is the place," Sleek said.

"How do you know?" Dickie finally asked.

"Hennessey told me long ago. It's where I'm going to put a plaque."

Duke stood behind Sullivan. He shook his head and crossed his hands over his heart . . . no.

"Never an ill wind . . ." Sullivan added. "*Casus natalis.* Accidents of birth. Sister Mary Riley used to say that. Up at St. Stephen's. Fifth grade."

Duke broke the silence. "Play the national anthem. Start the game." They dropped a ball apiece on the grass. "A judge we can trust," Duke said. "The senator will pull four blades of grass. We'll pick from him, shortest blade hits first, longest hits last." They chose: Temple, Hennessey, Singer, then Rose. "Let me hit one," the senator asked.

"Cost you too much," Dickie said. Sullivan insisted.

"Wait till we're done," Duke promised. Freddie hit a wedge over the road, way beyond the sign. But it stayed in the median strip. "Typical WASP hit, Freddie," Red said. "Never let it be said that you fire for the flag."

Temple answered, "Let's see yours."

Duke took a few practice swings, winked at the others, took half a backswing and completely shanked his chip. The ball hit the highway, kept bouncing right, hit a curb and rolled, eventually disappearing from sight as the road wound down and away. "That may be the longest chip in history," Red said. "Like hitting a shot on the moon."

"Fuck you, Stanley," Duke said, feeling the indigestion bubble form across his chest, uncomfortable rather than painful. He tried to calm himself down, deep breathing.

Red actually waited until he saw cars coming around the corner. He hit a nine iron as they went by, taking no chances on being short with a wedge. His ball soared over the traffic, but hooked slightly to the left. It fell into the tall grass, closer to the sign than Temple's shot, but still a good fifty feet away. "Wide open for the clutch player, Rosie," he said. Dickie could feel the sweat under his arms, sweat creeping down the small of his back. A simple chip shot. He offered his wedge to Sullivan. "Try one, Senator," he said. "I need a minute to get into my Zen go-for-the-gold mode."

Senator Sleek Sullivan took off his Armani suit jacket. He gripped the wedge, waggled his hips a few times, got ready to hit the ball Dickie had dropped on the grass for him.

"Piece of cake," thought Sullivan. But cars flowed by them, speeding, and he swung harder than he should, had to get the ball up. The swing was vicious, not smooth, and the ball flew almost straight up into the air, high, high. "Get legs," Sleek yelled at it. But the ball dropped like a small bomb onto the windshield of a passing red Jeep Cherokee, surprising the driver, a divorced father on the way to McDonald's with his kids, enough to make him slam on his brakes and lurch into a tree on the median strip near the traffic sign.

"Holy Jesus," Duke said, almost whispering. Traffic halted and backed up down the road.

The Jeep's passengers were shaken but unhurt, the divorced father actually pleased that he'd have something to talk with his children about over Big Macs. It would not be until later that he would consider how his lawyers might approach the deep pockets of a U.S. senator.

As Sleek was about to be driven off in the limousine, he looked at Hennessey and the others. "You and your fucking games," he said. "You and your fucking games."

*

"I never even had my turn," Dickie said.

They sat in the China Garden in South Brookwood drinking hard stuff and eating boneless spareribs, Chinese ravioli.

"You're like the flea floating down the river with a hard-on," Singer said, "yelling 'Open the drawbridge.' The height of conceit."

"Always on my case," Dickie said.

"We're on *all* of our cases," Duke answered. "A true democracy."

They laughed and then thought about that for a while in silence. Then Duke raised his Scotch. They clinked glasses.

"I didn't like coming here years ago," Temple said. "My parents never ate this food. I never eat Chinese food now."

"You're a white-rice guy, Freddie," Red told him. "What can I tell ya?"

"You guys can't leave, you know," Hennessey said, signaling for another round of drinks.

"You want pu pu platter?" the waiter asked.

"Just the drinks," Duke answered. "Tomorrow we go back. We have to finish the game."

"You never change," Dickie said. "Always the game."

"*We'll* never change," Red corrected him. "The guys never change. You know it's true. That's what makes life so interesting."

Management

RICHARD L. DAFT

Vanderbilt University

Management

RICHARD L. DAFT

Vanderbilt University

NINTH EDITION

SOUTH-WESTERN
CENGAGE Learning™

Australia • Brazil • Japan • Korea • Mexico • Singapore • Spain • United Kingdom • United States

SOUTH-WESTERN
CENGAGE Learning

Management, Ninth Edition
Richard L. Daft, with the assistance of
Patricia G. Lane

Vice President of Editorial, Business: Jack
W. Calhoun

Editor-in-Chief: Melissa S. Acuña

Executive Editor: Joe Sabatino

Managing Developmental Editor: Emma
Newsom

Developmental Editor: Erin Berger

Editorial Assistant: Ruth Belanger

Executive Marketing Manager: Kimberly
Kanakes

Marketing Manager: Clint Kernen

Sr. Marketing Coordinator: Sarah Rose

Sr. Marketing Communications Manager:
Jim Overly

Sr. Content Project Manager: Martha Conway

Media Editor: Rob Ellington

Sr. Frontlist Buyer, Manufacturing: Doug Wilke

Production Service: Macmillan Publishing
Solutions

Sr. Art Director: Tippy McIntosh

Cover and Internal Designer: Joe Devine, Red
Hangar Design

Cover Image: BLOOMimage, Getty Images

Photography Manager: Don Schlotman

Photo Researcher: Chris Caperton, O'Donnell
and Associates; Susan Van Etten

Text Permissions Manager: Margaret
Chamberlain-Gaston

Text Permissions Researcher: James Reidel

For product information and technology assistance, contact us at
Cengage Learning Customer & Sales Support, 1-800-354-9706

For permission to use material from this text or product,
submit all requests online at **www.cengage.com/permissions**
Further permissions questions can be emailed to
permissionrequest@cengage.com

Library of Congress Control Number: 2008943508

Student Edition ISBN 13: 978-0-324-59584-0

Student Edition ISBN 10: 0-324-59584-0

South-Western Cengage Learning
5191 Natorp Boulevard
Mason, OH 45040
USA

Cengage Learning products are represented in Canada by Nelson Education, Ltd.

For your course and learning solutions, visit **www.cengage.com**

Purchase any of our products at your local college store or at our preferred
online store **www.ichapters.com**

Printed in Canada
1 2 3 4 5 6 7 13 12 11 10 09

With deep appreciation to Dorothy,
the playwright and partner in my life,
and to my parents, who started my life
toward outcomes that I could not understand at the time.

About the Author

Richard L. Daft, PhD, is the Brownlee O. Currey, Jr., Professor of Management in the Owen Graduate School of Management at Vanderbilt University. Professor Daft specializes in the study of organization theory and leadership. Dr. Daft is a Fellow of the Academy of Management and has served on the editorial boards of *Academy of Management Journal, Administrative Science Quarterly,* and *Journal of Management Education.* He was the associate editor-in-chief of *Organization Science* and served for three years as associate editor of *Administrative Science Quarterly.*

Professor Daft has authored or co-authored 12 books, including *Organization Theory and Design* (South-Western, 2007), *The Leadership Experience* (South-Western, 2008), and *What to Study: Generating and Developing Research Questions* (Sage, 1982). He published *Fusion Leadership: Unlocking the Subtle Forces That Change People and Orga-*
nizations (Berrett-Koehler, 2000, with Robert Lengel). He has also authored dozens of scholarly articles, papers, and chapters. His work has been published in *Administrative Science Quarterly, Academy of Management Journal, Academy of Management Review, Strategic Management Journal, Journal of Management, Accounting Organizations and Society, Management Science, MIS Quarterly, California Management Review,* and *Organizational Behavior Teaching Review.* Professor Daft is currently working on a new book, *The Executive and the Elephant.* He also is an active teacher and consultant. He has taught management, leadership, organizational change, organizational theory, and organizational behavior.

Professor Daft served as associate dean, produced for-profit theatrical productions, and helped manage a start-up enterprise. He has been involved in management development and consulting for many companies and government organizations, including the American Banking Association, Bridgestone, Bell Canada, the National Transportation Research Board, Nortel, TVA, Pratt & Whitney, State Farm Insurance, Tenneco, the United States Air Force, the United States Army, J. C. Bradford & Co., Central Parking System, Entergy Sales and Service, Bristol-Myers Squibb, First American National Bank, and the Vanderbilt University Medical Center.

Preface

Managing for Innovation in a Changing World

In recent years, organizations have been buffeted by massive and far-reaching social, technological, and economic changes. Any manager who still believed in the myth of stability was rocked out of complacency when, one after another, large financial institutions in the United States began to fail. Business schools, as well as managers and businesses, were scrambling to keep up with the fast-changing story and evaluate its impact. This edition of *Management* addresses themes and issues that are directly relevant to the current, fast-shifting business environment. I revised *Management* with a goal of helping current and future managers find innovative solutions to the problems that plague today's organizations—whether they are everyday challenges or once-in-a-lifetime crises. The world in which most students will work as managers is undergoing a tremendous upheaval. Ethical turmoil, the need for crisis management skills, e-business, rapidly changing technologies, globalization, outsourcing, global virtual teams, knowledge management, global supply chains, the Wall Street meltdown, and other changes place demands on managers that go beyond the techniques and ideas traditionally taught in management courses. Managing today requires the full breadth of management skills and capabilities. This text provides comprehensive coverage of both traditional management skills and the new competencies needed in a turbulent environment characterized by economic turmoil, political confusion, and general uncertainty.

In the traditional world of work, management was to control and limit people, enforce rules and regulations, seek stability and efficiency, design a top-down hierarchy, and achieve bottom-line results. To spur innovation and achieve high performance, however, managers need different skills to engage workers' hearts and minds as well as take advantage of their physical labor. The new workplace asks that managers focus on leading change, harnessing people's creativity and enthusiasm, finding shared visions and values, and sharing information and power. Teamwork, collaboration, participation, and learning are guiding principles that help managers and employees maneuver the difficult terrain of today's turbulent business environment. Managers focus on developing, not controlling, people to adapt to new technologies and extraordinary environmental shifts, and thus achieve high performance and total corporate effectiveness.

My vision for the ninth edition of *Management* is to present the newest management ideas for turbulent times in a way that is interesting and valuable to students while retaining the best of traditional management thinking. To achieve this vision, I have included the most recent management concepts and research and have shown the contemporary application of management ideas in organizations. I have added a questionnaire at the beginning of each chapter that draws students personally into the topic and gives them some insight into their own management skills. A chapter feature for new managers, called the New Manager Self-Test, gives students a sense of what will be expected when they become managers. The combination of established scholarship, new ideas, and real-life applications gives students a taste of the energy, challenge, and adventure inherent in the dynamic field of management. The South-Western/Cengage Learning staff and I have worked together to provide a textbook better than any other at capturing the excitement of organizational management.

I revised *Management* to provide a book of utmost quality that will create in students both respect for the changing field of management and confidence that they can understand and master it. The textual portion of this book has been enhanced through the engaging, easy-to-understand writing style and the many in-text examples, boxed items, and short exercises that make the concepts come alive for students. The graphic component has been enhanced with several new exhibits and a new set of photo essays that illustrate specific management concepts. The well-chosen photographs provide vivid illustrations and intimate glimpses of management scenes, events, and people. The photos are combined with brief essays that explain how a specific management concept looks and feels. Both the textual and graphic portions of the textbook help students grasp the often abstract and distant world of management.

Focus on Innovation: New to the Ninth Edition

The ninth edition of *Management* is especially focused on the future of management education by identifying and describing emerging ideas and examples of innovative organizations and by providing enhanced learning opportunities for students.

Learning Opportunities

The ninth edition has taken a leap forward in pedagogical features to help students understand their own management capabilities and learn what it is like to manage in an organization today. New to this edition is an opening questionnaire that directly relates to the topic of the chapter and enables students to see how they respond to situations and challenges typically faced by real-life managers. New Manager Self-Tests in each chapter provide further opportunity for students to understand their management abilities. These short feedback questionnaires give students insight into how they would function in the real world of management. End-of-chapter questions have been carefully revised to encourage critical thinking and application of chapter concepts. End-of-chapter cases and ethical dilemmas help students sharpen their diagnostic skills for management problem solving.

Chapter Content

Within each chapter, many topics have been added or expanded to address the current issues managers face. At the same time, chapter text has been tightened and sharpened to provide greater focus on the key topics that count for management today. This tightening has resulted in a shortening of the text from 21 to 19 chapters. The essential elements about operations and technology have been combined into one chapter. An appendix on entrepreneurship and small business has been provided for students who want more information on managing in small businesses start-ups.

Chapter 1 includes a section on making the leap from being an individual contributor in the organization to becoming a new manager and getting work done primarily through others. The chapter introduces the skills and competencies needed to manage organizations effectively, including issues such as managing diversity, coping with globalization, and managing crises. In addition, the chapter discusses today's emphasis within organizations on innovation as a response to a rapidly changing environment.

Chapter 2 continues its solid coverage of the historical development of management and organizations. It also examines new management thinking for turbulent times. The chapter includes a new section on systemic thinking and an expanded discussion of post-World War II management techniques. The final part of the chapter looks at issues of managing the technology-driven workplace, including supply chain management, customer relationship management, and outsourcing.

Chapter 3 contains an updated look at current issues related to the environment and corporate culture, including a new section on issues related to the natural environment and managers' response to environmental advocates. The chapter also illustrates how managers shape a high–performance culture as an innovative response to a shifting environment.

Chapter 4 takes a look at the growing power of China and India in today's global business environment and what this means for managers around the world. The chapter discusses the need for *cultural intelligence,* and a new section looks at understanding communication differences as an important aspect of learning to manage internationally or work with people from different cultures. In addition, the complex issues surrounding globalization are discussed, including a consideration of the current globalization backlash. A new section on human resources points out the need for evaluating whether people are suitable for foreign assignments.

Chapter 5 makes the business case for incorporating ethical values in the organization. The chapter includes a new discussion of the *bottom-of-the-pyramid* business concept and how managers are successfully applying this new thinking. The chapter also has an expanded discussion of ethical challenges managers face today, including responses to recent financial scandals. It considers global ethical issues, as well, including a discussion of corruption rankings of various countries.

Chapter 6 provides a more focused discussion of the overall planning process and a new discussion of using strategy maps for aligning goals. This chapter also takes a close look at crisis planning and how to use scenarios. The chapter's final section on planning for high performance has been enhanced by a new discussion of intelligence teams and an expanded look at using performance dashboards to help managers plan in a fast-changing environment.

Chapter 7 continues its focus on the basics of formulating and implementing strategy. It includes a new section on diversification strategy, looking at how managers use unrelated diversification, related diversification, or vertical integration as strategic approaches in shifting environments. This chapter also looks at new trends in strategy, including the dynamic capabilities approach and partnership strategies.

Chapter 8 gives an overview of managerial decision making with an expanded discussion of how conflicting interests among managers can create uncertainty regarding decisions. A new section on why managers often make bad decisions looks at the biases that can cloud judgment. The chapter also includes a new section on innovative group decision making and the dangers of groupthink.

Chapter 9 discusses basic principles of organizing and describes both traditional and contemporary organizational structures in detail. The chapter includes a discussion of organic versus mechanistic structures and when each is more effective. Chapter 9 also provides a description of the virtual network organization form.

Chapter 10 includes a more focused discussion of the critical role of managing change and innovation today. The chapter includes a new discussion of the ambidextrous approach for both creating and using innovations and has expanded material on exploration and creativity, the importance of internal and external cooperation, and the growing trend toward open innovation.

Chapter 11 includes an expanded discussion of the strategic role of HRM in building human capital. The chapter has new sections on coaching and mentoring and the trend toward part-time and contingent employment. New ways of doing background checks on applicants, such as checking their pages on social networks, are discussed, and the chapter also looks at the changing social contract between employers and employees.

Chapter 12 has been revised and updated to reflect the most recent thinking on organizational diversity issues. The chapter looks at how diversity is changing the domestic and global workforce and includes a new section on the traditional versus inclusive models for managing diversity. This chapter also contains new coverage of the dividends of diversity; an expanded discussion of prejudice, discrimination, and stereotypes; and a new look at the difference between stereotyping and valuing cultural differences. The chapter includes a new five-step process for achieving cultural competence.

Chapter 13 continues its solid coverage of the basics of organizational behavior, including personality, values and attitudes, perception, emotional intelligence, learning and problem-solving styles, and stress management. Many exercises and questionnaires throughout this chapter enhance students' understanding of organizational behavior topics and their own personalities and attitudes.

Chapter 14 has been enriched with a discussion of followership. The chapter emphasizes that good leaders and good followers share common characteristics. Good leadership can make a difference, often through subtle, everyday actions. The discussion of power and influence has been expanded to include the sources of power that are available to followers as well as leaders. The discussions of charismatic, transformational, and interactive leadership have all been revised and refocused.

Chapter 15 covers the foundations of motivation and also incorporates recent thinking about motivational tools for today, including an expanded treatment of employee engagement. The chapter looks at new motivational ideas such as the importance of helping employees achieve work-life balance, incorporating fun and learning into the workplace, giving people a chance to fully participate, and helping people find meaning in their work.

Chapter 16 begins with a discussion of how managers facilitate strategic conversations by using communication to direct everyone's attention to the vision, values, and goals of the organization. The chapter explores the foundations of good communication and includes a new section on gender differences in communication, an enriched discussion of dialogue, and a refocused look at the importance of effective written communication in today's technologically connected workplace, including the use of new forms of manager communication such as blogs.

Chapter 17 includes a new section on the dilemma of teams, acknowledging that teams are sometimes ineffective and looking at the reasons for this, including such problems as free riders, lack of trust among team members, and so forth. The chapter then looks at how to make teams effective, including a significantly revised discussion of what makes an effective team leader. The chapter covers the types of teams and includes a new look at effectively using technology in virtual teams. The chapter also includes a section on managing conflict, including the use of negotiation.

Chapter 18 provides an overview of financial and quality control, including Six Sigma, ISO certification, and a new application of the balanced scorecard, which views employee learning and growth as the foundation of high performance. The discussion of hierarchical versus decentralized control has been updated and expanded. The chapter also addresses current concerns about corporate governance and finding a proper balance of control and autonomy for employees.

Chapter 19 has been thoroughly revised to discuss recent trends in operations management, information technology, and e-business. The chapter begins by looking at the organization as a value chain and includes an expanded discussion of supply chain management and new technologies such a radio frequency identification (RFID). The discussion of information technology has been updated to include the trend toward user-generated content through wikis, blogs, and social networking. The chapter explores how these new technologies are being applied within organizations along with traditional information systems. The chapter also discusses e-commerce strategies, the use of business intelligence software, and knowledge management.

In addition to the topics listed above, this text integrates coverage of the Internet and new technology into the various topics covered in each and every chapter.

Organization

The chapter sequence in *Management* is organized around the management functions of planning, organizing, leading, and controlling. These four functions effectively encompass both management research and characteristics of the manager's job.

Part One introduces the world of management, including the nature of management, issues related to today's chaotic environment, the learning organization, historical perspectives on management, and the technology-driven workplace.

Part Two examines the environments of management and organizations. This section includes material on the business environment and corporate culture, the global environment, ethics and social responsibility, and the natural environment.

Part Three presents three chapters on planning, including organizational goal setting and planning, strategy formulation and implementation, and the decision-making process.

Part Four focuses on organizing processes. These chapters describe dimensions of structural design, the design alternatives managers can use to achieve strategic objectives, structural designs for promoting innovation and change, the design and use of the human resource function, and the ways managing diverse employees are significant to the organizing function.

Part Five is devoted to leadership. The section begins with a chapter on organizational behavior, providing grounding in understanding people in organizations. This foundation paves the way for subsequent discussion of leadership, motivation of employees, communication, and team management.

Part Six describes the controlling function of management, including basic principles of total quality management, the design of control systems, information technology, and techniques for control of operations management.

Innovative Features

A major goal of this book is to offer better ways of using the textbook medium to convey management knowledge to the reader. To this end, the book includes several innovative features that draw students in and help them contemplate, absorb, and comprehend management concepts. South-Western has brought together a team of experts to create and coordinate color photographs, video cases, beautiful artwork, and supplemental materials for the best management textbook and package on the market.

Chapter Outline and Objectives. Each chapter begins with a clear statement of its learning objectives and an outline of its contents. These devices provide an overview of what is to come and can also be used by students to guide their study and test their understanding and retention of important points.

Opening Questionnaire. The text grabs student attention immediately by giving the student a chance to participate in the chapter content actively by completing a short questionnaire related to the topic.

Take a Moment. At strategic places through the chapter, students are invited to Take a Moment to apply a particular concept or think about how they would apply it as a practicing manager. This call to action further engages students in the chapter content. Some of the Take a Moment features also refer students to the associated New Manager Self-Test, or direct students from the chapter content to relevant end-of-chapter materials, such as an experiential exercise or an ethical dilemma.

New Manager Self-Test. A New Manager Self-Test in each chapter of the text provides opportunities for self-assessment as a way for students to experience management issues in a personal way. The change from individual performer to new manager is dramatic, and these self-tests provide insight into what to expect and how students might perform in the world of the new manager.

Concept Connection Photo Essays. A key feature of the book is the use of photographs accompanied by detailed photo essay captions that enhance learning. Each caption highlights and illustrates one or more specific concepts from the text to reinforce student understanding of the concepts. Although the photos are beautiful to look at, they also convey the vividness, immediacy, and concreteness of management events in today's business world.

Contemporary Examples. Every chapter of the text contains several written examples of management incidents. They are placed at strategic points in the chapter and are designed to illustrate the application of concepts to specific companies. These in-text examples—indicated by an icon in the margin—include well-known U.S. and international companies such as Toyota, Facebook, UPS, LG Electronics, Google, Unilever, Siemens, and eBay, as well as less-well-known companies and not-for-profit organizations such as Red 5 Studios, Strida, Genmab AS, ValueDance, and the U.S. Federal Bureau of Investigation (FBI). These examples put students in touch with the real world of organizations so that they can appreciate the value of management concepts.

Manager's Shoptalk Boxes. A Manager's Shoptalk box in each chapter addresses a specific topic straight from the field of management that is of special interest to students. These boxes may describe a contemporary topic or problem that is relevant to chapter content, or they may contain a diagnostic questionnaire or a special example of how managers handle a problem. The boxes heighten student interest in the subject matter and provide an auxiliary view of management issues not typically available in textbooks.

Video Cases. The six parts of the text conclude with video cases, one per chapter, that illustrate the concepts presented in that part. The 19 videos enhance class discussion, because students can see the direct application of the management theories they have learned. Companies discussed in the video package include Recycline, Flight 001, and Numi Organic Teas. Each video case explores the issues covered in the video, allowing students to synthesize the material they've just viewed. The video cases culminate with several questions that can be used to launch classroom discussion or as homework. Suggested answers are provided in the Media Case Library.

Exhibits. Several exhibits have been added or revised in the ninth edition to enhance student understanding. Many aspects of management are research based, and some concepts tend to be abstract and theoretical. The many exhibits throughout this book enhance students' awareness and understanding of these concepts. These exhibits consolidate key points, indicate relationships among concepts, and visually illustrate concepts. They also make effective use of color to enhance their imagery and appeal.

Glossaries. Learning the management vocabulary is essential to understanding contemporary management. This process is facilitated in three ways. First, key concepts are boldfaced and completely defined where they first appear in the text. Second, brief definitions are set out in the margin for easy review and follow-up. Third, a glossary summarizing all key terms and definitions appears at the end of the book for handy reference.

A Manager's Essentials and Discussion Questions. Each chapter closes with a summary of the essential points that students should retain. The discussion questions are a complementary learning tool that will enable students to check their understanding of key issues, to think beyond basic concepts, and to determine areas that require further study. The summary and discussion questions help students discriminate between main and supporting points and provide mechanisms for self-teaching.

Management in Practice Exercises. End-of-chapter exercises called "Management in Practice: Experiential Exercise" and "Management in Practice: Ethical Dilemma" provide a self-test for students and an opportunity to experience management issues in a personal way. These exercises take the form of questionnaires, scenarios, and activities, and many also provide an opportunity for students to work in teams. The exercises are tied into the chapter through the Take a Moment feature that refers students to the end-of-chapter exercises at the appropriate point in the chapter content.

Case for Critical Analysis. Also appearing at the end of each chapter is a brief but substantive case that provides an opportunity for student analysis and class discussion. Some of these cases are about companies whose names students will recognize; others are based on real management events but the identities of companies and managers have been disguised. These cases allow students to sharpen their diagnostic skills for management problem solving.

Continuing Case. Located at the end of each part, the Continuing Case is a running discussion of management topics appropriate to that part as experienced by General Motors Company. Focusing on one company allows students to follow the managers' and the organization's long-term problems and solutions in a sustained manner.

Supplementary Materials

Instructor's Manual. Designed to provide support for instructors new to the course, as well as innovative materials for experienced professors, the Instructor's Manual includes Chapter Outlines, annotated learning objectives, Lecture Notes, and sample Lecture Outlines. Additionally, the Instructor's Manual includes answers and teaching notes to end-of-chapter materials, including the video cases and the continuing case.

Instructor's CD-ROM. Key instructor ancillaries (Instructor's Manual, Test Bank, ExamView, and PowerPoint slides) are provided on CD-ROM, giving instructors the ultimate tool for customizing lectures and presentations.

Test Bank. Scrutinized for accuracy, the Test Bank includes more than 2,000 true/false, multiple-choice, short-answer, and essay questions. Page references are indicated for every question, as are designations of either factual or application so that instructors can provide a balanced set of questions for student exams. Each question is also tagged based on AACSB guidelines.

ExamView. Available on the Instructor's Resource CD-ROM, ExamView contains all of the questions in the printed Test Bank. This program is an easy-to-use test creation software compatible with Microsoft Windows. Instructors can add or edit questions, instructions, and answers, and select questions (randomly or numerically) by previewing them on the screen. Instructors can also create and administer quizzes online, whether over the Internet, a local area network (LAN), or a wide area network (WAN).

PowerPoint Lecture Presentation. Available on the Instructor's Resource CD-ROM and the Web site, the PowerPoint Lecture Presentation enables instructors to customize their own multimedia classroom presentation. Containing an average of 27 slides per chapter, the package includes figures and tables from the text, as well as outside materials to supplement chapter concepts. Material is organized by chapter and can be modified or expanded for individual classroom use. PowerPoint slides are also easily printed to create customized Transparency Masters.

Study Guide. Packed with real-world examples and additional applications for helping students master management concepts, this learning supplement is an excellent resource. For each chapter of the text, the Study Guide includes a summary and completion exercise; a review with multiple-choice, true/false, and short-answer questions; a mini case with multiple-choice questions; management applications; and an experiential exercise that can be assigned as homework or used in class.

Video Package. The video package for *Management*, ninth edition, contains two options: On the Job videos created specifically for the ninth edition of Daft's *Management* and BizFlix videos. *On the Job* videos use real-world companies to illustrate management concepts as outlined in the text. Focusing on both small and large business, the videos give students an inside perspective on the situations and issues that corporations face. *BizFlix* are film clips taken from popular Hollywood movies such as *Failure to Launch*, *Rendition*, and *Friday Night Lights*, and integrated into the ninth edition of Daft. Clips are supported by short cases and discussion questions at the end of each chapter.

Web Site (www.cengage.com/management/daft). Discover a rich array of online teaching and learning management resources that you won't find anywhere else.

Resources include interactive learning tools, links to critical management Web sites, and password-protected teaching resources available for download.

Premium Student Web Site (www.cengage.com/login). Give your students access to additional study aides for your management course. With this optional package, students gain access to the Daft premium Web site. There your students will find interactive quizzes, flashcards, PowerPoint slides, learning games, and more to reinforce chapter concepts. Add the ninth edition of *Management* to your bookshelf at www .cengage.com/login and access the Daft Premium Web site to learn more.

Acknowledgments

A gratifying experience for me was working with the team of dedicated professionals at South-Western who were committed to the vision of producing the best management text ever. I am grateful to Joe Sabatino, executive editor, whose enthusiasm, creative ideas, assistance, and vision kept this book's spirit alive. Emma Newsom, managing developmental editor, provided superb project coordination and offered excellent ideas and suggestions to help the team meet a demanding and sometimes arduous schedule. Kimberly Kanakes, executive marketing manager, and Clint Kernen, marketing manager, provided keen market knowledge and innovative ideas for instructional support. Martha Conway, senior content project manager, cheerfully and expertly guided me through the production process. Tippy McIntosh contributed her graphic arts skills to create a visually dynamic design. Ruth Belanger, editorial assistant, and Sarah Rose, marketing coordinator, skillfully pitched in to help keep the project on track. Joe Devine deserves a special thank you for his layout expertise and commitment to producing an attractive, high-quality textbook. Additionally, BJ Parker, Copyshop, USA, contributed the Continuing Case.

Here at Vanderbilt I want to extend special appreciation to my assistant, Barbara Haselton. Barbara provided excellent support and assistance on a variety of projects that gave me time to write. I also want to acknowledge an intellectual debt to my colleagues, Bruce Barry, Ray Friedman, Neta Moye, Rich Oliver, David Owens, Ranga Ramanujam, Bart Victor, and Tim Vogus. Thanks also to Deans Jim Bradford and Bill Christie who have supported my writing projects and maintained a positive scholarly atmosphere in the school. Another group of people who made a major contribution to this textbook are the management experts who provided advice, reviews, answers to questions, and suggestions for changes, insertions, and clarifications. I want to thank each of these colleagues for their valuable feedback and suggestions on the ninth edition:

David Alexander
Christian Brothers University

Reginald L Audibert
California State University—Long Beach

Burrell A. Brown
California University of Pennsylvania

Paula Buchanan
Jacksonville State University

Diane Caggiano
Fitchburg State College

Bruce Charnov
Hofstra University

Gloria Cockerell
Collin College

Jack Cox
Amberton University

Paul Ewell
Bridgewater College

Mary M. Fanning
College of Notre Dame of Maryland

Merideth Ferguson
Baylor University

Karen Fritz
Bridgewater College

Yezdi H. Godiwalla
University of Wisconsin— Whitewater

James Halloran
Wesleyan College

Stephen R. Hiatt
Catawba College

Betty Hoge
Bridgewater College

Jody Jones
Oklahoma Christian University